Media Audiences

Second Edition

Sara Miller McCune founded SAGE Publishing in 1965 to support the dissemination of usable knowledge and educate a global community. SAGE publishes more than 1000 journals and over 600 new books each year, spanning a wide range of subject areas. Our growing selection of library products includes archives, data, case studies and video. SAGE remains majority owned by our founder and after her lifetime will become owned by a charitable trust that secures the company's continued independence.

Los Angeles | London | New Delhi | Singapore | Washington DC | Melbourne

Media Audiences

Effects, Users, Institutions, and Power

Second Edition

John L. Sullivan
Muhlenberg College

Los Angeles | London | New Delhi
Singapore | Washington DC | Melbourne

FOR INFORMATION:

SAGE Publications, Inc.
2455 Teller Road
Thousand Oaks, California 91320
E-Mail: order@sagepub.com

SAGE Publications Ltd.
1 Oliver's Yard
55 City Road
London EC1Y 1SP
United Kingdom

SAGE Publications India Pvt. Ltd.
B 1/I 1 Mohan Cooperative Industrial Area
Mathura Road, New Delhi 110 044
India

SAGE Publications Asia-Pacific Pte. Ltd.
18 Cross Street #10-10/11/12
China Square Central
Singapore 048423

Acquisitions Editor: Lily Norton
Editorial Assistant: Sarah Wilson
Production Editor: Jyothi Sriram
Copy Editor: Amy Hanquist Harris
Typesetter: C&M Digitals (P) Ltd.
Proofreader: Ellen Brink
Indexer: Amy Murphy
Cover Designer: Ginkhan Siam
Marketing Manager: Victoria Velasquez

Printed in the United States of America

Library of Congress Cataloging-in-Publication Data

Names: Sullivan, John L. (John Lawrence), 1945- author.

Title: Media audiences : effects, users, institutions, and power / John L. Sullivan.

Description: Second edition. | Los Angeles : SAGE, 2019. | Includes bibliographical references and index.

Identifiers: LCCN 2019010245 | ISBN 9781506397405 (paperback : alk. paper)

Subjects: LCSH: Mass media—Audiences.

Classification: LCC P96.A83 S85 2019 | DDC 302.23—dc23
LC record available at https://lccn.loc.gov/2019010245

This book is printed on acid-free paper.

19 20 21 22 23 10 9 8 7 6 5 4 3 2 1

Brief Contents

Detailed Contents

SECTION III AUDIENCES AS ACTIVE USERS OF MEDIA   135

Preface

∙∙∙

We are confronted daily with a complex and potentially bewildering media environment. At any given moment, we can access a plethora of media inputs, ranging from giant digital cinema screens at the local multiplex movie theater to the 6-inch screen on the smartphone that we carry around in our pockets. In the 21st century, we are continually engaged as media audiences, yet the concept of "the audience" can be conceptually murky. This text explores the notion of media audiences from multiple theoretical perspectives: as victims, institutional constructions, users, and producers. This holistic approach is designed to introduce students to the history of the audience concept and to many of the important scholarly traditions in media audience research.

This book grew out of my own teaching experiences at Muhlenberg College in a course called Audience Analysis. Every year, I would cobble together a hodgepodge of sources for the course, which included overviews of effects research theories, ratings analysis, and British cultural studies, among other things. Like all professors who find themselves needing to teach from course readers, I attempted to bring all of these disparate scholarly sources together with a coherent framework through my lectures and slides, with varying levels of success. I regularly scoured publishers' catalogs, searching in vain for an overview text that would adopt an integrated approach to audience studies. After 10 years of waiting, I decided to take on the task of writing that text myself, and the result is before you now.

Readers and Courses

∙∙∙

This textbook is primarily intended for upper-division undergraduates, but it could also prove useful for first-year graduate students. Since the book covers quite a bit of complex theoretical ground, it would be most beneficial to students who have had at least one introductory course in media or communication studies. That said, the writing style is largely conversational, and I introduce numerous contemporary examples throughout the book to illustrate key concepts. Since the text provides an overview of a number of seminal theories about the relationship between media and society, this book can serve as a core text for a number of courses, including media theory, media effects, popular culture, television and society, audience measurement, advertising, and even marketing courses. In fact, I have often found a good number of business administration majors in my Audience Analysis course. This book was consciously written with American students in mind since it uses examples from the American media scene. However, the text should appeal to students everywhere since the theoretical ideas I explore can apply almost universally to our experiences as media audiences today.

Features and Organization: An Integrative Approach to Media Audiences

The overall purpose of this textbook is to provide a clear, concise overview and synthesis of major theories on media audiences, though organized and conceptualized in new ways to emphasize the connections between notions of the audience and social and economic power in postindustrial societies. As you can see from the Table of Contents, the book will be divided into four broad sections with individual chapters addressing major theoretical concerns in those areas. One of the most important features of this book is its integrative approach to audience studies. This text includes a wide variety of approaches, covering effects-based perspectives as well as active audience theories such as uses and gratifications, British cultural studies, and reception theory. The book also offers a comprehensive overview of media fandom, something that is missing from most audience textbooks. Another unique aspect of this text is its consideration of the institutional construction of audiences via public opinion polls and media ratings.

The central principle behind the book is that, while the concept of the audience is used frequently in the media and in common parlance, its meaning today is complex and deserves closer scrutiny by media scholars and students alike. As much as media professionals, pollsters, and institutions (such as the federal government, for instance) would like to imagine that the audience is a fixed, stable object that is measurable via numerical techniques, in fact the notion of the audience is a fluid, historically contingent concept that is inextricably bound with social and economic power. While I primarily focus on the central traditions of audience research, I continually emphasize the fact that audience studies are changing dramatically in an era when the decreasing price of powerful technology has emboldened individuals to become media producers themselves, thereby challenging their status as both objects and victims of media institutions and messages.

There are a number of features that should facilitate a deeper understanding of the field of audience studies. First, each chapter begins with an example that demonstrates an important idea that will be explored within that chapter. These real-world examples raise questions about our experiences with media that can be addressed through scholarly research. Second, many of the key terms and phrases are marked by bold lettering to facilitate their understanding and recall. Third, each chapter features stand-alone boxes that outline specific case studies to illustrate the theoretical ideas in the chapter. The goal here is to make audience theories relevant and accessible to students by using case study examples taken from the contemporary media scene. Fourth, the text features a short bibliography of "suggested further reading" at the end of each chapter to encourage students to delve deeper into the material. These suggested sources can provide a useful springboard for research papers and short essays. Finally, each chapter includes several discussion activities to help facilitate deeper thinking about the material and to spur classroom discussion. I hope that all of these tools will assist students and instructors in navigating this fascinating field.

Preface to the Second Edition

It seems difficult to believe that 6 years have elapsed since the release of the first edition of *Media Audiences*. But in that relatively short amount of time, our media environment has undergone enormous changes. In fact, the original concept for this book was hatched much earlier, at an international communications conference in Paris in 2007. When I think back to that time (which does not seem that far removed in my memory, but of course it is going on 12 years ago now), it is startling to think that some of the most transformative changes in our media landscape were in their embryonic stages during that pivotal year. For example, 2007 was the year that Netflix branched out of its direct-to-home DVD rental business and introduced its streaming service, which allowed customers to instantaneously access television and motion picture content over the Internet via broadband connections (Helft, 2007). Just over 10 years later, subscription video streaming accounted for $12.91 billion in annual revenues for companies like Netflix, Amazon, and Hulu (eclipsing motion picture box office gross revenue of $11.89 billion), while annual revenue from DVD and Blu-Ray rentals—Netflix's original business model—dropped to a lowly $360 million (Richter, 2019). Today, Netflix video streaming consumes roughly 15% of all Internet bandwidth globally and 19.1% of total downstream traffic within the United States (Spangler, 2018). For media scholars and the public, 2007 will probably be best remembered as the year that then-Apple CEO Steven P. Jobs unveiled the first iPhone, which he described at the time as "a magical product that is literally 5 years ahead of any other mobile phone" (Markoff, 2007). Just over 10 years later, a Pew Research Center poll found that the vast majority of the U.S. population (95%) owned a mobile phone of some kind, and 20% of those in the survey told Pew that they relied solely on their mobile phones for at-home Internet access (Pew Research Center, 2018). Social media giant Facebook opened up its platform to anyone (nonstudents) in 2007 and amassed 36 million users by the end of that year, adding new subscribers at the rate of 1 million per month (Vogelstein, 2007). In the third quarter of 2018, just over 10 years later, Facebook had roughly 2.27 billion active monthly users (Statista, 2018).

The year 2007 therefore marked something of a turning point for media—and for the study of media audiences as well. The rise of streaming services has given audiences instantaneous access to more than a lifetime's worth of media programming. The portability of Internet-enabled smartphones such as the iPhone have tethered us to media companies and to each other in ways that were difficult to imagine in 2007. Since 2007, of course, our mediated lives have also been transformed by the emergence and preeminence of social media platforms such as Facebook, Twitter, LinkedIn, Snapchat, and Instagram. Unlike the legacy media giants of the 20th century, these services produce no original content of their own. Rather, they provide a ready means for individual users to create, distribute, and share information of their own making. The ability of mobile phones to take photographs, input text, capture video, record audio, and accomplish a thousand more creative tasks has effectively blurred the distinction between media producers and audiences. In an era when we are constantly producing and consuming media via our hyperconnected mobile devices, is it even meaningful to speak anymore of the concept of an "audience"?

The second edition of *Media Audiences* has been expanded to consider these important trends in our media lives over the past decade. Throughout this new edition, examples have been updated to reflect some of the most important current events, while preserving the theoretical core of audience studies. Chapter 2, for example, explores enduring 20th century concerns about media effects by placing them into conversation with recent research about the impacts of mobile phones on our social lives and individual psyches. Chapter 3, which explores the construction of audiences as a public via opinion polls and institutional constructions, now considers these topics in light of the failures of pollsters to anticipate some of the most disruptive political shifts in our time, such as the Brexit vote in the United Kingdom and the 2016 election of President Donald J. Trump in the United States. As that chapter explores, the dramatic rise in news consumption via social media platforms has complicated the ability of readers to discern fact from hoax, spurring new concerns about the pernicious spread of conspiracies, propaganda, and "fake news."

The centrality of the Internet for circulating media has also altered the tools and methods that are employed by institutions for measuring audience activity, and later chapters in the second edition examine concepts such as social TV, audience engagement, and social media metrics. Readers interested in theories of audience interpretation and decoding will find many updates to Chapter 6 that aim to rework important theories from the 20th century for an interactive media age. The final chapter has also been updated to include recent discussions and reflections among audience researchers about maintaining the relevance of audience studies in an interactive, online world. There are many other small changes and updates throughout the book, of course, such as replacing broken web links, including new sources and scholarship, adding new discussion activities, reworking odd sentences, and so on. In sum, users of the first edition should find that the second edition maintains a broad overview of classic audience studies while including many relevant examples of recent research in the field.

References

Helft, M. (2007, January 16). Netflix to deliver movies to the PC. *The New York Times*. Retrieved from https://www.nytimes.com/2007/01/16/technology/16netflix.html

Markoff, J. (2007, January 10). Apple introduces innovative cellphone. *The New York Times*. Retrieved from https://www.nytimes.com/2007/01/10/technology/10apple.html

Pew Research Center. (2018, February 5). Demographics of mobile device ownership and adoption in the United States. Retrieved from http://www.pewinternet.org/fact-sheet/mobile/

Richter, F. (2019, January 24). Infographic: Streaming dominates U.S. home entertainment spending. *Statista Infographics*. Retrieved from https://www.statista.com/chart/7654/home-entertainment-spending-in-the-us/

Spangler, T. (2018, October 2). Netflix eats up 15% of all Internet downstream traffic worldwide. *Variety*. Retrieved from https://variety.com/2018/digital/news/netflix-15-percent-internet-bandwidth-worldwide-study-1202963207/

Statista. (2018). Facebook users worldwide 2018. Retrieved from https://www.statista.com/statistics/264810/number-of-monthly-active-facebook-users-worldwide/

Vogelstein, F. (2007, September 6). How Mark Zuckerberg turned Facebook into the web's hottest platform. *Wired*. Retrieved from https://www.wired.com/2007/09/ff-facebook/

Acknowledgments

Many of the additions and changes in this new edition were made in response to the thorough and extremely helpful reviews provided by four outside reviewers: Paula Hearsum at the University of Brighton, Nancy Worthington at Quinnipiac University, Robbie Smyth at Griffith College, and Robert Huesca at Trinity University. Their careful read of the first edition and thoughtful comments provided me with many valuable insights that have made the text more comprehensive and topical. I would like to sincerely thank them for their efforts. Of course, any mistakes, omissions, or errors in the text are mine alone. Thanks also to the team at SAGE for helping to keep this project on task, even when I fell behind on my own deadlines. Those folks include Matt Byrnie, Terri Accomazzo, Monica Eckman, Sarah Wilson, and Lily Norton. Extended thanks to the staff at SAGE includes Amy Hanquist Harris for her eagle-eyed copyediting and to Jyothi Sriram as well.

Second, I would also like to extend my appreciation to my departmental colleagues at Muhlenberg College for their steadfast support. Special thanks go to my colleague Jeff Pooley for cultivating a climate of collegiality and scholarly inquiry within the Media and Communication Department at Muhlenberg. I would also like to extend my appreciation to the Provost and Faculty Development and Scholarship Committee at Muhlenberg College for funding some of the work on this book revision.

Third, I would like to thank my students. This text was originally designed for students in my upper-division Audience Analysis class at Muhlenberg College. After 9 years of searching in vain for a suitable all-in-one textbook that covered media audience theories, I decided to simply write one myself. Over the years that I wrote this text, my students served as guinea pigs for draft chapters and offered enormously valuable feedback on writing style and organization. My goal in this text has always been to speak directly to an undergraduate reader. By "beta testing" many of the key chapters, my students have done a great service to future readers of this textbook.

Finally, members of my extended family were of enormous assistance throughout this project in helping me to find the time to research and write. For their encouragement, patience, and forbearance while I spent what seemed like countless hours hunched over my laptop, I would like to thank Sue Anne Basu, Krisna Basu, Linnea Basu, Josh Krell, Sarah Krell, Joseph Krell, Mary Jane Gilchrist, Jack Sullivan, and Vickie Sullivan. As with the first edition, none of this would be possible without the love and support of my family. To Andra, Cynthia, and Niva, thank you for continuing to keep me grounded in what's important. Like the first edition, this second edition is dedicated to you.

John L. Sullivan
Allentown, PA, USA
January 2019

CHAPTER 1

History and Concept of the Audience

This textbook is all about media audiences, so take a moment and consider perhaps one of the signature annual events in the television diets of audiences all over the world: the Super Bowl. Every year, individuals, families, and even strangers gather around television sets and (increasingly) mobile devices, becoming emotionally invested in the spectacle of American football, the commentary surrounding the game, and even the advertisements that occupy the gaps in the game. These days, if you're experiencing the Super Bowl, you may be doing other things at the same time, such as talking to others or texting a friend on a mobile phone, accessing the Internet for more stats, or interacting with tens of thousands of other fans in real time via social media. In fact, data from U.S. cell phone providers revealed that about 16.31 terabytes of information were transferred over wireless networks during the Super Bowl in 2018, with about 2.5 terabytes of data transferred through social media apps such as Snapchat, Facebook, and Twitter (Maddox, 2018). Watching the Super Bowl on television can also be a highly ritualized experience since our viewing experiences may incorporate a number of traditions that we repeat from year to year, such as eating certain types of foods or wearing particular clothes to support one team or another. There are other aspects to this experience that are important beyond your individual experience of the event as well. Let's not forget that the Super Bowl generates an enormous international viewership. The 2018 Super Bowl television audience was huge (though slightly decreased from the year previous), with over 103 million viewers (Otterson, 2018). This means that advertisers have paid millions of dollars for 15 or 30 seconds of airtime in order to reach this mass audience. Advertising is a major business that relies upon the presence of individuals in the audience, and the measurement of this audience is a crucial part of that business.

As this brief example illustrates, the media audience experience is rich and multifaceted. On the one hand, it's intensely personal; it takes place in our homes and other private spaces, and it becomes a topic of conversation and identification with others in our social circles. The audience experience is also informed by the logic of the marketplace since businesses spend hundreds of millions of dollars in the effort to reach us. This raises some interesting questions. To what extent are our experiences with media truly our own? When we interact with any kind of media today (via television, radio, online, or mobile devices), how much of that experience is driven by forces that are outside of our own control? How much leeway do we have as citizens and consumers to interpret the messages that form our daily cultural environment? Our media experiences are so integrated into our daily routines that they become part of what scholar Roger Silverstone (1999) has called our "texture of experience." This makes them more difficult to examine from an objective, detached perspective, but the centrality of the audience role in our media environment makes it vital to take a closer look at what it means to be an audience. This book will explore media audiences through history and contemporary media theory.

Situating the Audience Concept

The term *audience* is one that we use quite frequently in our everyday conversations, but it's one that has a multiplicity of meanings. If you were to say "I was in the audience" for a movie, you mean that you were one of a number of individuals witnessing a media event at the same time and place. Alternatively, if you noted that you were "part of the audience" for the season premiere of your favorite television program last night, you may be referring to the fact that you were viewing a particular media program in the comfort of your home at the same time as millions of other people in "the audience" were doing the same thing. In the first example, your audience experience was both a *temporal* (paying attention to the same thing at the same time as others) and a *physical* one: you were sitting along with other strangers in a darkened theater. In the second example, you were viewing the same media source as millions of other people, but you were not located in the same space. Indeed, cramming 6 million viewers of a television program into one physical location would create chaos and confusion. Now think about reading a book or perhaps an interesting blog you found online. Here, you are part of the reading "audience," yet you are having an intensely personal interaction with the author—who may or may not even be still writing or even still living at the time you encounter his or her words. In this final example, your experience with media is neither temporal nor geographical. You might think about how our audiovisual experiences via the Internet expand and challenge these notions as well.

Overview of the Chapter

This introductory chapter begins with an exploration of the term *audience* by explaining two different scholarly views of the audience: an information-based view and a meaning-based view. I'll outline the constructivist view of audience studies and explain its importance to our exploration of audiences in this textbook. Then we will get an overview of the field of audience studies, which can be broken down into at least three distinct categories. In order to better understand how our notions of the audience have shifted over time, we then explore some of the historical roots of the term from the Greeks and Romans up to the 20th century. At the end of the chapter, we will examine how the notion of the audience is closely bound to issues of power in society.

What Is an Audience?

Before getting further into the text, it's important to take a moment to describe the concept that is at its core: the audience. There are two basic notions of the audience, each with a core perspective about the communication process. The first is an **information-based** notion of the audience experience (Frey, Botan, & Kreps, 1999), which has also been described as a *transmission view of communication* (Carey, 1989). The Oxford English Dictionary defines *audience* as "the action of hearing; attention to what is spoken." The root of the word (*aud*) suggests the processing of verbal information (e.g., audio or auditory processing). In medieval times, hereditary rulers, monarchs, and feudal lords would often "grant an audience" to their constituents, using the term to indicate a disparity in social station between the two individuals in the conversation. This transmission view of the audience, then, emphasizes the verbal or other symbolic transaction between a speaker and a receiver. The focus is on both the *content* of the message as well as the *act* of sending and receiving messages (the purposes of which are intentional).

In its most simplified form, then, every act of communication requires two parties: a message sender (or creator) and a receiver (Shannon & Weaver, 1949). In this case, the "audience" would refer to the receiver of a particular symbolic message (see Figure 1.1 for an overview of this process). The sender transmits the message through a specific means (which is referred to as the *channel*), whether it be face-to-face speech or via mediated communication. As the message travels from the source to the intended receiver, it is subject to "noise," which refers both to literal interference from other ambient sounds or a rogue radio signal, as well as to psychological noise such as any competing thoughts or feelings that may interrupt or otherwise distort the original intent of the message. Communication with the audience is achieved when the message from the sender reaches its intended target. This model describes communication between a sender and a receiver either at the interpersonal or mass level. The model that we most often associate with "audience" in common parlance is that of a *mass audience*—where many anonymous individuals are receiving a particular message via some kind of media channel (either simultaneously or at different points in time).

There is an alternative notion of communication, however, that regards communication not as a transaction but instead as a process: the **meaning-based view** (Frey et al., 1999). In this model, the interaction between the sender and receiver is an ongoing process that may or may not be intentional. The message is de-emphasized here in favor of the *meaning* that is made of the message by the receiver—thus, this model regards the meaning-making activity of the receiver(s) as much more significant than the transmission of the message itself. A key aspect of this second model is the notion of *feedback* between receiver and sender. Take a simple conversation between two people as an example. There is a recursive nature to the interaction between the sender and the receiver because one person may be responding to the nonverbal signs from the other while the message is being transmitted. If your friend's attention begins to wander when you are describing to her

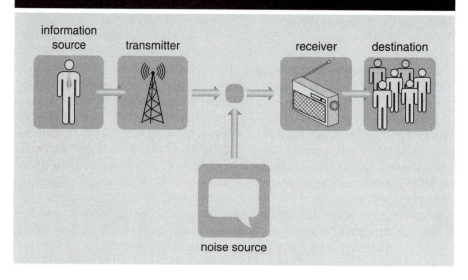

Figure 1.1 General Model of the Communication Process

information
source   transmitter   receiver   destination

noise source

Source: Adapted from Shannon, C. E., & Weaver, W. (1949). *The Mathematical Theory of Communication*. Urbana, IL: University of Illinois Press. Redrawn by Stephanie Plumeri Ertz.

a near miss you just had while driving your car, you would probably take that as a hint that she was not listening to your story and interrupt your recitation to ask her: "Are you all right? Why aren't you listening to me?" The feedback from sender to receiver here is immediate and changes according to the relationship between individuals in a face-to-face context.

In the case of mass media audiences, forms of feedback are still critical, but that feedback is inevitably delayed in time and relayed back to message producers via some third entity, such as the Nielsen ratings for television or a public opinion poll. This gap in the feedback loop is part of a much larger trend that began during the Industrial Revolution when industrialization opened up a rift between the production and consumption of goods. In the productive realm, individuals labored under the watchful eye of factory owners and capitalists, while workers' off-hours became a privatized sphere in which childrearing, cooking, and leisure took place outside of the eye of capital or the government. Thomas Streeter (1996, p. 287) argues that the Industrial Revolution "separated the public world of work, markets, and politics from the world of the nuclear family. Concretely, it enabled new arrangements of space, time, gender, and labor, with complex ramifications." The key shift that Streeter notes here is the social and physical separation of the production of goods and the private, domestic spaces in which they are consumed. The implications for media are profound: While these media are produced largely by for-profit companies in clearly observable ways, they are consumed by large, heterogeneous, and anonymous audiences in the privacy of their own homes.

How does one gauge the reaction of such mysterious and invisible receivers to specific media messages? As we'll explore in Chapter 4, industrial forms of mass audience feedback such as the Nielsen ratings system aim to re-create the notion of the mass audience, though this picture is delayed in time and far from complete.

As Figure 1.2 reveals, the larger the audience for a mediated communication experience, the longer the delay in obtaining feedback from that experience. The "media gap" is where community relationships and "small-group and special-interest group communications" are largely missing (Neuman, 1991, p. 9). Some scholars have lamented the erosion of these forms of civic involvement in modern times (most notably Putnam, 2000), but the rise of social networking via the Internet has opened up a new realm of possibilities for collapsing this "media gap" as well as rendering instantaneous feedback from millions of audiences to message producers, even

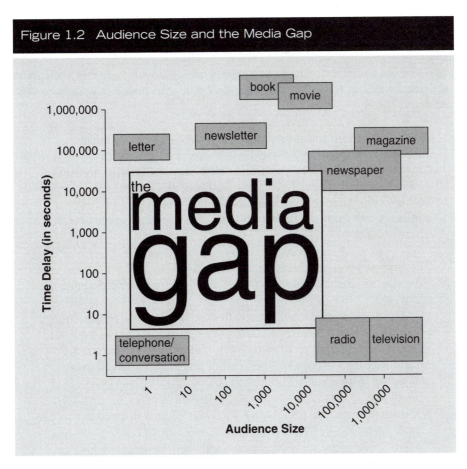

Figure 1.2 Audience Size and the Media Gap

Source: Adapted from Neuman, W. R. (1991). *The Future of the Mass Audience*, p. 10. Cambridge, United Kingdom: Cambridge University Press. Redrawn by Stephanie Plumeri Ertz.

allowing for extended conversations between these parties (Benkler, 2006; Castells, 2002). We'll address the burgeoning realm of online interactive media audiences in Chapter 10.

The effects of the Industrial Revolution were even more far-reaching for media audiences. The shift toward industrialization also spurred massive migration of workers from rural agricultural communities to cities in order to find work. For the first time, many individuals living in cities for the first time were confronted daily with a strange new environment, filled with people from many different walks of life, speaking different languages, eating different foods, and participating in many different cultural customs (Lowery & DeFleur, 1995, p. 11). Within this context, small cultural enclaves emerged within major cities, causing concern among scholars about the potential for forms of mass media to directly affect socially alienated audiences. These arguments about the power of the media for mass persuasion will be explored in Chapter 2.

Constructionism and the Notion of the Audience

There are a number of important perspectives that will guide this book about media audiences. Recent scholarship has decentered the notion of audiences as an ontological reality:

> Audiences are seen not as empirical actors to be examined in their concrete activity, but as discursive constructs, as effects of a variety of programs, institutions, and measuring instruments. **Constructionism** is a metatheoretical approach that treats audience as signifier and subject position rather than referent and autonomous subject. . . . To study audiences is to study the discourses that take audiences as their object. (Bratich, 2005, p. 243)

The first perspective, therefore, is that audiences are *abstractions* and not objective realities. Particularly since today's widely dispersed media audience is

> too large to be apprehended directly in experience, it is a construction of our research and theorizing. Different research methods and different manners of theorizing produce different understandings of the term. An audience then is not a fact but a set of pragmatics invoked in our perspective. (Anderson, 1996, p. 75)

Audience history scholar Richard Butsch (2008) puts this another way:

> The noun "audiences" makes it appear—and often makes us think—that audience is an identity that people carry into every situation and interaction. But audience is a situated role that people temporarily perform, and in their performance people produce representations of audiences. (p. 3)

Butsch's comment demonstrates another important aspect of the audience concept: that it is *situated* and *contingent*. In other words, the story of the audience is no more and no less than the story of the ways in which this concept has been imagined and used by communities and societies in specific historical and cultural contexts.

The notion that audiences are not observable, objective realities but instead constructed entities that emerge in popular memory, institutional practice, and academic research was crystallized in a review article by Martin Allor in 1988. Allor argued that

> the audience exists nowhere; it inhabits no real space, only positions within analytic discourses. . . . If we, as a discipline, are going to move forward on this issue, the central problematic of the field, we first have to deconstruct the "audience's" unity into constituent and constituting moments. (1988, pp. 228–229)

In this text, we'll use this constructivist approach to examine a number of "moments" in the history of media audience studies, paying close attention to the ways in which the concept of the audience is understood and utilized and how those constructions reveal notions of power in society. As we'll explore later in this chapter, for instance, the usage of the term *audience* and popular conceptions of audiences have changed dramatically over time. Competing conceptions of what it means to be an audience also illuminate broader political, economic, and cultural tensions in different historical moments.

Three Models of the Audience

Audience scholar James G. Webster (1998) argues that there are three basic models of the media audience that have animated scholarly inquiries since the early 20th century: audience-as-outcome, audience-as-mass, and audience-as-agent (see Figure 1.3). As you'll see when perusing the Table of Contents, these three categories map closely onto the structure of this text. First, the **audiences-as-outcome** model "sees people as being acted upon by media. Typically, it reflects a concern about the power of media to produce detrimental effects on individuals, and by implication on society as a whole" (Webster, 1998, p. 193).

The second model is the **audience-as-mass**. In this model, audiences are seen as "a large collection of people scattered across time and space who act autonomously and have little or no immediate knowledge of one another." Scholars and practitioners using this model typically ask questions such as these: What kinds of media do people consume? How many and what types of people are in the audience? How might specific groups of people respond to a particular issue or policy position? As we'll explore in the second section of the text (Chapters 3–4), public institutions (such as the government) and private organizations (like for-profit corporations) rely heavily on this notion of the audience, using quantitative measurement techniques such as public opinion surveys and television ratings to gauge mass responses to specific stimuli. Often, however, these audience

Figure 1.3 Three Models of the Audience

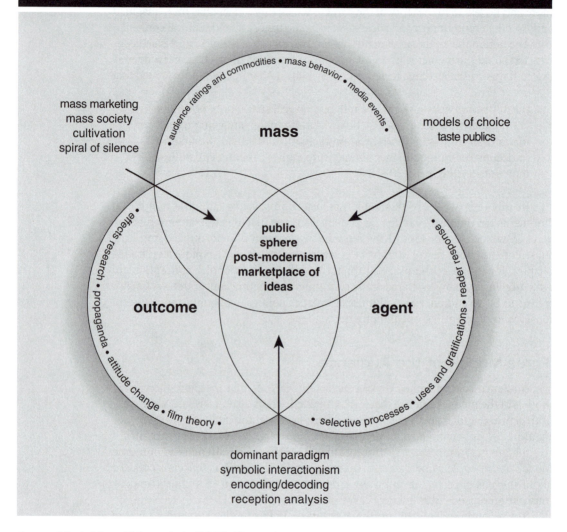

mass marketing
mass society
cultivation
spiral of silence

models of choice
taste publics

audience ratings and commodities • mass behavior • media events •

mass

• effects research • propaganda • attitude change • film theory •

• response

• reader response • uses and gratifications

public sphere post-modernism marketplace of ideas

outcome

agent

• selective processes •

dominant paradigm
symbolic interactionism
encoding/decoding
reception analysis

Source: Adapted from Webster, J. G. (1998). The audience. *Journal of Broadcasting & Electronic Media, 42*(2), 190–207. Redrawn by Stephanie Plumeri Ertz.

constructions say more about the logistical and strategic needs of the institutions creating them than they do about audiences' own self-images and concerns.

Finally, Webster outlines the notion of the **audience-as-agent**. Rather than imagining audiences as either objects that are acted upon by media stimuli or constructions of powerful institutions, in this mode "people are conceived of as free agents choosing what media they will consume, bringing their own interpretive skills to the texts they encounter, making their own meanings, and generally using media to suit themselves" (1998, p. 194). In this model, audience members are regarded to be reflexive about their own media use—selecting specific media and content to fit their own needs and desires and actively interpreting those media within the framework of their own personal experiences. The third section of this text, titled "Audiences as Users" (Chapters 5–7), covers these models of the audience experience, exploring uses and gratifications, reception theory, interpretation of media content, and media rituals. This perspective is then expanded further in the fourth section of the text, "Audiences as Producers" (Chapters 8–9). These chapters explore the blurring of the traditional dichotomy between message producers and receivers as seen through the lens of fan studies and online interactive audiences.

Although these models are divided into specific sections of the text, they don't necessarily fit so neatly into these three categories. As we'll see, theories about the audience often contain some aspects of the audience-as-mass model along with that of audience-as-agent. Nevertheless, these three conceptual categories serve as a useful organizing tool that will help you to navigate the book.

History of Early Audiences

As already noted, the notion of the audience has shifted continually throughout human history in response to the social and cultural dynamics of human societies. To understand our modern concept of the audience, it is important to see why this notion emerged and how it connected to issues of politics, race, and class. The history of the audience concept is closely intertwined with the notion of the public and public spaces. Individuals were colocated in time and space and participated in a collective ritual, whether it was spectating or actively engaging in the event itself. The shift away from real-time interaction toward more privatized, individualized spectatorship of mass media also reflects some of the profound technological changes that have redefined the notion of audiences in our modern era.

Greek and Roman Audiences: Public Performance and Oral Communication

It is difficult to overstate the importance of oral expression and communication in ancient Greek society. One of the chief advancements of Greek culture was the creation of the phonetic alphabet system, in which Greek words could be transferred onto portable media such as papyrus and parchment (made of animal skins) for preservation and transportation. As historian Eric Havelock explains,

> The introduction of the Greek letters into inscription somewhere around 700 BC was to alter the character of human culture, placing a gulf between all alphabetic societies and their precursors. The Greeks did not

just invent an alphabet, they invented literacy and the literate basis of modern thought. (2011, p. 38)

However, given the high cost of parchment and the fragile nature of papyrus reed, along with the relatively low levels of literacy, most communication was oral.

The Greeks not only pioneered early efforts to develop effective styles of public speaking (the introduction of the study of rhetoric), but they also institutionalized and ritualized public speech and audience participation through stage dramas and other public performances. As Thomas and Webb (1994, pp. 6–7) note, orality was one of the defining features of Greek culture since it was vital to the "preservation of important information. The need to be understood, even listened to, meant that expression was a vital skill." In a totally oral world, a premium was placed on the skills necessary to accurately and efficiently transfer information from one individual to the next. To maximize an individual's memory, long strings of information were woven together in the form of prose narratives, often with rhymes and meters to make them more memorable to listeners. This would ensure that the intended meaning of the original message would be preserved. In fact, poetic skill among Greeks was linked to divine inspiration and guidance. Critical to the success and brilliance of a speaker was "the effect his words have on his audience" (Thomas & Webb, 1994, p. 9). Even in ancient Greece, then, there was an acute awareness of the reception of speech by listeners that went hand in hand with the development of much more sophisticated techniques of organizing arguments and ideas to achieve maximum impact with the audience. As Greek philosopher and teacher Aristotle explained in his three-volume treatise *Rhetoric* (a collection of his thoughts about oral communication in the 335–322 BCE period), the art of rhetoric is different than didactic speech in that it is a form of "continuous discourse" that "usually addresses a large audience, and the orator must sense his hearers' reaction. . . . It avoids complex argumentation and often employs things like maxims or fables which will appeal to an audience" (Kennedy, 1980, p. 66). The interchange between individuals in the public realm was an integral part of Greek notions of citizenship on the model of "civic republicanism." This meant essentially that individuals who met a specific set of criteria—landowning, masculine, educated, and possessing strong moral character—were encouraged to participate in public discussions about political matters (Butsch, 2008, p. 4). The fact that a good number of citizens (including women and slaves) were actively excluded from these debates was entirely consistent with the notion that "civic virtue" was a quality found only among those individuals who had the time, ability, and commitment to devote to the interests of the community.

The importance of audiences in Greek society was also apparent in the traditions of public theater that were the focus of intellectual and political activity. Traditional Greek theater was defined by a large, arena-like outdoor space in which a live audience literally surrounded the players on a small stage. The space itself was quite intimate, with no physical or social separation between the players and the viewers. In this space, "the public was an active partner, free to comment, to be commented upon, to assist, or to intervene" with the onstage production (Arnott, 1989, p. 11). Indeed, historical evidence points to Greek audiences as "talkative and unruly," and there were "numerous stories of audiences disrupting performances by shouting, jeering, throwing fruit, and worse" (Arnott, 1989, p. 6). Greek playwrights were highly aware of the dynamics of the live audience experience and incorporated aspects of audience involvement into the plays themselves. The notion of the Greek "chorus" found in many tragedies and comedies is simply a fictional device meant to invoke the activities and responses of Athenian audiences, many of whom were familiar enough with many of the standard works to be able to recite lines from memory and to correct the actors when necessary.

The traditions of Greek theater were well known and celebrated throughout the Italian peninsula during the Roman Empire. As Beacham (1992) notes,

> Theater was a thriving institution throughout the Hellenistic world, and nowhere more so than in the Greek cities of southern Italy, which appear to have enjoyed regular visits from touring companies, and also mounted local productions of Greek dramatic fare. (p. 7)

However, unlike the socially transformative potential of Greek tragedies and other forms of public theater, Roman theater was designed for nonpolitical spectatorship—one which would not go too far in challenging the existing cultural and political status quo. As the political power of the artisans and the plebians in Roman society began to expand, the aristocracy found it ever more necessary to appeal to these lower societal classes in order to gain and retain political power through democratic processes. Since openly offering gifts and bribes to buy votes was a capital offense, one strategy for enhancing one's electoral prospects was to provide public entertainment for the voting members of the citizenry. These were called the "scenic games." Indeed, "public gatherings where argument and oratory could be used to impress and win support were crucially important, as was any gesture or deed which might win favorable publicity for a candidate" (Beacham, 1992, p. 16).

These games were also directly connected to Roman religious life, which both conditioned and heavily circumscribed the roles of the audience. This was seen most directly in the practice of "instauration, whereby if the play were in some way interrupted, or there was the smallest omission or mishap, it had to be repeated from the beginning just like any other formal religious ceremony" (Beacham, 1992, p. 21). As the Roman Empire began to wane around 400 BCE, large-scale public spectacles took on renewed importance for the political elite because they served to release sometimes volatile social and political tensions among the plebians. What had been a vital source of public interaction and communication during the height of Greek civilization, therefore, assumed the status of mere spectacle during the waning years of the Roman Empire. Instead of encouraging citizen participation, the goal was to stave off popular rebellion by refocusing the attention of the masses on ritualized violence and entertainment.

Figure 1.4 A Classic Greek Theater

Source: From the German encyclopedia Joseph Joseph Kürschner (editor): "Pierers Konversations-lexikon," 1891. PD—US—expired.

Taken together, Greek and Roman audiences shared a number of important aspects: First, they were organized, planned activities that were *public* in nature. That is, an integral feature of these theater and spectacle experiences was the "public-ness" of the encounter—citizens would attend in order to see both the event and each other. Social and cultural cohesion were achieved through the act of spectatorship itself. Secondly, these events were *colocated in time and space*, meaning that spectators gathered together at a set location and time to witness a shared event. Thirdly, the roles of authors, performers, and spectators were outlined and defined through these experiences, which shaped our notion of the spectator audience for the future (McQuail, 1997, p. 3).

Print and the Shift Toward Mediated Audiences

It is difficult to fully appreciate the transformative effect that the invention of the printing press had on both the production and distribution of knowledge. In addition to increasing the availability of cheaper books, the printing press also created a brand-new spectatorship experience for those fortunate enough to be able to read. Instead of needing the presence of the author or other person to relay the information, audiences far removed could now get access to another's ideas and stories. In addition, book readers no longer relied upon the spoken word for the transmission of others' thoughts—instead, mediated content could be experienced in the quiet and solitude of one's own surroundings. The book brought about the first *separation between the originator of a message and the message receiver*.

Separating the audience from the message sender both in time and space challenged the authority of the message as well as the messenger. In preliterate times, stories were transmitted from person to person via word of mouth. The fidelity of the original message was therefore only as good as the memory of the person who then relayed that story. Once books began to gain widespread circulation (after the invention of the printing press by Johan Gutenberg around 1440), the printed word could be reproduced in its exact original context hundreds of times over. You no longer needed to keep the original storyteller around to make sure the retelling was accurate. The sum total of people's knowledge and experience could be captured, preserved, and widely disseminated, lessening the absolute importance of the messenger. Older members of the community were no longer relied upon as the arbiters of "fact," and the power of monarchs and the church began to wane. When copies of the Bible were printed and circulated in languages other than Latin, local priests and parishioners were no longer bound to the Vatican for access to the Bible or to the news from around Europe, and the church's monopoly on information was disrupted. The Catholic Church ultimately factionalized over disparate local practices and theological interpretations, culminating in the Protestant Reformation (Febvre & Martin, 1990, pp. 287–319). As Eisenstein notes,

> As communion with the Sunday paper has replaced churchgoing, there is a tendency to forget that sermons had at one time been coupled with news about local and foreign affairs, real estate transactions, and other mundane affairs. After printing, however, news gathering and circulation were handled more efficiently under lay auspices. (2011, p. 84)

The *act of reading* also signaled a sea change in the audience experience itself. Readers began to scan the written text in silence, rather than read it aloud as was common during the Middle Ages when literacy was much rarer (Ong, 2002, p. 133). Additionally, simultaneous, physically colocated spectatorship was no longer required for an individual to receive a communication message. Instead, individuals could consume messages in private, and virtual communities of readers (who had access to the same printed material but who were neither physically adjacent nor even known to one another) began to develop. This represented both a shift *away* from groups of assembled people as the locus for discussion and debate as well as a shift *toward* new collectivities whose sense of identity and cohesion were forged through their shared experience of the print medium. Technology historian Elizabeth Eisenstein (2011, p. 85) writes that "printed materials encourage silent adherence to causes whose advocates could not be found in any one parish and who addressed an invisible public from afar." New forms of group identity began to compete with an older, more localized nexus of loyalties.

The creation of new geographically distant reading communities also had implications for the author or message creator: No longer was the act of communication connected to what Ong (1975, p. 10) calls the "present actuality" of the spoken word. Instead, the writer addressed him- or herself to an invisible collectivity of readers who may exist in different locales, historical time periods, and cultural contexts, resulting in a somewhat isolated, lonely communication experience. This notion of dispersed, anonymous audiences bears a closer resemblance to the mass mediated audience experiences of the present day. The invention of print allowed authors to extend their message well beyond the immediate reach of face-to-face oral communication while also preserving the message long after the authors themselves had ceased to exist (Kaufer & Carley, 1993, p. 254).

Liberalism, Democratic Participation, and Crowds in the 19th Century

The introduction of print was one of the first steps in the devolvement of power from centralized authorities (such as the Roman Catholic Church and feudal aristocracies) to smaller democratic collectives and reform movements throughout central Europe. The biggest philosophical and political shift toward "the people" occurred during the 18th-century Enlightenment period, when philosophers such as John Locke and John Stuart Mill emphasized that society should be governed by a social contract among individuals rather than under the auspices of an authoritarian state or regime. Mill's notion of liberalism argued that individuals were rational enough to make their own decisions and that government should intervene only when the individual liberties were at stake. The foundational documents of the new American nation contained many of these liberal concepts, such as the statement in the Declaration of Independence that governments derive "their just power from the consent of the governed" (Butsch, 2008, p. 5).[1]

Beginning in the 17th century, audience discourses were inextricably linked to race and class. They "tended to equate good audiences with the middle and upper classes, Euro-Americans, and males; bad audiences typically were identified with the working and lower classes, women, and subordinate races" (2008, p. 4). In the 17th and 18th centuries, for example, gatherings of individuals in public places became known as "crowds." The **audience as "crowd"** referred to working-class commoners who came together at specific times and places to experience some form of routinized behavior. Sometimes these behaviors centered on a specific elite-sanctioned (or sponsored) event, such as a public hanging or the annual ritual of *carnival*, where drunkenness, unruliness, and a lack of deference to hereditary rulers was tolerated for brief periods of time.

---

[1]Butsch argues, however, that authors of the U.S. Constitution such as James Madison also incorporated the ancient republican view of citizenship found in the Greek and Roman civilizations by restricting suffrage to those who were propertied and economically self-reliant enough to ensure that they would not place personal gain over the public interest.

These working-class crowds began to form a more coherent political force in the 19th century, however, particularly with the election of Andrew Jackson to the presidency in 1828. Jackson, himself a child of humble origins who taught himself to be a frontier lawyer, brought with him an era of expanded democratic access by eliminating land ownership as a requirement for suffrage. The Jacksonian era thereby became the "democratic moment" when working-class Americans began to form viable alternative political parties from the grassroots. This newfound political awareness of working-class Americans was also reflected in the cultural realm. More middle- and working-class Americans began attending theater performances, a form of entertainment that had hitherto been a solely patrician activity. During this period, "theater gained newfound legitimacy as one of few indoor gathering spaces for republican political participation" (Butsch, 2008, p. 25). Many theaters in the United States and Europe featured a "pit" immediately below the stage—an area where the less well-to-do could purchase standing-room-only theater tickets at greatly reduced prices. The popular imagination of the day was fired by the image of the *Bowery b'hoy*, a characterization of a good, hard-working young man who lived in the Bowery section of New York City and who regularly attended theater performances in a cheap suit coat and necktie (Butsch, 2008, p.7). During the 1830s and 1840s, these working-class tropes were celebrated in the popular press.

It was perhaps inevitable that the celebration of the working-class crowd would result in a backlash among the social and economic elite. Wealthy theater patrons who occupied the loges and box seats worried that these new unruly, uneducated interlopers would introduce disruption and chaos into what was hitherto a dignified and culturally uplifting experience. The term *crowd* began to creep into the popular lexicon, a term meant to associate groups of working-class citizens with a "mob"—a group of unruly individuals capable of riotous public acts designed to explicitly challenge the economic and political status quo. This more negative view of working-class audiences was crystallized after newspaper reports of the Astor Place Opera House riot in 1849 in New York City circulated throughout the United States. The riot was sparked by support for two different actors who were scheduled to star in Shakespeare's *Macbeth* during the same week. The working-class b'hoys supported the first actor, American-born Edwin Forrest. The social elite of New York preferred the interpretation of William Macready, an English actor who gave his performances at the upscale Astor Place Opera House. On the first night of Macready's *Macbeth* performance, supporters of Forrest attended and successfully disrupted the show. On the second night, a heavy police presence around the opera house was deployed to avoid a repeat of the previous night's disturbance. A crowd of Forrest supporters clashed with police outside the theater, throwing stones at the building and at police. Police and local militia fired into the crowd, killing 22 people and wounding over 100 (Butsch, 2008, p. 29).

The Astor Place Opera House Riot brought to an end the popular fascination with working-class audiences. What emerged in its place was the **psychopathology of the crowd**, which associated public collectivities of lower- and working-class citizens with violent mobs. French social psychologist Gustave Le Bon published perhaps the most developed and damning view of this new type of social being in his 1895 book *The Crowd*. Le Bon argued that individuals who converge in large groups in public spaces begin to lose their individual personalities and freewill in favor of a more collective, organic whole—guided not by reason, but by the baser instincts of humankind. Individuals become unconscious of their own acts and instead operate under the will of a collective, often with destructive and dangerous results. When part of a crowd, an individual's uniqueness and rationality devolves into mindless, wanton destruction, as Le Bon explains,

> [B]y the mere fact that he forms part of an organized crowd, a man descends several rungs in the ladder of civilization. Isolated, he may be a cultivated individual; in a crowd, he is a barbarian—that is, a creature acting by instinct. . . . The conclusion to be drawn from what precedes is, that the crowd is always intellectually inferior to the isolated individual. (1960, pp. 32–33)

Le Bon's conceptualization of crowds was not necessarily new, but his treatise effectively captured and condensed a number of strands of contemporary intellectual

Figure 1.5   Depiction of the Astor Place Opera House Riot of 1849

Source: New York Public Library Digital Library.

thought, such as Darwin's theory of natural selection and Freud's theories of the id and the unconscious. The remedy for the danger posed by crowds was clear: Authorities should exercise tight controls on the working class, particularly the expanding industrial underclass in the cities, and should disperse these crowds wherever they could be found in order to protect law-abiding citizens from potential destruction and political chaos. Thus, by the end of the 19th century, the popular view of public collectives had shifted radically from a celebration of the rational, democratic potential of "the common man" to outright fear and loathing of the potential destructive power of "the crowd."

Motion Pictures and the Rise of the Mass Audience

A number of societal changes in the United States, Britain, and Europe in the late 19th century once again redrew the cultural landscape for the audience concept. The first change came with large-scale industrialization, which was well under way in the United States by the late 1800s. New factories required legions of unskilled labor in the form of immigrant workers who had made the voyage to America in search of economic opportunity. What these immigrants found upon arrival, however, were hostile, balkanized urban environments with cramped, unsanitary living conditions. Low-wage immigrant workers "became scapegoats for the fears of native-born, middle-class Americans whose influence was slipping away" (Butsch, 2008, p. 442).

Despite this challenging social environment for immigrants and other unskilled workers living in industrial cities such as Baltimore, Chicago, and New York, Americans began experiencing something that had been largely impractical when they had been living in rural, agrarian settings: the emergence of leisure time. This increase in leisure time "encourage[d] the creation and use of all recreational forms, especially commercial amusements such as the motion picture, which required a more definite and specific commitment of free time" (Jowett, 1976, p. 17).

One of the most popular and historically important leisure time activities at the turn of the 20th century was unquestionably the motion picture. The first time that a moving picture was projected from behind onto a white screen was in the Grand Café in Paris in late 1895 by two French brothers, photographers Auguste and Louis Lumiere (Mast & Kawin, 2006). By 1908, an estimated 8,000 nickelodeon theaters (small storefronts that offered short 5- to 7-minute silent film screenings for the princely sum of 5 cents) were offering daily features to urban audiences. In 1910, the number of theaters had expanded to 10,000. Nickelodeons were found in cities and midsize communities all across the United States (Fuller, 1996, p. 48). By this time, movies "had clearly become a large industry, with three distinct phases of production, exhibition, and distribution; in addition, directing, acting, photography, writing, and lab work emerged as separate crafts" (Czitrom, 1982, p. 40). Silent films were particularly popular with urban immigrant workers who could not afford the higher ticket prices of stage and theater performances.

Additionally, since many of these early movie audiences could not speak English, the silent cinema offered an affordable, enjoyable entertainment experience regardless of viewers' native tongue. Concerns about the crowds and working-class collectives did not simply vanish with the introduction of new media like the movies, however. Instead, elite concerns regarding the power of demagogues over the suggestibility of the crowd mind shifted toward concerns over these new forms of mass media. These concerns are the focus of Chapter 2.

Audiences and Notions of Power

As we've seen in this chapter, the notion of the "audience" has a long history and has been subject to a number of important conceptual shifts—from the face-to-face participatory interactions of democratic citizenship in the Greek and Roman eras to the more dangerous notion of crowds and mobs in the late 19th century to the passive spectatorship of the mass in today's media environment. Apart from understanding the etymological history of the audience, these shifts also tell us something important about the nature of the audience concept; it is powerfully bound with the exercise of social and political power. In other words, *the story of the audience is always closely connected to the ways in which the audience is defined and by whom.* Some of these constructions afford the audience a great deal of power in their response to media messages. Others offer a rather dim view of audience power, identifying media sources as the dominant players in the media–audience relationship, often with negative consequences for receivers.

Structure and Agency

A good way to think about the notion of power is to consider these audiences in terms of *structure* and *agency*. These are the foundational building blocks of British sociologist Anthony Giddens's (1986, 1987) **structuration theory**, a fruitful perspective for understanding human societies from a sociological point of view. As we'll see, the concepts of structure and agency exist in a kind of dynamic tension with each other since the actions of individuals both reproduce and potentially alter existing forms of social structure. Let's deal with each of these in turn.

The concept of **structure** refers to any type of social behavior or set of interactions or relationships between human beings that is reproduced over time. Social structures are most visible when they are enshrined in an *institutional* form; in other words, there are organizations or institutions (such as the church, the government, the education system, etc.) that maintain a particular type of status quo in society, thereby circumscribing the actions of members of society in a particular way. These structures don't simply constrain our actions, however. In fact, in what Giddens terms the **"duality of structure"** (see Figure 1.6), structures effectively *enable* certain types of behaviors and social outcomes as well. Consider the fact that you are likely reading this text as part of a college- or university-level course in media audiences. The constructed nature of the coursework—the syllabus, paper assignments, deadlines, need for regular classroom attendance, and participation in class discussion—all work to effectively constrain the boundaries of your own individual activity in relation to the course. The same is true for the education system in general: Your freedom to navigate your own education, particularly from elementary through high school, is profoundly shaped by institutions and systems beyond your own immediate control, sometimes leaving students and their parents with a sense of helplessness about the system. On the other hand, along with all of this institutional constraint, the completion of a high school diploma or a college degree can be incredibly *enabling* as well. Think about it: That same education can make you a much more competitive applicant for higher-paying, more prestigious jobs, thereby opening access to a higher standard of living, along with

Figure 1.6 The Duality of Structure

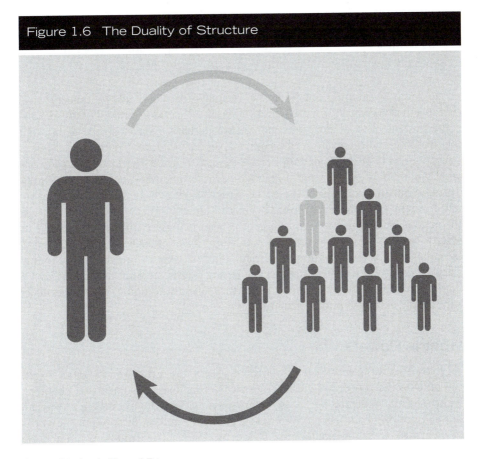

Source: Stephanie Plumeri Ertz.

a whole host of other social and cultural benefits. This is the reason why structures are simultaneously both constraining and enabling for individuals.

On the opposite side of the coin is the notion of **agency**. Agency refers to the actions of individuals in their environment. For Giddens, human beings are defined by their ability to freely make decisions and actions that serve the goals of the individual agent. Action, as Giddens suggests, "should be conceived as a continuous flow of interventions in the world which are initiated by autonomous agents" (Thompson, 1989, p. 58). Far from being blind to the consequences of their individual actions, says Giddens, human beings are instead "reflexive" about their actions. Individuals are aware of their environments, engage in active sensing of their environments, and gather information about the consequences of a partic-ular action that will inform and structure future decisions and actions. However, according to Giddens,

> It does not follow that [agents] know all there is to know about the consequences of what they do, for the activities of others or for their own activities in the future. Nor do they know all there is to know all about the conditions of their action, that is, the circumstances that are causally involved with its production. (1987, pp. 220–221)

Giddens is pointing out here that we make decisions all the time in ways that match our goals, but we may not know or fully understand all of the various consequences of those decisions, nor do we perhaps even grasp the reality that the available choices in front of us are shaped by other people and social forces that are outside of our own control. *Agency and structure are closely related to one another since through our actions we essentially alter and reproduce social structures.* Think about the example of the social structure known as the educational sys-tem from the previous paragraph. This institution continues to exist only because the actions of hundreds of thousands of human beings continually reinforce this system by recognizing the value of education, by financially supporting it, and by sanctioning those who do not participate in the system. Indeed, by attending classes, taking notes, writing papers, and taking exams, students also become will-ing participants in this institutional structure, and by so doing, they continually support the existence of that structure.

What Is Power?

Now that we have the preliminaries of agency and structure in front of us, we can address the concept of audience power. As we'll see in subsequent chapters, theories of the audience almost inevitably have packaged within them at least an implicit notion of audience power vis-à-vis media sources. Simply put, **power** is "the capacity to achieve outcomes" (Giddens, 1986). The more you can achieve your individual goals without hindrance from other structures or individuals or the more you can influence others in order to obtain those goals, the more power you have. We tend to think of power as vested in particular types of institutional authority, such as the police or the courts or even in political leadership. The classic view of power in political science involves "the making of decisions on issues over which there is an observable conflict of (subjective) interests, seen as express policy preferences, revealed by political participation" (Lukes, 1974, p. 12). However, a more sociological definition of power recognizes that *it is omnipresent and relational in nature*, enacted from individual to individual and from institution to individual, rarely with any kind of direct coercion from one agent toward another. A more precise definition of power, therefore, would be similar to the one offered by Bartlett (1989), who wrote that **power involves "the ability of one actor to alter the decisions made and/or welfare experienced by another actor relative to the choices that would have been made and/or welfare that would have been experienced had the actor not existed or acted"** (p. 30).

Sometimes power relationships can exist even without the explicit knowledge of an individual actor. For sociologist Steven Lukes, for instance, who crafted a powerful counterargument to more pluralist definitions of power found in political science, power is identified through the decision-making of individual agents, through the non–decision-making of agents (passive nonchoices), and through the ability of institutions to shape our decisions without our even knowing it. This kind of power recognizes that there are some social structures that go unquestioned by the vast majority of citizens. This means, however, that individuals may continue to lend their support and tacit approval to ruling systems even when it may not be in their best interest to do so. Italian Marxist Antonio Gramsci introduced the concept of hegemony to describe this process. **Hegemony** refers to the process by which political elites generate popular consensus via "the diffusion and popularization of the world view of the ruling class" (Bates, 1975, p. 352). In essence, Gramsci emphasized the role of civil society (schools, churches, clubs, and the media) in shifting our notions of common sense, thereby insulating those in power from dissent and revolution. As you read through the chapters of the book, we will return to the notion of audience power and ask how the theories and ideas of various scholars imagine the abilities of audience members to direct their own experiences with mass media.

Conclusion: Constructing Audiences Through History and Theory

There are two main points from this chapter. The first is that the notion of "the audience" is a theoretical abstraction, meaning that its nature and character are defined by the social, cultural, and political environment in which the audience concept arises. The second point is a corollary of the first: Because audiences are abstractions, the nature and character of what constitutes an "audience" are variable and subject to changes over time. Indeed, as we've seen in this chapter,

the audience experience during the Greek and Roman eras was radically different from the kind of audience experience to which we are accustomed today.
During those ancient times, the participation of citizens in public debate and in
response to dramatic stage presentations was a cornerstone of what it meant to
be a citizen of the republic. With the introduction of new technologies such as
the book in the 1500s, however, the oral traditions of audiences gave way to a
more personal, privatized experience with written text. During the 19th century,
the romanticized view of working-class audiences as direct participants in the
democratic experience gave way to a darker, more sinister view of these public
collectives as mobs and crowds. The Industrial Revolution and the arrival of
mass media such as motion pictures, radio, and (much later) television crystallized two long-developing trends: one toward the expansion of audience size
and the other toward the privatization of the audience experience into individuals' domestic spaces. The concepts of agency and structure help to contextualize
the notion of audience power, a key theme that will reemerge throughout the
book as we examine different schools of thought about media audiences and
their ability to direct their own experiences with the media.

DISCUSSION ACTIVITIES

1. Keep a daily log of your media experiences
for several days. Record when and where
you interact with media messages on any
technological platform such as radio,
television, books, magazines, and the Internet,
or on mobile devices such as your cellphone
or tablet computer. Make some notes about
what types of content you are accessing
(news, entertainment, sports, weather, or
other types of content) and whether or not
you are alone or with other people (make
note also of who those people are—friends,
family, authority figures, strangers, etc.).
Then compare your notes with a partner and
answer the following questions:

- Do you see any similarities in the types of
media experiences you had?

- Are there differences in the types of
content that you access on different sorts
of media?

- Does your social environment (other
audience members present or not) shape
your experiences with media? In what
ways?

- What might your experiences tell us about
the difficulties in identifying a single
definition of the term *audience*?

2. One of the central questions of this book
is how much power (or agency) individual
audience members have vis-à-vis media
producers or media messages. Take some
index cards or flashcards and write down a
media technology with which you interact
each day. On the back of each card, make
some notes about how much *agency* you have
in your interactions with that medium. How
much can you control the amount and type
of information that you receive from that
medium? Are the interpretations that you
make from the content you receive constrained

in any way, either by the technology or by the institutions (or companies) providing you with the technology? Make one card for each media technology you encounter daily. Once you're finished, arrange your cards in the order of audience freedom, from least to most. Which technology gives you the most autonomy as an audience member, and which gives you the least autonomy? Why did you say this?

3. Conduct a brief Internet search for two or three news articles that have to do with some aspect of the audience experience. You might start by thinking of a specific media technology (television, film, radio, Internet, social media, etc.) and then look for articles that specifically address audiences for that particular medium. Read each news article and answer the following questions: Which of James Webster's three models most accurately describe how audiences are being conceptualized in the article? What does this suggest about the kinds of information that we typically receive via the press about media audiences?

ADDITIONAL MATERIALS

Briggs, A., & Burke, P. (2009). *A social history of the media: From Gutenberg to the Internet.* Cambridge, United Kingdom: Polity Press.

Burke, J. (1979). *The day the universe changed: A matter of fact* [Video file]. Available at https://www.imdb.com/title/tt0964233/

Butsch, R. (2008). *The citizen audience: Crowds, publics, and individuals.* New York, NY: Routledge.

Folger Shakespeare Library. (2012). Expert voices on the Astor Place Riot. *Shakespeare in American life.* Available at http://www.shakespeareinamericanlife.org/stage/onstage/yesterday/expert.cfm

McQuail, D. (1997). *Audience analysis.* Thousand Oaks, CA: SAGE.

Reed College. (2012). Resources regarding ancient Greek theater. Available at http://academic.reed.edu/humanities/110tech/theater.html

Sanders, G. J. (2009, November 10). *Anthony Giddens presentation* [Video file]. Retrieved from https://www.youtube.com/watch?v=Zy_UzSm0NnY

REFERENCES

Allor, M. (1988). Relocating the site of the audience. *Critical Studies in Mass Communication, 5*(3), 217–233.

Anderson, J. A. (1996). The pragmatics of audience in research and theory. In J. Hay, L. Grossberg, & E. Wartella (Eds.), *The audience and its landscape, cultural studies* (pp. 75–93). Boulder, CO: Westview Press.

Arnott, P. D. (1989). *Public and performance in the Greek theatre.* London, England: Routledge.

Bartlett, R. (1989). *Economics and power: An inquiry into human relations and markets.* Cambridge, United Kingdom: Cambridge University Press.

Bates, T. R. (1975). Gramsci and the theory of hegemony. *Journal of the History of Ideas, 36*(2), 351–366. Retrieved from https://doi.org/10.2307/2708933

Beacham, R. C. (1992). *The Roman theatre and its audience.* Cambridge, MA: Harvard University Press.

Benkler, Y. (2006). *The wealth of networks: How social production transforms markets and freedom*. New Haven, CT: Yale University Press.

Bratich, J. Z. (2005). Amassing the multitude: Revisiting early audience studies. *Communication Theory, 15*(3), 242–265.

Butsch, R. (2008). *The citizen audience: Crowds, publics, and individuals*. New York, NY: Routledge.

Carey, J. W. (1989). A cultural approach to communication. *Communication as culture: Essays on media and society* (pp. 13–36). Boston, MA: Unwin Hyman.

Castells, M. (2002). *The Internet galaxy: Reflections on the Internet, business, and society*. Oxford, England: Oxford University Press.

Czitrom, D. J. (1982). *Media and the American mind: From Morse to McLuhan*. Chapel Hill: University of North Carolina Press.

Eisenstein, E. L. (2011). Aspects of the printing revolution. In D. Crowley & P. Heyer (Eds.), *Communication in history: Technology, culture, society* (6th ed., pp. 78–85). Boston, MA: Allyn & Bacon.

Febvre, L. P. V., & Martin, H.-J. (1990). *The coming of the book: The impact of printing 1450–1800*. London, England: Verve.

Frey, L. R., Botan, C. H., & Kreps, G. L. (1999). *Investigating communication: An introduction to research methods* (2nd ed.). Boston, MA: Allyn & Bacon.

Fuller, K. H. (1996). *At the picture show: Small-town audiences and the creation of movie fan culture*. Washington, DC: Smithsonian Institution Press.

Giddens, A. (1986). *The constitution of society: Outline of the theory of structuration* (1st paperback ed.). Berkeley: University of California Press.

Giddens, A. (1987). *Social theory and modern sociology*. Stanford, CA: Stanford University Press.

Havelock, E. (2011). The Greek legacy. In D. Crowley & P. Heyer (Eds.), *Communication in history: Technology, culture, society* (6th ed., pp. 38–43). Boston, MA: Allyn & Bacon.

Jowett, G. (1976). *Film: The democratic art*. Boston, MA: Little, Brown.

Kaufer, D. S., & Carley, K. M. (1993). *Communication at a distance: The influence of sociocultural organization and change*. Hillsdale, NJ: Lawrence Erlbaum Associates.

Kennedy, G. A. (1980). *Classical rhetoric and its Christian and secular tradition from ancient to modern times*. Chapel Hill: University of North Carolina Press.

Le Bon, G. (1960). *The crowd: A study of the popular mind*. New York, NY: Viking Press.

Lowery, S. A., & DeFleur, M. L. (1995). *Milestones in mass communication research* (3rd ed.). Boston, MA: Allyn & Bacon.

Lukes, S. (1974). *Power: A radical view*. London, England: Macmillan.

Maddox, T. (2018, February 9). *Data usage at Super Bowl 52 grows 48% as social media use skyrockets*. Retrieved from https://www.techrepublic.com/article/data-usage-at-super-bowl-52-grew-48-as-social-media-use-skyrockets/

Mast, G., & Kawin, B. F. (2006). *A short history of the movies* (9th ed.). White Plains, NY: Longman.

McQuail, D. (1997). *Audience analysis*. Thousand Oaks, CA: SAGE.

Neuman, W. R. (1991). *The future of the mass audience*. Cambridge, UK: Cambridge University Press.

Ong, W. J. (1975). The writer's audience is always a fiction. *PMLA, 90*(1), 9–21.

Ong, W. J. (2002). *Orality and literacy: The technologizing of the word*. London, England: Routledge.

Otterson, J. (2018, February 5). TV Ratings: Super Bowl LII slips 7% from 2017 to 103.4 million viewers. *Variety*. Retrieved from https://variety.com/2018/tv/news/super-bowl-lii-ratings-1202687239/

Putnam, R. D. (2000). *Bowling alone: The collapse and revival of American community*. New York, NY: Simon & Schuster.

Shannon, C. E., & Weaver, W. (1949). *The mathematical theory of communication*. Urbana: University of Illinois Press.

Silverstone, R. (1999). *Why study the media?* Thousand Oaks, CA: SAGE.

Streeter, T. (1996). *Selling the air: A critique of the policy of commercial broadcasting in the United States*. Chicago, IL: University of Chicago Press.

Thomas, C. G., & Webb, E. K. (1994). From orality to rhetoric: An intellectual transformation. In I. Worthington (Ed.), *Persuasion: Greek rhetoric in action* (pp. 3–25). London, England: Routledge.

Thompson, J. B. (1989). The theory of structuration. In D. Held & J. B. Thompson (Eds.), *Social theory of modern societies: Anthony Giddens and his critics* (pp. 56–76). Cambridge, UK: Cambridge University Press.

Webster, J. G. (1998). The audience. *Journal of Broadcasting & Electronic Media, 42*(2), 190–207.

Audiences as Objects

The first section of the text examines audience constructions from a particular perspective: as a collective of individuals who are potentially susceptible to outside media influence. The orientation here is one that considers **audiences as objects** that are acted upon by media messages. The implied audience is one that is ill-equipped to adequately argue against or process harmful media messages or is perhaps misled into actions, beliefs, or behaviors that threaten the general social fabric. This notion places the audience in a largely reactive mode by arguing that messages disrupt individuals' normal states of being and introduce foreign and potentially damaging influences on attitudes, behaviors, and other psychological variables. This view of the audience has been historically dominant in the history of the field of media and communication, though scholarship at the end of the century began to offer strong challenges to this idea.

The notion that audiences can be "imagined" as a loose confederation of faceless, anonymous masses has its roots in the Industrial Revolution, when rural communities (which privileged face-to-face communication and informal social ties) were forever altered by waves of urban migration to the city. In the early 20th century, the concern over the "crowd" mentality shifted to the faceless power of the "mass." The definition of the **mass audience** concept was most famously outlined by early 20th-century sociologist Herbert Blumer (1954, p. 370), who argued that this new type of audience included two distinguishing features: (1) membership from "all walks of life, and from all distinguishable social strata" and (2) anonymity marked by little interaction or exchange among individuals. In contrast to the 19th-century notion of crowds, a mass audience is loosely organized and unable to act as a unified whole because individuals are geographically dispersed, connected only via their spectatorship of a particular medium. Consequently, Blumer's notion of the mass is largely that of an undifferentiated, impersonal collective that is "devoid of the features of a society or a community" (1954, p. 370).

The idea that an audience of anonymous millions could be created as a result of media spectatorship also made sense in the context of the increased use of statistics to understand the behavior of very large groups of people by both business and government throughout the 1800s (Webster & Phalen, 1997, p. 4). By the time that corporations began mass producing consumer goods in the latter half of the

19th century, product surveys and statistical models were already in widespread use as tools to predict consumer demand. As new forms of mass media emerged in the 20th century (such as radio in the 1920s and television in the late 1940s), the notion of mass audiences as agglomerations of individual behaviors and opinions was entrenched enough to be dubbed the "dominant model" of the audience. We will explore this notion of the mass audience much more in Chapter 2.

Effects of
Media Messages

On June 12, 2016, at roughly 2:00 a.m., a 29-year-old security guard named Omar Mateen entered Pulse, a gay nightclub in Orlando, Florida, and began firing into the crowd with a semiautomatic rifle and a pistol, leaving 49 people dead and over 50 people wounded (Mozingo, Pearce, & Wilkinson, 2016). Mateen staged a 3-hour hostage standoff before police stormed the nightclub and killed him. At the time, it was the worst mass shooting in U.S. history. On June 3, 2017, pedestrians on the London Bridge were left scrambling when a van deliberately drove into them before crashing on the south bank of the River Thames, after which the three occupants of the van ran to a nearby market and began stabbing people around nearby pubs and restaurants (Dearden, 2017). Police shot dead the three attackers about 8 minutes into the emergency, but not before eight innocent civilians were killed and 48 people were wounded.

Aside from the infliction of mass casualties and a sense of terror among civilians, these two horrific events had something in common: They were perpetrated by individuals—all native-born citizens in their respective countries—who had reportedly become "radicalized" by consuming Islamist extremist videos on YouTube. In the London Bridge case, Khuram Shazad Butt, one of the attackers and a Pakistani-born British citizen, had been an outspoken proponent of the Islamic State in Iraq and Syria (ISIS) after watching online videos of Ahmad Musa Jibril, an American preacher of Palestinian descent who preached a radically conservative ideology of Islam (Moore, 2017). In the Pulse nightclub shooting, FBI Director James Comey as well as President Barack Obama confirmed that Mateen had been "self-radicalized" via his exposure to extremist views over the Internet (Pilkington & Roberts, 2016). These two terrorist incidents in two different countries raise a host of thorny questions about the media: Did these two individuals seek out extremist content online after they had become radicalized? Or did watching YouTube videos really alter the political views of Mateen and Butt, leading them to violently reject their home countries in favor of a dangerously extreme and brutal sect of Islam? YouTube's parent company Google responded to the London Bridge incident by promising to remove videos that clearly violated its community guidelines (such as those promoting terrorism) and would make other changes with regard to videos that denigrated other religions or races. For example, Google changed its policies to prevent extremist videos from to prevent extremist videos from selling advertising and from being promoted, endorsed, or commented on by users (Wakabayashi, 2017). Google noted that its new policy was intended to balance the need to promote free expression via YouTube with the desire to protect audiences from damaging and potentially radicalizing content.

Overview of the Chapter

These examples of radicalization via consumption of extremist content on YouTube and other sites online illustrate a style of reasoning that stretches back more than a century: that media messages carry potentially damaging information for the audience and that these messages need to be carefully monitored and potentially restricted. The idea that media messages can lead to changes in individual audience members is the thrust behind the "effects perspective," which emerged in the 20th century as the dominant paradigm in the field of media studies. This chapter orients you to some of the major strands in media effects theories, beginning with the origins of mass society theory in the early 20th century. We then focus on early concerns over film and radio. The chapter then moves on to examine some key studies in media exposure and persuasion in the World War II era. The final section focuses on concerns with mediated violence and its effects on society, particularly children. This is examined via the U.S. television violence studies from the late 1960s and early 1970s (especially the Surgeon General's Report). The chapter concludes with some examples of more recent research into the effects of mediated violence on children, specifically that from video games and mobile media.

Origins of Media Effects Theories in the Early 20th Century

The early 20th century was a time of extraordinary change in the United States and elsewhere in the industrialized world. Manufacturing was rapidly becoming the largest source of job creation, supplanting agricultural labor. The mechanization of farming drove millions to urban centers where they formed a giant pool of cheap labor to fuel the industrial machine. Human migration and immigration were also a part of the story, with waves of new immigrants pouring into the United States from Europe, Ireland, and elsewhere, creating new cultural diasporas in urban centers up and down the East Coast of the United States. New media technologies also emerged during this time period, from motion pictures in the late 1890s to consumer radio in the 1920s. Perhaps not surprisingly, with all of these extraordinary social, economic, and technological changes, there was a good deal of anxiety expressed among elites, scholars, and politicians about the impacts of these changes and the uncertain future direction of society. As discussed in Chapter 1, in the first decade of the 20th century the notion of crowds as dangerous, gullible collectives propelled deep suspicions about the common people among both economic elites and progressive reformers. These fears of the crowd coincided with the emergence of a new media technology that captivated audiences: motion pictures. The rapid rise of the movies as a dominant leisure-time activity in burgeoning urban areas became a focal point for fascination and alarm among scholars, progressive reformers, and politicians. The importance of film in American life was accompanied by the near simultaneous emergence of new academic disciplines, most notably sociology, which arose to understand and contextualize the enormous changes under way as a result of industrialization, rapid urbanization, and immigration. The seeds of the media effects paradigm were sown during this chaotic and dynamic period.

Charles Horton Cooley and the Emergence of Sociology

In the early 20th century, the field of sociology was beginning to emerge. For the first time, a number of thinkers were considering some of the ramifications of Gustave Le Bon's theories about crowd psychology. In particular, fascination developed over the dynamics between the individual and social groups, how such groups developed and sustained themselves, and the impact of group membership on the psychology of individuals within the group.

One of the first observers of the impacts of media on society was Charles Horton Cooley, a professor at the University of Michigan (and later at the University of Chicago) and key founding figure in American sociology. In two early books, *Human Nature and the Social Order* first published in 1902 (1964) and *Social Organization: A Study of the Larger Mind* first published in 1909 (1962), Cooley outlined the significance of "communication" in giving societies a sense of themselves, beginning with observation and imitation processes that children adopt as they mature. Cooley described **communication** as follows:

The mechanism through which human relations exist and develop—all the symbols of the mind, together with the means of conveying them through space and preserving them in time. It includes the expression of the face, attitude, and gesture, the tones of the voice, words, writing, printing, railways, telegraphs, telephones, and whatever else may be the latest achievement in the conquest of space and time. (1962, p. 61)

Cooley was one of the first intellectuals to link the development of individuals' psyches and worldviews with (a) their immediate surroundings, including social feedback from peers, parents, and other authority figures, and (b) the messages carried by communications media via print, telegraph, and telephones, to name a few.

Of particular interest to Cooley were newer forms of mass media such as newspapers and motion pictures. Each of these new technologies, argued Cooley, would not only encourage the dissemination of more information among the populace, but they would also catalyze a "growth of a sense of common humanity, of moral unity, between nations, races, and classes" (1962, p. 88). Alongside this newfound social uniformity, however, Cooley noted that modern forms of communication had dramatically lowered barriers to information, allowing individuals to pursue their own individual interests and goals to a greater degree than ever before. In spite of some of these positive impacts of new forms of communication, Cooley also voiced some concern about the potentially negative effects of media. In particular, he surmised that newspapers and other media forms would give the public only a superficial understanding of (and concern with) public issues and other people. The problem, he noted, is that we learn so much about so many things that we develop only the most rudimentary understanding of those things (because our time and attention are necessarily limited). Cooley's early scholarship paved the way for future systematic analysis of the impacts of media, particularly the Payne Fund Studies in the late 1920s.

Concern Over Film Audiences: Hugo Münsterberg and Mass Suggestibility

The movies were rapidly becoming one of the most popular leisure-time activities for lower-class immigrants and other unskilled labor in major cities in the United States and elsewhere. This development raised numerous red flags for elites and progressive reformers. Gustave Le Bon's theories about the suggestibility of large crowds to unscrupulous demagogues were quickly adapted to the motion pictures. The capability of this new medium to reach tens of thousands of people sparked new controversy about the susceptibility of the "masses" to dangerous thoughts and emotions. Film historian Garth Jowett (1976, p. 13) argues that these concerns were fueled not necessarily because there was any substantive evidence to support them but instead because "there were no established mechanisms of cultural or social control" to rein in the perceived excesses of the motion picture. In fact, the "movies represented a threat to the established hegemony of the Protestant groups that had imposed their morality and values on American life and culture" (Jowett, Jarvie, & Fuller, 1996, p. 22). In cities and towns all over the United States, small, silent motion picture houses called "nickelodeons" began appearing that offered short 10- to 15-minute silent films for a 5-cent ticket price (see Figure 2.1). Particularly in urban areas, working-class Americans (many of them recent immigrants) flocked to nickelodeons as their main leisure-time activity, which caused consternation among politicians, elites, and other cultural critics (Fuller, 1996; Peiss, 1986).

Scholars and social commentators of the time were concerned with how motion pictures integrated into the modern city. They worried about the effect of the movies and popular amusements in general on other sociological changes such as childhood delinquency, a rise in teenage pregnancy rates, and the health and safety of the movie theaters themselves (Edwards, 1915; Phelan, 1919). As McDonald (2004, p. 185) notes, notions of media effects in these early years "were conceived of as learning effects" and other potential effects on children and other populations emerged out of the learning process. However, Harvard psychologist Hugo Münsterberg was the first to consider how motion pictures were beginning to alter

Source: Library of Congress.

human beings' sense of reality. His 1916 book *The Photoplay* closely examined the perceptual processes that were found among audiences when they encountered the moving image on the screen. In order to understand and engage with a film's plot and characters, he argued, audiences must first place themselves within the conceptual world of the visual images on the screen. They must accept, at least temporarily, the reality of the images they encounter in order to make some kind of sense of the events unfolding on the film screen. For Münsterberg, "This confusion of reality and content is a necessary condition for understanding communication and a crucial part of how mediated communication works" (McDonald, 2004, p. 185). For instance, even though the images flickering on the screen are two-dimensional, Münsterberg argued that audiences cannot help but see them as "strongly plastic forms. . . . We feel immediately the depth of things" (1916, p. 47).

Perhaps the most explosive aspect of Münsterberg's analysis of film viewers, however, was his suggestion that the unique cognitive and emotional state experienced by audiences during a motion picture performance left those individuals vulnerable to forms of psychological suggestion. Films introduced an altered reality for audiences, which was a concern, according to Münsterberg:

> The sight of crime and of vice may force itself on the consciousness with disastrous results. The normal resistance breaks down and the moral balance, which would have kept under the habitual stimuli of the narrow routine of life, may be lost under the pressure of the realistic suggestion. (1916, p. 95)

Over time, Münsterberg worried, the deeply moving cinematic world of images and faraway places would slowly begin to displace real-world social interaction. Additionally, Münsterberg's warning that the movies could be used to implant ideas into unsuspecting audiences marked "the beginnings of an effects approach that would become the dominant paradigm for audience researchers, for government investigation, and for the public for over fifty years. Much of the research would be driven by public concern and *moral panics*" (Butsch, 2008, p. 45). British sociologist Stanley Cohen (2002) used the term **moral panics** to describe very strong negative public reactions to the spread of a new social behavior. This response is generally an overreaction, which makes finding an accommodation to the new behavior difficult. **Media panics** are a specific type of moral panic that surround the introduction of a new type of media or content genre (Drotner, 1992). Audiences are typically imagined as vulnerable to negative influences from this new medium or content since messages are assumed to have a direct influence on each individual.

The rapid expansion of new media technologies in the 20th century was largely characterized by a cycle of media panics and subsequent actions, including scholarly research, elite activism, and even public policy responses. Münsterberg's book was one of the first to facilitate a media panic surrounding the motion picture and in so doing effectively replaced Le Bon's idea of crowd psychology with the notion of a **mass society**. This concept of the isolated, anonymous, and vulnerable mass became the dominant view of media audiences throughout much of the 20th century.

Mass Society Theory and the Payne Fund Studies

Much of the concern surrounding new forms of media had its roots in the social and economic upheavals of the 19th century. With the rise of industrialization in the United States and elsewhere around the world, farm workers found that their labor was being displaced by faster, more efficient machinery, which drove them into urban environments where there were available factory jobs. In 1887, a young German sociologist named Ferdinand Tönnies (1957) began an analysis of the large-scale shifts going on around him and published them in an influential book titled *Community and Society*. Tönnies observed an ongoing transition between **Gemeinschaft** (community) and **Gesellschaft** (society). The concept of Gemeinschaft referred not just to small rural communities that were increasingly disintegrating because of urban migration but also to a way of living in these communities. Tönnies noted that social relationships were deeply intertwined in these small communities, and webs of reciprocal trust and cooperation bound these communities to one another. These strong interpersonal networks were fueled by a shared heritage or cultural traditions (such as religious or ethnic ties). In the cities, however, recent transplants from these tight-knit, rural settings were confronted with a completely different social environment. Industrialization and the move toward factory labor resulted in a different kind of social organization, a Gesellschaft. **Gesellschaft** refers to a much larger group of individuals living together in an urban environment. Here, the informal webs of interpersonal trust are replaced by formal contracts, which are required since almost all daily social and economic transactions take place between strangers. Instead of feeling closely connected with one's peers, individuals in a Gesellschaft are largely anonymous and experience a sense of displacement because they are unmoored from their traditional cultural environments. In a Gesellschaft, Tonnies' wrote,

> Everybody is by himself and isolated, and there exists a condition of tension against all others. Their spheres of activity are sharply separated so that everybody refuses to everyone else contact with and admittance to his sphere; i.e., intrusions are regarded as hostile acts. (1957, p. 64)

Tonnies' ideas about the shift from Gemeinschaft to Gesellschaft had a profound impact on the development of the field of sociology in the 20th century (Kamenka, 1965). They also shaped a new way of thinking about the vulnerability of audiences to forms of mass media in urban, industrialized environments by giving rise to the **mass society theory**. Mass society theory assumes that Tonnies' claims about the isolated nature of individuals living in modern, urban environments are correct and then imagines the role that media such as newspapers, magazines, and motion pictures might play in such a society. The theory posits that these forms of media are a malignant force in society because they have the capacity to directly influence the attitudes and behaviors of individuals. Modern audiences are vulnerable to media influence precisely because they are anonymous city dwellers who have been cut off from their families, communities, cultural traditions and other social institutions. Forms of mass media, then, serve to further isolate individuals, debase culture as a whole, and generally result in social decline (for a recent overview of the notion of the mass, see Lang & Lang, 2009).

The Payne Fund Studies (1929–1932)

The tenets of mass society theory were well accepted by social theorists, progressives, and educators who focused their concern on the potentially negative influence of motion pictures in the 1920s. Their suspicion that the movies could implant ideas into the minds of unsuspecting audiences motivated one of the most ambitious early audience research projects in the history of the field. While the movies had been a source of concern during the first two decades of the 20th century, "there was very little scientific evidence to substantiate the often hysterical claims of the reform group" (Kamenka, 1965). The Payne Fund, a philanthropic organization founded to encourage adolescents to take up reading, took up the cause against the movies by hiring William Short, the executive director of the Motion Picture Research Council (another private educational group), to organize a large-scale research project to generate scientific evidence about the deleterious effects of the movies. Short himself was "convinced that commercial interests had captured what was a powerful tool for education and morality and were producing movies that undermined the moral education of youth" (Jansen, 2008, p. 82). In 1927, Short began the process of inviting scholars from a number of fields such as education, sociology, and psychology to conduct systematic research into the effects of motion pictures on America's youth. The Payne Fund Studies, as they came to be known, explored numerous types of effects of the movies, including physical and emotional impacts, effects on racial attitudes and beliefs, self-identity, and factual learning and retention. The project culminated in a sizeable 13-volume report, which was published in 1933. While an extensive overview of the studies is beyond the scope of this chapter, some highlights of the findings are outlined here.

One of the questions addressed by the research was the influence of motion pictures on adults' and children's retention of factual information. George Stoddard, director of the Iowa Child Welfare Research Station at the University of Iowa, and a graduate student, P. W. Holaday, conducted a series of experiments in which they showed feature-length films to children in different age groups (Holaday and Stoddard, 1933). To measure information retention, the researchers gave the children a fact quiz 6 weeks and 3 months after they had seen the films. They found that 60% of children could recall specific details about the films they saw, though the retention of information increased for films with exciting action sequences and for films that featured contexts that were beyond the world experiences of the children.

In another study, psychologists Shuttleworth and May (1933) developed a questionnaire with inventories of children's attitudes toward categories of people and ethical situations, including questions about their own moviegoing habits and performance in school. After conducting surveys with approximately 1,400 children and comparing movie "fans" to those with sparse movie attendance, only small differences were observed: Movie fans had slightly lower grades in school but were more liked by their peers. The lack of conclusive results about the impact of movie attendance on these behavioral and attitude measures was a source of concern for William Short, who urged the researchers to keep looking for a connection (Jowett et al., 1996, p. 68).

A clearer link between film exposure and attitude change was observed by Ruth Peterson and L. L. Thurstone (1933). This study loomed particularly large in the larger Payne Fund research project because Thurstone's pioneering work on quantifying and measuring attitudes was considered crucial to finding specific evidence of motion picture effects (Jowett et al., 1996, p. 67). In their experiments, Peterson and Thurstone selected 16 different feature films that presented either favorable or unfavorable views about one of a number of topics, such as antiwar sentiment (*All Quiet on the Western Front*, 1930) or anti-Black sentiment (*Birth of a Nation*, 1915). In experiments that investigated both single and multiple film effects on different children ranging in age from sixth through 12th grades, children's attitudes were measured 2 weeks before exposure to films and then again afterward. While some individual films had little if any effect on attitudes toward themes or ethnic groups portrayed in the films, other films demonstrated a measurable impact. In a study that measured attitudes of more than 400 high school students with little exposure to African Americans, for instance, exposure to the racist film *Birth of a Nation* substantially lessened viewers' favorability toward Blacks. Peterson and Thurstone (1933) discovered a cumulative effect as well: When two or three films were shown that expressed very similar views, the effects on children's attitudes were much more pronounced than with single film exposures.

The Payne Fund Studies also contained research on more immediate and visceral impacts of the movies. Christian Ruckmick and graduate student Wendell Dysinger, both from the University of Iowa psychology department, were fascinated by the physiological and emotional responses of children to motion pictures (Dysinger and Ruckmick, 1933). In their studies, they attached children to heart monitors and galvanometers in order to capture real-time measurements of children's heart rates, blood pressure, and sweaty palms as indicators of excitement, arousal, and fear. Children in their study screened adventure and romance films that were in circulation at the time, such as *Charlie Chan's Chance* (1932) and *The Feast of Ishtar*. Responses to films varied according to the children's age. For instance, scenes of danger and tragedy had a powerful effect on children up to age 9, but then began decreasing steadily among teens and adults. On the other hand, responses to erotic or romantic scenes were muted among 7- to 10-year-olds, but grew in intensity among 10- and 11-year-olds, only to peak in the 16-year-old viewers.

Consequences of the Payne Fund Studies

Despite the somewhat mixed results regarding the impacts of motion pictures on children's attitudes, emotional health, and behaviors, the lasting impression left by the Payne Fund Studies was that the movies represented a powerful and inherent danger to American youth. This perception was fueled mainly by Short's public interpretation of the findings and by some of the more reformist-minded scholars who contributed research to the project. Chief among these reformers was University of Chicago sociologist Herbert Blumer, who conducted a qualitative study that compared the autobiographical reflections of middle-class high school students with those of juvenile delinquents (Blumer, 1933). A reformer by nature and a critic of the movies, Blumer was interested to see if he could uncover a connection between motion picture exposure and delinquency. In one of his two reports submitted to the Payne Fund Studies, Blumer built upon Le Bon's ideas about emotional contagion by using a concept called "emotional possession" to describe the sway that the moviegoing experience had on young viewers. The effects of this on the individual were so strong, argued Blumer, that "even his efforts to rid himself of it by reasoning with himself may prove of little avail" (Butsch, 2008, p. 45). While Blumer ultimately discovered only a tenuous connection between juvenile delinquency and moviegoing, the notion of **emotional contagion**—the viral-like spread of emotional states and attitudes from one individual to another, facilitated through mass media—captured the public's concern once again, drawing attention back to earlier concerns that had been so powerfully perpetuated by Le Bon's and Münsterberg's research. Fears about the persuasive impact of motion pictures were largely transferred to the medium of radio, which began to rise in importance in the late 1920s.

The War of the Worlds Broadcast and the Direct Effects Model
• •

By the time the Payne Fund Studies were published in 1933, a new medium was emerging for delivering news and entertainment to millions of Americans: radio. According to estimates provided by the Columbia Broadcasting System, by 1935 roughly 70% of all American households (some 21.5 million homes) possessed a radio set, and some 78 million Americans described themselves as habitual radio listeners (Cantril & Allport, 1935, p. 85). Even during the depths of the Great Depression, Americans clung to their radio sets as a source of information, entertainment, and even comfort. The first systematic attempt to take stock of the effects that radio listening was having on audiences was *The Psychology of Radio* (1935), written by Harvard psychologist Gordon Allport and his former graduate student Hadley Cantril. Cantril and Allport argued that the rhetorical conventions of radio radically oversimplified many complex issues, reducing them to "black or white" dichotomous terms (Pandora, 1998). They worried that this was narrowing the minds of American listeners, particularly since many radio programs were dominated by so-called experts who instructed their listeners on "what to eat, what to read, what to buy, what exercise to take, what to think of the music we hear, and how we treat our colds" (Cantril & Allport, 1935, p. 23). They also noted that the radio could function as a tool of propaganda, which they described as the "systematic attempt to develop through the use of suggestion certain of the listener's attitudes and beliefs in such a way that some special interest is favored" (1935, p. 48). With start-up funds from the Rockefeller Foundation in 1937, Cantril was one of several prominent scholars (such as Paul Lazarsfeld and Theodor Adorno) to found the first large-scale research institute dedicated to understanding the impacts of radio on society. At the Office of Radio Research at Princeton University, Cantril and his colleagues began to map out methodological strategies for tracking who was listening to radio and why.[1]

---

[1]One of these studies, coauthored by Herta Herzog, explored the uses of daytime radio serials by American women. It is discussed in full detail in Chapter 5.

The War of the Worlds Broadcast (1938)

The event that crystallized critics' concerns about the power of radio was *The War of the Worlds* broadcast on October 30, 1938. The broadcast was a production of a radio drama program titled *Mercury Theatre on the Air* on the CBS network: a weekly program of audio-only stage dramas (including classic works by Shakespeare) that featured the vocal and artistic talents of director Orson Welles and his troupe of classically trained actors. During this particular week, Welles and his creative collaborator John Houseman had decided to dramatize British author H. G. Wells's science-fiction classic from 1898, *The War of the Worlds.* Wells's first-person narrated novel follows the events of an imagined invasion of London by Martians. Welles and Houseman reimagined the novel for their radio drama by making several small but fateful changes to the narrative. They adopted the first-person narration of the original novel but changed the setting of the drama to take place in the United States and made the small town of Grover's Mill, New Jersey, the landing site for the fictional Martian invasion. After an initial introduction to the program by Welles himself to set the stage for the drama, a fictional radio announcer took the microphone and informed listeners that they would be listening to a selection of musical pieces played by Ramon Raquello and his orchestra in the Meridian Room in the Hotel Park Plaza in downtown New York. The drama quickly shifted, however, when multiple news bulletins interrupted the music to inform listeners that a strange object had landed from space near Princeton, New Jersey. The broadcast skillfully wove in supposed eyewitness accounts of Martians attacking passersby and spreading their extraterrestrial conquest throughout the country.

Radio listeners who had tuned into the Mercury Theatre program from the 8:00 p.m. start time were likely aware that the musical program they were listening to was part of the plot of the drama. There were many more, however, who tuned in late, thanks to a much more popular program on rival network NBC. Many of these "dial-twisting" listeners believed that the broadcast was a real news program and that accounts of alien invaders in New Jersey were happening in real time. Primed to believe in the radio as a trustworthy source of news, hundreds of thousands of listeners panicked when they heard Welles's broadcast. The reaction was strongest in the area immediately surrounding Princeton, New Jersey, where news reports indicated that families were rushing out of their homes with wet handkerchiefs and towels around their heads to ward off a gas attack (Cantril, 1940, p. 49). In all, Cantril estimated that roughly 1 million people out of the several million who tuned into the broadcast were frightened by what they heard, though historical reexamination has challenged this mass panic narrative (Socolow & Pooley, 2013).

Cantril's Study of Mass Panic Among Radio Audiences

Cantril immediately recognized the unique opportunity that had presented itself to gather data on the "psychology of panic" and its relationship to radio broadcasting. In the preface to the 1939 book that detailed the results of his research, Cantril wrote, "Such rare occurrences are opportunities for the social scientist to study mass behavior. They must be exploited when they come" (1940, p. ix). Given the inability to carefully plan a research project in advance, Cantril relied upon several sources of available data, including a nationwide telephone survey conducted by the American Institute of Public Opinion (founded by George Gallup; see Chapter 3), another telephone survey conducted by CBS itself, and 135 listeners who were interviewed by Cantril and his research team in the weeks following the broadcast. Cantril was interested in how many people panicked and why. In particular, he wondered why some audiences had panicked while others did not.

The results of the telephone surveys indicated that fewer than 1-in-3 listeners (28%) thought that the broadcast was a news report. However, of those who did believe that they were hearing breaking news, 70% reported that they were frightened or disturbed by the broadcast. In his follow-up interviews with panicked listeners living near Princeton, Cantril discovered a number of psychological characteristics and personality factors that helped to explain why they became frightened. For instance, listeners who were less self-confident, less emotionally secure, or were fatalistic were much more likely to panic when they heard the broadcast. Additionally, listeners who were more religious than others were also more likely to be frightened by the broadcast. As to why some listeners panicked while others did not, Cantril posited that some audiences possessed "critical ability," which he defined as "a capacity to evaluate the stimulus in such a way that they were able to understand its inherent characteristics so they could judge and act appropriately" (1940, pp. 111–112). Cantril reasoned that critical ability was likely related to an individual's level of education but admitted that there was no direct way to measure it.

As with the Payne Fund Studies earlier in the decade, the results of Cantril's study revealed that the effects of media messages were contingent on specific characteristics of the audience. This nuance was largely lost on the popular media, however, which saw the broadcast as yet another example of the dangerous power of the mass media to affect millions of innocent people.

Mass Propaganda Concerns and World War II Communication Research

The panic that ensued following the *War of the Worlds* broadcast demonstrated the potential power of the mass media to provoke an immediate, emotional response to a message. But aside from these types of short-term emotional responses, could media messages also change the way we think about the world? Could forms of media actually change audiences' attitudes, beliefs, and behaviors? A number of key early figures in the use and study of media effects were fascinated by the media's potential for mass persuasion.

Early Concerns With Mass Persuasion

One of the key early texts to explore the relationship between the media and audiences was *Public Opinion*, published in 1922 by journalist and public intellectual Walter Lippmann. While Lippmann is most remembered for his reflections upon news and politics (he was extensively consulted by numerous U.S. political figures, including presidents), he is also "arguably the most important single figure in the immediate prehistory of academic communication research" (Jansen, 2008, p. 82). The title of Lippmann's 1922 classic is a bit misleading—his book did not consider public opinion in our modern sense of that phrase (statistical measurements of collective sentiment). Instead, Lippmann painted a broad picture of how modern forms of mass communication such as newspapers and motion pictures affected the psychological outlook of individuals and therefore their ability to effectively participate in a democratic society.

Specifically, Lippmann outlined the notion of **stereotypes**, which described the predominant method through which all individuals perceived the world. He wrote that "we are told about the world before we see it. We imagine most things before we experience them" (Lippmann, 1922, p. 90). Individuals' sense of reality is therefore mediated by their expectations of reality, and these expectations are formed through their exposure to the media. Journalists, who conduct what Lippmann called "intelligence work" on behalf of the public by gathering information about national events, policies, and people, provide an incomplete picture of political and world events for the public. The public, therefore, makes decisions and evaluates their political leaders according to the "pictures in their heads," which are composed of the narratives and images that are provided by the news media. This presented an important problem: If there existed "some barrier between the public and the event," then this barrier could create a "pseudo-environment" that could be effectively managed by those with specific interests in mind. In essence, Lippmann foreshadowed the dangers posed by **media propaganda**. The term *propaganda* refers to the means to "disseminate or promote particular ideas," and it stems from the Latin term meaning "to propagate" or "to sow" (Jowett & O'Donnell, 2011, p. 2). In its modern usage, however, *propaganda* has taken on a more negative connotation, describing a deliberate attempt by one party to control or manage the information environment of another (or group) through the manipulation of symbols or psychology.

The power of the media to direct the American public's understanding and evaluation of world events was demonstrated strikingly during World War I (1917–1918). Then-President Woodrow Wilson recognized from an early stage that he faced a highly skeptical public and Congress regarding the potential entry of the United States into a costly and dangerous foreign conflict. To rally public support and to put pressure on Congress and American businesses to cooperate with his administration in its war policy, Wilson established the Committee on Public Information (CPI) by executive order in April 1917. The committee was chaired by George Creel, who worked closely with the Secretaries of War, State, and the Navy to carefully coordinate the first wide-scale public relations effort in American history (Jowett & O'Donnell, 2011, pp. 124–125). The CPI carefully crafted messages about the U.S. war efforts and communicated them through an enormous range of media outlets: news stories, motion pictures, books, magazines, posters, billboard advertisements, speeches, and phonograph records. In a series of billboards and posters, Creel's committee not only informed Americans of their responsibilities to preserve food and to buy war bonds, but it also depicted the German army as evil and barbaric, which generated hard feelings among the public for the enemy (see Figure 2.2). The wartime propaganda effort was regarded by many to be highly successful in mobilizing the U.S. public and the industrial interests in the United States to fight a long, protracted war in Europe.

Figure 2.2   U.S. World War I Poster

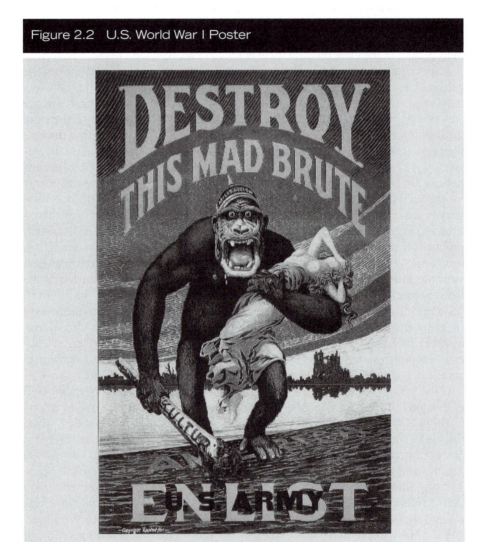

Source: "Destroy this Mad Brute," US Government. H.R. Hopps, 1917.

After the armistice was signed in 1918, bringing an end to the war, a number of lawmakers in Congress began to call for an investigation into the CPI since they believed that it had systematically deceived the American public during the war. Creel staunchly defended his work on the CPI in the 1920 book *How We Advertised America*, arguing that he had simply engaged in

> plain publicity proposition, a vast enterprise in salesmanship, the world's greatest adventures in advertising. . . . We did not call it propaganda. . . . Our effort was educational and informative throughout, for we had such confidence in our case as to feel that no other argument was needed than the simple, straightforward presentation of the facts. (1920, pp. 4–5)

The experience of World War I also solidified the notion that media forms could persuade millions of people to change their attitudes and behaviors.

World War II Communication Research

The apparent success of Creel's propaganda efforts coupled with rising concerns over the persuasive power of radio (seen in *The War of the Worlds* broadcast, for instance) crystallized the view that specific media messages could alter audiences' attitudes and behaviors. Although the institutional propaganda apparatus within the U.S. government was dismantled after the end of the war, the "psychological warfare projects of World War I left their strongest legacy in academic circles, particularly in the embryonic field of communication research" (Simpson, 1996, p. 16). Scholars became fascinated by the prospect that individuals might be susceptible to persuasive messages distributed via the mass media. A myriad number of questions remained, however: What types of media and what aspects of the specific media message would prove most persuasive for audiences? Under what conditions might audiences shift their attitudes and behaviors as a result of experiencing a message?

When World War II erupted in Europe, answers to these questions were of interest not only to social scientists but to those in the highest echelons of the U.S. armed forces. Social psychologists and sociologists were hastily recruited by the federal government to study how to perfect propaganda and counterpropaganda. The U.S. War Department was particularly concerned about the seeming effectiveness of the German propaganda machine in persuading Germans to back the policies of Hitler's Nazi government. It was clear that some media messages could achieve powerful effects under certain conditions, but the researchers working under the auspices of the government attempted to determine which "magic bullets" could alter attitudes on a mass scale. This wartime research was spearheaded by University of Chicago sociologist Sam Stouffer and Yale University psychologist Carl Hovland (Hovland, Lumsdaine, & Sheffield, 1949; Stouffer, Lumsdaine et al., 1949; Stouffer, Suchman, Devinney, Star, & Williams, 1949).

One of the key problems for the U.S. military at the outset of the war was the enormity of the task of training millions of young civilians to become soldiers. One challenge was the widespread ignorance of world affairs among the recruits. To combat this problem and to counter German propaganda, the U.S. Army recruited famous Hollywood director Frank Capra to develop "pro-democratic" propaganda to support the U.S. cause. Rather than shoot new footage, Capra had the novel idea of reediting Axis propaganda footage to tell a much different story about how Germans were being misled by their government and how Hitler's aims were a direct threat to the United States. Capra produced seven 50-minute documentary features in a series called *Why We Fight*, and they were screened in movie theaters all over the United States (see Figure 2.3).

Hovland and his team used controlled field experiments to better understand soldiers' knowledge about the war, opinions about the war and the Allies, and attitudes about their willingness to fight in the conflict. Different methods of transmitting persuasive messages were used: lectures, screenings of the *Why We Fight* films, and written documentation of the information contained in the

Figure 2.3 Compilation of Screen Images From *Divide and Conquer* (*Why We Fight Film No. 3*)

Source: "Divide and Conquer" (1943), Frank Capra. Images compiled by Stephanie Plumeri Ertz.

films. After more than 4,000 Army soldiers participated in the experiments, Hovland discovered that the *Why We Fight* films were by far the most effective at expanding soldiers' *knowledge* about the history and geopolitics surrounding the conflict. The soldiers' knowledge was tested via a factual quiz related to the themes and specific historical material provided in the films. However, while Capra's films were heralded as masterfully persuasive about the just nature of the American cause, the films did little to alter soldiers' initial attitudes or overall motivation to fight in the war. The development of the concept of attitude was a major contribution of Hovland's WWII-era studies. An **attitude** refers to an internal psychological orientation toward an external entity, typically expressed in terms of the degree of favor or disfavor toward that entity (Eagly & Chaiken, 1993). In the case of the *Why We Fight* studies, soldiers were asked about their orientation toward the British Allies both before and after viewing the *Battle of Britain* (1943) documentary, which depicted the determination of the British military despite the campaign of Nazi air bombardment. Hovland measured attitudes with a Likert scale, which consisted of a series of statements to which respondents indicated their agreement on a scale of 1 to 5 (where 1 is *very much disagree* and 5 was *very much agree*, for example). Hovland found little attitude change in soldiers' overall attitude toward the British Allies after watching the films.

The lack of strong evidence for persuasion in these studies made it clear that there were no magic keys that could unlock mass persuasion. Hovland's research methods—use of a controlled setting and experimental techniques to measure soldiers' knowledge, attitudes, and beliefs—had a profound effect upon the study of mass media for many decades following his World War II research.

Postwar Communication Research: The Rise of the Limited Effects Paradigm

The takeaway message from the extensive research conducted during World War II was clear: It was actually quite difficult to persuade audiences through the use of mass media, regardless of the skill of the message producer. The once-pervasive concern about the propagandistic qualities of the media seemed less problematic than before. In the wake of Hovland's research findings, scholars began to search for new models to explain the effects of media messages on audiences. In postwar research, the perspective on media effects underwent an important shift. Now, scholars were interested in exploring the specific conditions under which media messages might be influential, but they no longer expected to find universal effects among all audiences. Two key theories that emerged in this postwar period—selectivity and the two-step flow of communication—are explored next.

Persuasion Research:
Selectivity and the Elaboration Likely Model (ELM)

Carl Hovland returned to Yale University after the war, recruited a group of 30 colleagues, and continued his research into attitude change by using the experimental approach he had pioneered during the war (Jowett & O'Donnell, 2011, p. 132). Fresh from the seeming lack of evidence for mediated persuasion from the *Why We Fight* films, Hovland's goal was to develop a systematic theory of persuasion. He wanted to carefully isolate and explore the mechanisms through which humans made decisions about their environment. Hovland and his colleagues studied a number of variables that may have an influence on the persuasion process, including audience personality traits, susceptibility to persuasive appeals, the order of arguments in a message, and fear-based appeals. One of the surprising results from this research was that weak fear appeals seemed to be more influential than moderate and strong fear appeals (Hovland, Janis, & Kelley, 1953). The researchers also discovered that communications from a source perceived to be low in credibility would be seen as more biased and unfair than from a high credibility source. Thus, **source credibility**, or the degree to which a message receiver perceived the source of the message to be credible, emerged as a major factor in determining whether or not attitude change took place in the receiver. This effect was a short-term effect, however, since people tended to disassociate a message from its source over time (Kelman & Hovland, 1953).

One of the major theoretical advances to come out of Hovland's Yale research group was **consistency theory**. Consistency theorists argued that the human being's drive for cognitive consistency (the mental agreement between someone's beliefs about an object or event) was the prime motivator for all human behavior. The assumption of the theory was that when individuals are exposed to information that is inconsistent with their previously held beliefs, they will experience confusion and tension. For example, if you are a cigarette smoker and you have a desire and expectation that you will live a long life, when you encounter information that provides conclusive evidence that smoking causes cancer, then you will be motivated to resolve this inconsistency by changing your behavior (e.g., giving up cigarettes). The most famous and controversial theory of cognitive consistency is Leon Festinger's (1957) **theory of cognitive dissonance**. Festinger's claim was that the need for cognitive consistency was so strong (and the discomfort felt by individuals by inconsistency was so great) that individuals will rationalize their actions to relieve the inconsistency. To take the previous smoking example, if smokers were confronted with information about the health dangers of cigarettes, then they might decide that they actually smoke so little that the negative effects are going to be quite small (and therefore the decision to smoke is rationalized). This process of reinterpreting the world to match one's previously held beliefs is called **selective perception** (see Box 2.1). Additionally, Festinger argued that individuals would actively avoid a state of cognitive dissonance. So the smoker may consciously avoid communication messages about the health hazards of smoking. This process is called **selective exposure**.

BOX 2.1
Selectivity at Work in *The Colbert Report* Audience

One of the more popular programs on cable television in the early 2000s was *The Colbert Report*, a satirical news program on the Comedy Central cable network that masqueraded as a conservative news and interview program. The show's host and creator, Stephen Colbert, who left Comedy Central to take over as the host of *The Late Show* on CBS, relentlessly parodied the self-indulgence of conservative news personalities, and his on-air persona is specifically modeled on then-Fox News commentator Bill O'Reilly. Part of the show's continual comic appeal was Colbert's "explicit rejection of the need for facts in engaging in political debate and assessing political arguments" (Baumgartner & Morris, 2008, p. 623).

Given the popularity of *The Colbert Report*, one might assume that its tongue-in-cheek humor was widely appreciated by its audience. However, scholarly research suggested that different viewers may have distinctly different reasons for appreciating the program. Two studies of *Report* viewers attempted to understand how audiences were interpreting the satirical humor on the program. These studies took their cue from an earlier postwar study of selective perception in audiences. Cooper and Jahoda's 1947 study "The Evasion of Propaganda" evaluated a public information campaign designed to lessen prejudice against minorities in American society. The campaign featured a cartoon character named "Mr. Biggott" who illustrated a number of prejudiced opinions in the comics but was then the object of the humor at the end of the message. Cooper and Jahoda measured respondents' initial level of prejudice (their attitude toward minorities) and then asked them about their interpretation of the cartoon. Contrary to their initial suspicions that prejudiced individuals would recognize their own biases in the character of Mr. Biggott, those individuals instead distanced themselves from the character or noted that people are entitled to their prejudices. Some prejudiced readers failed to understand the core message about tolerance and understanding. Instead of changing their views, therefore, some readers had effectively "evaded" this prosocial propaganda and kept their initial attitudes intact.

The story was much the same with viewers of *The Colbert Report*. Baumgartner and Morris (2008) found, for example, that Colbert's satirical critiques of the George W. Bush administration had the effect of actually *increasing* support for President Bush, for Republicans in Congress, and for Bush's national security policies. Another study by LaMarre, Landreville, and Beam (2009) found that both conservative- and liberal-minded college students found *Colbert* equally funny, but for different reasons. The researchers concluded that the conservative students were selectively perceiving the program in a way that matched their existing ideological beliefs. These studies demonstrate some of the inherent difficulties in persuading audiences with strong initial attitudes.

Sources: Baumgartner, J. C., & Morris, J. S. (2008). One "nation," under Stephen? The effects of *The Colbert Report* on American youth. *Journal of Broadcasting & Electronic Media, 52*(4), 622–643; Cooper, E., & Jahoda, M. (1947). The evasion of propaganda: How prejudiced people respond to anti-prejudice propaganda. *The Journal of Psychology, 23*(1), 15–25; LaMarre, H. L., Landreville, K. D., & Beam, M. A. (2009). The irony of satire. *The International Journal of Press/Politics, 14*(2), 212–231.

The investigation into the process of persuasion is ongoing—not only in communication studies but in the field of psychology as well. A significant advance in the study of the persuasion process occurred with the discovery of the **elaboration likelihood model (ELM)** (Petty & Cacioppo, 1986a, 1986b). The model maps out the process by which an individual forms an attitude about an object, event, or experience. Petty and Cacioppo's significant contribution to the study of persuasion was their contention that an individual's susceptibility to a persuasive message was directly related to their *motivation to process the message.* If the message is of perceived relevance to the receiver and the receiver is able to process the message, then she may engage in *central processing.* In this case, the receiver carefully attends to the message, evaluates the information, and makes a reasoned judgment based on a number of factors (including the arguments made and the credibility of the source) and, ultimately, may accept or reject the information. Central processing represented the type of classic learning theory that had been characteristic of earlier work in persuasion, including Hovland's World War II research. The model also suggested a secondary route to persuasion, however, called *peripheral processing.* When the motivation or ability to process a message is low, then the receiver is likely to take a "cognitive shortcut" to process the message by making a quick decision about the message based on a peripheral cue (such as the background music or other emotional cue; Petty, Brinol, & Priester, 2009). Peripheral processing could therefore provide a "back door" for a weak argument to persuade a receiver, though the persuasive effects of this type of processing are typically not as long lasting as centrally processed messages.

The People's Choice (1944) and Personal Influence (1955)

While postwar communication research shifted toward the notion that the effects of media messages were limited in scope, a number of studies that were already under way during the war were drawing similar conclusions. One of the most important studies conducted during the wartime years was *The People's Choice* (Lazarsfeld, Berelson, & Gaudet, 1944). The project was spearheaded by Paul F. Lazarsfeld, an Austrian émigré who fled to the United States to escape persecution shortly before the annexation of Austria by Nazi Germany. A mathematician by education, Lazarsfeld was fascinated by quantitative techniques to explore social phenomena (Rogers, 1994). Unlike Hovland's focus on carefully controlled experiments, Lazarsfeld's research relied largely on survey methods to study attitudes. Lazarsfeld was the director of the Office of Radio Research at Princeton when Hadley Cantril conducted his famous study of *The War of the Worlds* broadcast. After a falling out with Cantril, Lazarsfeld moved the office to Columbia University where he renamed it the Bureau of Applied Social Research (BASR). The bureau became a major hub of communication research in the postwar years. Lazarsfeld and his colleagues at the bureau, most notably sociologist Robert Merton, played an important role in shaping the direction of communication research in the second half of the 20th century (Katz, 1987).

The study that became *The People's Choice* was designed to answer a basic question: To what extent did the radio and newspapers shape voters' choice in a presidential election? The test case was the 1940 presidential election between the incumbent president, Democrat Franklin Delano Roosevelt, and Republican Wendell Willkie. Lazarsfeld and his team selected Erie County, Ohio, as the main research site for a number of reasons. First, the small county of 43,000 residents was culturally homogeneous and had changed little in population size or character for 40 years. Secondly, the county had deviated little from national voting trends, making it a convenient microcosm for the country as a whole. Six hundred randomly selected respondents were given a telephone survey at various points throughout the 1940 campaign season, and their responses were compared with four control groups in different months to make sure that the repeated surveys were not biasing the results. Lazarsfeld wanted to know when voters made up their minds about how they would vote in the November election and whether their exposure to the news media affected their decisions. The results revealed that very few voters actually changed their minds over the course of the campaign. In fact, voters' ultimate choices could be largely inferred in advance by looking at their socioeconomic status, religious affiliation, and age (a combined metric that was dubbed the "index of political participation"). With regard to media exposure, Lazarsfeld's team discovered that voters' reported news exposure served mainly to reinforce their latent predisposition to vote either Democratic or Republican.

The key finding of *The People's Choice* study—that the media may simply reinforce rather than persuade citizens about their voting choice—foreshadowed much of the postwar selectivity research. One interesting and unexpected finding from the Erie County study was that many respondents indicated that their conversations with others were more influential in their voting decisions than their media exposure. It was clear from the results that some individuals had acted as **opinion leaders** for others. In other words, these individuals were regarded to be knowledgeable about a particular issue and were consulted by others as a source on that issue. Lazarsfeld vowed to follow up on this insight in subsequent research.

The opportunity to explore the role of interpersonal relationships in media effects presented itself to Lazarsfeld when the head of McFadden Publications, a company that published women's gossip and fashion magazines, contracted with the bureau to perform market research on women readers. McFadden wanted to know what kinds of products his readers were buying so that he could more effectively market his magazines to advertisers. Ever the intellectual entrepreneur, Lazarsfeld agreed to do the study but added additional survey questions so that he could study the process of opinion leadership. The findings from the research were released in a book, *Personal Influence*, which was coauthored by Lazarsfeld and graduate student Elihu Katz.

The research was based on interviews with 800 women in the Decatur, Illinois, area. By using the survey, the research team was able to discover 693 reported opinion leaders (Katz & Lazarsfeld, 1955). Who were these opinion leaders, and what distinguished them from the rest? They discovered that women's "position in the life cycle" (their age and role as single or married, for example), their socioeconomic

Figure 2.4 The Two-Step Flow Model of Communication

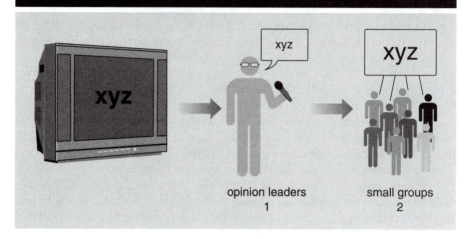

opinion leaders
1

small groups
2

Source: Stephanie Plumeri Ertz.

status, and the extent of their social contacts were largely responsible for their position as opinion leaders. Additionally, different women acted as opinion leaders for different kinds of products. For household items, older married women were cited most often as opinion leaders, while younger women acted as opinion leaders for fashion and movie selection. Along with their role as informal persuaders for others, Katz and Lazarsfeld discovered that opinion leaders were also more likely to closely monitor the media for trends and information. This led to a new theory of media effects called the **two-step flow of communication**. Katz and Lazarsfeld reasoned that the impact of media messages flows through opinion leaders, who then pass along this influence to other audiences (see Figure 2.4). The two-step model suggested that the lack of media influence found in previous research studies (such as *The People's Choice*) was likely because scholars had not adequately understood the role that person-to-person communication played in media effects. The close connection between interpersonal communication and mass media impact was an important contribution of *Personal Influence*.

Is the two-step flow model still operative today in an era of online news and social media? Bennett and Manheim (2006) argue that audiences today have radically altered their information consumption patterns. Instead of face-to-face discussions around the proverbial "water cooler," contemporary audiences have "gained greater command of their own information environments" by seeking out small, niche groups of people online via social media. Advertisers and marketers can therefore target their messages to a very particular group of people who they know will be listening. In these scenarios, social media has therefore given rise to the *one-step flow of communication* (Bennett & Manheim, 2006, p. 216). We will discuss the impacts of social media on audiences and public opinion in Chapter 3.

Effects of Media Violence

As the previous section illustrated, the orientation of media effects research shifted markedly after World War II. The theories of the mass audience that animated much early concern about motion pictures and radio gave way to the limited effects paradigm in the postwar years. This did not mean, however, that concerns about the potentially dangerous effects of media messages evaporated. In fact, during the 1960s and 1970s the increasingly important role of television in American households sparked new concerns about mediated violence, sexuality, and hypercommercialization. A few of the major research projects conducted during the television era are outlined here. The main focus of concern was the potential impacts of television exposure on children— more specifically, how images of violence on television affected children's attitudes and behaviors. Many of these questions about the impacts of media violence have been transferred to the newer technology of computer and video games.

Rise of Public Concern Over Television and the Surgeon General's Report (1971)

The arrival of television in American homes in the 1950s heralded a new era for the media. Now, audiences could experience visuals as well as sound right in their own living rooms. Along with the immersive experience of the movies, television carried the immediacy of radio with continually updated news, live sporting events, and entertainment programming. By 1959, approximately 88% of all American households owned a television set (roughly 50 million sets), making television the fastest-growing media technology in history at that time (Schramm, Lyle, & Parker, 1961, p. 12). During the 1960s, however, parents, educators, and cultural critics became concerned that much of the television diet available on the three networks (ABC, NBC, and CBS) consisted of cheap, overcommercialized fare, such as game shows, violent dramas, and mindless comedies. The lack of quality programming on American television received nationwide attention in 1961 when the then-chairman of the Federal Communications Commission (FCC), Newton Minow, gave a speech to the National Association of Broadcasters in which he dubbed TV programming "a vast wasteland" (Minow, 2002). Concerns about television in the 1960s were in part a reflection of the growing unrest in American society. Americans were witnessing increasingly stark images of violence in the news, thanks to the deepening U.S. involvement in the Vietnam War; antiwar demonstrations on university campuses around the nation; and acts of civil disobedience to protest segregation policies against Blacks and other minorities. After the deeply troubling assassinations of key American political figures such as President Kennedy, his brother Robert, and civil rights leader Martin Luther King Jr., many began wondering whether violence was becoming a nationwide epidemic.

U.S. Sen. John O. Pastore of Rhode Island suggested that violence had become a "public health risk," and he worried that images of violence on television (both in news and entertainment) were prompting children to be more aggressive. At the urging of Congress and the U.S. Secretary of Health, Education, and Welfare, the surgeon general of the United States and the National Institute of Mental Health (NIMH) recruited 40 experts in the field and commissioned 23 independent studies of television's effects on children (Surgeon General's Scientific Advisory Committee on Television and Social Behavior, 1972, p. 18). This rich collection of research, which spans five volumes, was referred to as the "Surgeon General's Report."

One of the key questions asked by the report was "Does mediated violence encourage aggressive behaviors in children?" One of the most memorable studies included in the report was by psychologist Albert Bandura, who was interested in **social learning theory**, or how children are socialized by their environment. In Bandura's (1965) study, children observed an adult model beating an inflatable plastic Bobo doll in an experimental setting. In one experimental condition, the adult model was chastised for this behavior, and in another condition the adult model was not chastised. Children who did not witness the adult model being reprimanded for the aggressive behavior were more likely to play aggressively when left alone in a room with the Bobo doll. Bandura observed, however, that even children who did not demonstrate aggressive play could still reproduce the behavior when asked to do so by an adult. Bandura's research was the first to provide empirical evidence that children imitate adult models, which suggested that children were internalizing behaviors they witnessed on television. Another study by Liebert and Baron (1972) determined that children who watched even a short selection from a violent television program were more willing to show aggression to other children. This aggression was measured by children turning a handheld dial that they were told would either help or hurt another child's chance to get a prize. Like the Payne Fund Studies 40 years earlier, the Surgeon General's Report stoked fears that children were uniquely vulnerable to the powerful influence of the media. The fact that children's access to television was only as far away as their living rooms prompted further discussions in government and industry about how to protect children from potentially damaging content.

Long-Term Media Effects and Cultivation Theory

Scholars also began looking closely at the long-term effects of television exposure on children for evidence of media effects. For example, a 10-year longitudinal study of 436 children was conducted by Eron, Huesmann, Lefkowitz, and Walder (1972) to understand the impact of television exposure on later childhood development. The researchers discovered that the TV viewing habits of 8-year-old boys were predictive of their aggressive behavior throughout their childhood and later into adolescence. The research team continued to follow the children into their 20s (Huesmann, 1986) and even their 30s (Huesmann, Moise-Titus, Podolski, & Eron, 2003), and the findings remained strikingly consistent: Children who were in the upper 20% of television exposure were significantly higher on measures of aggression than the study's other participants. Thus, negative impacts of television violence may last much longer than some scholars had anticipated.

Another key research tradition that focuses on the long-term impacts of television is **cultivation theory**. Developed by Dr. George Gerbner of the Annenberg

School for Communication, cultivation theory argues that audiences' conceptions of reality are developed through exposure to television over a period of months and years (Gerbner & Gross, 1976). Through surveys, Gerbner and his colleagues found evidence for what they termed **cultivation process**: that heavy television viewers (those who watched more than 4 hours per day) were more likely to perceive the world in ways that mirrored television reality rather than other, objective measures of social reality. They found, for example, that individuals who watched more television were much more likely to believe that the world was a violent and dangerous place, even if they themselves had not personally experienced violence (Gerbner, Gross, Morgan, & Signorielli, 1980; Signorielli, 1990). These effects were found regardless of the genre of television watched by viewers. Cultivation research was a significant shift in the effects paradigm because it turned the focus on the *stability of attitudes over time rather than attitude change*, thus turning on its head the central thrust of the persuasion research of the World War II era. Since it found significant **cumulative, long-term** effects of media, cultivation analysis also reignited debate about the potential for media stimuli to have powerful impacts on audiences.

Video Game Violence and Effects

Television continues to be a dominant source of news and entertainment in people's lives; our 21st-century lives are now full of technologies that can reach audiences anywhere, anytime. School shooting incidents in the United States and elsewhere have focused the public's attention on relative newcomers to the media scene: computer and video games. In the 1980s, American children played video games roughly 4 hours per week, but more recent estimates indicate that the average is now around 13 hours per week (Anderson et al., 2008). There is an expanding volume of scholarly work that examines the impacts of video games on audiences. Many of these studies have adopted the effects theories from earlier research on television and aggression to consider what types of impacts modern video games might have on child and adult audiences.

For example, Anderson and Dill (2000) surveyed college students about their use of various types of video games. They found that the students who said they spent more time playing video games also reported more aggressive and delinquent behaviors. They also set up a laboratory experiment in which students were assigned to play either a violent or a nonviolent video game. In the laboratory setting, those playing the violent video game displayed more aggressive behaviors toward peers. A comparative study of American and Japanese children also found that respondents who indicated a higher level of violent video game play were more likely to report aggressive actions and feelings over time (Anderson et al., 2008). A meta-analysis of the research on video games and aggression in 2001 found that data from about 30 independent investigations seemed to show a "small effect of video game play on aggression, and the effect is smaller than the effect of violent television on aggression" (Sherry, 2001, p. 427). A follow-up review later in the decade (Lee, Peng, & Park, 2009) found that Sherry's conclusion was still relevant for research on the transference of emotional or behavioral aggression from violent video games to audiences. Lee, Peng, and Park noted, however, that video game addiction (an inability to stop playing video games) had become a source of concern. Scholars have also begun investigating the effects of video games through magnetic resonance imaging (MRI) to detect whether the areas of the brain that control aggression are activated during exciting, first-person shooter games (Weber, Ritterfeld, & Mathiak, 2006). It's important to note here that the research setting itself may contribute to the discovery of some of the video game effects observed. As Perse (2001, p. 9) notes, research subjects may assume that the experimenter approves of media content that is used during a research study, even if that material is violent or pornographic in nature. This form of research bias, called an **experimenter effect**, could cause research subjects to behave differently in research settings than in the real world, thereby unintentionally magnifying the observed effects of specific types of media on audiences. Thus, despite the intense public interest in isolated cases—such as the shootings at Columbine High School in 1999 and Virginia Tech in 2007—the research has found only small, negative effects from video game play, even in experimental settings.

Mobile Media and Effects

The research findings on the effects of violent video games should certainly give us pause, but the reality is that violent video game play represents a relatively small slice of overall media consumption among audiences. But what about our exposure to mobile devices like smartphones and tablets? These portable devices are easy to carry with us, allowing us to be instantly connected to friends, family, and to online media wherever we go. Mobile devices are also ubiquitous: A 2017 Pew Research Center survey found that 77% of Americans owned a smartphone, and 20% of Americans relied on their mobile devices for access to the Internet (in other words, they did not have access to broadband Internet at home; Pew Research Center, 2018). Scholar Sherry Turkle has argued that today's teenagers are "tethered" to their mobile phones, which allows for constant connection to parents as well as to friends and peers (Turkle, 2008). The fact that millions carry their mobile phones on their physical person 24 hours a day and that these devices are perpetually connected to the Internet means that we are "always on" and available for private communications, even in public spaces (Katz & Aakhus, 2002). As Turkle has discovered in her research, teenagers feel a sense of safety and security from being "connected" to their parents via mobile technology, but they are also more distracted, become anxious when they feel as if they are missing out on communications from peers, and sometimes engage in risky behaviors such as sexting, texting while driving, and even cyberbullying (Turkle, 2008).

There are a number of potential effects of mobile communications that scholars have investigated. Negative effects of smartphones are becoming more and more acute since mobile phone use is on the rise, particularly among teenagers. A 2015 Pew Research Center survey found that 24% of U.S. teens are online "almost constantly," using social media apps like Facebook, Snapchat, Instagram, and Twitter

Source: iStock.com/nemke.

(Lenhart, 2015). According to a recent report issued by Common Sense Media (2016), half of teens report feeling "addicted" to their smartphones. In 2002, media scholar Todd Gitlin warned that the torrent of constant media messages into the home "has swelled into a torrent of immense force and constancy, an accompaniment *to* life that has become a central experience *of* life" (emphasis in original; 2002, p. 17). Focus group research has found that mobile phone users are continually annoyed and distracted by trivial messages (Hargittai, Neuman, & Curry, 2012). In addition to this rise in "infoxification" (or intoxication by too much information), other researchers have discovered that adolescents often develop stress related to the perpetual contacts from peers since they are expected to return messages immediately, leading to anxiety about keeping up with this constant barrage (Mascheroni, 2017). In addition, all this anxiety about keeping up with our mobile devices leads us to disengage from our face-to-face conversations, negatively affect our moods, and cause spinal curvature from looking down at small screens over a long period of time (Popescu, 2018). One recent analysis of 300 adolescent narratives about friendships found that mobile communications intensified emotions of meanness, betrayal, and harassment by amplifying the number of people who can potentially see these interactions unfold in the social media space (called **scalability**; White, Weinstein, & Selman, 2018). The constant need to respond to friends and acquaintances can lead to feelings of guilt for not keeping up, thus lowering our levels of satisfaction with these friendships as a result (Hall & Baym, 2012).

Lastly, the accessibility of social media via mobile phones has encouraged more potentially problematic and risky behaviors among adolescents. For instance, young people with mobile phones have reported using their phones while doing other important tasks, such as homework or even driving. This attention to multiple simultaneous stimuli is called **multitasking**. Research by David, Kim, Brickman, Ran, and Curtis (2015) found that college students who owned mobile phones and had lots of Facebook friends were more likely to multitask while completing homework, leading to more distractions. Adolescents have also engaged in sexting, or the exchange of sexually explicit messages via social media and texting, or short messaging service (SMS). There have been numerous studies of adolescent sexting, many of which ask the question "Does teen sexting lead to other risky sexual behaviors?" A meta-analysis of sexting research (Kosenko, Luurs, & Binder, 2017) found somewhat weak results on the question of whether sexting causes risky behaviors such as unprotected sex, though there was a clear connection between sexting behavior and sexual activity among young people. The increase in screen time afforded by widespread access to smartphones may even be increasing rates of adolescent depression. For example, research by a team of scholars found a connection between the rising rate of teen suicides in the United States between 2010 and 2015 and increased screen time via mobile devices (Twenge, Joiner, Rogers, & Martin, 2018).

The effects of mobile communications on audiences are not all negative, however. In fact, access to mobile technologies has been transformative in a number of ways that directly benefit society. For example, mobile phones can be vital in emergencies to call for help or to increase the sense of safety for those who carry them. There are broader social and political implications as well. For instance, the capability of mobile phones for texting has expanded democratic participation around the world by enabling what Howard Rheingold (2002) calls "smart mobs," or groups of citizens that can rally almost instantly for social or political change. One such example is in Turkey, where in 2013 citizens used the social messaging service Twitter on their mobile phones to quickly organize pro-democracy protests in Gezi Park (Tufecki, 2017). In the United States, advocacy groups like Black Lives Matter have used the video cameras on mobile phones to document police brutality of African Americans in order to bring worldwide attention to continued civil rights abuses there (Stephen, 2015). There is also evidence that individuals who use smartphones are more likely both to consume news and political information, as well as to share their own views about politics in online forums and social media, thus increasing their own political participation (Campbell & Kwak, 2010; Kim, Chen, & Wang, 2016).

All of these studies point to the complex character of mobile device effects, particularly on young people. Mobile smartphones can become important tools for social and political expression, yet they can also make us anxious, induce depression and loneliness, affect our friendship dynamics, and distract us from our surroundings by keeping us constantly tethered to our devices. Since Internet-enabled smartphones are still just over a decade old, scholarly research into the effects of these technologies is still in its infancy.

Conclusion: Enduring Concern Over Media Effects

This chapter has mapped out a very brief history of some of the major media effects studies and theories in the 20th century. The rise in the importance of motion pictures as a major leisure-time activity, along with urbanization and radical shifts in Americans' work lives, catalyzed early concerns about the power of media messages to shift attitudes and behaviors. After World War I, the notion that mass opinion could be shaped and managed by media messages was widespread. This logic was evident in the findings on both the impact of *The War of the Worlds* broadcast and Hovland's wartime propaganda research. The focus of postwar research may have shifted to more limited effects, but concern about the vulnerability of children to violent media was transferred from motion pictures to newer forms of media, such as television and video games.

While the scope of the research in the effects tradition is vast, there are some clearly identifiable characteristics that define this research tradition. The operative notion in the effects paradigm is that the audience exists in a naturally occurring state that can be interrupted and dramatically changed, thanks to specific media messages. The notion of the anonymous, powerless mass audience is no longer the dominant assumption in effects research. Nevertheless, the media effects literature approaches the audience as a collective that potentially requires protection from dangerous outside influences. Butsch (2008, p. 127) notes that "the effects paradigm sustained the image of audiences as passive individuals, even while the research itself often contradicted fears about the power of media." In the next section of the book, we'll explore how audiences are constructed by institutions and the impacts of those constructions on our roles as citizens and consumers.

DISCUSSION ACTIVITIES

1. Either individually or in groups, conduct a brief online search for news articles that deal with some kind of media (TV, radio, film, video games, and social media are some examples) and the potential effects on audiences. Once you have gathered several stories, read them carefully and then discuss the following questions:

- What types of effects are suggested by these articles? Are they negative or positive effects or both?

- According to these articles, what is the extent of the media's effect on audiences? Are the effects serious (such as significant changes in audiences' attitudes or behaviors) or minimal?

- What inherent assumptions do these articles make about audiences and their ability to process messages? Are audiences seen as relatively passive or active in their capability to process media messages?

- Do you see a consistent pattern in news coverage of media effects?

2. Take 10 to 15 minutes and recall an episode from your childhood when you had a strong emotional, physiological, or psychological response to something that you saw in the media (on TV, in the movies, or on the Internet, for example). Write a brief first-person narrative about this episode: What particular program, film, or message made an impression on you and why? Once your narrative is complete, select a partner and exchange your narratives with each other to read. Once you have done so, answer the following questions in a brief discussion:

- What types of responses have you and your partner outlined? Are they positive or negative responses to media? Which type of response do you think is more memorable and why?

- Which medium (TV, film, Internet, etc.) did you and your partner remember most vividly? Why do you think this is the case?

- Do you see any similarities between the two narratives? What are they?

- Do any of the media effects theories outlined in this chapter help to explain you or your partner's experiences? Which one(s) and why?

3. Reread the portion of the chapter that outlines Albert Bandura's *social learning theory.* Next, think about how this theory might apply to newer forms of online social networking, such as Facebook, Twitter, Reddit, Instagram, Snapchat, and others. How might the interactivity offered by these forms of social media affect children's social learning as outlined by Bandura? Do you think Bandura's research on social modeling from the 1970s has relevance for these online services today? Why or why not?

4. How "tethered" are we to our mobile devices? Try this exercise to evaluate your own exposure to mobile phones. First, install a free "app tracker" for your mobile phone (Moment for iOS, or simply use the built-in features of Screen Time; Quality Time for Android). After you create a free account and enable it on your phone, these apps will run in the background and track your usage of the phone (onscreen time; apps used; amount of time on each app, etc.). Do this as soon as possible and have the app running in the background of your phone for several days (3–4 days is optimal). After several days, look at your patterns of smartphone use and make some notes. Then answer the following questions in a brief paragraph or in classroom discussion:

- How much screen "on" time did you have daily (on average)? Did it change from day to day? What times of day did you have more concentrated use of the phone? Why do you think this is?

- What types of apps did you use most often on your smartphone during this time? (Give some specifics about which apps and how much time). What does this tell you about the uses or affordances that you value most in the phone?

- Lastly, does anything surprise you about your use of the phone (either amount or type of use)? Are you concerned about this at all?

ADDITIONAL MATERIALS

Bryant, J., & Oliver, M. B. (Eds.). (2009). *Media effects: Advances in theory and research.* Communication series. Communication theory and methodology (3rd ed.). New York, NY: Routledge.

Butsch, R. (2008). From crowds to masses: Movies, radio, and advertising. In *The citizen audience: Crowds, publics, and individuals* (pp. 41–57). New York, NY: Routledge.

Czitrom, D. J. (1982). *Media and the American mind: From Morse to McLuhan.* Chapel Hill: University of North Carolina Press.

Gameheadz: History of video games [Discovery Channel documentary]. Retrieved from https://www.youtube.com/watch?v=5QD098LVZI0

Jean Kilbourne's webpage: http://jeankilbourne.com/

Library of Congress. Collection of World War I posters. Retrieved from http://www.loc.gov/pictures/collection/wwipos/

The long road to Decatur: A history of personal influence [Video documentary]. Retrieved from https://www.unm.edu/~balas/

Lowery, S. A., & DeFleur, M. L. (1995). *Milestones in mass communication research* (3rd ed.). Boston, MA: Allyn & Bacon.

Nabi, R. L., & Oliver, M. B. (Eds.). (2009). *The SAGE handbook of media processes and effects.* Los Angeles, CA: SAGE.

Park, D. W., & Pooley, J. (Eds.). (2008). *The history of media and communication research: Contested memories.* New York, NY: Peter Lang.

PBS Newshour. (2010, May 4). The drug-like effect of screen time on the teenage brain. Washington, DC. Retrieved from https://www.pbs.org/newshour/show/the-drug-like-effect-of-screen-time-on-the-teenage-brain

Ross, J. (Director). *The day that panicked America: The H. G. Wells' War of the Worlds scandal* [Video documentary]. Retrieved from http://www.highlandvideo.com/movies/panic_am.php

Rushkoff, D., & Dretzin, R. (2010, February 2). Digital nation: Life on the virtual frontier. *Frontline.* Boston, MA: PBS. Retrieved from http://www.pbs.org/wgbh/pages/frontline/digitalnation/

Signorielli, N. (2005). *Violence in the media: A reference handbook.* Contemporary world issues. Santa Barbara, CA: ABC–CLIO.

Vorderer, P., & Bryant, J. (Eds.). (2006). *Playing video games: Motives, responses, and consequences.* LEA's communication series. Mahwah, NJ: Lawrence Erlbaum Associates.

REFERENCES

Anderson, C. A., & Dill, K. E. (2000). Video games and aggressive thoughts, feelings, and behavior in the laboratory and in life. *Journal of Personality and Social Psychology, 78*(4), 772–790.

Anderson, C. A., Sakamoto, A., Gentile, D. A., Ihori, N., Shibuya, A., Yukawa, S., Naito, M. (2008). Longitudinal effects of violent video games on aggression in Japan and the United States.

Pediatrics, 122(5), e1067–e1072. doi:10.1542/peds.2008-1425

Bandura, A. (1965). Influence of models' reinforcement contingencies on the acquisition of imitative responses. *Journal of Personality and Social Psychology, 1*(6), 589–595. doi:10.1037/h0022070

Baumgartner, J. C., & Morris, J. S. (2008). One "nation," under Stephen? The effects of *The Colbert*

Report on American youth. *Journal of Broadcasting & Electronic Media, 52*(4), 622–643. doi:10.1080/08838150802437487

Bennett, W. L., & Manheim, J. B. (2006). The one-step flow of communication. *The ANNALS of the American Academy of Political and Social Science, 608*(1), 213–232.

Blumer, H. (1933). *Movies and conduct*. New York, NY: Macmillan.

Blumer, H. (1954). The crowd, the public, and the mass. In W. Schramm (Ed.), *The process and effects of mass communication* (pp. 363–379). Urbana: University of Illinois Press.

Butsch, R. (2008). *The citizen audience: Crowds, publics, and individuals*. New York, NY: Routledge.

Campbell, S. W., & Kwak, N. (2010). Mobile communication and civic life: Linking patterns of use to civic and political engagement. *Journal of Communication, 60,* 536–555.

Cantril, H. (1940). *The invasion from Mars: A study in the psychology of panic*. Princeton, NJ: Princeton University Press.

Cantril, H., & Allport, G. (1935). *The psychology of radio*. New York, NY: Harper.

Cohen, S. (2002). *Folk devils and moral panics: The creation of the mods and rockers* (3rd ed.). Abingdon, Oxfordshire: Routledge.

Common Sense Media. (2016, May 3). New report finds teens feel addicted to their phones, causing tension at home. Retrieved June 15, 2018, from https://www.commonsensemedia.org/about-us/news/press-releases/new-report-finds-teens-feel-addicted-to-their-phones-causing-tension-at

Cooley, C. H. (1962). *Social organization: A study of the larger mind*. New York, NY: Schocken Books.

Cooley, C. H. (1964). *Human nature and the social order*. New York, NY: Schocken Books.

Creel, G. (1920). *How we advertised America: The first telling of the amazing story of the Committee on Public Information that carried the gospel of Americanism to every corner of the globe*. New York, NY: Harper & Brothers. Retrieved from http://www.archive.org/details/howweadvertameri00creerich.

David, P., Kim, J.-H., Brickman, J. S., Ran, W., & Curtis, C. M. (2015). Mobile phone distraction while studying. *New Media & Society, 17*(10), 1661–1679.

Dearden, L. (2017, June 4). Isis claims responsibility for London terror attack. *The Independent*. Retrieved from http://www.independent.co.uk/news/uk/home-news/london-terror-attack-isis-claims-responsibility-borough-market-bridge-a7772776.html

Drotner, K. (1992). Modernity and media panics. *Media cultures: Reappraising transnational media* (pp. 42–64). London, England: Routledge.

Dysinger, W. S., & Ruckmick, C. A. (1933). *The emotional responses of children to the motion picture situation* (Vol. 3). New York, NY: Macmillan.

Eagly, A. H., & Chaiken, S. (1993). *The psychology of attitudes*. Fort Worth, TX: Harcourt Brace Jovanovich College.

Edwards, R. H. (1915). *Popular amusements*. New York, NY: Association Press.

Eron, L. D., Huesmann, L. R., Lefkowitz, M. M., & Walder, L. O. (1972). Does television violence cause aggression? *American Psychologist, 27*(4), 253–263.

Festinger, L. (1957). *A theory of cognitive dissonance*. Stanford, CA: Stanford University Press.

Fuller, K. H. (1996). *At the picture show: Small-town audiences and the creation of movie fan culture*. Washington, DC: Smithsonian Institution Press.

Gerbner, G., & Gross, L. (1976). Living with television: The violence profile. *Journal of Communication, 26*(2), 172–194.

Gerbner, G., Gross, L., Morgan, M., & Signorielli, N. (1980). The "mainstreaming" of America: Violence profile no. 11. *Journal of Communication, 30*(3), 10–29.

Gitlin, T. (2002). *Media unlimited: How the torrent of images and sounds overwhelms our lives.* New York, NY: Henry Holt.

Hall, J. A., & Baym, N. K. (2012). Calling and texting (too much): Mobile maintenance expectations, (over)dependence, entrapment, and friendship satisfaction. *New Media & Society, 14*(2), 316–331.

Hargittai, E., Neuman, W. R., & Curry, O. (2012). Taming the information tide: Perceptions of information overload in the American home. *Information Society, 28*(3), 161–173.

Holaday, P. W., & Stoddard, G. D. (1933). *Getting ideas from the movies.* New York, NY: Macmillan.

Hovland, C. I., Janis, I. L., & Kelley, H. H. (1953). *Communication and persuasion: Psychological studies of opinion change.* New Haven, CT: Yale University Press.

Hovland, C. I., Lumsdaine, A. A., & Sheffield, F. D. (1949). *Experiments on mass communication.* (Studies in social psychology in World War II, Vol. 3.). Princeton, NJ: Princeton University Press.

Huesmann, L. R. (1986). Psychological processes promoting the relation between exposure to media violence and aggressive behavior by the viewer. *Journal of Social Issues, 42*(3), 125–139.

Huesmann, L. R., Moise-Titus, J., Podolski, C. L., & Eron, L. D. (2003). Longitudinal relations between children's exposure to TV violence and their aggressive and violent behavior in young adulthood: 1977–1992. *Developmental Psychology, 39*(2), 201–221.

Jansen, S. C. (2008). Walter Lippmann, straw man of communication research. In D. W. Park & J. Pooley (Eds.), *The history of media and communication research: Contested memories* (pp. 71–112). New York, NY: Peter Lang.

Jowett, G. (1976). *Film: The democratic art.* Boston, MA: Little, Brown.

Jowett, G., Jarvie, I. C., & Fuller, K. H. (1996). *Children and the movies: Media influence and the Payne Fund controversy—Cambridge studies in the history of mass communications.* New York, NY: Cambridge University Press.

Jowett, G., & O'Donnell, V. (2011). *Propaganda & persuasion* (4th ed.). Thousand Oaks, CA: SAGE.

Kamenka, E. (1965). Gemeinschaft and Gesellschaft. *Political Science, 17*(1), 3–12. doi:10.1177/003231876501700101

Katz, E. (1987). Communications research since Lazarsfeld. *The Public Opinion Quarterly, 51,* S25–S45.

Katz, E., & Lazarsfeld, P. F. (1955). *Personal influence: The part played by people in the flow of mass communications.* New York, NY: The Free Press.

Katz, J. E., & Aakhus, M. A. (Eds.) (2002). *Perpetual contact: Mobile communication, private talk, public performance.* Cambridge, United Kingdom: Cambridge University Press.

Kelman, H. C., & Hovland, C. I. (1953). "Reinstatement" of the communicator in delayed measurement of opinion change. *The Journal of Abnormal and Social Psychology, 48*(3), 327.

Kim, Y., Chen, H.-T., & Wang, Y. (2016). Living in the smartphone age: Examining the conditional indirect effects of mobile phone use on political participation. *Journal of Broadcasting & Electronic Media, 60*(4), 694–713.

Kosenko, K., Luurs, G., & Binder, A. R. (2017). Sexting and sexual behavior, 2011–2015: A critical review and meta-analysis of a growing literature. *Journal of Computer-Mediated Communication, 22*(3), 141–160.

LaMarre, H. L., Landreville, K. D., & Beam, M. A. (2009). The irony of satire. *The International Journal of Press/Politics, 14*(2), 212–231.

Lang, K., & Lang, G. E. (2009). Mass society, mass culture, and mass communication: The meaning of mass. *International Journal of Communication*, 3, 998–1024.

Lazarsfeld, P. F., Berelson, B., & Gaudet, H. (1944). *The people's choice: How the voter makes up his mind in a presidential campaign*. New York, NY: Columbia University Press.

Lee, K. M., Peng, M., & Park, N. (2009). Effects of computer/video games and beyond. In J. Bryant & M. B. Oliver (Eds.), *Media effects: Advances in theory and research* (3rd ed., pp. 551–566). New York, NY: Routledge.

Lenhart, A. (2015, April 9). *Teens, social media & technology overview 2015*. Retrieved June 15, 2018, from http://www.pewinternet.org/2015/04/09/teens-social-media-technology-2015/

Liebert, R. M., & Baron, R. A. (1972). Some immediate effects of televised violence on children's behavior. *Developmental Psychology*, 6(3), 469–475.

Lippmann, W. (1922). *Public opinion*. New York, NY: Harcourt, Brace.

Mascheroni, G. (2017). Addiction or emancipation? Children's attachment to smartphones as a cultural practice. In J. Vincent & L. Haddon (Eds.), *Smartphone cultures* (pp. 121–134). London, England: Routledge.

McDonald, D. G. (2004). Twentieth-century media effects research. In J. Downing, D. McQuail, P. Schlesinger, & E. Wartella (Eds.), *The SAGE handbook of media studies* (pp. 183–200). Thousand Oaks, CA: SAGE.

Minow, N. N. (2002). Television and the public interest. *Fed. Comm. LJ*, 55, 395–406.

Moore, J. (2017, June 5). London attacker had watched videos from a radical U.S. preacher and influential ISIS recruiter. *Newsweek*. Retrieved from http://www.newsweek.com/london-bridge-attacker-followed-radical-preacher-isis-recruiter-online-youtube-620682

Mozingo, J., Pearce, M., & Wilkinson, T. (2016, June 13). "An act of terror and an act of hate": The aftermath of America's worst mass shooting. *The Los Angeles Times*. Retrieved from http://www.latimes.com/nation/nationnow/la-na-orlando-nightclub-shooting-20160612-snap-story.html

Münsterberg, H. (1916). *The photoplay: a psychological study*. New York, NY: D. Appleton.

Pandora, K. (1998). Mapping the new mental world created by radio: Media messages, cultural politics, and Cantril and Allport's *The Psychology of Radio*. *Journal of Social Issues*, 54(1), 7–27.

Peiss, K. L. (1986). *Cheap amusements: Working women and leisure in turn-of-the-century New York*. Philadelphia, PA: Temple University Press.

Perse, E. M. (2001). *Media effects and society*. Mahwah, NJ: Lawrence Erlbaum Associates.

Peterson, R. C., & Thurstone, L. L. (1933). *Motion pictures and the social attitudes of children*. New York, NY: Macmillan.

Petty, R. E., Brinol, P., & Priester, J. R. (2009). Mass media attitude change: Implications of the elaboration likelihood model of persuasion. In J. Bryant & M. B. Oliver (Eds.), *Media effects: Advances in theory and research* (3rd ed., pp. 125–164). New York, NY: Routledge.

Petty, R. E., & Cacioppo, J. T. (1986a). The elaboration likelihood model of persuasion. *Advances in experimental social psychology* (Vol. 19, pp. 123–205). New York, NY: Academic Press.

Petty, R. E., & Cacioppo, J. T. (1986b). *Communication and persuasion: Central and peripheral routes to attitude change*. New York, NY: Springer/Verlag.

Pew Research Center. (2018, February 5). *Mobile fact sheet*. Retrieved June 15, 2018, from http://www.pewinternet.org/fact-sheet/mobile/

Phelan, J. J. (1919). *Motion pictures as a phase of commercial amusement in Toledo, Ohio*. Toledo, OH: Little Book Press.

Pilkington, E., & Roberts, D. (2016, June 14). FBI and Obama confirm Omar Mateen was radicalized on the internet. *The Guardian*. Retrieved from http://www.theguardian.com/us-news/2016/jun/13/pulse-nightclub-attack-shooter-radicalized-internet-orlando

Popescu, A. (2018, January 25). Keep your head up: How smartphone addiction kills manners and moods. *The New York Times*. Retrieved from https://www.nytimes.com/2018/01/25/smarter-living/bad-text-posture-neckpain-mood.html

Rheingold, H. (2002). *Smart mobs: The next social revolution*. Cambridge, MA: Perseus.

Rogers, E. M. (1994). *A history of communication study: A biographical approach*. New York, NY: The Free Press.

Schramm, W. L., Lyle, J., & Parker, E. (1961). *Television in the lives of our children*. Palo Alto, CA: Stanford University Press.

Sherry, J. L. (2001). The effects of violent video games on aggression: A meta-analysis. *Human Communication Research*, 27(3), 409–431.

Shuttleworth, F. K., & May, M. A. (1933). *The social conduct and attitudes of movie fans*. New York, NY: Macmillan.

Signorielli, N. (1990). Television's mean and dangerous world: A continuation of the cultural indicators perspective. In N. Signorielli & M. Morgan (Eds.), *Cultivation analysis: New directions in media effects research* (pp. 85–106). Newbury Park, CA: SAGE.

Simpson, C. (1996). *Science of coercion: Communication research and psychological warfare, 1945–1960*. New York, NY: Oxford University Press.

Socolow, M., & Pooley, J. (2013, October 29). The Myth of the War of the Worlds Panic. *Slate Magazine*. Retrieved from https://slate.com/culture/2013/10/orson-welles-war-of-the-worlds-panic-myth-the-infamous-radio-broadcast-did-not-cause-a-nation-wide-hysteria.html

Stephen, B. (2015, October 10). Get up, stand up: How Black Lives Matter uses social media to fight the power. *Wired*. Retrieved March 5, 2018, from https://www.wired.com/2015/10/how-black-lives-matter-uses-social-media-to-fight-the-power/

Stouffer, S. A., Lumsdaine, A. A., Lumsdaine, M. H., Williams Jr., R. M., Smith, M. B., Janis, I. L., Star, S. A., & Cottrell, L. S., Jr. (1949). *The American soldier: Combat and its aftermath*. (Studies in social psychology in World War II, Vol. 2.). Princeton, NJ: Princeton University Press.

Stouffer, S. A., Suchman, E. A., Devinney, L. C., Star, S. A., & Williams, R. M., Jr. (1949). *The American soldier: Adjustment during army life*. (Studies in social psychology in World War II, Vol. 1.). Princeton, NJ: Princeton University Press.

Surgeon General's Scientific Advisory Committee on Television and Social Behavior. (1972). *Television and growing up: The impact of televised violence*. Washington, DC: US Department of Health, Education, and Welfare.

Tönnies, F. (1957). *Community & society (Gemeinschaft und Gesellschaft)*. East Lansing: Michigan State University Press.

Tufekci, Z. (2017). *Twitter and tear gas: The power and fragility of networked protest*. New Haven, CT: Yale University Press.

Turkle, S. (2008). Always-on/always-on-you: The tethered self. In J. E. Katz (Ed.), *Handbook of mobile communication studies* (pp. 121–137). Cambridge, MA: The MIT Press.

Twenge, J. M., Joiner, T. E., Rogers, M. L., & Martin, G. N. (2018). Increases in depressive symptoms, suicide-related outcomes, and suicide rates among U.S. adolescents after 2010 and links to increased new media screen time. *Clinical Psychological Science*, 6(1), 3–17.

Wakabayashi, D. (2017, June 18). YouTube sets new policies to curb extremist videos. *The New*

York Times. Retrieved from https://www.nytimes .com/2017/06/18/business/youtube-terrorism .html

Weber, R., Ritterfeld, U., & Mathiak, K. (2006). Does playing violent video games induce aggression? Empirical evidence of a functional magnetic resonance imaging study. *Media Psychology*, 8(1), 39–60. doi:10.1207/S1532785XMEP0801_4

Webster, J. G., & Phalen, P. F. (1997). *The mass audience: Rediscovering the dominant model*. LEA's communication series. Mahwah, NJ: Lawrence Erlbaum Associates.

White, A. E., Weinstein, E., & Selman, R. L. (2018). Adolescent friendship challenges in a digital context. *Convergence: The Journal of Research Into New Media Technologies*, 24(3), 269–288.

Audiences as Institutional Constructions

The next two chapters mark a new section of the book. In this section, we will examine audiences not as objects of media power, but instead as *artifacts of social processes* such as public opinion polling (Chapter 3) and commercial audience ratings (Chapter 4). We will focus our attention on the strategies with which institutions actively construct notions of the audience through different research methodologies. The term **institution** here refers to "complex social forms that reproduce themselves, such as governments, the family, human languages, universities, hospitals, business corporations, and legal systems" (Miller, 2011). Sociologist Anthony Giddens (1986, p. 24) notes that institutions "by definition are the more enduring features of social life." We will be considering a number of important institutions in our society, such as the government, the press, and the media marketplace.

If we wish to have governments and market systems that respond to the will of the people, it is vital for our institutions to obtain feedback about the public's wants and needs. However, the method by which these institutions gather intelligence about the audience is often fraught with conceptual and logistical pitfalls. The source of these problems can be traced to the Industrial Revolution. As outlined in Chapter 1, the Industrial Revolution created an artificial separation between the workspace and the home (or leisure space). This meant that audience consumption of media messages took place in private, domestic spaces (such as the home) that were not under the direct supervision of private companies or the government. As we'll discuss in this section of the text, the fact that our product consumption, voting, and other forms of political engagement now take place outside of the public realm poses some thorny problems for institutions. These institutions want to ascertain our behaviors, attitudes, wishes, and desires but are often blocked by the legal and social protections that we have set up to protect our private spaces from outside influence. Indeed, the Declaration of Independence takes language from Enlightenment philosopher John Locke that the goal of government should be to enable citizens' unfettered access to "life, liberty, and the pursuit of happiness."

Since individuals in democracies do not live under the constant surveillance of a police state, institutions must turn to more indirect means for gathering feedback from the citizenry. This feedback takes many forms, such as public opinion polling, audience ratings, market surveys, and, increasingly, an analysis of "trending" topics on social media like Facebook and Twitter. There are some important implications to consider here. First, institutionalized forms of feedback always involve a time delay because of the nature of the process: Measuring audiences is complicated, costly, and sometimes slow; therefore, the feedback provided always reflects the past rather than the present. Secondly, because most modern, industrialized societies are extremely large, formal feedback solicited by institutions will always be incomplete since there are simply too many people in the audience to provide input on any one issue (and institutions would not be able to adequately process all of that information even if it were possible to gather it all). Sampling the audience is therefore necessary.

Thirdly, the process for gathering feedback from the audience is often *subject to institutional pressures*. This means that social institutions have particularized ways of knowing about message receivers because their techniques for information gathering and processing often *reflect institutional motives and needs*. For example, you might experience a plethora of complex reactions to a program that you see on television, but those reactions are of little concern to audience measurement firms like the Nielsen Corporation. These firms need to know only who was present in the audience in order to fulfill a business contract with an advertiser. Likewise, major social media platforms like Facebook and Twitter present their users in ways that privilege and emphasize certain kinds of hyperpartisan discourse that does not necessarily capture the complexity of our political discourse.

This disconnect between how you understand yourself and how audience measurement firms or social media platforms understand you might not seem that strange or problematic until you realize that institutions make critical decisions that can constrain the universe of actions or choices available to you. Indeed, governments, law enforcement, and the legal system have the power of life or death in their hands (Douglas, 1986). Returning to Giddens's theory of structuration, this means that institutions are powerful *structures* that can affect individual agency. Thus, while forms of audience measurement may be crude and imprecise, these constructions have real power to change decisions that affect millions of people. For this reason, it is critical that we understand how and why these institutions construct audiences.

CHAPTER

3

Public Opinion and Audience Citizenship

The year 2016 was marked by two major elections that reshaped the global political landscape. The first was the referendum (also known as Brexit) in the United Kingdom on June 23, 2016, on whether to withdraw the country from the European Union (EU; Asthana, Quinn, & Mason, 2016). In an extremely close vote after a 72.2% turnout of eligible voters, the United Kingdom voted 51.9% to 48.1% to leave the EU (BBC News, 2016), stunning many political observers. The vote to leave the EU had widespread implications, ranging from the resignation of then-Prime Minister David Cameron to the reemergence of political strife in Northern Ireland over the potential of a new customs border between it and the Irish Republic (still an EU member). The effects of Brexit will continue to ripple until and after the U.K.'s formal withdrawal date of March 29, 2019. The second major political earthquake of 2016 was the U.S. presidential election on November 8, 2016, which saw Republican and political neophyte Donald J. Trump defeat former Secretary of State and U.S. Senator Hillary Clinton with 306 Electoral College votes to 232, respectively (Kirk, Scott, & Graham, 2016). Trump won the election despite Clinton winning a slim majority of the popular vote, 48% to 46%.

Both of these elections in two major economic and geopolitical powers have upset the global status quo. But these two elections had something else in common: Social media platforms may have played a significant role in shaping the outcomes. In both the United Kingdom and the United States, Facebook and Twitter were enormously active with debate in the weeks and days leading up to the elections. Research in the aftermath of the Brexit vote found significant polarization among Facebook groups in the run up to the vote. For example, Facebook users tended to "like" posts that agreed with their previous beliefs about Brexit, forming vast echo chambers of similar viewpoints online (Del Vicario, Zollo, Caldarelli, Scala, & Quattrociocchi, 2017). Another analysis of millions of tweets leading up to the Brexit vote found that pro-Brexit Twitter accounts were roughly four times more effective than pro-remain groups in getting their message out and that pro-Brexit messages were more widely distributed via retweeting throughout the campaign (Grčar, Cherepnalkoski, Mozetič, & Kralj Novak, 2017). In the 2016 U.S. election, social media were leveraged extensively by both the Trump and Clinton campaigns, though Trump's campaign used a more amateur (and therefore more potentially "authentic") and unprofessional approach to reach out to potential supporters (Enli, 2017). Social media were so instrumental to Donald Trump's media coverage, voter outreach, and fundraising strategies, in fact, that one Trump campaign manager noted shortly after the election that "Facebook and Twitter were the reason we won this thing" (Lapowsky, 2016).

But something was amiss in the run up to the 2016 U.S. election. As Special Counsel Robert J. Mueller III's investigation later uncovered, many of the pro-Trump tweets and Facebook messages that trended on social media in days and weeks before the election were actually generated by hundreds of fake accounts created by a Russian front company called the Internet Research Agency, head-quartered in St. Petersburg, Russia (Shane & Mazzetti, 2018). These social media accounts posed as average Americans, and almost all of them were decidedly pro-Trump (or anti-Clinton). The sheer volume of these social media posts distorted the online debate by making it seem that there were many more vocal Trump supporters than there were Clinton supporters (Bessi & Ferrara, 2016). Particularly during key events, the Russian Twitter "troll" accounts fomented hatred of Muslims and distrust of the mainstream media, all to the benefit of the Trump campaign (Popken, 2017). Similar to the U.S. election cycle, in the Brexit case Russian Twitter "bots" (or automated message accounts) sent roughly 45,000 pro-Brexit tweets in the 48 hours before the referendum vote in the United Kingdom (Lomas, 2017). An investigative report issued by the U.S. Senate in early 2018 concluded that these two incidents of social media manipulation amounted to nothing less than a state-sponsored effort by Russia to spread disinformation and to destabilize the politics of the United States and the United Kingdom (Wintour, 2018). These inci-dents also demonstrated that we, the public, were potentially vulnerable to "brain hacking" by taking advantage of our tendency to believe that trending topics on social media were a true representation of the public mood.

Overview of the Chapter

The two examples of potential election tampering through the manipulation of public opinion via social media demonstrate some of the pitfalls associated with the centrality of technology in our modern political debate. They also point to the power inherent in representing (or, in this case, misrepresenting) public opinion since it can profoundly shape our political discourse and, indeed, political out-comes as well. In this chapter, we will explore how the audience is identified and measured as a "public." The key mechanism by which this concept is defined in our society today is through the machinery of quantitative, cross-sectional surveys of the population. This is a relatively recent innovation, however. We will explore the definition of public opinion by first tracing the development of notions of "the public" from ancient times until the 20th century. Next, the chapter turns to an overview of some of the key organizations and measurement techniques that are responsible for assessing public opinion today. Although the measurement of public opinion has become quite sophisticated in our modern era, there are nevertheless some inherent problems with the survey technique that can skew our perception of the public's wishes. Some of these problems are outlined in the next section of the chapter. Despite this reality, measurements of public opinion are very powerful in shaping decision-making in important institutions such as government and commerce. Next, the chapter focuses on some of the impacts of public opinion polling on the audience. In particular, we'll explore how our views on politics can be shaped by our perceptions of others' opinions. Finally, the chapter returns to the example of Brexit and the 2016 election to consider how the prospect of "fake news" and social media bots can create online echo chambers that mislead the public about the nature of public opinion itself.

A Brief History of Public Opinion

To understand the concept of public opinion in today's political discourse, we need to step back a moment and realize that this idea has undergone numerous historical shifts. We tend to think of public opinion in terms of poll results that we read about in the newspapers or online. However, the notion that the public is essentially created via the machinery of polling is a relatively recent innovation. In its more general meaning, public opinion refers to "group consensus about matters of public concern which has developed in the wake of informed discussion" (Graber, 1982, p. 556). The purpose of this group consensus is to communicate public sentiment and policy preferences back to government. For example, Speier (1950) understands public opinion as "primarily a communication from the citizens to their government" (p. 376). Feedback from the citizenry to those in power is an essential feature of a participatory democracy. As we'll see in this brief overview, the type of feedback from citizens to the state has wide-reaching implications.

Although the term *public opinion* is used quite often in our popular discourse, scholars have devised numerous definitions of the term. In part, this has to do with the goals of the people defining the public in particular ways. As Glynn, Herbst, Shapiro, and O'Keefe (1999, p. 56) note, "*Who* is a member of the public is always shifting, depending upon historical context and the agendas of those measuring public opinion" (see Figure 3.1). We'll trace the development of some of these meanings in this section of the chapter. This historical discussion incorporates the important scholarship of German sociologist and political philosopher Jürgen Habermas. Habermas's notion of the "public sphere" is key to understanding the historical transformations in the notion of public opinion during the Enlightenment and beyond, and his ideas are found throughout this brief historical overview.

Greco-Roman Notions of Public Opinion

Although the term *public opinion* was not actually in widespread use before the 19th century, the concept of the public was an important one to political philosophers in ancient times. As outlined in Chapter 1, the notion of the public was quite important to the political life of Greek and Roman societies. Groups of citizens would assemble in specially designated spaces to debate the issues of the day,

Figure 3.1 Historical Techniques for the Expression and Assessment of Public Opinion

Techniques	Time of Appearance
Oratory/rhetoric	5th century BCE
Printing	16th century
Crowds	17th century
Petitions	Late 17th century
Salons	Late 17th century
Coffeehouses	18th century
Revolutionary movements	Late 18th century
Strikes	19th century
General elections	19th century
Straw polls	1820s
Modern newspapers	Mid-19th century
Letters to public officials and editors	Mid-19th century
Mass media programming (political)	1920s–1930s
Sample survey	1930s

Source: Numbered Voices: How Opinion Polling Has Shaped American Politics by Susan Herbst, 1993. Reproduced with permission of University of Chicago Press.

and a premium was placed on the ability of individuals to clearly articulate their rhetorical arguments. Of course, it is important to point out that not everyone had access to these spaces. Since ancient Greek society was essentially a "patrimonial slave society," the male landowning citizens were freed from productive labor such that they could participate in these public discussions (Habermas, 1991, p. 3).

The history of thinking about the concept of public opinion starts with Plato, the Greek philosopher from the 4th century BCE. Plato was respectful of the powers of the public to make decisions, but he was generally skeptical about the wisdom of common people to make decisions in their own best interest or to "strive toward the creation of a morally sound state" (Glynn et al.,

1999, p. 34). Plato drew a contrast between two types of thinking: **doxa** (opinion) and **epistêmê** (knowledge). *Doxa* referred to popular belief that was fickle and "unshaped by the rigors of philosophy" (Peters, 1995, p. 4). On the other hand, *epistêmê* was sure knowledge about the true, unchanging nature of the world, which was informed by scientific principles. Plato believed that politics should not be clouded by the ephemeral nature of opinion. The task of governing should be reserved for experts, scientists, and philosopher-kings who rule according to the guidelines of epistêmê.

Plato's student Aristotle was more favorably disposed toward the body politic. Aristotle admired the universal laws behind epistêmê, but he believed that politics represented a more practical area of human activity that did not lend itself well to universal truths. In fact, Aristotle believed that the collective will could be superior to the opinions of individual men. The notion of public opinion was somewhat different than today's meaning, however. Public opinion for Aristotle did not constitute the ideas and sentiments of the common people. Instead, it was a more holistic term that encompassed "the values, norms, and tastes of a civilization" (Glynn et al., 1999, p. 35). When the Romans translated the Greek word *doxa* as *opinio*, the meaning of **opinion** as "judgment resting on grounds insufficient for complete demonstration" was transferred to the English language (Peters, 1995, pp. 4–5).

Feudal Europe and the Representative Public Sphere

By the Middle Ages, the Greco-Roman notion of the public as a collection of citizens who come together to discuss important civic topics was effectively dead. In its place, kings and feudal lords were the only individuals who were truly part of the "public." There were still events that were held in public such as marriages, trials, and hangings, but these events were largely ceremonial in nature. In his book *The Structural Transformation of the Public Sphere*, Jürgen Habermas (1991) describes this feudal period in Europe as the **representative public sphere**. By *representation*, Habermas did not mean that individual citizens had the capacity to select other citizens who would represent their interests with the monarchy. Instead, representation in the Middle Ages referred to the "public-ness" of the king, which was continually staged before the people in elaborate rituals and ceremonies such as coronations, festivals, and jousting tournaments. According to Habermas, "This *publicness* (or *publicity*) *of representation* was not constituted as a social realm—that is, as a public sphere; rather, it was something like a status attribute" (1991, p. 7). The king therefore "represented" the body politic by being the single embodiment of the society. The commoners were meant to participate in public events only as spectators, and the purpose of these events was to bolster the divine right of the monarchic ruler by continually demonstrating the glory and honor of the monarch. Peters writes that "in 'representation,' Habermas sees the epitome of public life modeled on the theater: the elite few have speaking parts while the many groundlings can only hiss or cheer" (1995, p. 8).

The 18th-Century Enlightenment and the Bourgeois Public Sphere

It was not until the latter half of the 18th century that the meaning of "the public" changed once again. In revolutionary England and France, the notion of public opinion as the collective will of the citizenry emerged for the first time. Habermas explains that the old feudal order began to collapse, thanks to the rise of capitalism and the merchant middle classes. As citizens grew less reliant on the generosity of the feudal lord for their land and material well-being, they began to gain more independence from the state. The concentrated authority of the monarch was slowly redistributed among multiple individuals and agencies (such as the police, army, and local entities), and the social distance between the state and the people shrank, which created new opportunities for bourgeois citizens and merchants to challenge those in power. In this way, "civil society came into existence as the corollary of a depersonalized state authority" (Habermas, 1991, p. 19). Habermas argues that the press had a vital role to play here since it broke the previous monopoly on information distribution enjoyed by the monarchy and the church. For the first time in centuries, citizens were transacting business and politics with one another without the direct influence of the state. This new form of social organization is defined as the **bourgeois public sphere**.

The key aspect of the bourgeois public sphere was that the location wherein citizens could constitute a "public" was not centralized in any one location or controlled by any one entity. In fact, the public emerged as a social process that was created *through conversation* between citizens (Peters, 1995, p. 9). These conversations were facilitated through the development of the English coffeehouse and the French salon (see Figure 3.2). Salons provided a physical space wherein men (and sometimes women) could gather for conversation that was not sponsored or controlled by the state. The salon "was an experiment in equality that assumed paradigmatic importance within a hierarchically organized society" (Speier, 1950, p. 381). Salons were important not just because citizens could speak together about politics, but because these were some of the first places where the citizens' opinions could be assessed by other citizens as well as by the ruling regime (Herbst, 1995a, p. 52). We should be clear that the 18th-century notion of the public did not refer to universal citizenship. Rather, the concept of the public reflected the growing economic and political power of the middle class, which emerged as a potential threat to the entrenched monarchies and aristocracies of the feudal period. The notion of the public was therefore "less a signifier of democracy than a shift in power toward an educated, property-owning middle class" (Lewis, 2001, p. 23). Some scholars have critiqued Habermas's celebration of the bourgeois public sphere as a model for democratic citizenship because of the restricted access of many citizens to the political arena, particularly women and minority groups (Benhabib, 1992; Fraser, 1990).

The press began to play an increasingly important role in these new private discussion spaces. While monarchs had vigorously controlled printing during the feudal era, private printers emerged during the Enlightenment, thanks to increased patronage

Figure 3.2   Depiction of a 17th-Century English Coffeehouse

Source: 1674 woodcut.

from the merchant middle class. Rather than extol the virtues of the feudal lord, this new liberated press aimed for a more realistic description of events in order to make the functions of the state more transparent. Ordinary citizens became the primary subject of the news. The goal of the press was simply to "publicize" or to provide a record of what individuals had said to one another in public places like coffeehouses, taverns, and salons. The press, therefore, did not necessarily serve the kind of watchdog role that is most common today. Instead, it served as a vehicle of publicity and a "reflector of animated public conversation and argument" (Carey, 1995, p. 382). In this sense, the press facilitated the expansion of public conversation beyond the confines of the salons and coffeehouses, thereby creating a broader awareness of political issues. The press not only made things public, but it actually "made publics" by "opening up the affairs of state to citizens who had no other way of knowing" (Lewis, 2001, p. 25).

The newfound autonomy of the citizens from the aristocracy inspired the political theorists of the time. British philosopher John Locke (1988) argued in the late 1600s that human beings are creatures of reason and tolerance and that all men were created equal in the eyes of God. This fundamental truth was carried forward by Enlightenment political philosopher Jean-Jacques Rousseau. In his 1767 book *The Social Contract*, Rousseau (1967) was one of the first to use the term *public opinion* to argue that the state should be governed by the "general will" and not by the whim of centralized autocracies. This system would be practical, he argued, because citizens were honest and expected honesty from others. However, Rousseau was convinced that the public could become too unwieldy if it grew too large in size. Writing in the 19th century, British philosopher John Stuart Mill (1859/1999) emphasized that individual free will was paramount and that government should act only to circumscribe individual freedom when the "law of opinion" was not functioning effectively. In his visit to the United States in the 1830s, Alexis de Tocqueville was impressed by the degree of social equality he witnessed among American citizens. He famously observed that

> in times of equality men, being so like each other, have no confidence in others, but this same likeness leads them to place almost unlimited confidence in the judgment of the public. For they think it not unreasonable that, all having the same means of knowledge, truth will be found on the side of the majority. (1969, p. 435)

De Tocqueville effectively captured the growing sentiment that relying upon the collective will of the public can enhance democracy. His observation also pointed to a growing recognition that obedience to the **will of the majority** represented the most democratic means of governance.

Quantification of Public Opinion in the 19th Century

Our modern notions of public opinion as the accumulation of individual political voices into a collective whole were developed during the 19th century. A number of citizen-sponsored forms of political expression such as *petitions* and *public rallies* were recurring features of political life as early as the 1640s in England. In the late 18th century, *rioting* also emerged as a common form of political expression. In England, riots and other popular uprisings were typically linked to economic issues such as food shortages, food price spikes, and tax policies. Political agitators in the American colonies also adopted many of these strategies to protest what they saw as unfair policies from the British crown.

All of these forms of collective political expression were directly observable in the public spaces, but the **rise of quantification** in the 19th century marked an important shift in the definition of the public. The definition of public opinion shifted to mean the majority sentiment as measured by numerical counts. Although political opinions had been counted back in ancient Greece, "It was not until the eighteenth and nineteenth centuries that quantification became a significant element of political discourse in the West" (Herbst, 1995a, p. 7). The roots of quantification come from the 17th century when it became attractive to measure and accumulate social data. Historians believe that the rise in importance of quantifiable social data is likely due to a number of factors, including growth in the insurance industry, the expansion of foreign trade, and concern over the numbers of dead in the Great Plague of 1665 (Herbst, 1995a, p. 9). Public opinion in the modern sense was first measured thanks to the development of the general election in the American colonies in the late 1700s (Mackenzie, 1972). The key innovation at that time was the use of *secret balloting* for all public elections. For the first time, citizens' political voices were not heard orally in public but were instead registered in private at the ballot box. The benefits of this technique were clear: In increasingly large societies where universal political participation was the hallmark of a democracy, balloting was a much more efficient and reasonable method to achieve this goal.

The private nature of secret ballot elections created some trepidation among political leaders who could not directly access the public mood in advance of these elections. This uncertainty motivated politicians, political parties, and journalists to create a crude, quantitative form of opinion polling in the 19th century called **the straw poll** (Herbst, 1995a, p. 69). Straw polls are oral or pen-and-paper surveys that measure the popularity of a political candidate or policy. This form of measurement seemed much more scientific than a political discussion held in a tavern or coffeehouse. However, there was little regularity to the methodology behind these polls, which led to sometimes conflicting results. In the highly partisan era of the mid-19th century, political candidates could always find a particular straw poll that favored their interests (Herbst, 1995a, pp. 80–83). Nevertheless, straw polls often animated citizen discussions about the results, thereby building on the strong tradition of public discussion from earlier centuries (Herbst, 1995b).

The Rise of Surveys in the 20th Century

Straw polls continued to be popular into the early decades of the 20th century, though they began to compete with the technique of **systematic surveys** beginning in the 1920s. Surveys differed from straw polls in their methodology. While straw polls reported the political whims of groups of people in specific contexts, surveys measure their respondents more scientifically by using the statistical technique of sampling (more on sampling in the next section). Surveys were also capable of measuring larger groups of citizens more accurately. When the Herbert Hoover administration determined in 1929 that the U.S. government needed to gather more scientific information about the economic and social conditions of the nation in order to better identify the causes of the nation's economic woes, a group of social scientists gathered in Washington, DC, to create new measures for this purpose (Converse, 1987). When they released their report, called *Recent Social Trends*, in 1933, it became a model for the numerous social research projects that were undertaken as part of Franklin Roosevelt's New Deal policies.

At the same time, the political tradition of conducting straw polls ahead of elections to gather the pulse of the public came to a somewhat abrupt end. In 1936, the news magazine *Literary Digest* conducted a straw poll by mailing out millions of ballots to lists of citizens it had gathered from telephone directories and auto registration records. The *Literary Digest* poll predicted that Republican Alf Landon

Figure 3.3   World War II–Era Poster Created by the U.S. Office of War Information

Source: Office for Emergency Management, Office of War Information, Domestic Operations Branch, Bureau of Special Services. (1943–1945).

would soundly defeat incumbent Democrat Roosevelt. A much smaller opinion organization run by George Gallup conducted a poll as well, though Gallup used *random sampling* to gather his respondents and predicted that Roosevelt would win handily (see the following sections for full discussion). When Roosevelt captured 61% of the popular vote, the *Literary Digest* ran a public apology and unsystematic straw polls gave way to the scientific survey (Glynn et al., 1999, pp. 61–62). After 1936, Gallup's polling organization emerged as a major factor in the U.S. political landscape. Scientific surveys became the dominant form of public opinion measurement and a potent symbol of American democracy (see Figure 3.3).

Survey Methods and the Public Opinion Industry

Beginning in the 1930s, the **survey** became the most widely used research method for measuring public opinion. A survey (or poll) refers to a quantitative research technique for counting or describing characteristics of a population (Glynn et al., 1999, p. 68). Public opinion surveys are guided by a number of methodological considerations that are described in the following sections. In general, opinion surveys construct "the public" as a numerical aggregate of individual, private opinions in response to questions about political issues and policies. This means that quantification is a critical aspect of the process of measuring public opinion today. Surveys are most often *cross-sectional*, meaning that they are conducted at a single point in time to capture a snapshot of the public's views on issues. This model is far removed from the types of political discussions that took place in the salons and coffeehouses of the 18th century, but it has come to define the parameters of "public opinion" in our modern era.

Sampling and Survey Participation

Modern public opinion surveys consist of a number of components. First, surveys are designed to measure a **population** of individuals. A *population* refers to a group of individuals (citizens of a community or nation, for instance) who may have an opinion relating to the subject of the survey (Miller, 1995). With most populations, especially in a nationwide study, it is impossible to include everyone in the survey. Pollsters therefore select a **sample** (or subset) of individuals from the population to complete the survey. The experience of the *Literary Digest* magazine in the 1936 presidential election demonstrated that the method of selecting the sample is critically important in determining the validity of the survey results. Like George Gallup in the 1930s, survey methodologists today use **probability sampling** to select the individuals for the sample. This means that individuals are selected *at random* from the population such that there is a known chance of being included in the sample. This assures that the sample is roughly *representative* of the population as a whole and increases the likelihood that the results are generalizable. Pollsters attempt to be cost-conscious by assembling the smallest possible sample that will still be representative of the population.

Another important issue in survey research is that the individuals chosen randomly to participate often choose not to do so. Large, professional polling organizations typically obtain survey participation rates of 70% to 80% (meaning that 70–80% of respondents who are initially contacted choose to participate in the survey; Glynn et al., 1999, p. 71). Low response rates can endanger the generalizability of the findings, particularly when the types of individuals who decline to participate are systematically different from the survey participants. Selecting potential survey respondents became much easier beginning in the 1930s and 1940s because most Americans were listed in public records such as telephone books and mailing lists (Glynn et al., 1999, p. 66). More recently, however, pollsters have become worried that representative samples of Americans will become more difficult to find in the next decade. The problem is that many Americans are canceling their landline telephones in favor of mobile phones, which are not listed in telephone directories. A recent study by the Pew Research Center for The People and the Press found that approximately 7.1% of Americans were from "cell-only" households (Keeter, 2007). Worse yet, the Pew Center study revealed that these cell-only citizens differed systematically from their landline peers: They were much younger, more likely to be African American or Hispanic, and less likely to be married or own a home. Although the net impact of cell-only individuals on nationwide poll results is still small, this sampling problem will continue to increase as more Americans adopt mobile phones over landlines.

Data Gathering and Survey Design

Public opinion surveys use a number of methods for gathering data on audience attitudes and beliefs. The ideal situation is the **person-to-person interview**, in which the researcher sits down with a respondent, establishes a rapport, and asks in-depth questions. This type of interaction allows for the best "read" of the complexities of individuals' thoughts about the issue in question. The major downside of this method is the time and excessive cost involved, which is why few national polling organizations gather their data this way. Instead, polling firms use **telephone interviews** as the primary means of gathering survey data. Telephone surveys are relatively quick and easy to organize, and computers are employed to dial telephone numbers randomly in order to achieve a probability sample of the population. Since telephone survey questions can be difficult for the respondent to understand, they are designed to be as straightforward as possible, and the length of the interview is typically kept short (fewer than 20 minutes) to maintain the attention and cooperation of the respondent. By far the cheapest method to gather data is the **mail-administered survey**, but response rates for this method are often so low (lower than 5% return rates, as opposed to the minimally acceptable 50% response rate) that polling firms hardly ever resort to this technique (Glynn et al.,

1999, p. 73). In fact, most surveys that you typically receive in the mail are not scientific surveys at all but thinly disguised marketing messages meant to raise awareness of a political candidate or product, or to appeal for money.

One of the most significant challenges in conducting survey research is crafting the language of each question to be clear, concise, and understandable to a broad range of respondents. Survey questions that initially seem straightforward can potentially lead to respondent confusion, thereby obscuring the "true" opinion that is being measured. For example, pollsters attempt to avoid **leading questions**, which can steer respondents to give a particular answer even if it is not the best representation of their views. So if a survey question asks "What do you see as the benefits of a tax cut for the American economy?" the respondent may be primed to think only about the positive aspects of a reduction in the tax rate rather than other negative consequences. Pollsters also try to avoid *double-barreled questions*, which occur when two separate issues are inadvertently combined into a single question, leading to respondent confusion. An example of a double-barreled question might be "Do you support the president's economic stimulus proposal, or do you think it doesn't provide enough tax cuts?" Here, there are two questions rolled into one: whether or not the respondent supports the stimulus proposal and what specific aspects of the proposal are individually supported. To correct the problem, questions such as these need to be broken into their constituent parts and reframed as separate issues to avoid respondent confusion. We'll address some of the problems with question wording in the next section.

Public Opinion Organizations

Like the Gallup organization in the 1930s, there are a number of important institutions in society today that issue regular reports about Americans' opinions about a whole range of topics. Although the field of survey production in the United States is vast, there are several broad types of institutions that generate public opinion data about American citizens on an ongoing basis. For example, *governmental agencies* such as the Department of Labor, the Department of Justice, and the National Center for Health Statistics account for over a million survey interviews each year (Lewis, 2001, p. 41). There are numerous *private polling companies* that contract with government and other firms to provide polling data. Two such companies, the Wirthlin Group and Market Opinion Research (MOR), are Republican-leaning organizations that have worked with numerous congressional and Senate candidates to conduct polling in advance of elections (Miller, 1995, p. 116). Private polling companies may choose not to release the results of their polls to the public, depending upon the wishes of their clients.

The most visible survey organizations today are generally those that regularly release their results to the public. *Academic institutions* such the National Opinion Research Center (NORC) at the University of Chicago and the Institute for Social Research at the University of Michigan are important because they make their raw datasets widely available so that scholars can mine those data to answer their own research questions. NORC is responsible for the General Social Survey (GSS), an annual nationwide public opinion survey that asks Americans a battery of demographic, behavioral, and attitudinal questions. Since many of the questions have remained the same since 1972, scholars can conduct sophisticated longitudinal (time-series) analyses of American opinions. *News corporations* such as *The New York Times* and CBS News or the *Washington Post* and ABC News also conduct opinion polling on an ongoing basis about politics, economics, and social trends. A more recent entrant into this cadre of polling organizations is YouGov, which has partnered with the British newspaper *The Economist* (http://today.yougov.com/). These polls are some of the most widely recognized by average citizens simply because the results are often given extensive coverage in the news outlets that sponsor them.

Finally, there are numerous *independent companies or organizations* such as the Gallup, Roper, and Harris organizations. These private companies produce opinion polls that are a matter of public record, but they earn their revenue by conducting market research for clients. It's important to note that opinion polling is not a large money-making business (Miller, 1995). In fact, revenues of organizations like Harris and Gallup pale in comparison with firms like Nielsen or Arbitron that measure audience demographics and size for the commercial media (there is much more on these firms in Chapter 4). Some independent polling organizations, such as the Pew Research Center for The People and the Press (http://pewresearch.org/), are supported by foundations and thereby release all of their reports to the public. Opinion polls conducted by these organizations are often cited by the news media in their reports as well.

Public Opinion and the Limits of Audience Constructions

The success of Gallup and other polling organizations in developing scientific survey techniques in the early 20th century has irrevocably changed our popular notion of public opinion. Although modern surveys conducted using probability sampling techniques have been shown to be quite accurate reflections of the attitudes and behaviors of large populations, critics and scholars have continued to debate whether these new techniques enhance or undermine our political discourse. This section briefly lays out some important criticisms of public opinion as expressed through quantitative surveys. These critiques focus on two key claims: (1) that the institutionalization of opinion polling in the 20th century has carried us far afield from the type of engaged, rational discussion of the Enlightenment period; and (2) that some of the inherent weaknesses of the survey method can skew the findings, thereby creating a false and artificial sense of public opinion today.

Public Opinion as a Fictional Construct

For the most cogent and durable critique of the notion of public opinion, it is instructive to consider Walter Lippmann's writings during the 1920s (see Chapter 2 for details). In his book *Public Opinion*, Lippmann (1922) argued that individual citizens had neither the time nor the resources to be able to develop complex and reasoned responses to national or international events. Instead, they relied chiefly on elites in the news media to gather intelligence on those events in their place. In this sense, it was somewhat misleading to claim that public opinion was an independent entity. In his follow-up to *Public Opinion* called *The Phantom Public*, Lippmann (1993, p. 147) took his argument further to suggest that the entire notion of the public is an artificial fiction based upon a "mystical notion of Society." The public, he argued, most often performed the role of bystanders who are more interested in their own personal lives than they are in the affairs of state. Indeed, two researchers in the 1990s found that a sample of American citizens could answer only four out of 10 basic questions about civics, such as the name of their U.S. representative, the stands of key politicians, or what party controlled the U.S. Senate (Carpini & Keeter, 1997). Lippmann argued that there was a small number of knowledgeable people who possessed the power to make changes in economic and political affairs (called "agents"). Thus, Lippmann urged the abandonment of the myth contained in public opinion polling that all citizens were equally engaged in the issues.

Sociologist Herbert Blumer (1969, pp. 201–202) was similarly critical of the concept of public opinion, though he was much more concerned with the mechanics of the survey methodology itself. Blumer argued against the notion of public opinion as a "quantitative distribution of individual opinions." Instead, he considered public opinion to be an organic outgrowth of social relationships between everyday people. What surveys accomplished, he argued, was the transformation of democratic debate into columns of numbers and symbols. Not only did this rob the public of the ability to have a vigorous debate about the issues, but the survey instrument essentially denied its own existence and presented polling data as fact. It also removed the need for public discussion of the issues since public opinion is registered anonymously. In this sense, "citizens do not themselves produce public opinion today; it must be generated through the machinery of polling. The power to constitute the public space, then, falls into the hands of the experts, not of the citizens" (Peters, 1995, p. 20). Habermas (1991) added that opinion polling reintroduces the representative public sphere by placing the power to define public opinion in the hands of elite pollsters.

The Manufacture and Management of Public Opinion

Even scholars who accept the premise that aggregations of individual opinions can be valid representations of the public have noted that surveys are fraught with methodological challenges. Zaller (1992) notes several inherent problems with the quantitative measurement of public opinion. For instance, the public may seem overly fickle since their responses on similar questions will seem to shift markedly over time. This might simply be an indication that individuals carefully monitor events in the media and adjust their views on an ongoing basis. However, psychological research on attitudes (see Chapter 2) has found strong evidence that individuals' true attitudes are quite stable over time. A more plausible explanation is that the shift in responses is due to "**measurement error.**" Stated differently, because surveys (1) measure a small sample of the population and (2) attempt to measure complicated concepts through a questionnaire, then there is a "chance variation" that can creep into the results. This means that the survey is not measuring the public's "true" opinion as accurately as we might wish.

There will always be some amount of random error in quantitative surveys. However, public opinion surveying is also prone to more systematic forms of error that results from the mechanics of the measurement process, something that Zaller (1992, pp. 32–33) calls "response effects" and "question-wording effects." **Response effects** occur when some questions on a survey affect respondents' answers on others. For example, a survey in 1984 asked respondents about their interest in politics and then followed that question with more specific questions about some obscure political issues (Bishop, Oldendick, & Tuchfarber, 1984). The researchers then reversed the question order and found that, when asked the obscure policy issues first, respondents were much less likely to describe themselves as interested in politics. **Question-wording effects** occur when shifts in survey responses are the result of the way in which the question is asked (see Box 3.1). Finally, surveys can create what Philip Converse (1964) calls *nonattitudes* by asking respondents to express a sentiment about something about which they have no opinion. Pressed by the interviewer, the respondent will make up something to satisfy the demands of the survey, but this type of public opinion measure is also highly suspect.

Surveys that aim to estimate the views of a large population are also reliant on a model of what that population looks like. In the 2016 election, for instance, pre-election polls predicted an "over 90%" likelihood that Hillary Clinton would win the presidency, with estimates of the probability of her election ranging between 71% and 99% (Kennedy et al., 2017). Indeed, Trump's victory surprised even the pollsters working for his campaign since they had also predicted that Trump would lose the election, albeit by a small margin (Mills, 2016). So why were the public opinion polls wrong in predicting the outcome of the election in 2016? Shortly after the election, pollsters for the Pew Research Center offered some potential explanations (Mercer, Deane, & McGeeney, 2016). One possible cause was **nonresponse bias**. In essence, some groups of potential respondents are difficult for pollsters to reach or are more hesitant to respond to requests to fill out polls (particularly if their chosen candidate regularly maligns public opinion polls as biased and unfair). When there is a systematic bias in their inability to reach those individuals, the resulting opinion poll will not accurately reflect the population. A follow-up investigation and report by the American Association for Public

BOX 3.1
Question Wording and the Manufacture of Public Opinion

There are numerous problems posed by survey question wording that can end up skewing measures of public opinion or, worse yet, *manufacturing* opinions where none exist. In his book *Constructing Public Opinion*, scholar Justin Lewis describes a 1991 nationwide survey conducted by a Boston polling agency for the Anti-Defamation League (during the Gulf War in Iraq). The survey asked two questions in order to understand the opinion of the American public about the establishment of a Palestinian state. The first question was phrased as follows:

> *Do you favor or oppose giving the Palestinians a homeland of their own in the West Bank?*

When the question was asked this way, 58% of the sample favored the proposal, with 20% opposed. Later on in the survey, the question was asked in a more specific manner:

> *Many people feel that if the West Bank were under Palestinian control, Iraq or other enemies might be able to use it as a base for attacking Israel. With this in mind, which of these opinions about a Palestinian homeland is closer to yours:*
>
> *The Palestinians should have a homeland on the West Bank, even if the risk to Israel's security cannot be completely eliminated, or the Palestinians should not be allowed to have a West Bank homeland because the risk to Israel's security can never be completely eliminated.*

Once the question was framed quite specifically, public opinion seemed to be radically transformed. In response to the second question, 44% supported a Palestinian homeland while 41% opposed it. It is doubtful that the respondents shifted their political views midway during the survey, so what happened here? The first question was more broadly posed with no mention of the complex political situation in the Middle East. This may have encouraged more positive responses. In the second example, the potential impact on Israel of a Palestinian state and the phrase *Many people feel . . .* likely encouraged more respondents to view the creation of a Palestinian homeland more dimly. But what if the respondents in the poll had never given a second thought to the situation in the Middle East before being asked these questions? There would be no way to tell whether or not these opinions were simply manufactured by the process of asking the question (also called "nonattitudes"). Lewis concludes that the questions in this poll were therefore "structured interventions into public discourse rather than independent verifications of it" (Lewis, 2001, p. 13).

Source: Lewis, J. (2001). *Constructing Public Opinion: How Political Elites Do What They Like and Why We Seem to Go Along with It* (pp. 12–13). New York, NY: Columbia University Press.

Opinion Research (Kennedy et al., 2017) found that, in fact, pollsters in several key Midwest states (such as Wisconsin and Michigan) underestimated the number of less-educated, working-class voters in their models of likely voters and therefore underestimated support for Donald Trump in these key battleground states.

Another potential culprit of the misleading public opinion polls leading up to the 2016 presidential election was what researchers call **social desirability bias**. This occurs when survey respondents give an answer to the interviewer that they believe is the more socially acceptable answer, even if that does not accurately reflect their own attitudes or behaviors. For example, it is well-known to survey researchers that some respondents will tell them that they voted in the last election even when they did not, because this response is seen to be more socially acceptable (Holbrook & Krosnick, 2010). After the results of the 2016 election became clear, some pollsters suspected that some opinion poll respondents who intended to vote for Trump had misrepresented their intentions to interviewers because they believed this to be the less socially desirable response. The investigative report of the American Association for Public Opinion Research found little evidence for this so-called shy Trumper effect, however (Kennedy et al., 2017). The failures of opinion polling in 2016 demonstrated some of the natural pitfalls of measuring public opinion. In some cases, the method of gathering and measuring public opinion may have the effect of *artificially generating* the very thing it is trying to measure, in effect manufacturing public opinion in the process. These challenges mean that it is often difficult to equate survey analysis with "true" public sentiment.

Given these problems, why does public opinion polling remain such a powerful force in our political conversation today? Margolis and Mauser (1989, pp. 6–7) suggest that surveys provide the measurement of audience opinions with a "greater aura of science" and therefore they seem more objective than relying on rhetorical claims. Opinion surveys are therefore quite useful as a neutral touchstone for political debate: Individuals can disagree on policies and ideologies, but no one can dispute the "facts" about what the public thinks. Belief in the value of opinion polling also fits in nicely with the democratic ideal that those in government are responsive to the will of the people. When one looks closely at the process of opinion polling, however, it's clear that the organizations and individuals who construct the surveys are socioeconomic elites who have been socialized into the existing system of political values (Dye, 2002; Margolis & Mauser, 1989; Mills, 1956). We should not be surprised, then, when polls seem to express popular support for the existing status quo. Finally, public opinion surveys are *relatively simple to accomplish and are cost-effective*, which has made them the dominant form of citizen feedback in our modern era. More colleges, universities, private foundations, and other organizations have begun surveying the American electorate because there are few if any barriers to doing so.

Some political scientists have questioned the very notion that public opinion polling represents an entity that is independent of the systems of power and authority that govern the populace. Margolis and Mauser (1989) argue that public opinion is, in fact, a *dependent variable*. What they mean is that public opinion is generally inextricable from the policy proposals and positions of elites in both government and private think tanks, such that when the members of the public are asked questions on surveys, their views often simply reflect the range of debates among these elites (therefore, public opinion is dependent on those elites, as opposed to being separate or organic from those elites). Benjamin Ginsberg (1986) has focused on the ways in which opinion polling actually facilitates elite agendas in a democracy by reshaping the potentially transformative power of group political behavior into a manageable phenomenon of individual opinions. According to Ginsberg, polls shift responsibility for raising issues from the people to the elites who formulate survey questions, thereby enhancing the power of those elites in our political system. Bennett (1989) has found that the news media contribute to this dependent relationship of the public by continually highlighting the views of elites and experts in their coverage, which also serves to marginalize the views of the public. As these perspectives make clear, our political lives are shaped and buffeted by a sea of public opinion polls, but many of these polls may be more suited to addressing elite and institutional needs than to providing a reliable conduit from citizens to policy makers.

How News Shapes Public Opinion

Thus far in the chapter, we have explored the history of the concept of public opinion as well as the current survey methods for measuring it. But where do the public's opinions come from? Communication research has produced compelling evidence that citizens' political awareness and information environment are profoundly shaped by the news media. Walter Lippmann first suggested that the press creates a "pseudo-environment" by selecting only certain events, perspectives, and ideas to present to the public. In this section, we'll briefly explore how news coverage affects the public's opinions about the importance of political issues and how that perception feeds back into the policy arena and into the news media as well.

News and the Public Agenda

In the classic democratic model, citizens discuss issues that are relevant to their lives, and these issues are then dutifully reported by the news media so that they can filter up to political elites. This is reminiscent of the type of press found back in the 18th and 19th centuries, when the news consisted of summaries of what citizens talked about in public places such as taverns and salons. However, groundbreaking research in the early 1970s discovered that this classic model had been reversed in our modern era. McCombs and Shaw (1972) examined national and regional news coverage of the 1968 presidential election to compile a list of the top issues of the presidential campaign, which they dubbed the *news agenda*. They compared the news agenda with public opinion polls asking a representative sample of voters which issues were more salient to them (the *public agenda*) and found that the news agenda profoundly shaped what voters thought was important. The ability of the mass media to transfer the salience of items and their attributes from the news agenda to the public was called the **agenda-setting effect** (see Figure 3.4). In the past 40 years, hundreds of research studies have found empirical support for agenda setting (Dearing & Rogers, 1996; McCombs & Reynolds, 2009). More recent studies have demonstrated that media agenda setting can even trump our own personal experiences in directing our opinions about important public issues. For example, a survey conducted in Washington, DC, found that exposure to local news stories about city crime

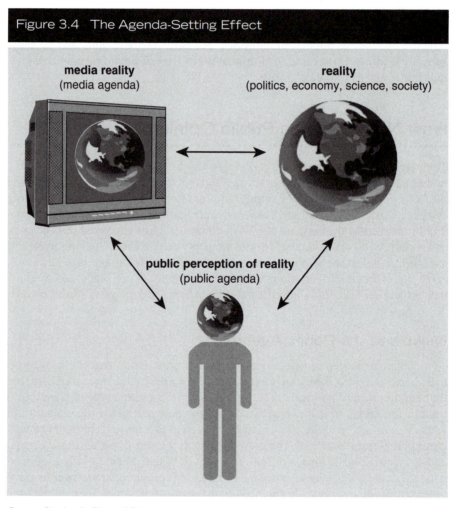

Figure 3.4 The Agenda-Setting Effect

media reality
(media agenda)

reality
(politics, economy, science, society)

public perception of reality
(public agenda)

Source: Stephanie Plumeri Ertz.

increased respondents' awareness of crime as an important local political issue (Gross & Aday, 2003). Interestingly, Gross and Aday found that respondents' personal experiences with crime had no agenda-setting effect.

Further research has uncovered the ability of the news media to affect not just the salience of particular issues for the public but also the types of conclusions that the public draws about those issues. A number of studies have closely examined *news framing*. **Framing** occurs when journalists or media producers "select some aspects of a perceived reality and make them more salient in a communicating text, in such a way as to promote a particular problem definition, causal interpretation, moral evaluation, and/or treatment recommendation" (Entman, 1993, p. 52). For example, in political campaigns some candidates may be considered by the press as the "front-runner" in the race, and this particular media frame has consequences for voter perceptions of the candidate. A number of studies in the 1980s and 1990s uncovered empirical evidence that media frames can affect "how people interpret the news and the judgments they form after viewing or reading the news" (Perse, 2001, p. 106). For instance, a classic book by Iyengar and Kinder (1987) found that news reports not only shape citizens' awareness of public issues, but they also provide citizens a conceptual framework within which to understand these stories. A follow-up book (Iyengar, 1994) found that media frames directed respondents toward specific policy solutions for social and economic problems.

Opinion Polling and the News Media

Both agenda setting and framing research demonstrate that the news media can affect the public's perception of political issues. How, then, might news reports of public opinion polls affect citizens' awareness of issues? Could news reports of opinion polls ultimately shape how citizens think about these issues? German scholar Elisabeth Noelle-Neumann (1984, 1991) contended that the reporting of public opinion in the news media may reduce the number of divergent opinions in society. Her theory, called the **Spiral of Silence**, claims that individuals naturally fear social isolation and will therefore monitor the political views expressed in the media and repress their own opinions if they are in the minority. While Noelle-Neumann pointed to experiences in the German political scene as examples of this effect, it has not received widespread empirical support in the United States.

Research has also shown evidence for **bandwagon effects**. This occurs when individuals hear news reports of opinion polls that differ from their own opinions, which causes them to shift their outlook to match the majority opinion. **Underdog effects** are the opposite of bandwagon effects. This happens when the public shifts its support to a minority position or political candidate. For example, if voters do not expect a political candidate to win (since opinion polls show that candidate trailing), they may vote for the candidate anyway. During election seasons when opinion polls are reported quite often in the news media, bandwagon effects are much more commonly found (Marsh, 1984). Morwitz and Pluzinski (1996) found evidence that both the bandwagon and underdog effects were contingent upon whether voters were paying close attention to the polls in an election, as well as their degree of support for a particular candidate. The more uncertain voters were about their candidate choice, the more likely they were to join the perceived majority opinion. During elections, the news media provide continual updates about which candidate is leading in the opinion polls. This is called **horse race coverage**. In a series of controlled experiments, Cappella and Jamieson (1997) discovered that poll-centered, strategy-oriented news coverage of elections (as opposed to issue-oriented coverage) actually increased voter cynicism about politics in general.

There are a number of insights to be gained from the research on the news and public opinion. First, opinion polls give us a sense of how our fellow citizens think about important issues, allowing us to understand how our views compare with those of the majority. Second, these surveys are critical information tools for the press, which regards them as unproblematic mirrors of citizen sentiment and gives them wide exposure via news outlets. Third, agenda-setting theory demonstrates that the extent of news coverage about a particular event or issue can have a powerful effect on whether or not the public thinks carefully about that issue. Thus, there is a kind of reciprocal, mutually reinforcing relationship between the news media and public opinion. Finally, a number of scholars have found evidence that both the media and public agendas can impact the **policy agenda,** or the actions of political elites and policy makers (Dearing & Rogers, 1996; Rogers & Dearing, 1988).

Social Media as Public Opinion Barometers: Filter Bubbles, Fake News, and Conspiracy Theories

Agenda-setting theory came about during a time when the information sources available to citizens, while abundant in Western democracies, nevertheless pale in comparison to the sheer volume and information sources available via the Internet. Now, in addition to major news websites and news aggregators such as Apple News, Google News, and Yahoo News, more and more individuals are consuming their news via social media platforms like Facebook and Twitter. A 2017 Pew Research Center survey found that 26% of Americans get their news from two or more social media sites, and half of all Americans who use Facebook for their news rely solely on Facebook to get their news (Grieco, 2017). What types of news about politics, the economy, and social issues are available on social media? As the beginning of this chapter outlined in the case of Brexit and the 2016 presidential election, the information we receive via social media can be false, manipulated, and can cater to our existing beliefs and biases.

As discussed in Chapter 2, researchers have found that audiences tend to engage in selectivity when they consume media, meaning that they tend to seek out information that supports their preexisting attitudes about the world. We live in an era where Internet companies like Google, Microsoft, and Yahoo can easily filter our information environment in order to deliver news that might be relevant to our particular interests or points of view, thereby creating a personalized information environment. On social media like Twitter, Facebook, Snapchat, and

Instagram, these predispositions toward selective exposure, in particular, can be extreme. Thanks to the sophisticated filtering algorithms used by Facebook, for instance, resulting in a kind of "algorithmic visibility," some people, ideas, and sentiments are more relevant in an individual's newsfeed than others (Bucher, 2012). Eli Pariser (2012) has dubbed this carefully manicured information environment a "filter bubble" and has warned that these bubbles are isolating us from one another and contributing to the polarization of society. The problem with most technologies that consumers use to access the Internet today, argues Pariser, is that computer algorithms are continually working in the background to filter our information environment in ways that are mostly invisible to us, which makes these bubbles difficult to escape. Scholar Cass Sunstein (2017) has similarly argued that in today's information environment, we are more likely to segregate ourselves into echo chambers of partisan opinion, thus damaging our roles as citizens. In the course of watching Donald Trump campaign rallies on YouTube, Media scholar Zeynep Tufecki even found the site's recommendation algorithm began recommending right-wing videos from White supremacist groups and Holocaust deniers, and other fringe content, essentially "radicalizing" her information feed (2018). The research evidence on online opinion filter bubbles has been decidedly mixed. One research study that examined the web-browsing histories of 50,000 U.S. online news readers found that, indeed, social media and web searches lead news readers to more ideologically polarized sources of information, yet these sources of information were (strangely) often from the readers' less preferred side of the ideological spectrum (Flaxman, Goel, & Rao, 2016). This same study found that most online news readers actually visited the homepages of their favorite mainstream news outlets, thus exposing them to differing points of view. The primary concern regarding access to political information today is that some individuals might not realize that their news environment is being artificially edited and restricted, something scholars call "preselected personalization" (Borgesius et al., 2016). One study of over 10 million Facebook accounts (Bakshy, Messing, & Adamic, 2015) found some important effects of friend networks and the algorithmic filtering of "cross-cutting" (or likely-to-cause-disagreement) news for readers, but the overall effect was quite modest, with fewer than 10% of all cross-cutting news stories being filtered out by social connections (Tufecki, 2015). Another recent study looked carefully at actual web usage data and found no evidence of "partisan selective exposure" to political information, suggesting that fears of polarization resulting from social media are perhaps overblown (Nelson & Webster, 2017).

One of the chief concerns with self-segregating our news and information consumption is that we can be more easily misled by false information. During the 2016 election, then-candidate Donald J. Trump continually lambasted the mainstream press for indulging in what he called "fake news" when it ran stories that were unflattering. The term *fake news* has subsequently been deployed so routinely that it has begun to lose its meaning, but the reality is that fake news is a serious problem. Fake news can be understood as "news articles that are intentionally and verifiably false, and could mislead readers" (Allcott & Gentzkow, 2017, p. 213).

Fake news can not only propagate false information about policies or statistics, but it can also spur extreme behavior. On December 4, 2016, for instance, a man carrying an assault rifle walked into a Comet Ping Pong pizzeria restaurant in Washington, DC, believing that Democratic candidate Hillary Clinton and her former campaign chair, John Podesta, were running a child sex ring in the basement of the restaurant (Lopez, 2016). Dubbed "Pizzagate," this false conspiracy theory had emerged from the online chat website 4Chan, then was promoted by right-wing Twitter followers and boosted by conservative talk show host Alex Jones on his program *Infowars*. This type of fake news was essentially a "fabricated news story" (Tandoc, Lim, & Ling, 2018) that was distributed so widely on social media that some conservative, pro-Trump news readers began to believe the story.

How could this happen? How might an online news reader like the Pizzagate shooter become convinced by such a far-fetched conspiracy theory? Part of the answer may lie in the ways in which social media distorts our sense of public opinion. One study found, for example, that when individuals received external news stories that had more recommendations on Facebook from individuals in their social circle, they found those stories more trustworthy regardless of their factual nature (Turcotte, York, Irving, Scholl, & Pingree, 2015). Once this fact is paired with the reality that so many social media users' newsfeeds were manipulated by fake accounts and bots in the 2016 election, it's easy to see how this problem can distort and poison our political discourse. There are psychological elements involved here as well. One reason that individuals indulge in conspiracy theories, suggest Gorman and Gorman (2016), is that they are seeking to overcome feelings of powerlessness. They write, "Studies have shown that people who feel that they lack control over situations are prone to *illusory pattern perception*, essentially seeing what is not really there (emphasis in original; Gorman & Gorman, 2016, p. 42). Individuals who are mistrustful of science and who have low self-esteem are also more prone to believing conspiracy theories, note Gorman and Gorman (2016). For instance, a study of attitudes toward the H1N1 flu vaccine in the United States found that individuals living in areas where Twitter messages tended to be more positive about the vaccine had higher vaccination rates than regions where tweets were more negative about the benefits of H1N1 and vaccines in general (Southwell, 2013). When biased information we may encounter online reinforces our previously held beliefs, audiences are less apt to employ reason in evaluating the quality of that information (Mercier & Sperber, 2017).

Conclusion: The Construction of Public Opinion and Its Implications for Democracy

In this chapter, we've explored the concept of public opinion by tracing the history of different conceptualizations of this term, from the ancient ideals of rhetorical argument to the idealized rationality of the 18th century bourgeois public sphere.

Public opinion today bears little resemblance to the bourgeois public sphere primarily because the tools with which we define *the public* have radically changed. The introduction of probability sampling and telephone surveying in the 1930s transformed the meaning of public opinion into an aggregation of individual, private opinions. Critics have argued that these aggregate opinions (1) bear little resemblance to private political discourse and (2) may actually manufacture opinions, thanks to the mechanics of the survey method itself. Finally, scholars exploring agenda-setting and Spiral-of-Silence theories have discovered that citizens' views of political and social issues are directly affected by news media. These findings call into question the "organic" nature of the opinions that are reflected in the polls. Despite the many potential shortcomings of surveys, they have come to define public opinion in our modern era. The implications of these quantitative audience constructions for our democracy are wide-reaching. Opinion polls not only shape our sense of ourselves as citizens but also the kinds of policies that impact our lives. In the next chapter, we'll examine how another type of audience construction—media ratings—largely determines the structure of commercial media in the United States.

DISCUSSION ACTIVITIES

1. Watch this 10-minute video interview with Andrew Kohut, former president of the Pew Research Center, an important public opinion polling organization, on why public opinion surveys matter: http://bigthink.com/ideas/4255. Once you have watched it, discuss the following questions:

   • What assumptions (either explicit or implicit) do you see about modern public opinion polling in this video?

   • How does Kohut justify or explain the *form of measurement* of public opinion? How important is quantitative polling and why?

   • What does Kohut suggest about the connection between public opinion polling and democratic citizenship? How do his ideas compare to Habermas's notion of a *public sphere*?

2. Locate a print news article from a newspaper, news magazine, or online source (such as NYTimes.com or WSJ.com) that directly uses or somehow references a public opinion poll in relation to some social or political issue (for example, how Americans will vote, what they think about certain policies, etc.). Your news article should feature a table or chart presenting the results along with a discussion of the nature of the questions asked, who was surveyed, and how many people were surveyed, as well as margins of error in the results. Then discuss the following questions in relation to your article:

   • What are the results of the poll, and how does the reporter interpret these results? What conclusions does the reporter draw from these numbers?

   • What does the journalist suggest about the impact of the patterns discussed above for the country? In other words, what is the potential importance of these numbers for the issue or topic being discussed in the article?

- Finally, is there any discussion in the article about how these results should or will affect outcomes? Is it discussed explicitly or not by the journalist? The goal here is to think critically about whether the means for feedback from the audience are meaningfully discussed or addressed.

3. Obtain a national daily newspaper (*The New York Times* or *The Washington Post*, for example) or a large urban metropolitan daily newspaper (such as the *Los Angeles Times* or *The Boston Globe*) for a particular weekday. Then, for that same weekday, view or record a national television news broadcast (such as *NBC Nightly News*, *ABC World News Tonight*, or *CBS Evening News*). Then compare the two by discussing the following questions:

- How many stories were on the front page of the newspaper you located? How many stories were contained in the news broadcast that you viewed?

- What types of news stories did you see across both outlets? Were they national, international, regional, or local stories? Was the type and extent of information provided similar or different across the two media outlets? Explain.

- How similar was the selection of top news stories in both news outlets? Do you see any evidence of media agenda setting here?

- What might audiences conclude about the most important news of the day by reading the newspaper or watching the television news? What impacts do you think exposure to one or both of these news outlets might have on audiences' opinions about what's important in the news?

4. Watch the brief 2011 TED Talk by Eli Pariser about filter bubbles. It can be found at https://www.ted.com/talks/eli_pariser_ beware_online_filter_bubbles. Then briefly discuss these questions:

- How might technology play a role in how we filter information that we receive online? Give one example from your own life.

- How do you access news and information about what's happening in the world? Do you think you might be trapped in the kind of filter bubble that Pariser describes?

- What are some of the potential implications of filter bubbles for democracies around the world? Do you see any evidence of the fallout from filter bubbles in the news?

ADDITIONAL MATERIALS

C-Span. (2012, October 30). Understanding polling: Interview with Scott Keeler, Director of Survey Research, Pew Research Center. [Information on public opinion polls]. Available at https://www .c-span.org/video/?309018-3/understanding-polling

Ericsson, S. (2001). *Constructing public opinion: How politicians & the media misrepresent the public*. Media

Education Foundation. [Video documentary]. More information at https://shop.mediaed.org/constructing-public-opinion-p78.aspx

The General Social Survey (NORC). Available at http://gss.norc.org/

Glynn, C. J., Herbst, S., Shapiro, R., & O'Keefe, G. (1999). *Public opinion*. Boulder, CO: Westview Press.

Herbst, S. (1995). *Numbered voices: How opinion polling has shaped American politics.* Chicago, IL: University of Chicago Press.

Interview with Jürgen Habermas [Video documentary]: https://www.youtube.com/watch?v=jBl6ALNh18Q

Inter-University Consortium for Political and Social Research (ICPSR). [Online survey data resource]. Available at http://www.icpsr.umich.edu/icpsrweb/ICPSR/

Pariser, E. (2011). Beware online "filter bubbles." TED 2011. Available at https://www.ted.com/talks/eli_pariser_beware_online_filter_bubbles

Price, V. (1992). *Public opinion.* Newbury Park, CA: SAGE.

Stimson, J. A. (2004). *Tides of consent: How public opinion shapes American politics.* Cambridge, MA: Cambridge University Press.

Weaver, D. H., McCombs, M. E., & Shaw, D. L. (Eds.). (1997). *Communication and democracy: Exploring the intellectual frontiers in agenda-setting theory.* LEA's communication series. Mahwah, NJ: Lawrence Erlbaum Associates.

REFERENCES

Allcott, H., & Gentzkow, M. (2017). Social media and fake news in the 2016 election. *Journal of Economic Perspectives, 31*(2), 211–236.

Asthana, A., Quinn, B., & Mason, R. (2016, June 24). UK votes to leave EU after dramatic night divides nation. *The Guardian.* Retrieved from http://www.theguardian.com/politics/2016/jun/24/britain-votes-for-brexit-eu-referendum-david-cameron

Bakshy, E., Messing, S., & Adamic, L. (2015). Exposure to ideologically diverse news and opinion on Facebook. *Science, 348*(6239), 1130–1132.

BBC News. (2016). *EU Referendum Results.* Retrieved June 21, 2018, from https://www.bbc.com/news/politics/eu_referendum/results

Benhabib, S. (1992). Models of public space: Hannah Arendt, the liberal tradition, and Jürgen Habermas. In C. Calhoun (Ed.), *Habermas and the public sphere* (pp. 73–98). Cambridge, MA: MIT Press.

Bennett, W. L. (1989). Marginalizing the majority: Conditioning public opinion to accept managerial democracy. In M. Margolis & G. A. Mauser (Eds.), *Manipulating public opinion: Essays on public opinion as a dependent variable* (pp. 321–362). Pacific Grove, CA: Brooks/Cole.

Bessi, A., & Ferrara, E. (2016). Social bots distort the 2016 U.S. presidential election online discussion. *First Monday, 21*(11). Retrieved from http://firstmonday.org/ojs/index.php/fm/article/view/7090

Bishop, G. F., Oldendick, R. W., & Tuchfarber, A. (1984). What must my interest in politics be if I just told you "I don't know"? *Public Opinion Quarterly, 48*(2), 510–519.

Blumer, H. (1969). *Symbolic interactionism: Perspective and method.* Englewood Cliffs, NJ: Prentice-Hall.

Borgesius, F. J. Z., Trilling, D., Möller, J., Bodó, B., de Vreese, C. H., & Helberger, N. (2016). Should we worry about filter bubbles? *Internet Policy Review, 5*(1). Retrieved from https://policyreview.info/articles/analysis/should-we-worry-about-filter-bubbles

Bucher, T. (2012). Want to be on the top? Algorithmic power and the threat of invisibility on Facebook. *New Media & Society, 14*(7), 1164–1180.

Cappella, J. N., & Jamieson, K. H. (1997). *Spiral of cynicism: The press and the public good.* New York, NY: Oxford University Press.

Carey, J. W. (1995). The press, public opinion, and public discourse. In T. L. Glasser & C. T. Salmon (Eds.), *Public opinion and the communication of consent* (pp. 373–402). New York, NY: The Guilford Press.

Carpini, M. X. D., & Keeter, S. (1997). *What Americans know about politics and why it matters*. New Haven, CT: Yale University Press.

Converse, J. M. (1987). *Survey research in the United States: Roots and emergence, 1890–1960*. Berkeley: University of California Press.

Converse, P. (1964). The nature of belief systems in mass publics. In D. E. Apter (Ed.), *Ideology and discontent* (pp. 206–261). Ann Arbor: University of Michigan Press.

De Tocqueville, A. (1969). *Democracy in America*. (J. P. Mayer, Trans.). New York, NY: Anchor Books.

Dearing, J. W., & Rogers, E. M. (1996). *Communication concepts 6: Agenda-setting*. Thousand Oaks, CA: SAGE.

Del Vicario, M., Zollo, F., Caldarelli, G., Scala, A., & Quattrociocchi, W. (2017). Mapping social dynamics on Facebook: The Brexit debate. *Social Networks, 50*, 6–16. Retrieved from https://doi.org/10.1016/j.socnet.2017.02.002

Douglas, M. (1986). *How institutions think*. Frank W. Abrams lectures. Syracuse, NY: Syracuse University Press.

Dye, T. R. (2002). *Who's running America? The Bush restoration* (7th ed.). New York, NY: Prentice Hall.

Enli, G. (2017). Twitter as arena for the authentic outsider: Exploring the social media campaigns of Trump and Clinton in the 2016 US presidential election. *European Journal of Communication, 32*(1), 50–61.

Entman, R. M. (1993). Framing: Toward clarification of a fractured paradigm. *Journal of communication, 43*(4), 51–58.

Flaxman, S., Goel, S., & Rao, J. M. (2016). Filter bubbles, echo chambers, and online news consumption. *Public Opinion Quarterly, 80*(S1), 298–320.

Fraser, N. (1990). Rethinking the public sphere: A contribution to the critique of actually existing democracy. *Social Text,* (25/26), 56–80.

Giddens, A. (1986). *The constitution of society: Outline of the theory of structuration* (1st paperback ed.). Berkeley: University of California Press.

Ginsberg, B. (1986). *The captive public: How mass opinion promotes state power*. New York, NY: Basic Books.

Glynn, C. J., Herbst, S., Shapiro, R., & O'Keefe, G. (1999). *Public opinion*. Boulder, CO: Westview Press.

Gorman, J. M., & Gorman, S. E. (2016). *Denying to the grave: Why we ignore the facts that will save us*. Oxford, United Kingdom: Oxford University Press.

Graber, D. A. (1982). The impact of media research on public opinion studies. In D. C. Whitney, E. Wartella, & S. Windahl (Eds.), *Mass communication review yearbook* (Vol. 3, pp. 555–563). Beverly Hills, CA: SAGE.

Grčar, M., Cherepnalkoski, D., Mozetič, I., & Kralj Novak, P. (2017). Stance and influence of Twitter users regarding the Brexit referendum. *Computational Social Networks, 4,* 6.

Grieco, E. (2017, November 2). More Americans are turning to multiple social media sites for news. Retrieved June 26, 2018, from http://www.pewresearch.org/fact-tank/2017/11/02/more-americans-are-turning-to-multiple-social-media-sites-for-news/

Gross, K., & Aday, S. (2003). The scary world in your living room and neighborhood: Using local broadcast news, neighborhood crime rates, and personal experience to test agenda setting and cultivation. *Journal of Communication, 53*(3), 411–426.

Habermas, J. (1991). *The structural transformation of the public sphere: An inquiry into a category of bourgeois society*. Cambridge: The MIT Press.

Herbst, S. (1993). *Numbered voices: How opinion polling has shaped American politics*. Reproduced with permission of University of Chicago Press—Books in the format Textbook via Copyright Clearance Center.

Herbst, S. (1995a). *Numbered voices: How opinion polling has shaped American politics*. Chicago: University of Chicago Press.

Herbst, S. (1995b). On the disappearance of groups: 19th- and early 20th-century conceptions of public opinion. In T. L. Glasser & C. T. Salmon (Eds.), *Public opinion and the communication of consent* (pp. 89–104). New York, NY: The Guilford Press.

Holbrook, A. L., & Krosnick, J. A. (2010). Social desirability bias in voter turnout reports tests using the item-count technique. *Public Opinion Quarterly*, 74(1), 37–67.

Iyengar, S. (1994). *Is anyone responsible? How television frames political issues*. Chicago, IL: University of Chicago Press.

Iyengar, S., & Kinder, D. R. (1987). *News that matters: Television and American opinion—American politics and political economy*. Chicago, IL: University of Chicago Press.

Keeter, S. (2007). *How serious is polling's cell-only problem?* Washington, DC: Pew Research Center for The People & the Press. Retrieved from http://pewresearch.org/pubs/515/

Kennedy, C., Blumenthal, M., Clement, S., Clinton, J. D., Durand, C., Franklin, C., . . . Rivers, D. (2017). *An evaluation of 2016 election polls in the US*. Washington, DC: American Association for Public Opinion Research.

Kirk, A., Scott, P., & Graham, C. (2016, November 8). US election results: The maps and analysis that explain Donald Trump's shock victory to become President. *The Telegraph*. Retrieved from https://www.telegraph.co.uk/news/0/us-election-results-and-state-by-state-maps/

Lapowsky, I. (2016, November 15). This is how Facebook actually won Trump the presidency. *Wired*.

Retrieved from https://www.wired.com/2016/11/facebook-won-trump-election-not-just-fake-news/

Lewis, J. (2001). *Constructing public opinion: How political elites do what they like and why we seem to go along with it*. New York, NY: Columbia University Press.

Lippmann, W. (1922). *Public opinion*. New York, NY: Harcourt, Brace.

Lippmann, W. (1993). *The phantom public: The library of conservative thought*. New Brunswick, NJ: Transaction. (Originally published in 1925)

Locke, J. (1988). *Two treatises of government*. (P. Laslett, Ed.). Cambridge, United Kingdom: Cambridge University Press. (Originally published in 1690)

Lomas, N. (2017, November 15). Study: Russian Twitter bots sent 45k Brexit tweets close to vote. *Techcrunch*. Retrieved June 20, 2018, from http://social.techcrunch.com/2017/11/15/study-russian-twitter-bots-sent-45k-brexit-tweets-close-to-vote/

Lopez, G. (2016, December 5). Pizzagate, the totally false conspiracy theory that led a gunman to a DC pizzeria, explained. *Vox*. Retrieved July 10, 2018, from https://www.vox.com/policy-and-politics/2016/12/5/13842258/pizzagate-comet-ping-pong-fake-news

Mackenzie, W. J. (1972). The functions of elections. In D. L. Sills (Ed.), *International encyclopedia of the social sciences*. New York, NY: Macmillan.

Margolis, M., & Mauser, G. A. (1989). Introduction: Public opinion as a dependent variable. In M. Margolis & G. A. Mauser (Eds.), *Manipulating public opinion: Essays on public opinion as a dependent variable* (pp. 1–16). Pacific Grove, CA: Brooks/Cole.

Marsh, C. (1984). Back on the bandwagon: The effect of opinion polls on public opinion. *British Journal of Political Science*, 15(1), 51–74.

McCombs, M. E., & Reynolds, A. (2009). How the news shapes our civic agenda. In J. Bryant & M. B. Oliver (Eds.), *Media effects: Advances in theory and research* (3rd ed., pp. 1–16). New York, NY: Routledge.

McCombs, M. E., & Shaw, D. L. (1972). The agenda-setting function of mass media. *Public Opinion Quarterly*, 36(2), 176–187.

Mercer, A., Deane, C., & McGeeney, K. (2016, November 9). *Why 2016 election polls missed their mark*. Retrieved June 28, 2018, from http://www.pewresearch.org/fact-tank/2016/11/09/why-2016-election-polls-missed-their-mark/

Mercier, H., & Sperber, D. (2017). *The enigma of reason*. Cambridge, MA: Harvard University Press.

Mill, J. S. (1999). *On liberty*. (E. Alexander, Ed.). Broadview literary texts. Orchard Park, NY: Broadview Press. (Original published in 1859)

Miller, P. V. (1995). The industry of public opinion. In T. L. Glasser & C. T. Salmon (Eds.), *Public opinion and the communication of consent* (pp. 105–131). New York, NY: The Guilford Press.

Miller, S. (2011). Social institutions. In E. N. Zalta (Ed.), *The Stanford encyclopedia of philosophy* (Spring 2011.). Stanford, CA: Stanford University. Retrieved from http://plato.stanford.edu/archives/spr2011/entries/social-institutions/

Mills, C. (2016, December 14). Trump reveals some surprise at winning. *US News & World Report*. Retrieved from https://www.usnews.com/news/politics/articles/2016-12-14/donald-trump-admits-he-was-a-little-surprised-at-election-outcome

Mills, C. W. (1956). *The power elite*. New York, NY: Oxford University Press.

Morwitz, V. G., & Pluzinski, C. (1996). Do polls reflect opinions or do opinions reflect polls? The impact of political polling on voters' expectations, preferences, and behavior. *Journal of Consumer Research*, 53–67.

Nelson, J. L., & Webster, J. G. (2017). The myth of partisan selective exposure: A portrait of the online political news audience. *Social Media + Society*, 1–13.

Noelle-Neumann, E. (1984). *The spiral of silence: Public opinion, our social skin*. Chicago, IL: University of Chicago Press.

Noelle-Neumann, E. (1991). The theory of public opinion: The concept of the spiral of silence. In J. A. Anderson (Ed.), *Communication yearbook* (Vol. 14, pp. 256–287). Newbury Park, CA: SAGE.

Pariser, E. (2012). *The filter bubble: How the new personalized web is changing what we read and how we think*. London, England: Penguin Books.

Perse, E. M. (2001). *Media effects and society*. LEA's communication series. Mahwah, NJ: L. Erlbaum Associates.

Peters, J. D. (1995). Historical tensions in the concept of public opinion. In T. L. Glasser & C. T. Salmon (Eds.), *Public opinion and the communication of consent* (pp. 3–32). New York, NY: The Guilford Press.

Popken, B. (2017, December 20). Russian Twitter trolls exploited key election moments. *NBC News*. Retrieved June 22, 2018, from https://www.nbcnews.com/tech/social-media/russian-trolls-went-attack-during-key-election-moments-n827176

Rogers, E. M., & Dearing, J. W. (1988). Agenda-setting research: Where has it been, where is it going? In J. A. Anderson (Ed.), *Communication yearbook* (Vol. 11, pp. 555–594). Newbury Park, CA: SAGE.

Rousseau, J.-J. 1967. *The social contract and the discourse on the origins of inequality*. New York, NY: Washington Square Press. (Original work published 1767)

Shane, S., & Mazzetti, M. (2018, February 20). Inside a 3-year Russian campaign to influence U.S. voters. *The New York Times*. Retrieved from https://www.nytimes.com/2018/02/16/us/politics/russia-mueller-election.html

Southwell, B. G. (2013). *Social networks and popular understanding of science and health: Sharing disparities*. Baltimore, MD: Johns Hopkins University Press.

Speier, H. (1950). Historical development of public opinion. *American Journal of Sociology*, 55(4), 376–388.

Sunstein, C. (2017). *#Republic: Divided democracy in the age of social media*. Princeton, NJ: Princeton University Press.

Tandoc, E. C., Lim, Z. W., & Ling, R. (2018). Defining "fake news." *Digital Journalism*, 6(2), 137–153.

Tufekci, Z. (2015, May 7). How Facebook's algorithm suppresses content diversity (modestly) & how the newsfeed rules the clicks. *Medium*. Retrieved July 9, 2018, from https://medium.com/message/how-facebook-s-algorithm-suppresses-content-diversity-modestly-how-the-newsfeed-rules-the-clicks-b5f8a4bb7bab

Tufekci, Z. (2018, June 8). YouTube, the Great Radicalizer. *The New York Times*. Retrieved from https://www.nytimes.com/2018/03/10/opinion/sunday/youtube-politics-radical.html

Turcotte, J., York, C., Irving, J., Scholl, R. M., & Pingree, R. J. (2015). News recommendations from social media opinion leaders: Effects on media trust and information seeking. *Journal of Computer-Mediated Communication*, 20(5), 520–535.

Wintour, P. (2018, January 10). Russian bid to influence Brexit vote detailed in new US Senate report. *The Guardian*. Retrieved from http://www.theguardian.com/world/2018/jan/10/russian-influence-brexit-vote-detailed-us-senate-report

Zaller, J. (1992). *The nature and origins of mass opinion*. Cambridge, MA: Cambridge University Press.

CHAPTER 4

Media Ratings and the Political Economy of Audiences

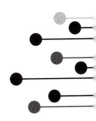

As the previous chapter illustrated, social, political, and media institutions routinely gather information about the public through a variety of measurements, although these measurements sometimes speak more to the goals of the institutions in question than to the specific needs and self-conceptions of the public. Corporations and other commercial institutions also have a vested interest in measuring media audiences. In order to be responsive to consumer needs and desires and ultimately generate revenue, advertisers and marketers have devised elaborate means for obtaining feedback.

Walmart, the largest retailer in the United States, stands out in the industry when it comes to turning information into profit. It is perhaps obvious to say that Walmart is in the business of selling products such as electronics, toys, and clothing to consumers. What is less obvious, however, is Walmart's other business, which emerges out of its primary retail function. The firm uses the transaction records of millions of customers to compile a vast database of purchasing behavior by American consumers. Most national retail businesses today routinely gather and store information about consumer purchases. However, Walmart's sheer size, volume of business, and almost universal penetration into the U.S. market allow the company to monitor the purchasing patterns of American consumers on a much larger scale. What does Walmart do with all of this customer information? By matching customer purchasing records, universal product codes (UPC), and radio frequency identification tags (RFIDs) on products, Walmart knows what customers are purchasing, in which stores these products are being bought, and in what quantities. One way Walmart keeps prices and overhead low (besides purchasing cheaper goods from China and keeping wages and benefits for employees to a minimum) is by using its profile of customer behavior to minimize warehousing costs. As soon as a product is purchased from a Walmart store, an order to refill that item is communicated instantaneously to the warehouse (Smith & Young, 2004).

In fact, one of the keys to Walmart's market success (and its most jealously guarded proprietary asset) is the ability to use this massive information source to track and, yes, *predict* consumer behavior. Shortly before the landfall of Hurricane Frances in Florida in 2004, Walmart consulted its vast customer databases to predict that demand for certain types of products would increase. In short order, truckloads of flashlights, batteries, blankets, strawberry Pop-Tarts (this was a top-selling item in previous hurricanes), and beer were rushed down to the areas in the path of the hurricane. These goods quickly sold out (Hays, 2004).

Walmart's use of consumer information demonstrates two fundamental principles that are the foundation of this chapter: (1) Sophisticated surveillance mechanisms have been put into place in modern postindustrial economies to be able to measure and track individuals' thoughts, attitudes, and behaviors; and (2) these tools are often used by powerful institutions and organizations to advance their own goals, thus bringing into play fundamental issues of power.

Overview of the Chapter

As the Walmart example suggests, the concentration of information about the behavior of individuals in the hands of a single organization or corporation can have powerful consequences for consumers, even though we may not even realize that we are being monitored. A research tradition that examines these fundamental issues of power and access to resources in the communications industries is called the **political economy of communication**. This chapter will briefly outline the field of political economy of communication in broad strokes and explore how it connects to the study of audiences by outlining the theory of the "commodity audience." Next, we will examine some of the methods by which major corporations such as The Nielsen Corporation (formerly A. C. Nielsen) and Nielsen Audio (formerly Arbitron) measure and therefore imagine media audiences. While these are both American companies and their focus is on audience measurement in the United States, the principles behind their techniques are the same that are used in audience research worldwide. Next, we'll explore newer forms of target marketing and "relationship marketing" via the use of personal consumer information. What does the collection, analysis, and strategic use of this audience information mean for us and for the economy? Unfortunately, as we'll see, the end result is not necessarily the kind of consumer- or audience-oriented media environment that corporations often tout as the payback for increasingly intrusive forms of audience surveillance. Instead, as the case of minority audiences and the increased focus on data-driven consumer relations demonstrate, narrower targeting of media audiences often encourages exclusionary business practices that threaten to further marginalize some members of our society.

One final note: The goal of the chapter is to introduce the political economy approach to audiences and to link that approach to the methodology and logics of measuring audience consumption of mass media such as television and broadcast radio. Metrics for online media, such as social media, video sharing (such as YouTube), and podcasting, are discussed further in Chapter 9.

The Political Economic Approach to Communication

Political economy is a long-standing intellectual tradition, dating back to Adam Smith's *The Wealth of Nations*, published in 1776 and the foundation of modern economics today. At its core, political economy focuses broadly on social theory by connecting the systems of the economy—the organization of corporations, the structures of a marketplace, and the behavior of market players—with notions of resource availability and power. Renowned scholar Vincent Mosco has defined **political economy** as "the study of *the social relations, particularly the power relations, that mutually constitute the production, distribution, and consumption of resources*" (emphasis in original; Mosco, 1996, p. 25). Political economy examines society through a number of different lenses, but this perspective is generally identified through its focus on three particular aspects: (1) profound historical shifts, particularly the transformation from agrarian- to industrial-based economies in the late 19th century and the rise of capitalism; (2) understanding the connections between systems of the larger economy and social forces such as race, class, and gender; and (3) a connection to what Mosco calls "moral philosophy"—that is, social values and the notion of ethics when discussing issues of resource allocation in society. This means that political economy is critical in nature, centering on problems of inequality and social justice by exploring the economic, social, and institutional forces that support the status quo. Political economists also explore avenues for expanding democratic access to scarce resources, thereby going beyond a strictly functional understanding of the workings of modern economies to "engage with basic moral questions of justice, equity, and the public good" (Golding & Murdock, 1991, p. 20). Rather than simply describing or analyzing economic systems in society, or what *is*, political economy engages these issues from the standpoint of social critique, or what *ought to be* (Wasko, 2004, p. 322).

As you can see, political economic theory covers quite a bit of ground. The **political economy of communication** uses the tradition of this general theory to explore a few key issues, most notably the history, development, and current structure of mass communication technologies and their close connections with profit-seeking organizations in capitalist societies. Scholars such as Robert McChesney and Ben Bagdikian, for instance, have charted the increasing consolidation among media companies in the United States (Bagdikian, 2004; McChesney, 1999, 2008). What distinguishes political economic analyses from other types of inquiry, however, is the fact that these scholars focus on many of the challenges that the increasing commercialization and corporatization of the mass media pose for citizen choice, access to information, and participatory democracy. The internationalization and global domination of American media products have also been topics of concern for scholars writing in the political economic tradition (see Herman & McChesney, 1997; Schiller, 1992).

Political economy is closely attuned to the relations between management and labor. As you might suspect given this overview, political economists tend to concentrate their focus on the labor side. These scholars pay close attention to the impacts of the consolidation of media and the rapid globalization of American media production on communication workers. Take the U.S. motion picture industry, for example. Janet Wasko's political economic look at Hollywood, *How Hollywood Works* (2003), explores the institutions responsible for making movies today, from the studios and distributors to the bankers and the unions that still serve as a powerful voice for labor in this industry. Other political economists have noted that the production of Hollywood motion pictures is increasingly being shifted outside of the United States so that the studios can avoid union rules and pay scales, resulting in a "new international division of cultural labor" (Miller, Govil, McMurria, Maxwell, & Wang, 2005). More recently, in their edited book *Knowledge Workers in the Information Society*, Catherine McKercher and Vincent Mosco (2007) have documented major shifts occurring in a number of "knowledge" industries whereby the Internet and instant global telecommunications have begun to spread out labor across the globe. These shifts in information work have been presented in the popular press and among business elites as the natural evolution of a globalized economy. Political economists have observed, however, that this new economic environment forces many media workers into precarious, temporary employment. The easy movement of capital from countries where wages and labor standards are high to those where salaries and governmental oversight of working conditions are low has facilitated both unskilled and skilled job outsourcing. These labor shifts, in turn, have reshaped the economic lives of millions of information workers.

Political Economy and the Commodity Audience

As you can see from this brief introduction, political economy is a rich theoretical tradition that explores many key aspects of our social and economic lives in modern, industrialized economies. But what does it have to do with the study of audiences? The connections between media audiences and political economy may seem tenuous, but there are a number of central insights that political economy has added to our understanding of media audiences.

Political economic analyses place particular emphasis on the social and economic transformations that have occurred as a result of industrialization and rise of corporations within a capitalist system. What the industrialization and shift to a wage–labor system has created, argues Thomas Streeter (1996), is an artificial divide between the realm of *production* (in other words, our work lives, where we are economically productive) and *consumption* (our leisure time, where we are consuming instead of being productive). Streeter (1996, pp. 287–288) uses Raymond Williams's (1975) notion of **mobile privatization**, which refers to "a pattern of social life characterized by high mobility, a consequent uprootedness, and the construction and valorization of privatized family homes whose contents were both easily transportable and conducive to isolation from the surrounding community." Unlike agrarian economies where work (production) and leisure (consumption) happen in the same physical and social spaces, capitalism has created a divide between the spaces of production—where workers expect to be closely monitored by their employers—and spaces of leisure—where the home and domestic sphere are separated from the public realm and individuals are granted autonomy and privacy. This divide, notes Streeter, has been engrained into the fabric of our modern lives in terms of space (we live sometimes far away from work sites) and time (days are for work, nights are for leisure), as well as in the social structure.

This divide has some fundamental consequences for the mass media as well. Since our experiences as media audiences occur largely within the domestic, privatized sphere—after work, on our "leisure" time—the production/consumption divide has created a profound crisis for capitalist institutions that want to continually monitor our viewing habits and purchasing activities. Media corporations must find some way to break into this private realm to measure and catalog consumers' behaviors for commercial purposes. This corporate desire to penetrate the home made it necessary to develop sophisticated measurement practices to try to understand, quantify, and monitor the behaviors of the audience. Overcoming this divide is the primary purpose behind the types of audience ratings and market research strategies that we'll explore later on in this chapter. What's important to note here is that the political economy perspective can help us to contextualize these audience measurement regimes and to realize their historical, economic, and social origins.

Dallas W. Smythe and the "Blindspot" Debate

It is perhaps most obvious that the core business of profit-driven mass media is to produce communication *products* (such as television programs, radio shows, motion pictures, etc.) and market those products to consumers. The price that consumers pay for "free," over-the-air TV programming is the advertising that they are forced to endure during each show. However, like the earlier Walmart example, the transaction between producer and consumer is not the only one happening when you turn on your television. At the same time that the television program is being "sold" to the audience, the attention of the audience is being "sold" to advertisers.

This dual transaction idea first emerged from the writings of Canadian media scholar Dallas W. Smythe. Smythe sparked a spirited debate among political economists in 1977 when he argued that the mass media, rather than simply serving an ideological function supportive of capitalism, was instead part of the economic system of capital itself. While Marxist scholars for years had identified the media as part of a larger ideological apparatus charged with supporting the capitalist status quo, Smythe considered the content of the media to be rather less important, calling it instead "an inducement (gift, bribe, or 'free lunch') to recruit potential members of the audience and to maintain their loyal attention" (1977, p. 5). The real value of audiences to media producers was their viewership. Viewers essentially became a new product that media corporations could sell to advertisers: **the audience commodity**. The key to understanding the audience commodity lies in the fact that audiences perform *labor* for advertisers by learning about brands of consumer goods featured in the commercials. While we are socialized to think that our media consumption is primarily a leisure-based activity, Smythe suggested that audiences continue to generate economic value to the system of commercial broadcasting by internalizing advertising messages and turning them into demand for consumer goods and services. Smythe described the phenomenon of audience labor as the "blindspot" in Western Marxist thinking.

Smythe's ideas about the audience as a commodity within the capitalist system were highly influential among political economists. While some disagreed with Smythe's premise that the audience is part of the capitalist system, critical scholar Sut Jhally believed that Smythe's argument did not go nearly far enough. Smythe had argued that the audience's purchasing decisions (and perhaps the mental energy required to remember brand names and slogans, etc.) constituted the "productive" aspect of audience economic activity. Jhally, however, was keen to clarify that advertisers were actually buying viewers' attention and time in front of the television and not their potential future brand loyalty. He noted that "when media sell 'time' to a sponsor, it is not abstract time that is being sold but the time of particular audiences. . . . That is all the media have to sell" (Jhally, 1987, p. 72). And what was precisely occurring during this time that audiences devoted to their favorite television shows and to the commercial advertising that was nestled among the programming? Jhally's answer to this question took Smythe's original contention to its logical conclusion: The audience was *working as a labor force*. Without the labor of the audience to actually watch the advertising, he reasoned, the very structure of commercial media was threatened. Far from the popular notion of listless couch potatoes in front of the television, Jhally connected the act of watching commercials to a form of productive labor that generates economic value (and surplus value) for broadcasters, for which the audience receives "payment" in the form of the programming itself. The sale of the audiences' attention to advertisers then becomes part of the integral functioning of the commercial broadcasting system.

Ratings and the Construction of the Audience Product

By now, it should be clear that commercial media companies rely heavily on the viewership of millions of people so that they can sell their attention to advertisers for a profit. Although a number of scholars have disputed the precise nature of what is being sold to advertisers, political economists are in general agreement that media audiences in capitalist societies are incorporated into the economic system of exchange. But what precisely is being bought and sold here? Given the inability of television broadcasters to reach through the television screen and physically monitor the individual behaviors of millions of anonymous viewers, how is the commodity audience defined and by whom?

Toothpicks and Trees: The "Natural" Audience as Taxonomic Collectives

The answer to this question about the measurement and definition of the audience turns out to be critical to understanding the centrality of the audience concept to commercial media systems. As Smythe's blindspot argument continued to spark debate and discussion in the early 1980s over whether or not the audience was truly a commodity of exchange, Eileen Meehan (1984), herself a political economist of communication, argued that no picture of the audience is complete without a close analysis of the systems for measuring those audiences. Her main targets of inquiry were the most widely used metrics for calculating the size and the composition of television and radio audiences in the United States: the ratings.[1]

One of Meehan's key insights was to shine the spotlight on the ratings themselves. She argued that the ratings are not a simple numerical representation of a real audience out there. Instead, she argued, the ratings are a very specialized form of information about the television audience. Not all viewers are equally in demand, and therefore, not all viewers are valuable (or even measured) by the ratings companies. Ratings numbers exist to create a saleable commodity that advertisers will buy—this is the key to their importance and centrality in the broadcast television industry. So, she argued, "at the level of cross-industrial analysis, neither messages nor audiences are exchanged: only ratings" (1984, p. 223). Since "actual" audiences were captured only through the ratings systems, the transaction between media companies and advertisers was guided by the ratings numbers themselves, not actual audience viewing, as Smythe and Jhally suggested.

Media professionals assume that the audience is a "naturally occurring phenomenon" that can be accurately measured with the right tools. By this reasoning, "measuring the audience becomes analogous to measuring trees" (Meehan, 1993, p. 385). However, as Meehan pointed out, the ratings numbers themselves are not simply mirror reflections of the audience since different types of measurement strategies will offer different types of errors in the calculation—this is a natural by-product of statistical measurement and estimation. The type of measurement technique that is selected to generate audience research numbers "becomes a matter of corporate strategy" (p. 387). Instead of measuring something that occurs in the natural environment, ratings serve as extensions of the needs of media corporations and advertisers—to facilitate financial transactions. Therefore, according to Meehan,

> The relationship of the commodity audience to the general audience is rather like that of toothpicks to trees: one, a manufacture, is whittled out of the other, a natural phenomenon. The commodity audience and commodity ratings are entirely artificial and manufactured. (1993, p. 389)

Audience ratings, in Meehan's view, are analogous to toothpicks—manufactured entities carved from the actual audience.

Australian critical scholar Ien Ang addressed similar issues in her 1991 book *Desperately Seeking the Audience*. She argued that television broadcasters seek to "freeze" the ever-changing behaviors of the audience into a fixed, static concept,

---

[1]Given the continued importance of ratings for the structure of commercial media in the United States, a more detailed discussion of the ratings is included later on in the chapter.

thereby "colonizing" the audience into a durable, reliable entity that can be relied upon for steady profits. Broadcasters create what Ang called a **taxonomic collective**, which is "an entity of serialized, in principle unrelated individuals who form a group solely because each member has a characteristic—in this case, spectatorship—that is like that of each other member" (Ang, 1991, p. 33). The notion of the audience here is a very particular one: geographically dispersed, too large ever to be observed (since you could not even fit most groups of viewers for a U.S. television program into a single location at the same time), and imagined as a mass or undifferentiated collective. Individuality is subsumed in this notion of the audience: The only thing that commercial broadcasters care to know about the audience is whether or not they were watching a particular message at a particular time. As we'll see later in the chapter, the connection between the "actual" audience and the audience created through the ratings has been a flashpoint for confrontations between media companies and advertisers in recent years.

Measuring Audiences: The Ratings System

As the discussion thus far in this chapter has revealed, the notion of the audience is critical to the economic structure of profit-driven, advertiser-supported media. The theories of political economic scholars have laid bare the economic underpinnings of the role of the audience commodity, while Meehan's and Ang's research suggests that an analysis of the audience is not complete without a closer examination of the ways in which the audience is imagined by media corporations. In the United States, the United Kingdom, and elsewhere around the world, the bedrock of audience measurement for the broadcast television, cable, and radio industries is the ratings system. In this section of the chapter, we will briefly explore how audiences are operationalized by the ratings, how the Nielsen companies sample the viewing population, and how audiences are assigned different economic value according to their appeal to major advertisers. This section is meant to be a basic primer on the methodology of the ratings system and not a detailed overview of the ratings, which can be found in a number of other excellent sources (such as Buzzard, 1992; Webster, Phalen, & Lichty, 2006).

Audience Research and the Ratings

The history of research into the size and composition of media audiences stretches back to the 1930s during the heyday of network radio in the United States. Today, there are a plethora of companies offering what Peter Miller calls "made-to-order" audience research studies, which are customized studies to investigate specific questions, such as how many *Grey's Anatomy* viewers drink Pepsi or whether *Outside* magazine readers are more likely to purchase RV trailers (Miller, 1994). For media companies and consumer product manufacturers, conducting research on consumers has been integrated into their organizational structures. Almost every modern corporation selling products or services directly to consumers has a department of "research" that conducts studies of consumer preferences, desires, and exposure to advertising messages. Even in the television, cable, and radio industries, there are a number of syndicated research studies that examine different aspects of audience response to media from both quantitative (numerical) and qualitative (observational, conversational, or written) data. The most important tool for audience measurement in the electronic mass media industries, however, is the ratings system.

The ratings are dominated by two primary companies in the United States: The Nielsen Corporation in television and cable TV ratings (and increasingly in online audience measurement) and Nielsen Audio in broadcast radio. Because these forms of audience measurement are the most important in terms of setting advertising rates for individual programs and for packaging audiences into saleable commodities, they occupy the central focus of this chapter. Nielsen and Nielsen Audio operate as essentially monopoly suppliers of audience data within their respective media, despite the availability of many smaller niche audience research studies. Their monopoly status has been preserved for decades because the enormous upfront cost of launching a nationwide survey of audience viewership serves as a natural deterrent to new competitors (Webster et al., 2006, p. 108). Additionally, advertisers and media companies must agree upon a currency or "coin of exchange" that will allow for smooth financial transactions with one another. The ratings serve this purpose. Despite some of their methodological shortcomings, ratings continue to dominate the decision-making about mass media.

Operationalization of the Audience Concept: Quantification

In the spirit of the critical and political economic theories explored earlier in the chapter, it is worthwhile to examine the assumptions that lurk behind this widely influential system of audience measurement. The logic of the ratings is identical to that of public opinion surveys (see Chapter 3): It aims to estimate the size and composition of the audience as clearly and accurately as possible. It's important to keep in mind that all information about audiences is meaningless without interpretation or judgments on behalf of those who gather and use this information. In other words, the numbers do not speak for themselves. The figures can be understood only within the specific contexts in which they are generated and analyzed.

Let's first look at how the audience is operationalized. **Operationalization** is a term used to describe *how to specify empirical "things" that are taken to represent an outside construct under consideration.* Since social scientists cannot possibly capture all of the complexity of our social lives in their analyses, they must simplify complex realities into more generalized concepts for easier understanding and comparison. This turns out to be quite important because audience research can tell you information only about something that has been operationalized in the research itself. In the case of audience ratings, for example, we cannot make any claims or statements about viewers' critical responses to television programming (such as what they thought about it) because these types of responses are not included in Nielsen's *operational definition* of viewing. If this kind of information were important to advertisers, Nielsen would certainly alter the way it constructs the concept of television viewing to address this question. In the absence of this data, media executives and advertisers have typically equated audience size with quality or viewer satisfaction.

Like public opinion surveys, the ratings operationalize viewing by **quantifying** audience responses. The ratings structure essentially reduces audience viewing to a simplistic binary choice: watching or not watching. If you are "watching" television (and the definition of this is very nebulous), then you are counted as part of the viewing audience. Nielsen does collect quite a bit of other information about television viewers, such as demographic details (age, gender, socioeconomic status, education, etc.), but the core of the ratings system is a highly simplified method of counting who is in the audience for a particular television program at a particular moment.

Reducing television viewing to a single binary (viewing/not viewing) is quite a limited way of understanding the audience, of course. If you think about how you watch television, there are probably times when you are sitting rapt with attention when your favorite program is airing and other times when the television serves merely as background while you focus on other tasks such as reading, checking e-mail, or cleaning. These nuances of audience behavior are lost by simplifying the notion of television viewing to "on" or "off." So why don't audience research firms like Nielsen develop more sophisticated and qualitative measures of audience response to television? The answer, as Ien Ang (1991) pointed out, is that this type of simplified quantification is "institutionally enabling." Media companies can more easily assimilate and understand hard numbers. These figures can also be easily plugged in to mathematical formulas for analysis. Quantification of the audience is also a *practical* choice because it eliminates by design any particularities of audiences or their responses to media by reducing all media interactions to homogeneous data. This allows audiences to be easily exchanged as commodities in financial transactions between media companies and advertisers. Finally, and not least, numbers take on a life of their own—they are *seen as legitimate* by industry practitioners because hard figures carry with them an air of objectivity. When push comes to shove, it becomes difficult to "argue with the numbers," as the phrase goes, even though they may arise from highly questionable sampling and data-gathering techniques. For all of these reasons, quantification of audience response to media is the foundation of the audience construct in media industries today.

Constructing the Nielsen Sample

As with public opinion polling, it is a practical impossibility to measure every single viewer of a television program or listener of a local radio broadcast. So the

Nielsen companies must *sample* the population of viewers and listeners in order to arrive at an estimate of total media exposure that has any connection to actual audience behaviors. Audience researchers must first select a **sampling unit** from the population at large. Since radio listening often occurs individually, Nielsen Audio uses a single individual as a sampling unit. Although Nielsen is moving in the direction of sampling individual television usage (see later on in this section regarding personal people meters, or PPMs), the sampling unit that is used in the ratings is the *television household.* Households that have been included as part of the Nielsen sample are commonly referred to as "Nielsen families." According to Nielsen, as of September 2007 there were roughly 113 million TV households in the United States (Nielsen Media Research, 2008). Nielsen's national sample for its overnight ratings service consists of about 14,000 television households from local markets across the country (Story, 2008).

Once a sampling unit has been selected for calculating TV ratings, Nielsen begins the process of selecting families. Those familiar with statistics will recall that the best method of sampling a population is to conduct a *simple random sample.* This would mean that every television household in the United States would be known and would have an equal chance of being selected for the sample. While this sampling technique is clearly the most valid (in terms of being able to accurately estimate the size of the audience in the population as a whole), the impossibility of creating a list of every American household makes this sampling technique unavailable. Instead, Nielsen breaks down the complexity of sampling TV households by using two sampling techniques: **multistage cluster sampling** and **stratified sampling** (see Figure 4.1). Let's take the first technique. While it may be impossible to generate a list of every television household in the United States, it is possible to compile a list of every county in the United States and then to randomly sample those counties. This is what Nielsen actually does. Nielsen then divides those counties into city blocks and streets and randomly samples from those smaller groupings to arrive at a list of households to approach for inclusion in its sample. Since the population is divided into separate sections or clusters that are used for random sampling, this technique is called *multistage cluster sampling.* Instead of organizing a simple random sample of the population, Nielsen randomly samples different clusters of the population. It is important to realize, however, that at each clustering stage, some amount of sampling error can occur. Certain regions of the country could be overrepresented, for example, which could call into question the accuracy of the sample.

Some of this type of error can be addressed by incorporating the second sampling technique, **stratified sampling**. Nielsen divides the viewing public into specific homogeneous groups called *strata.* The strata of most interest to the ratings companies are specific demographic categories such as gender, income, age, and race. By dividing the population into the strata of "male" and "female," for instance, Nielsen can randomly sample a category of individuals to get an appropriate number from each group to match the proportion in the population at large. Combining the sample obtained through this technique with the sample

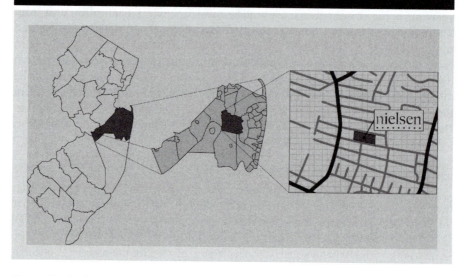

Figure 4.1   Multistage Cluster Sampling for the Nielsen Ratings

Source: Stephanie Plumeri Ertz.

drawn through multistage cluster sampling ensures that the resulting sample better resembles the general population (in terms of gender, age, etc.). The Nielsen ratings use both of these sampling techniques in order to arrive at a national sample of television viewing across the United States.

As you might imagine, there are a number of potential sources of error that can emerge in the final ratings sample. The most common one is **sampling error**, which is built into the process of conducting any type of survey research. As with public opinion surveys, ratings also have margins of error built into them, though we rarely hear about these other figures. For example, if the overnight rating for a program like *American Idol* were a 10, depending upon the sampling error, it could mean that the true rating might actually be a 9 or 11. While that may be a difference of only one rating point, that rating point represents roughly 1.1 million viewers, which translates into a lot of advertising dollars. In order to determine how far off the estimate might be from the true number, researchers can compute the sampling error. Although an extended discussion of sampling error is beyond the scope of this basic introduction to ratings methodology (for that see Buzzard, 1992; Webster et al., 2006), it is enough to note that the goal of any survey is to obtain the lowest sampling error possible to be confident of the estimate that you generate. Furthermore, sample size is inversely related to sampling error. In other words, the larger your sample size, the less likely it is that your estimate will deviate from the true rating for a program. Given the size and heterogeneity of the U.S. broadcast and cable television audience, companies like Nielsen must have rather large samples to maintain the credibility of their numbers, which can become quite a costly undertaking.

Another potential source of error is what we might call a **conceptual error**, or an error that results from conceptualizing the notion of television viewing in a particular way. By sampling television households instead of individual viewers, for example, Nielsen simplifies the process of operationalizing viewing at the cost of leaving out up to 44 million potential viewers who are watching TV in nondomestic spaces like bars, restaurants, airports, and on college campuses (Consoli, 2006; see Box 4.1).

A third source of error that can occur in the sampling stage is **nonresponse error**. Once Nielsen has decided upon the sampling technique, it goes out into the field to recruit participants, offering a nominal stipend as an incentive. Due to

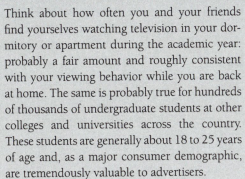

BOX 4.1
The Nielsen Ratings and Undergraduate Students

Think about how often you and your friends find yourselves watching television in your dormitory or apartment during the academic year: probably a fair amount and roughly consistent with your viewing behavior while you are back at home. The same is probably true for hundreds of thousands of undergraduate students at other colleges and universities across the country. These students are generally about 18 to 25 years of age and, as a major consumer demographic, are tremendously valuable to advertisers.

Now, consider this: Up until January 2007, the value assigned to you by Nielsen was zero. That was because college and university dormitories were not included in the operational definition of a "television household" used by Nielsen. After years of complaints and inquiries from TV and cable networks that actively targeted young people with their programming (such as Turner Broadcasting, owner of cable networks Cartoon Network and TBS), Nielsen relented in

early 2007 and began installing people meters on televisions in student dormitories across the country. Interestingly, Nielsen did not create a new sample of college students but instead contacted their existing Nielsen "families" and asked if they had sons or daughters in college who would be willing to have their viewing patterns measured while on campus.

The result of this shift in the operationalization of the television audience was quite dramatic in some cases. Some programs were much more appealing to college-aged audiences than to the general population of viewers. Comedy Central's animated program *Drawn Together*, for example, emerged as a very popular program for 18- to 24-year-old male viewers, increasing its audience size by roughly 60% after the inclusion of college audiences (see Figure 4.2). This case is just one concrete demonstration of the significant impact that different sampling techniques can have on the ultimate size and definition of the television audience.

Source: Adapted from Story, L. (2007, January 29). "At last, television ratings go to college." *The New York Times.* Accessed at http://www.nytimes.com/2007/01/29/business/media/29nielsen.html. Redrawn by Stephanie Plumeri Ertz.

Figure 4.2

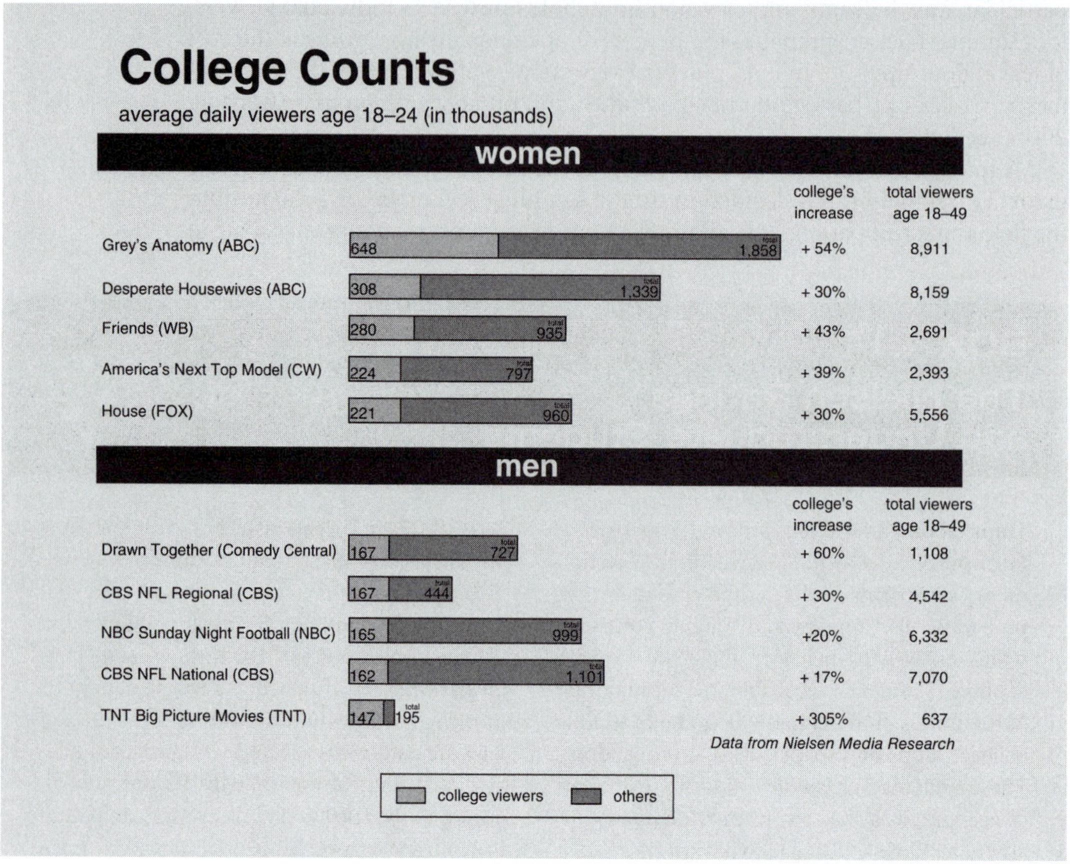

College Counts

average daily viewers age 18–24 (in thousands)

women

	college's increase	total viewers age 18–49
Grey's Anatomy (ABC) — 648 ... total 1,858	+ 54%	8,911
Desperate Housewives (ABC) — 308 ... total 1,339	+ 30%	8,159
Friends (WB) — 280 ... total 935	+ 43%	2,691
America's Next Top Model (CW) — 224 ... total 797	+ 39%	2,393
House (FOX) — 221 ... total 960	+ 30%	5,556

men

	college's increase	total viewers age 18–49
Drawn Together (Comedy Central) — 167 ... total 727	+ 60%	1,108
CBS NFL Regional (CBS) — 167 ... total 444	+ 30%	4,542
NBC Sunday Night Football (NBC) — 165 ... total 999	+20%	6,332
CBS NFL National (CBS) — 162 ... total 1,101	+ 17%	7,070
TNT Big Picture Movies (TNT) — 147 ... total 195	+ 305%	637

Data from Nielsen Media Research

Legend: ☐ college viewers ■ others

Source: Adapted from Story, L. (2007, January 29). "At last, television ratings go to college." *The New York Times.* Accessed at http://www.nytimes.com/2007/01/29/business/media/29nielsen.html. Redrawn by Stephanie Plumeri Ertz

the rather invasive nature of having an outside company monitor your everyday television viewing habits, however, it is not surprising that just about half of all households asked to join the Nielsen ratings survey refuse to do so. This could very quickly become a major source of bias in the Nielsen sample because those households that agree to become part of the sample may have inherent qualities that make their members different from other viewers. They might watch more television, for example, or perhaps they are in greater need of the money that Nielsen offers, thereby skewing the sample to favor lower-income groups. To deal with this problem, Nielsen recruits extra households to add to its sample when some households decline to join the sample. Ideally, the replacements are as similar as possible in key demographic categories to the original households to avoid any kind of systematic bias.

Measuring Audience Viewership: Diaries, Household Meters, People Meters, and PPMs

As you can see, arriving at a sample of viewers is a challenging task. But the difficulty in capturing viewing behaviors does not stop there. Nielsen and Nielsen Audio must also *measure* actual audience viewing patterns, which turns out to be a lot more complicated than it appears at first glance. What we mean here by **measurement** is "a process of assigning numbers to objects, according to some rule of assignment" (Webster et al., 2006, p. 126). The objects of interest here are specific viewing behaviors, such as tuning in to a program at a certain time of day. Here, we are confronted with another thorny problem: What does it mean to be "watching television"? Does a viewer need to be paying close attention to the set in order to be counted as part of the audience for a particular program? Since most of us tend to channel surf with the remote control while viewing, how much attention do we need to pay to a particular program to be counted as part of the audience?

In answering these questions, the ratings attempt to strike a balance between *validity* and *reliability*. First, the ratings attempt to capture the real behaviors of viewers as accurately as possible—this is an attempt to maximize **validity**. The more specific information you gather about each individual's viewing behaviors, however (thereby maximizing validity), the more difficult it becomes to compare one person's viewing with another's, which would make the entire process of gathering viewing information rather useless for advertisers. Consequently, the tools for measuring viewing behavior must be general enough to be able to be applied consistently to different audience groups in multiple settings. This is called **reliability**. Nielsen threads this needle by defining *television viewing* as exposure to a particular program, thereby assuming that viewers are attending closely to the screen whether or not they are actually doing so.[2] Additionally, Nielsen measures viewing in four 15-minute time blocks. So if you have your TV set tuned to a particular channel for a majority of that 15-minute time period, Nielsen counts you as having been exposed to that particular program for that quarter-hour block. One other interesting aspect of the Nielsen ratings is the use of the household as the **unit of analysis.** This means that the ratings are actually a measurement of household television viewing, which is then extrapolated back to determine the actual number of viewers that watched a particular program. It's important to realize here that there is nothing "natural" about these definitions of television viewing. These are arbitrary decisions made by Nielsen that allow it to quantify human behaviors in a way that is useful and meaningful for its prime customer—advertisers.

---

[2]Efforts were made in in the 1980s by the Corporation for Public Broadcasting and Arbitron to devise a system of *qualitative* ratings by measuring viewers' preferences for and level of attention to specific television programs. This type of ratings system never caught on with advertisers and was subsequently abandoned.

There are a number of techniques that Nielsen uses to measure television viewing. We will briefly explore each of them and some of their potential limitations. The most traditional and widely used technique is to distribute **diaries** to Nielsen families. Thousands of diaries are distributed by Nielsen to generate viewing estimates in local TV markets across the country. The diary is a small paper pamphlet that records viewing of a single TV set over the course of one week. The diary keeper must track the time spent viewing (broken down into quarter-hour time segments on the left-hand side), the station and program that was viewed during that time period, and the members of the household who were present at the time of viewing. This technique can provide a wealth of data, but the quality of information depends upon the willingness of the viewer to put in a significant amount of work to maintain an accurate snapshot of viewing within the household. This can lead to some significant errors as a result of natural human tendencies. For example, most people aren't terribly diligent about filling in their viewing choices as they are watching TV, waiting until the end of the week to do so and relying upon their memory of what they watched. A more serious problem with the diary technique in recent years has been the proliferation of channels on most Americans' cable and satellite boxes, making it difficult for viewers to determine what channel they are on when they are watching a program. When it comes time to fill out the diary, viewers may report that they watched a program on a more familiar channel (usually a broadcast network affiliate station) rather than on a more obscure cable network, thereby skewing the ratings in favor of local network stations and recognizable cable networks such as CNN and HBO. Indeed, beginning in the early 1980s cable networks urged Nielsen to abandon the diary method, arguing that it vastly underestimated audiences for their channels.

To combat this problem, in the late 1980s Nielsen began using **household meters** to measure TV set tuning. The household meter is a small electronic box that sits on top of the TV and measures what channel the set is tuned to at any given moment. The box is plugged into a telephone line, and the data are downloaded by Nielsen at the end of the day. Since this is a passive monitoring system, it requires no human intervention to record viewing and is therefore a much more reliable tool for generating the ratings. What was missing when this system was implemented was any indication of *who* was in the room during viewing. This problem was addressed in the fall 1987 with the introduction of the **people meter**. People meters are household meters with an extra remote control added. Using the remote, viewers enter a special code for themselves when they are in the room with the TV set. They press another button when they leave the room, thus giving Nielsen a tally of who is watching a particular program. Despite their widespread use today in generating the all-important overnight TV program ratings, people meters are not without their own measurement errors. For instance, the people meters have not been terribly effective at measuring the viewing behaviors of children, who are much less likely to be conscientious about logging themselves in and out of the system. Additionally, Nielsen has found that, over time, the average amount of television viewing in a Nielsen household decreases. This has been interpreted not as a gradual decrease in television viewing but as the increasing "button fatigue" of viewers within the household who grow weary of logging themselves into the system each time they wish to watch television. This problem became so acute that Nielsen decreased the time that it metered its television households from 5 years to 2 years, though this has done little to quiet critics of this method.

Newer technology attempts to develop an even more comprehensive measurement of television exposure without the persistent problem of reliance upon the viewer to register his or her own media use. In 2005, in response to advertisers' increasing dissatisfaction with people meter data, Nielsen introduced the **portable people meter (PPM),** which was meant to defy the limitations of set-top metering within TV households. Arbitron, the radio ratings company at the time, began using portable people meters as well (see Figure 4.3). The PPM consists of a small device the size of a pager, which is worn at all times by viewers in a Nielsen household. Small, inaudible tones, embedded within both television and radio programming, can be picked up by the PPM, which indicates that a person is within range of a particular media program. At the end of the day, viewers deposit their pagers in a base that both charges the PPM and uploads the viewers' data to Nielsen. There are two enormous advantages to this type of technology: It is nearly completely passive, requiring little effort on behalf of viewers, and it measures media exposure *both inside and outside* of the household (Gertner, 2005). Nielsen began pursuing the widespread implementation of PPMs as part of a proposed overhaul of its audience measurement in 2006, which it dubbed Anytime Anywhere Media Measurement, or A2/M2 (Higgins, 2006). Through its A2/M2 initiative, Nielsen determined to eliminate diaries in all of its local market ratings measurement. PPMs also allowed the company

Figure 4.3 Personal People Meter (PPM)

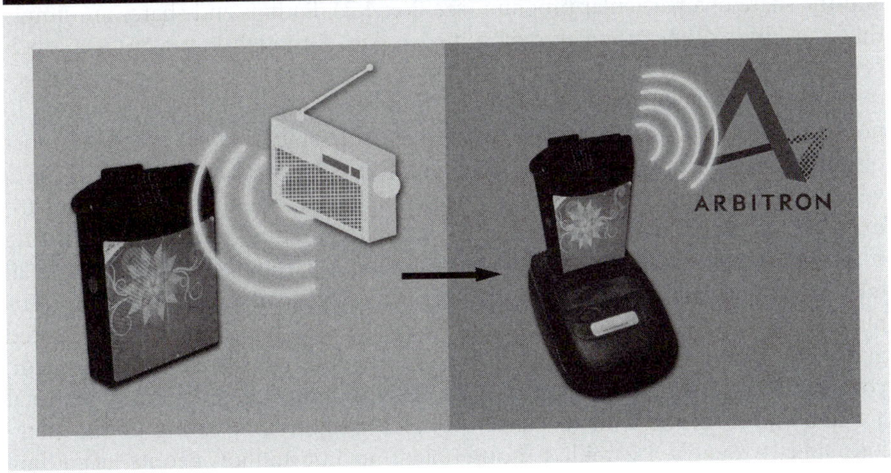

Source: Stephanie Plumeri Ertz.

to do two other important things: track "time-shifted" television viewing via digital video recorders (DVRs, discussed later in the chapter) and link television viewership with Internet usage data (Nielsen Media Research, 2008; Elliott, 2006). This effort hit some initial snags, however, since Nielsen discovered that most viewers did not want their web usage tracked along with their television viewing behaviors (Story, 2008).

Nielsen has also begun matching its ratings data with other forms of information about the individuals in its ratings sample, especially their geographic locations (usually their zip codes or postal codes) and credit card purchasing data, which they obtain from credit agencies. Nielsen purchased a company called Claritas in the early 2000s that gave the ratings giant access to quite detailed consumer purchasing data that it bundled into a service called NielsenPRIZM. The goal was to offer advertisers and media companies a comprehensive overview of audiences' viewing and purchasing habits. Although Claritas was sold off to the Carlyle Group in 2017 (Neff, 2017), it remains a powerful player in target marketing by consumer location (see the Claritas discussion activity at the end of this chapter for more details).

Ratings and Shares in the Television Industry

Now that you have a basic overview of the methodology of ratings systems and some of their shortcomings, we will turn briefly to the actual outcome of all of this concentrated effort—the ratings numbers themselves. In order to compute two of the most important numbers used by advertisers and television networks, *ratings* and *shares*, we need to have two other numbers in hand. First, we need to know the total number of television households (HHs) in the United States (or Total TV HHs) and the number of television *households using television* (HUTs) at a particular moment in time. From these numbers, we can then compute both the rating and the share of a particular program (see Box 4.2). Ratings and shares are simply different kinds of measurements of audience size. Although you won't see a percentage sign after them, ratings and shares are calculated as ratios or percentages.

Let's break down each of these key numbers, one at a time. One thing to notice right away is that ratings and shares have the same numerator—the number of households watching a particular program or station at any one time. This is what is measured by Nielsen through the people meter, or diary. The denominator in each equation determines the difference between ratings and shares. A **rating** is a ratio of how many households are watching a particular program out of all television households in the United States. As of September 2018, Nielsen estimated that there were roughly 119.9 million television households in the United States (Nielsen Media Research, 2018). To get the rating for a particular program, you would divide the number of households watching that program by the total TV households in the United States, or 119.9 million. One rating point, therefore, equals roughly 1.2 million households, or 3.06 million people, according to Nielsen estimates. A program with a 10 rating, for example, would represent 11.99 million households (10 x 1.199) watching a particular program.

BOX 4.2
Important Audience Numbers and Their Computations

$$\text{Rating (R)} = \frac{\textit{Number of TV HHs watching a program or station}}{\text{Total TV HHs}}$$

$$\text{HUT} = \frac{\textit{Households using television}}{\text{Total TV HHs}}$$

$$\text{Share} = \frac{\textit{Number of HHs watching a program or station}}{\text{HUTs}}$$

$$\text{Gross Rating Points (GRP)} = R_1 + R_2 + R_3 + \dots R_n$$

$$\text{Cost Per Thousand (CPM)} = \frac{\textit{Cost advertisement (\$)} \times 1{,}000}{\text{Audience size}}$$

$$\text{Cost Per Point (CPP)} = \frac{\textit{Cost advertisement (\$)}}{\text{Audience rating (R)}}$$

Ratings are useful in generating a numerical value of audience size, but advertisers often want to know the popularity of a program in relation to other programs that are being seen at the same time. To do this, Nielsen provides data about the share of a program. A **share** is a ratio of how many households are watching a particular program out of all households that are watching television at that particular moment (or HUTs). Let's say that only about half of all television households are on during a particular program (roughly 50 million HHs—this is our HUT number). If 10 million TV households were watching a particular program at that moment, then the share would be a 20 (10 ÷ 50 x 100 to express it as a percentage). This would mean that roughly 20% of all televisions turned on during that time period were watching that program. If a program has a low rating but a 20 or 30 share, for instance, it could indicate that the program was garnering a significant part of the audience during a time of day when not many people are watching television (such as during late-night TV or early in the morning).

There are a number of ways in which ratings and shares are used to assist advertisers in making decisions about purchasing time on various media outlets. Although there are many computations that use both ratings and shares, we will only explore a few here. First, many advertisers will want to know approximately how many people (or households) were exposed to their commercial message, which may have run across different television channels and time periods. To do this, they compute the **gross rating points** (or GRP) for the ad campaign by simply adding up the rating points of each time period in which the advertisement was placed. Advertisers also measure the efficiency of their media buys by calculating how much it costs them to reach each individual viewer. The standard measurement of efficiency is to calculate the **cost per thousand** (or CPM, where M is the Roman numeral for 1,000), which is computed by dividing the cost of the commercial by the audience size, multiplied by 1,000. Advertisers can also evaluate for the cost of each ratings point that their advertisement garnered (called the **cost per point,** or CPP) by dividing the cost of the commercial by the rating for the channel and time period in which it appeared on screen.

DVRs, C3, STBs, SVOD, and Shifting Audience Metrics in the 2000s

Audience measurement companies like Nielsen have relied historically on a relatively stable media environment in order to track viewership. This stability was built on a few core technologies—broadcast television, cable television, and broadcast radio—that provided consumers access to media programming. The introduction of the video cassette recorder (VCR) in the 1980s had the potential to disrupt viewing by allowing viewers to time-shift their viewing and potentially skip commercial breaks, but research in the United States at the time revealed that few viewers were severely changing their viewing habits (Lotz, 2014). The real shift came in 1999 with the introduction of TiVo and the **digital video recorder (DVR).** Because of the relative ease and the digital nature of the recording (no costly videotapes), consumers began recording more and more programming, and viewing habits shifted correspondingly. Although the growth of DVR adoption was relatively slow at first, a marketing study in 2017 found that 53% of all U.S. households had a DVR (Spangler, 2017). More and more viewers now consumed programming after it had officially aired, severely complicating the process of audience measurement. Nielsen also now had clients with competing visions of audience metrics: Program providers wanted Nielsen to measure DVR viewing up to 7 days after it officially aired, while advertisers were pressuring Nielsen to rely only on consumption data from the first 24 hours after air.

The resulting negotiation among these stakeholders resulted in a compromise metric called **C3 ratings**. C3 ratings gave advertisers something important, which was a rating based upon the actual commercial rather than an average rating for the overall program for each quarter hour, as had been the practice by Nielsen during the network era of the 20th century (Buzzard, 2012). Networks were worried that this per-minute commercial rating would decrease their profits since audiences presumably might switch channels during commercial breaks and thereby lower the rating. Because commercial-based ratings were the practice in other countries, advertisers insisted that Nielsen adjust its measurement practices accordingly. U.S. advertisers did compromise with programmers, however, by agreeing to count audience exposure to programming and commercials up to 3 days beyond the original air date. Any viewing outside of that window is not included in the official ratings count (Napoli, 2011). It took Nielsen 4 years to finally implement this new standard to begin to report time-shifted viewing in 2005, though the advertising industry itself did not formally adopt the C3 ratings standard until 2009 since it was expensive to install in the more than 10,000 local cable systems around the United States (Lotz, 2014).

There were other major changes afoot in audience ratings as well. Beginning in the mid-2000s, local cable operators around the United States began rolling out digital television services. These services required a device that decoded the compressed and scrambled digital signal called a **set-top box** (STB). STBs offered the potential to revolutionize the gathering of audience viewing data by offering audience measurement firms a moment-by-moment measure of television tuning, including advertising measurement. Unlike Nielsen's people meter, however, STBs cannot detect who is in the room when the television is on. Companies like TNS Media Research and Rentrak emerged as competitors to Nielsen in the late 2000s. These companies harvested data from digital STBs and sold it directly to advertisers and program networks, cutting Nielsen out of the process. STB data was particularly valuable because it was entirely passive—it transmitted viewing data in the background without the necessity for effort from viewers. Resistance to Nielsen's increasingly dated panel and diary techniques reached a crescendo in 2009 when 14 of its largest clients formed a consortium called the Coalition for Innovative Media Measurement (Napoli, 2011, p. 143). The goal of the coalition was to pressure Nielsen to incorporate STB data into its ratings service. By August of 2013, 231 local U.S. television stations in 54 media markets had subscribed to Rentrak's TV essentials service, though most used it as a supplement to Nielsen's ratings rather than a replacement (Lotz, 2014). Rentrak merged with web analytics company ComScore in 2015 to solidify its status as a major competitor to Nielsen's ratings service (Steinberg, 2015). As Buzzard explains, "Nielsen realized that if another company could collect STB data from millions of U.S. cable subscribers, it could pose a serious threat to its core business (2012, p. 143). Nielsen responded to this industry pressure by making deals with large cable carriers such as AT&T (Lieberman, 2017) and Comcast (Lafayette, 2017) to access their STB data and to include those numbers in its overall ratings data portfolio, while simultaneously attempting to publicly argue that single-source data like STB metrics were incomplete and prone to potential errors.

Audience viewing habits have continued to shift. Not only are more audiences accessing television via STBs, but **subscription-video-on-demand (SVOD)** services such as Netflix, Hulu, and Amazon Prime are rapidly eclipsing cable television as a source for viewing, particularly since many of these services are becoming bundled into digital televisions themselves. In 2016, 50% of all U.S. TV households had access to some kind of SVOD service, which equaled adoption of DVRs (Mandese, 2016). The very next year, a marketing survey found that 54% of U.S. adults reportedly had access to Netflix in their households, just slightly higher than the 53% who noted that they had a DVR (Spangler, 2017). Nielsen has endeavored to stay on top of the rise of streaming video services. In 2017, the company announced a new service called SVOD Content Ratings, which allowed for measurement of television content from Netflix, Amazon Prime, YouTubeTV, and Hulu (Steinberg, 2017). This move was particularly significant given the fact that audiences are increasingly "cord-cutting," or eliminating their monthly cable television services and relying entirely on **over-the-top (OTT)** devices like Apple TV, Amazon Fire TV, Roku, Sling, and Google's Chromecast to stream video content over the Internet. Given these important changes in viewing behaviors, the audience measurement industry will continue to be in a competitive flux, particularly since passive, technology-based solutions for tracking media consumption are no longer controlled by a single monopoly supplier, Nielsen. The rising importance of social media and other web-based analytics (discussed more fully in Chapter 9) is further accelerating some of these major changes in audience measurement.

Ratings, Market Research, and the Audience Commodity: Assigning Market Value to Mass Audiences

So far in this chapter, we have explored the theory of political economy and sketched out its importance in developing a critical understanding of audiences as commodities in a capitalist media system. We have also outlined the operationalization and methodology of the Nielsen television ratings, one of the most important forms of mass audience feedback used in today's commercial media environment. In the last section of this chapter, we will use the political economic perspective to explore how the process of commodifying the audience in many ways challenges taken-for-granted freedoms in liberal democracies, such as equality of opportunity and nondiscrimination. This section will explore how ratings companies and market research firms have developed highly sophisticated constructions of media audiences that go well beyond simple notions of audience size and exposure to media stimuli. These new techniques aim to split the audience into smaller niche segments so that advertisers and marketers can target pitches more specifically at these segments. Audiences are also assigned differential market values according to their desirability to advertisers, threatening to polarize an increasingly diverse society.

The Importance of Audience Demographics: Age, Gender, and Income

The main goal of the ratings is to provide advertisers and television programmers with an estimate of audience size. However, total audience size is rarely the most important number for advertisers these days. Instead, advertisers look at the size of specific subgroups that are of particular interest, based upon certain basic social features of these audiences such as age, income, gender, geographic location, and race. These social groupings are called **demographics**. Demographic groupings are so fundamental to the ways in which advertisers direct their appeals to potential consumers that Nielsen routinely reports the ratings for particular programs by listing the audience size for key demographic groups such as gender (men, women) and age (18–24, 25–49). As scholar Philip Napoli has observed, "Because most predominant systems of audience measurement do not link individual audience members' media consumption habits with their product-purchasing behaviors, demographics are the proxy used by both advertisers and content providers" (2003, p. 104).

The three most important demographics for advertisers are age, gender, and income (Napoli, 2003). In the case of age, it is not surprising that Madison Avenue places a higher premium on younger viewers than on older ones. Even though there is little evidence that older viewers consume less than their younger counterparts, advertisers assume that older viewers have built decades of brand loyalty and are therefore less likely to change their habits in response to advertising messages. It is important to realize that the "brand loyalty" argument is a supposition on behalf of the advertising community and not established fact, yet it results in some stark market realities. Because consumers over 50 years old are of little interest to advertisers, the ratings for this group are not reflected in the standard reports that Nielsen provides to television networks and advertisers. As a consequence, television programmers are not looking to cater to an over-50 audience.

Gender is another critical form of demographic segmentation that affects the value of audiences to advertisers. In general, male audiences are valued more highly in the marketplace than women, though type of product being advertised plays a large role (see Figure 4.4). Why would advertisers value men more highly than women, particularly when market research demonstrates that women generally make a majority of household purchases on a day-to-day basis? The answer may lie in the scarcity of male audiences. Because women typically consume more media than men, they are easier to reach with advertising messages. This in turn "exerts downward pressure on their value, while the greater scarcity of men raises their value to many advertisers" (Napoli, 2003, p. 105). The same pattern occurs for income—those with lower income typically consume more media, thereby decreasing the value of their attention to advertisers.

As each of these examples demonstrates, advertisers assign different market values to certain audience members because of their demographic makeup. What is important to note, however, is that these distinctions and valuations are not natural but are instead the creations of advertisers and media companies. In fact, as Napoli diplomatically argues, more often than not these demographically based valuations are based upon flimsy or nonexistent evidence. He writes that "the valuations of audiences on the basis of demographic distinctions bear an uncertain relationship to the true value of these audiences to advertisers" (Napoli, 2003, p. 107). Here, political economists such as Eileen Meehan would notice that the process of assigning value to audiences is fraught with problematic suppositions and tendencies on behalf of advertisers. The consequence of this is that profit-driven media companies will gear their content toward the types of audiences that are most valuable, thereby discouraging program diversity in our media environment.

Figure 4.4 CPM Estimates for the 2017–2018 Television Season (30-Second Commercials)

	Sex		Age		
	Men	Women	18–34	18–49	25–54
Broadcast Networks					
Early AM	$41.35	$26.47	$74.58	$36.58	$31.47
Daytime	–	12.41	26.56	17.47	18.81
Early News	29.34	23.06	72.90	33.39	31.12
Prime	61.13	44.65	83.69	51.14	53.03
Late Fringe	60.77	52.70	67.49	40.89	47.24
Syndication					
Daytime	–	9.95	24.48	13.83	15.67
Early Fringe	32.57	22.16	48.90	26.02	25.02
Prime Access	56.53	42.00	117.60	50.68	51.57
Late Fringe	35.89	30.65	51.98	25.43	27.21
Cable Networks					
Daytime	11.94	4.71	17.50	11.13	10.51
Early/Late Fringe	27.74	20.40	35.83	20.00	21.95
Prime	36.42	29.75	59.18	34.19	28.93

Source: Reprinted from *TV Dimensions 2018* with permission from Media Dynamics, Inc. For more information, visit www.mediadynamicsinc.com

The Role of Psychographic and Lifestyle Measurements in Targeted Marketing Appeals

As the number of media choices has expanded for consumers, including more cable channels, satellite channels, and online media options such as YouTube, Apple TV, and Google Chromecast, among others, media audiences have fragmented into smaller and smaller pieces, making it much more difficult for advertisers to reach them in large numbers. Advertisers and marketers have coped with this trend by devising even more particularized methods of identifying media audiences, breaking them down into ever-smaller marketing niches in order to direct more personalized advertising appeals to these segments (in the hopes that those audiences will pay more attention to them). This process of directing promotional messages to a specific subsection of the audience is called **target marketing**, and it is the primary focus of today's advertising community (Turow, 1997).

Besides demographics, another tool used by marketers and advertisers to segment audiences is called **psychographics**. Psychographics, a term that merges two words, *demographics* and *psychology*, refers to the general association of personality or psychological traits with groups of consumers in an effort to create even finer distinctions among them (Vyncke, 2002). Marketers may define audiences in terms of personality qualities such as leadership, sociability, independence, conformity, status-seeking, or compulsiveness, to name a few examples. More recently, psychographics has been combined with what marketers call **lifestyle measurements.** These measurements essentially define a group of individuals according to their product and media consumption habits. Individuals might be classified as "frequent travelers" if they make more than four airline trips per year. Moreover, if someone is willing to take risks and enjoys new experiences, the individual might be identified by marketers as an "adventurer" and then actively sold to retailers who specialize in outdoor merchandise, such as Eddie Bauer or L.L.Bean.

Marketing and Social Stereotypes: Minority Audiences Struggle With Big Media

What are the consequences of these increasingly detailed institutional constructions of the audience? You might conclude, as many advertisers and marketers do, that all of these new methods of defining audiences as increasingly tiny niches allow companies to more narrowly define their target audiences in order to provide customers with higher-quality services and products that meet their specific needs. In fact, the dynamics of this new system of "narrowcasting" to ever-tinier audience groups mean that the individuals who are most valuable to advertisers are more likely to receive targeted messages about products they are more interested in. These sought-after customers may also receive substantial discounts that are not available to the general public (Turow, 2006, pp. 183–185). But what about the flip side of this coin? What happens to those audiences that are of little interest to advertisers? What are the consequences for them in a commercial media system designed to cater to the desires of small subsections of the audience?

Minority audiences have found themselves precisely in this situation: ignored by advertisers and thereby rendered essentially invisible to the commercial media apparatus. The case of Hispanic and Latino audiences in the United States is indicative of some of the ways in which ethnic and racial minorities have had to struggle with marketers to raise awareness of their needs. These groups have been attempting to carve out a notion of their own identity that challenges the type of demographic, psychographic, and lifestyle categories that had relegated them to marketplace footnotes in the past. As critical scholar Oscar Gandy points out,

For the most part, when Whites identify minority audience segments, either for commerce or for public service, there is a tendency to be guided more by convenience than by consideration for the identities actually held by members of target populations. (2000, p. 51)

The story of advertisers' awareness of U.S. Hispanic consumers began in advertising and trade magazines in the late 1960s, in which Hispanic business executives complained that their customers were ignored and neglected by major advertisers, partially as a result of their invisibility in the mainstream media (Astroff, 1988). One of the major reasons for the lack of desirability of Hispanic audiences to advertisers was the persistence of negative social stereotypes of U.S. Hispanics and Latinos. According to Arlene Dávila,

Dominant stereotypes of Hispanics in mainstream society revolve around the poor and welfare-dependent population—views that repel corporate clients, who are interested in middle-class and affluent consumers, and have long challenged advertising executives to convince them that Hispanics are indeed a worthy target population. (2001, p. 68)

The goal of Hispanic community leaders was both to raise awareness of their community such that they would gain visibility and greater acceptance among advertisers and to dispel some of the persistent social stereotypes of Hispanics as poor.

The first marketing research study of the U.S. Hispanic population was completed in 1979 by the marketing firm Yankelovich, Skelly, and White (Rodriguez, 1997). For the first time, this study constructed the Hispanic audience in terms that Madison Avenue could understand—as demographic, psychographic, and lifestyle categories. The study concluded that Hispanics were a good investment because

(1) as a group, Hispanics were younger than the general population and so ripe for instilling "brand loyalty"; (2) Hispanics had larger households than the general market and so bought more food, disposable diapers, and many other consumer items; (3) Hispanics spoke Spanish, patronized Spanish-language media, and so were easily "targetable" through the Spanish-language media offerings. (Rodriguez, 1997, p. 290)

This study heralded the beginning of advertiser interest in U.S. Hispanics as a potential target market for consumer goods and eventually led to a pilot study by Nielsen in Los Angeles in 1990 that focused on generating a more valid measure of Hispanic television viewing.[3] The downside of this new interest in U.S. Hispanics,

---

[3]Because Nielsen had not used bilingual neighborhood recruiters in the past, for instance, the Hispanic audience size had been grossly underestimated by the national TV ratings sample. The results of this pilot study demonstrated that the size of the actual Hispanic television viewing audience was 64% larger than previously reported.

however, was that the desire of advertisers and Nielsen to capture and compare audiences with one another meant that specific subcultural groupings within this diverse community (such as Cuban Americans, Puerto Ricans, and Mexican Americans) were lumped together as one umbrella ethnic group by advertisers. Rather than spend money on separate marketing plans to reach each of these communities with different histories and cultures, advertisers developed a generic "Hispanic" audience construct, even going so far as to replace Spanish-speaking on-camera actors' accents with a "Walter Cronkite Spanish" that masked national origins (Rodriguez, 1997, p. 290).

The case of U.S. Hispanics is just one of many that involves the struggle of minority groups to achieve visibility in the mainstream media. As this episode demonstrated, overcoming invisibility among advertisers and marketers was achieved only by perpetuating Latino stereotypes. This process, which Astroff terms **racial formation**, occurs when "social, economic, and political forces determine the content and importance of racial categories" (1988, p. 156). As a result of their newfound visibility through marketing categories, Hispanics saw their individual social and cultural characteristics subsumed within a "denationalized, racialized U.S. Latino panethnicity" (Rodriguez, 1997, p. 291). These images may have also shaped how millions of non-Latinos perceived this minority group. In this instance, the ability of minority communities to define themselves was hampered by advertisers' stereotypes, illustrating the disconnect between institutional constructions and notions of self-identity. The fact that many of these audience misconceptions persist points to the unequal power distribution between media producers and audiences.

Audience Engagement and the Rise of Social TV

The previous examples of target marketing had several things in common: They were all based upon industry-initiated data-gathering, they relied upon somewhat intrusive techniques to gather that data, and they privileged measurements of audience *exposure* to program and commercial content. Increasingly, however, as more and more of us consume media content online, there has been an explosion in the amount of data about audience behaviors and attitudes that are potentially available to measurement firms. New technologies like DVRs and digital set-top boxes have reduced the reliance of measurement companies on surveys and audience panels because these technologies allow for passive monitoring of viewing behaviors. Like the portable people meter (PPM), this type of technology-enhanced passive monitoring also eliminates the potential for recall and recording errors that were a problem with diary data from the 20th century. These errors became more acute as the number of digital cable and satellite channels increased into the hundreds. Digital set-top boxes allowed advertisers to demand even more specific metrics that went beyond demographics, psychographics, and lifestyle data. In this brave new world of audience data, advertisers demand data that goes far beyond simply measuring who was exposed to a specific media message. This change amounts to nothing less than a wholesale shift in what scholars call a "market regime" for audience data.

Advertisers are demanding measures of audience **engagement**. What exactly defines an engaged consumer of a television program, radio show, or a podcast? Advertisers increasingly wanted to distinguish between those viewers who were fully invested in the program content and those who were simply casual viewers. Webster, Phalen, and Lichty (2014) define engagement as the following:

> Broad, ill-defined, term encompassing measures designed to assess user's liking of or involvement with various media products and services. Sometimes these are derived from more conventional measures of exposure (e.g., repeat viewing or time spent metrics). Sometimes they are derived from actions taken on social media sites (e.g., comments, sharing, etc.). Sometimes engagement is measured directly with dedicated surveys. (p. 270)

There are two different meanings of engagement here: The first is essentially a direct outgrowth of the exposure measure, such as repeat viewing or time spent with a particular media message. Engagement can also mean whether or not audiences recall information from an advertising message from one day to the next (Napoli, 2012). Some Internet websites, for example, have used "time spent" on their pages in place of clicks or "pageviews" as a proxy for audience engagement (Ingram, 2014). While it seems logical that audiences who spend more time on a website are more engaged with the content, a systematic study of online news consumption found that there was little connection between the most popular sites (measured by pageviews) and the amount of time that each unique visitor spent on those sites (Nelson & Webster, 2016).

The second meaning of engagement in Webster et al.'s (2014) definition refers to specific actions that are taken by audiences as a result of their interest in or enthusiasm for a particular media message. One study by Yang and Coffey (2014), for example, conducted an online survey to ask individuals about their consumption of online videos. They identified deeper engagement among those individuals who watched entire videos (an exposure metric) and found that those who did were more likely to tell others about their viewing experiences via e-mails and social media (something they describe as electronic word of mouth, or e-WOM). Advertisers have also noted with intense interest that audiences often consume multiple media simultaneously. Social media sites like Twitter and Facebook are often used by viewers to connect with others during specific programming events. Called **social TV**, this form of audience interactivity became a focus for programmers and advertisers beginning in 2007 as another potential metric of audience engagement (Kosterich & Napoli, 2016). Social TV metrics are generated in much different ways than ratings data. Instead of counting exposures, social TV analysis uses computer algorithms to collect comments, opinions, and reactions posted to social media about specific programs or events. According to one marketing study by Twitter, for example, more than 24.9 million tweets were posted during the 2014 Super Bowl (Midha, 2014). While there were over 100 start-up companies aiming to provide social media

Figure 4.5 Top 10 Most-Social TV Series of 2018 (USA, Nielsen)

Rank	Network	Program Name	Number of Episodes	Average Total Interactions (000)	Average Facebook Interactions (000)	Average Twitter Interactions (000)
1	ABC	*The Bachelor*	8	611	14	596
2	USA Network	*WWE Monday Night RAW*	46	518	188	330
3	NBC	*America's Got Talent*	23	459	151	308
4	ABC	*American Idol*	19	346	238	108
5	USA Network	*WWE SmackDown!*	45	274	96	178
6	FX	*American Horror Story: Apocalypse*	10	271	27	243
7	ABC	*The Bachelorette*	11	255	4	251
8	NBC	*This Is Us*	15	229	65	163
9	The CW	*Riverdale*	19	207	7	200
10	VH1	*RuPaul's Drag Race: All Stars*	5	206	20	187

Source: Nielsen Media Research. (2018, December 20). Tops of 2018: Social TV. Retrieved from http://www.nielsen.com/us/en/insights/news/2018/tops-of-2018-social-tv

metrics to programmers and advertisers in 2013, Kosterich and Napoli (2016) argue that social TV metrics are becoming widely adopted in the industry. Commercial TV networks in the United States regularly take the pulse of Twitter and other social media when deciding whether to renew programs. Not to be left behind, Nielsen acquired the company Social Guide (which provided social media analytics) in 2012 and launched its own rebranded Social Content Ratings service in 2016 (Steel, 2016). Nielsen now monitors Twitter, Facebook, and Instagram posts for reactions to popular programs (see Figure 4.5 on the previous page for an example).

These audience research trends reveal that the measurement of audience data is a rapidly shifting media landscape in flux. The attempt to measure social media use and other types of online activity during traditional media consumption is just one indication that advertisers and program providers are continually adjusting to try to model and sample the habits of a new generation of media audiences. Advertising industry watchers are convinced that more targeted approaches to reaching audiences—through demographics, psychographics, and engagement metrics—point to the future of the media ratings industry.

Conclusion: How Effective Is Institutional Control Over Audiences?

In this chapter, we have explored the institutional construction of media audiences by focusing on the most prominent forms of commercial audience measurement—the Nielsen ratings and marketing research. The political economy of communication perspective, which frames the issues in this chapter, is quite useful for understanding these trends because it foregrounds issues of the economy and power. Because of the separation between the zones of production and consumption in modern capitalist societies, advertisers and media producers will continually struggle to monitor and measure media audiences. The ratings, the dominant form of audience feedback in a commercial media system, are prone to numerous types of error, which calls into question the notion that the market is responsive to the will of consumers. As advertisers and marketers have tried to wrestle with an ever-fragmenting audience, newer forms of segmentation through demographic, psychographic, and lifestyle categories have further problematized the connection between commercial audience constructions and our own sense of identity. The rise of STBs and SVOD services like Amazon Prime and Netflix have further complicated the landscape for accurately measuring audience media consumption.

Given the shortcomings in these forms of commercial audience measurement, then, how effective is institutional control over audiences? Scholars such as Ien Ang (1991) argue that, because institutional surveillance of the audience is always fleeting and incomplete, audiences will continue to enjoy power over media institutions due to their relative anonymity. However, as political economists point out, while the connections between the ratings and the "natural" audience may be fleeting at best, we must realize that these numbers are the basis upon which decisions about most of the programming available to American audiences are made. Indeed, the flow of millions of dollars between advertisers and media conglomerates is predicated on the notion that the ratings numbers are meaningful and represent a real connection to the invisible viewing public out there, despite some of the methodological criticisms of the ratings that erupt from time to time.

Outside of debates among scholars about the role and function of the audience commodity in capitalist societies, does it really matter to the average American how the ratings construct audiences? As the examples about the sampling of college students and the construction of Latino consumers should make clear, the choices that ratings companies make about imagining the audience can have significant real-world consequences. Fundamental aspects of life in a democratic society, such as access to goods, services, and information, are to a large extent determined by the image of the audience that is fed back to media companies through the ratings. Without reform of the ratings system, it is unlikely that market-driven media corporations will have any incentive to offer alternative types of programming that will appeal to audiences who are of less interest to advertisers (older television viewers, for example). As this chapter has outlined, the political economy perspective helps us to uncover the economic underpinnings of the ratings system and the structural features that keep it more or less resistant to change.

DISCUSSION ACTIVITIES

1. Look at some of the headline results provided by Nielsen about media usage in the United States that was provided as part of its 2018 Q1 Nielsen Total Audience Report: https://radioconnects.ca/wp-content/uploads/2018/08/Nielsen-Q1-2018-Total-US-Audience-Report.pdf. After reading over the report, answer the following questions:

   • What are some of the key trends in audience data highlighted by this report? What do we learn about media consumption trends?

   • What assumptions (either implicit or explicit) are being made about media audiences in this report? Is there a connection being made between *quantity* (audience size) and *quality of the media experience?* If yes, how is this connection made?

   • Do you see any connection between these findings and your own media consumption experiences? What kind of information do you feel is missing, if anything, from this overview of media consumption? Can you link this to the theory of political economy?

2. Have a look at an overview of the Fall 2018 American broadcast TV schedule at this link: https://tvseriesfinale.com/tv-show/check-fall-2018-television-schedule/. Pay close attention

to the grid at the bottom of the page, which shows all programs on the major U.S. television networks as well as the ratings and shares for those programs. Look carefully at this grid and answer the following questions:

- What five shows on the weekly schedule had the highest *rating*, and which network aired those programs?

- Which five shows on the weekly schedule had the highest *share*, and which network aired those programs? Were they the same shows that had the highest rating? If not, why do you think there was a discrepancy?

- Do you see any patterns in audience viewership (across networks, times, or days of the week)? What are they? What might these patterns reveal about audience viewing habits?

3. Take a sheet of graph paper and make five columns from left to right across the top, one for each weekday (Monday–Friday). Then, on the left-hand side, create one row for each hour of the day, beginning at 9:00 a.m. and ending at 11:00 p.m. You have now created a basic time diary similar to those used by Nielsen. Use this sheet to track your media exposure as precisely as you can for an entire week. Write down what you watched on television, what network it was on, and how long you watched the program. If you streamed a program on the Internet (on sites such as YouTube, Netflix, Hulu, and ComedyCentral.com, for example), then indicate that as the source of the video. At the end of the week, discuss the following questions:

- What patterns did you notice about your viewing behaviors? How much television did you watch and when? Compare your viewing to others' in the class.

- Reflect on the process of keeping the viewing diary: How difficult was it to keep up with the diary? Did you fill it out as you went along or go back later in the week to record your viewing? Were you able to recall specifically what you watched and on what channels or networks? Talk with others in the class about some of the challenges involved in keeping the diary.

- What lessons can you draw from this experience about the accuracy of diaries in measuring audience viewing?

4. Watch this brief 5-minute promotional video for the segmentation and marketing services by Nielsen: https://www.youtube .com/watch?v=qH9W6ONEztE. After you watch this video, make some notes about the following questions:

- How does Nielsen "construct" the notion of the audience? In other words, what types of information does Nielsen claim to provide to marketers and advertisers about consumers?

- Who is "John"? What do we learn about this consumer? What types of segmentation categories are being used to describe him?

- What do you think of these types of segmentation strategies? Do they concern you? Why or why not?

5. This activity asks you to explore forms of market segmentation of audiences. Go to Claritas's "My Best Segments" website: https:// claritas360.claritas.com/mybestsegments/. When on the website, look at the top of the page and click either on the "Zip Code Lookup" link (you can see all segments and their definitions if you click on the "Segments Details" link). Enter in your own home zip code or any 5-digit U.S. postal code to

explore what marketing segments live in that geographic area. Answer the following questions in writing or in discussion:

- What segmentation categories did you find? Locate the names of two of them and type or write down a brief description of them.

- Identify two different segments that you discovered on the website and a brief

description of each segment. What types of segmentation categories were used (geographic, demographic, psychographic, etc.)?

- How do these segments construct a particular view of the audience? Do any of the terms or descriptions used make you uncomfortable? Why or why not?

ADDITIONAL MATERIALS

Buzzard, K. (2012). *Tracking the audience: The ratings industry from analog to digital*. Abingdon, Oxfordshire: Routledge.

Buzzard, K. S. F. (2015). The rise of market information regimes and the historical development of audience ratings. *Historical Journal of Film, Radio & Television, 35*(3), 511–517.

Lotz, A. D. (2007). *The television will be revolutionized* (Ch. 6). New York: New York University Press.

Mosco, V. (2009). *The political economy of communication: Rethinking and renewal* (2nd ed.). London, England: SAGE.

Nielsen ratings 101: Designing the sample [Video presentation]. Available at https://www.youtube.com/watch?v=2AZ3ftjcJU4

Nielsen ratings 101: Introduction [Video presentation]. Available at https://www.youtube.com/watch?v=r4jyhQnl5Vo

Smith, H., & Young, R. (2004, November 16). Is Wal-Mart good for America? *Frontline*. WGBH Boston: PBS. [Video presentation]. Available at http://www.pbs.org/wgbh/pages/frontline/shows/walmart/

Turow, J. (2006). *Niche envy: Marketing discrimination in the digital age*. Cambridge, MA: MIT Press.

Wasko, J. (2004). The political economy of communications. In J. D. H. Downing, D. McQuail, P. Schlesinger, & E. Wartella (Eds.), *The SAGE handbook of media studies* (pp. 309–329). Thousand Oaks, CA: SAGE.

Webster, J. G., & Nelson, J. L. (2015). Accounting for attention minutes. *Digital Content Next*. Retrieved from https://digitalcontentnext.org/blog/2015/05/11/accounting-for-attention-minutes-as-a-currency/

Webster, J. G., Phalen, P. F., & Lichty, L. W. (2014). *Ratings analysis: Audience measurement and analytics* (4th ed.). New York, NY: Routledge.

REFERENCES

Ang, I. (1991). *Desperately seeking the audience*. London, England: Routledge.

Astroff, R. J. (1988). Spanish gold: Stereotypes, ideology, and the construction of a U.S. Latino market. *The Howard Journal of Communication, 1*(4), 155–173.

Bagdikian, B. H. (2004). *The new media monopoly*. Boston, MA: Beacon Press.

Buzzard, K. (1992). *Electronic media ratings: Turning audiences into dollars and sense*. Boston, MA: Focal Press.

Buzzard, K. (2012). Tracking the audience: the ratings industry from analog to digital. Abingdon, Oxon; Routledge.

Consoli, J. (2006, April 21). 44 mil. watch TV in unmeasured places. *Mediaweek.com*. Retrieved from http://www.mediaweek.com/mw/esearch/article_display.jsp?vnu_content_id=1002383527

Dávila, A. M. (2001). *Latinos, Inc.: The marketing and making of a people*. Berkeley: University of California Press.

Elliott, S. (2006, February 13). How to value ratings with DVR delay? *The New York Times*. Retrieved from http://www.nytimes.com/2006/02/13/business/media/13adcol.html

Gandy, O. H. (2000). Race, ethnicity, and the segmentation of media markets. In J. Curran & M. Gurevitch (Eds.), *Mass media and society* (3rd ed., pp. 44–69). New York, NY: Arnold.

Gertner, J. (2005, April 10). Our ratings, ourselves. *The New York Times Magazine*.

Golding, P., & Murdock, G. (1991). Culture, communication, and political economy. In J. Curran & M. Gurevitch (Eds.), *Mass media and society* (pp. 15–32). London, England: Arnold.

Hays, C. L. (2004, November 14). What Wal-Mart knows about customers' habits. *The New York Times*. Retrieved from http://www.nytimes.com/2004/11/14/business/yourmoney/14wal.html

Herman, E. S., & McChesney, R. W. (1997). *The global media: The new missionaries of corporate capitalism*. London, England: Cassell.

Higgins, J. M. (2006, June 19). Nielsen: Follow the video. *Broadcasting & Cable*. Retrieved from http://www.broadcastingcable.com/article/CA6344824.html?display=News&q=%22Nielsen%3A+Follow+the+Video%22

Ingram, M. (2014, June 23). Is time spent a better metric than pageviews? Upworthy says it is, and open-sources its code for attention minutes. Retrieved from https://gigaom.com/2014/06/23/is-time-spent-a-better-metric-than-pageviews-upworthy-says-it-is-and-open-sources-its-code-for-attention-minutes/

Jhally, S. (1987). *The codes of advertising: Fetishism and the political economy of meaning in the consumer society*. New York, NY: St. Martin's Press.

Kosterich, A., & Napoli, P. M. (2016). Reconfiguring the audience commodity: The institutionalization of social TV analytics as market information regime. *Television & New Media*, 17(3), 254–271.

Lafayette, J. (2017, November 9). Nielsen to include Comcast set-top box data in ratings. *Multichannel News*. Retrieved from https://www.multichannel.com/news/nielsen-include-comcast-set-top-box-data-ratings-416440

Lieberman, D. (2017, January 18). Nielsen lands deal to tap set-top box data from AT&T's DirecTV and U-Verse. *Deadline*. Retrieved from https://deadline.com/2017/01/nielsen-deal-set-top-box-data-att-directv-uverse-1201888699/

Lotz, A. D. (2014). *The television will be revolutionized* (2nd ed.). New York: New York University Press.

Mandese, J. (2016, June 27). SVOD reaches critical mass, surpasses DVR penetration. *MediaPost*. Retrieved from https://www.mediapost.com/publications/article/279049/svod-reaches-critical-mass-surpasses-dvr-penetrat.html

McChesney, R. W. (1999). *Rich media, poor democracy: Communication politics in dubious times—The history of communication*. Urbana: University of Illinois Press.

McChesney, R. W. (2008). *The political economy of media: Enduring issues, emerging dilemmas*. New York, NY: Monthly Review Press.

McKercher, C., & Mosco, V. (Eds.). (2007). *Knowledge workers in the information society*. Lanham, MD: Lexington Books.

Meehan, E. R. (1984). Ratings and the institutional approach: A third answer to the commodity question. *Critical Studies in Mass Communication*, *1*(2), 216–225.

Meehan, E. R. (1993). Commodity audience, actual audience: The blindspot debate. In J. Wasko, V. Mosco, & M. Pendakur (Eds.), *Illuminating the blindspots: Essays honoring Dallas W. Symthe* (pp. 378–397). Norwood, NJ: Ablex.

Midha, A. (2014, February 5). TV x Twitter: New findings for advertisers and networks. Retrieved from https://blog.twitter.com/marketing/en_us/a/2014/tv-x-twitter-new-findings-for-advertisers-and-networks.html

Miller, P. V. (1994). Made-to-order and standardized audiences: Forms of reality in audience measurement. In J. S. Ettema & D. C. Whitney (Eds.), *Audiencemaking: How the media create the audience* (pp. 57–74). Thousand Oaks, CA: SAGE.

Miller, T., Govil, N., McMurria, J., Maxwell, R., & Wang, T. (2005). *Global Hollywood 2* (Rev., p. 442). London, England: BFI.

Mosco, V. (1996). *The political economy of communication: Rethinking and renewal*. London, England: SAGE.

Napoli, P. M. (2003). *Audience economics: Media institutions and the audience marketplace* (pp. x, 235). New York, NY: Columbia University Press.

Napoli, P. M. (2011). *Audience evolution: New technologies and the transformation of media audiences*. New York, NY: Columbia University Press.

Napoli, P. M. (2012). Audience evolution and the future of audience research. *JMM: The International Journal on Media Management*, *14*(2), 79–97.

Neff, J. (2017, January 5). Carlyle buys Claritas from Nielsen, installing team from Catalina Venture. *Advertising Age*. Retrieved from https://adage.com/article/datadriven-marketing/carlyle/307364/

Nelson, J. L., & Webster, J. G. (2016). Audience currencies in the age of big data. *JMM: The International Journal on Media Management*, *18*(1), 9–24.

Nielsen Media Research. (2008). Top TV ratings. *Nielsen Media Research*. Retrieved from http://www.nielsenmedia.com/nc/portal/site/Public/menuitem.43afce2fac27e890311ba0a347a062a0/?vgnextoid=9e4df9669fa14010VgnVCM100000880a260aRCRD

Nielsen Media Research. (2018, September 7). Nielsen estimates 119.9 million TV homes in the U.S. for the 2018–2019 TV season. Retrieved from http://www.nielsen.com/us/en/insights/news/2018/nielsen-estimates-119-9-million-tv-homes-in-the-us-for-the-2018-19-season

Rodriguez, A. (1997). Commercial ethnicity: Language, class and race in the marketing of the Hispanic audience. *The Communication Review*, *2*(3), 238–309.

Schiller, H. I. (1992). *Mass communications and American empire* (2nd ed.). Boulder, CO: Westview Press.

Smith, H., & Young, R. (2004, November 16). Is Wal-Mart good for America? *Frontline*. Retrieved from http://www.pbs.org/wgbh/pages/frontline/shows/walmart/

Smythe, D. W. (1977). Communications: Blindspot of Western Marxism. *Canadian Journal of Political and Social Theory*, *1*(3), 1–27.

Spangler, T. (2017, March 6). More U.S. households now have access to Netflix than a DVR. *Variety*. Retrieved from https://variety.com/2017/digital/news/netflix-dvr-us-households-survey-1202002673/

Steel, E. (2016, January 20). Nielsen to use Facebook and Twitter in new ratings system. *The New York Times*. Retrieved from https://www.nytimes.com/2016/01/20/business/media/nielsen-to-use-facebook-and-twitter-in-new-ratings-system.html

Steinberg, B. (2015, September 30). Media measurement madness: Can ComScore-Rentrak go toe-to-toe with Nielsen? *Variety*. Retrieved from https://variety.com/2015/tv/news/media-measurement-comscore-rentrak-nielsen-1201606166/

Steinberg, B. (2017, October 18). Nielsen says it will measure audiences for TV episodes that stream via Netflix. *Variety*. Retrieved from https://variety.com/2017/tv/news/nielsen-measurement-netflix-1202592985/

Story, L. (2008, February 26). Nielsen looks beyond TV and hits roadblocks. *The New York Times*. Retrieved from http://www.nytimes.com/2008/02/26/business/media/26nielsen.html?_r=1&oref=slogin&ref=media&pagewanted=print

Streeter, T. (1996). *Selling the air: A critique of the policy of commercial broadcasting in the United States*. Chicago, IL: University of Chicago Press.

Turow, J. (1997). *Breaking up America: Advertisers and the new media world*. Chicago, IL: University of Chicago Press.

Turow, J. (2006). *Niche envy: Marketing discrimination in the digital age*. Cambridge, MA: MIT Press.

Vyncke, P. (2002). Lifestyle segmentation: From attitudes, interests and opinions, to values, aesthetic styles, life visions and media preferences. *European Journal of Communication*, 17(4), 445–463.

Wasko, J. (2003). *How Hollywood works* (p. 248). London, England: SAGE.

Wasko, J. (2004). The political economy of communications. In J. D. H. Downing, D. McQuail, P. Schlesinger, & E. Wartella (Eds.), *The SAGE handbook of media studies* (pp. 309–329). Thousand Oaks, CA: SAGE.

Webster, J. G., Phalen, P. F., & Lichty, L. W. (2006). *Ratings analysis: The theory and practice of audience research—LEA's communication series* (3rd ed.). Mahwah, NJ: Lawrence Erlbaum Associates.

Webster, J. G., Phalen, P. F., & Lichty, L. W. (2014). *Ratings analysis: Audience measurement and analytics* (4th ed.). New York, NY: Routledge.

Williams, R. (1975). *Television: Technology and cultural form*. New York, NY: Schocken Books.

Yang, Y., & Coffey, A. J. (2014). Audience Valuation in the New Media Era: Interactivity, Online Engagement, and Electronic Word-of-Mouth Value. JMM: The International Journal on Media Management, 16(2), 77–103.

Audiences as Active Users of Media

Up to this point in the text, we have been examining media audiences primarily through the lenses of outside agents, considering audiences as they are imagined by scholars (in effects-oriented research), public opinion pollsters, advertisers, and media companies. As we have seen, these agents have different and sometimes competing motivations for "constructing" the audience, resulting in complex and sometimes contradictory characterizations. The theories in the previous two sections of the book also tend to objectify audiences and place them into neat conceptual categories. While these categories are useful for the purposes of systematic study, they are potentially limited in their ability to accurately capture the complexity of audience responses to media messages. These perspectives also tend to regard audiences as objects of media influence or control—as if audiences existed in a "null" state and were activated only when exposed to media stimuli. The upshot of these theories is that audiences are relatively powerless vis-à-vis media content and institutions to determine their own thoughts and behaviors.

This section of the book will outline a number of theories that ask not *what media do to people*, but rather *what people do with the media and why*. Instead of considering media audiences as inert entities that are activated in some way by media, uses and gratifications theory (Chapter 6), notions of audience interpretation (Chapter 7), and reception theory (Chapter 8) all consider audiences to be alert, active participants in their media use. These models operate under the assumption that viewers bring with them a preexisting set of beliefs, experiences, and expectations about what they hope to gain from watching a particular TV program or listening to a particular song. The usefulness of media choices does not stop at the individual, however. Active audience theories also explore how our immediate social environment—such as the presence of friends, family, or strangers—can shape our experiences with media at any particular point in time. Scholars using these "active audience" paradigms assume that individual audience members are the best source of data on their own decisions and actions. While active audience theories had been a part of audience research since the 1920s, they became increasingly visible in the scholarly literature beginning in the 1970s. As we'll see, the gist of audience theories began to focus more on notions of agency than on the structures that constrain audience responses.

CHAPTER 5

Uses and Gratifications

It is no secret that professional football generates tens of millions of dollars in annual economic activity in the United States. Vocal, passionate fans are an important part of the experience of attending a National Football League (NFL) game. Players like Tampa Bay Buccaneers receiver Mike Williams are accustomed to being booed and taunted by opposing fans during away games. However, at the start of the 2011 football season, Williams experienced something new. When his team played a preseason game in Kansas City against the Chiefs, Williams was greeted with a different kind of verbal assault from the sidelines. As Williams recounted to the *Tampa Tribune*, one Chiefs fan kept shouting at him: "I don't like you, Mike Williams, but I need you to play good because you're on my fantasy team" (Richardson, 2011). Along with their avid enthusiasm for professional sports, an increasing number of fans are participating in *fantasy sports leagues.* Fantasy sports allow fans to create mock teams of real-life players that can "compete for statistical advantage over other fake franchises" that are created by other fans (Schouten, 2011). Participants in fantasy sports leagues (many of whom wager money on their teams, something that has been specifically allowed by U.S. law) keep a watchful eye on the statistical performance of every player on their mock teams in order to compete against other fan-created teams. Approximately 32 million people ages 12 and over played some type of fantasy sports in 2010, representing a 60% increase since 2006 (Richardson, 2011). In 2008, fantasy sports generated about $1.9 billion in revenue, according to the Fantasy Sports Trade Association (Schouten, 2011).

Traditional sports fandom has been a major part of American culture for over a century, so what could account for the more recent rise in the appeal of fantasy sports? Instead of watching a game unfold on the field or on television, the drama of fantasy sports games plays out in the statistical charts listing individual players' performance after every game. What motivates so many people to seek out this type of imaginary play? Researchers Lee Farquhar and Robert Meeds (2007) surveyed 42 fantasy sports participants to find some answers to these questions. They discovered that fantasy sports motivations fell into one of two categories. Some fans participated in fantasy sports because they enjoyed following the statistical trends and expressed a desire to outsmart their opponents (the *surveillance* motivation). Others perceived fantasy sports as a game of chance and enjoyed the thrill of victory, though they were much less involved in the daily monitoring of sports statistics (the *arousal* motivation). They also noted that most fantasy sports enthusiasts are men between the ages of 18 and 34.

The Farquhar and Meeds study is a good example of the **uses and gratifications approach** to audience studies. Uses and gratifications theorists consider *how and why individuals use the media* rather than considering the ways in which they are acted upon by outside forces. The theory presupposes an engaged, creative audience that makes conscious decisions about media exposure. The development of this approach represented a key turning point in late 20th-century audience studies because it opened up new possibilities for considering media consumers as something other than objects of outside influence (see Chapter 2). Additionally, as we'll see in Chapters 6 and 7, the perceived deficiencies of uses and gratifications inspired audience researchers to explore new paradigms and methodologies.

Overview of the Chapter

This chapter outlines the theory of uses and gratifications by examining both historical and current research. We will first explore the genesis of uses and gratifications, beginning with the Payne Fund Studies in the 1930s and Herta Herzog's work on women radio listeners in the early 1940s. User-oriented inquiry into communication audiences reemerged in the late 1960s and early 1970s and developed into the "uses and gratifications" approach. This chapter outlines the main tenets of the theory, followed by an explanation of some important additions to the theory in the 1980s. Although uses and gratifications has been criticized by some as focusing too heavily on individual needs, we will explore how James Lull's family-oriented media studies expanded uses and gratifications to include the social aspects of media use. Finally, the uses and dependency model is explored, which once again trains the spotlight on the role of the media in generating some of the needs that individual audience members bring to their media experiences.

Early Examples of Uses and Gratifications in Communication Research

Like many theoretical traditions in academic research, the uses and gratifications approach to understanding audience behavior was identified and labeled as a distinct form of audience inquiry long after some of the first user-oriented studies of media reception had been completed. Many have traced the origin of this new theoretical direction to Elihu Katz's response to a 1959 editorial by communication scholar Bernard Berelson. In that article, Berelson put forth an incendiary hypothesis: that communication research was "withering away" and that "the great ideas that gave the field of communication research so much vitality ten and twenty years ago have to a substantial extent worn out. No new ideas of comparable magnitude have appeared to take their place" (Berelson, 1959, pp. 1, 6). A number of prominent communication scholars responded to Berelson's claims, including Elihu Katz. While others strongly disputed Berelson's conclusions about the state of crisis in the field, Katz (1959) agreed that perhaps the study of the potentially persuasive influence of media campaigns on audiences had indeed run its course. Katz argued that the field, in the wake of the abandonment of questions about corrosive media influence (see Chapter 2), should instead reframe issues of media power to more fully document the conditions under which individuals choose to consume particular types of media and media content. Instead of asking what the media do to the people, Katz reasoned, communication scholars should focus on *"what do people do with the media?"* (emphasis in original; 1959, p. 2). Katz essentially advocated a shift toward a more **functional audience inquiry**, asking *why* people chose to consume various media messages. His uses approach

> begins with the assumption that the message of even the most potent
> of the media cannot ordinarily influence an individual who has no
> "use" for it in the social and psychological context in which he lives.
> The "uses" approach assumes that people's values, their interests, their
> associations, their social roles, are prepotent and that people selectively
> "fashion" what they see and hear to those interests. (1959, pp. 2–3)

The shift advocated by Katz was a significant one. He argued that audiences bring their own sets of beliefs, values, and needs, some of which may be shaped by their social environment, to their media exposure.

Although his article gave this new thrust of inquiry a name, Katz noted that this kind of work was already ongoing in some corners of the field. Ironically, one of the scholars cited by Katz was Berelson himself, who conducted a study of how readers responded to a newspaper strike (Berelson, 1954). Other early uses studies cited by Katz included Cantril and Allport's book on radio audiences (1935), audiences for the *Professor Quiz* radio quiz show (Cantril, 1942; Herzog, 1940), and child comic book readers (Wolfe & Fiske, 1949). Perhaps the most widely remembered early uses studies of media audiences were those conducted by Herta Herzog (1941, 1944), who explored the uses of radio daytime serials for female listeners in the 1940s. Herzog's work has been subsequently cited by others as the genesis for a new realm of research on media use by audiences. However, the earliest type of user-oriented study in fact emerged out of the Payne Fund Studies of motion picture effects in the late 1920s.

Motion Picture Autobiographies and Media Motivations in the 1920s

Though generally not noted by scholars as such, perhaps the earliest example of a user-oriented perspective on media emerged out of the Payne Fund Studies, an academic endeavor with a decidedly effects-driven model of media influence (see Chapter 2 for a full discussion). While the findings of these studies raised the level of public concern about the persuasive and physical impacts of the movies, University of Chicago sociologist Herbert Blumer's contribution to the Payne Fund studies was slightly different. His contribution, published in 1933 as *Movies and*

Conduct, was notable because he eschewed the kind of "scientific" methods such as surveys and experiments that were used by other scholars in this research project (1933). Instead, Blumer solicited and collected written autobiographical statements from 1,115 college undergraduates and 583 high school students, asking them to write "life histories, describing the movies' impact on their developing emotional, social, and intellectual lives during childhood and adolescence" (Jowett, Jarvie, & Fuller, 1996, p. 237). Many of the responses that Blumer obtained indicated the degree to which motion pictures, and particularly the personalities of movie stars, infiltrated the daily lives of his adolescent subjects. Popular entertainment films, as Blumer learned from his participants, served as the focus of romantic fantasies, role modeling, and information about faraway people and places.

While the majority of these autobiographical narratives no longer exist, some that were written by Blumer's undergraduate students were preserved and have subsequently been published (Jowett et al., 1996). Upon reading the rich, original narratives written by these college students, the degree to which these individuals were actively choosing media content to suit their own needs and desires becomes clear. One male student describes his use of the movies to learn about social etiquette and how to behave with members of the opposite sex:

> I watched for the proper way in which to conduct oneself at a night club, because I began to have ideas that way. . . . The technique of making love to a girl received considerable of my attention, and it was directly through the movies that I learned to kiss a girl on her ears, neck and cheeks, as well as on the mouth, in a close huddle. (Jowett et al., 1996, pp. 278–279)

Though Blumer and the other Payne Fund scholars interpreted this as evidence of the power of the movies on impressionable young minds, the data he collected nevertheless foregrounded individual audiences' motivations for seeing popular movies. First, given free rein to talk about the role of the movies in their lives, the respondents reflected on how they used and understood movies in ways that suited their own desires and needs. As we will see, this is a distinct hallmark of the uses and gratifications approach. Second, rather than experiment on his students, Blumer asked them to offer their own reflections on their interpretations of the movies and how the movies affected them. Self-reports like these are also an important characteristic of the uses and gratifications approach.

Female Radio Serial Listeners in the 1940s

Perhaps the most oft-cited example of early uses and gratifications research emerged from the Office of Radio Research at Columbia University (which would later become the Bureau of Applied Social Research). This larger project on radio audiences was created by a grant from the Rockefeller Foundation in 1937 with the goal of studying "what radio means in the lives of listeners" (Lazarsfeld & Stanton, 1944, p. vii). The research was directed at quantitatively measuring the size of the radio audience and developing a technology for assessing audience reactions to a particular program. However, another aspect of these studies asked a different set of questions about the radio audience. Herta Herzog, a former student of Paul Lazarsfeld and one of the directors of the Radio Research project, brought together data about women radio listeners from four much larger studies of radio exposure (one of which was the study of the role of radio during the 1940 presidential election, published as *The People's Choice*, in 1948). She specifically gathered data on women's response to daytime radio serials (today these are called daytime soap operas; see Figure 5.1). Herzog's interests in the audience were quite different from the standard questions of the effects tradition. She wanted to know this:

> What satisfactions did listeners say they derive from daytime serials? As psychologists, what is our judgment on these assertions? . . . In addition to content analyses, then, we wish to examine the structure of the audience and the gratifications derived from daytime serials. (Herzog, 1944, p. 4)

Figure 5.1   Young Woman Tunes In to a Radio Program in the Early 1930s

Source: National Photo Company Collection.

Herzog's project aimed to answer two basic questions: What are the social characteristics of female daytime radio listeners? And what uses did these women have for these particular programs?

Herzog's initial guesses about these women were firmly rooted in the effects tradition. She hypothesized that women who listened regularly to daytime radio serials (1) would be isolated from their community due to the time they spent listening to the radio; (2) would exhibit a more narrow range of intellectual interests; (3) would be less interested in public affairs; (4) would be characterized by "anxieties and frustrations" about their life situations and would therefore turn to the radio for compensation; and (5) would tend to listen to the radio more in general than the rest of the population. In examining the responses from the different datasets that she gathered, Herzog found no differences between radio serial listeners and nonlisteners in their levels of social isolation, concern with public affairs, or levels of anxiety about their life situations. She concluded that "there is no vacuum in the lives of listeners for which they compensate by turning to daytime serial dramas" (Herzog, 1944, p. 8). The only differences in terms of range of intellectual interests that emerged between listeners and nonlisteners in the surveys were that women who regularly listen to radio serials preferred mystery novels over historical novels and were more likely to read magazines that have content that is "notably similar to that of the serial (the 'true story') or it centers on home life" (p. 8). Herzog linked women serial listeners' desire for more "confessional magazines" to their relatively low level of education and suggested that "these serials provide the more naïve individual with a much-desired, though vicarious, contact with human affairs which the more sophisticated person obtains at first hand through her wider range of experience" (pp. 8–9).

Herzog also noticed that radio serial listeners tended to use radio as a source of news and information over traditional print news sources (see Figure 5.2). But why would radio listeners favor that medium over newspapers and magazines? To answer that question, Herzog reanalyzed some of the data that she had gathered earlier as part of interviews with 100 female radio serial listeners in the New York City area (Herzog, 1941). Herzog posited three distinct "gratifications" for listening to radio serials. First, she argued that some listeners used these programs as a kind of "emotional release." Secondly, she noted that one of the central enjoyments of radio serials for women was the chance to engage in "wishful thinking"—or to fantasize—about others in order to fill gaps in their own personal lives or to "compensate for their own failures through the success pattern of the serials" (Herzog, 1944, p. 24). Thirdly, women listeners turned to radio serials as a source of advice, particularly regarding social etiquette.

The questions that Herzog asked about these women radio audiences were noteworthy because they explored *why* these programs appealed to specific women rather than *what these programs were potentially doing* to these women. Typical effects-style questions were reinterpreted here as questions about the utility of these programs to their listeners. Although Herzog herself was ultimately quite skeptical about the social utility of radio for these women (see Liebes, 2003), the shift from questions of widespread media influence to those regarding the utility of the media for individual viewers heralded an early shift toward a uses-oriented view of audience experience.

Figure 5.2 Sources of Political Information for Listeners and Nonlisteners of Radio Serials

Source of Information	Percentage for Listeners	Percentage for Nonlisteners
Radio	40.2	33.3
Newspapers and magazines	32.4	41.7
Friends and relatives	25.4	22.0
Public speakers and newsreels	2.0	3.0
Total percentages	100.0	100.0
Total number of cases	299.0	363.0

Source: Based on Herzog, H. (1944). What do we really know about daytime serial listeners? In P. F. Lazarsfeld & F. N. Stanton (Eds.), *Radio Research* 1942–1943 (pp. 3–33). New York, NY: Duell, Sloan & Pearce.

The Uses and Gratifications Approach

What distinguishes a uses and gratifications (U&G) approach to audiences from other types of inquiry? First and foremost, as the early studies demonstrate, the theory reorganizes the traditional notion of the media–audience relationship, which presupposes that media have some type of effect on the audience (usually in the form of some type of harmful influence). U&G reverses these roles, proposing instead that the audience members actively choose media channels and content to suit their own needs at a particular moment. Uses and gratifications takes an essentially *functional* **perspective on audience activity**. Functional theory looks to understand why people do what they do. It considers individuals to be rational, decision-making creatures whose actions can be understood within particular social contexts (see Wright, 1959, for an overview of this perspective in mass communication research). There are five basic assumptions of the uses and gratifications approach (Katz, Blumler, & Gurevitch, 1974, p. 21):

- The audience is considered *active*, and media use is directed toward particular goals of the individual.

- The audience member takes the lead in linking need gratification with specific media choices. In other words, the individual selects different types of media in order to satisfy a particular need or desire.

- Mass media compete with other sources of need satisfaction. If you were looking to relax, for example, you could watch TV, play Xbox 360, or have a conversation with a friend.

- Audience members are aware of their own individual needs and motivations in selecting certain media and are able to report their needs accurately to media researchers when asked.

- Scholars using the U&G approach do not make value judgments about peoples' media choices. Instead, they try to understand the audiences' orientation to certain media "on their own terms."

These five criteria distinguish uses and gratifications as a user-centered approach to understanding media audiences. Audiences are constructed here as thoughtful and purposive in their media use and self-aware enough to tell outside researchers why they have made particular media choices. The U&G approach is also sensitive to the social environment of audience members by realizing that some of the explanations for why people do what they do can be heavily influenced by their immediate social environment. For example, you might choose to watch a movie with a friend because you would like to spend time with that person, even though you have absolutely no interest in the film. You are choosing the watch the film, but for reasons that lie outside of its interest for you. We'll explore the social dimensions of media use later on in the chapter.

Israeli Media and Their Uses (Katz, Gurevitch, and Haas, 1973)

Early user-oriented audience studies were interesting examples of this new type of uses and gratifications research. However, they acted as "one-off" studies that did not attempt to map out a coherent theory. Even Katz's 1959 article suggesting the "uses" approach was only the kernel of an idea that could suggest future research. It was not until the early 1970s when studies designed specifically with the uses and gratifications framework were conducted (Katz et al., 1973; McQuail, Blumler, & Brown, 1972).

One of these early studies, by Elihu Katz and his colleagues, investigated audience uses for a number of different mass media. Katz et al. started with the notion that individuals bring to their media use a preexisting set of desires and expectations—what they termed *needs*. In order to come up with a list of these needs to better understand the use of media among audiences in Israel, they consulted the "(largely speculative) literature of the social and psychological functions of mass media" (Katz et al., 1973, p. 166). They organized these needs into five specific groups:

- Cognitive needs: Needs related to "strengthening information, knowledge, and understanding"

- Affective needs: Needs related to "strengthening aesthetic, pleasurable, and emotional experience"

- Integrative needs: Needs related to "strengthening credibility, confidence, stability, and status"

- Social needs: Needs related to "strengthening contact with family, friends, and the world"

- Escape: Needs related to escape or tension release, also "weaken[s] contact with self and one's social roles"

They then surveyed 1,500 Israelis, asking them to rate how well different forms of mass media (such as newspapers, books, radio, television, and films) satisfied each of these groups of needs. The results of this study indicated that different media fulfilled different kinds of needs. For individuals who made it a priority to closely follow national issues and affairs of state (cognitive needs), the medium most important to them was newspapers, followed by radio and television.[1] The media associated with self-integrative needs varied according to the specific type of need being gratified. For example, Katz et al. (1973) found that "knowing oneself" was best served through reading books, while television and the movies were best for "enjoying oneself." Television was often mentioned by subjects as a good way to kill time, but not to escape from reality; that was left to the magic of the movies.

Interestingly, Katz et al. (1973) examined the gratification derived from both media and nonmedia sources used to satisfy the five need groups outlined above. While some forms of mass media were more useful than others, the researchers discovered that, across the board, social contacts and connections were more gratifying than the mass media. Sources of gratification such as interactions with friends, family, and work colleagues emerged as critical alternatives to mass media. From this early study, then, social interaction emerged as a competitor for media in terms of need gratification.

Uses and Gratifications and the Notion of Needs

The concept at the core of the uses and gratifications approach is that of **needs**. The U&G approach maps out a series of logical steps that begins with the "social and psychological origins" of needs, which then "generates expectations" of the mass media, leading to "differential patterns of media exposure" and resulting in "need gratifications" along with other unintended consequences (Katz et al., 1974, p. 20). But what exactly is a need? There are lots of things that we may think we *need*—like the latest iPod or that shiny new sports car—but is a need something that we simply want, or is it something that we cannot survive without? This haziness about the concept of needs within the uses and gratifications approach has

---

[1]The importance of newspapers in distributing information could be a historical anomaly. The centrality of newspapers as a medium that satisfies cognitive needs of citizens is likely diminished in today's media environment. Not only are newspapers in the United States struggling to retain their readership, but new forms of continual "24/7" news sources such as the 24-hour cable news networks and the Internet have emerged to usurp the primacy of newspapers for new generations of information-hungry citizens.

been a catalyst for criticism of the theory from those who argue that it is vague and imprecise (Elliott, 1974; Katz, 1987; Lometti, Reeves, & Bybee, 1977).

The key to unlocking the notion of needs, argued Rosengren (1974) in one of the early books on uses and gratifications, was to turn to psychological literature. Rosengren noted that Abraham Maslow's (1970) theories of needs and human motivations could serve as the foundation for understanding how needs related to media uses. Maslow outlined a basic **need hierarchy** as the foundation for the motivation of all human beings, beginning with "physiological drives" that are necessary to maintain **homeostasis** ("the body's automatic efforts to maintain a constant, normal state of the blood stream"; 1970, p. 15). Once basic survival needs such as food, water, and shelter were met, he argued, new "higher order" needs would emerge for the individual (see Figure 5.3). These included *safety needs* (or "security; stability; dependency; protection; freedom from fear, anxiety, and chaos"), followed by *belongingness and love needs* (such as "giving and receiving affection"), *esteem needs* (a "desire for a stable, firmly based, usually high evaluation of themselves, for self-respect or self-esteem, and for the esteem of others") and *self-actualization needs* (which "refers to people's desire for self-fulfillment, namely, the tendency for them to become actualized in what they are potentially"; Maslow, 1970, pp. 20–22). Added to these higher-order needs were basic "cognitive needs," such as the desire to know and understand (pp. 23–24) and "aesthetic needs" (p. 25).

Rosengren (1974) took Maslow's theories as the starting point for understanding the uses and gratifications associated with media use. The fulfillment of some needs as a precondition for the satisfaction of other needs became a central tenet of the uses and gratifications paradigm. As Maslow argued,

> Our needs usually emerge only when more prepotent needs have been gratified. Thus gratification has an important role in motivation theory. Apart from this, however, needs cease to play an active determining or organizing role as soon as they are gratified. (1970, p. 30)

Rosengren (1974) added to this individualistic notion of needs intraindividual characteristics such as personality variables and extraindividual characteristics such as social position, along with other variables such as the structure of the media to arrive at a more complete paradigm for modeling how and why people choose different sorts of media.

Audience Activities and Media Motives

As some of the earliest research by Herzog and Katz, Gurevitch, and Haas demonstrated, individual media users bring their own needs to their media experiences. These needs, in turn, shape users' motivations for experiencing different kinds of media. But what kinds of motivations can shape audience decision-making about media? Early studies of media use proposed various typologies for

Figure 5.3 Maslow's Hierarchy of Needs

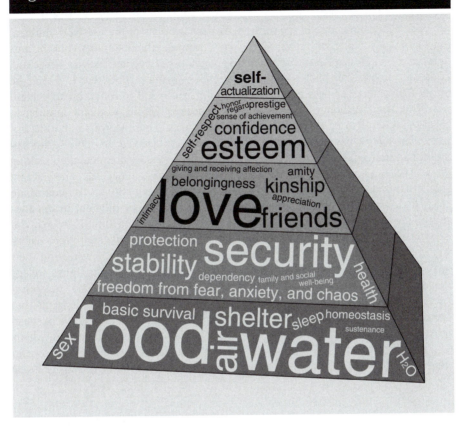

Source: Image created by Stephanie Plumeri Ertz from information in Maslow, A. H. (1970). *Motivation and Personality* (2nd ed., p. 20). Upper Saddle River, NJ: Pearson Education.

understanding the functions of media for audiences. Writing before the paradigm of uses and gratifications had been outlined by Katz, Harold Lasswell (1948) and Charles Wright (1960) identified four functions of the media for audiences: surveillance, correlation, entertainment, and socialization. Other scholars began adding dimensions to these media uses, including diversion, social relationships, personal identity (McQuail et al., 1972), reinforcement, guidance, relaxation, and alienation (McLeod & Becker, 1974). The plethora of media uses identified in these early efforts made the comparison of research studies with one another difficult at best. Was there a single, uniform set of media uses that cut across different kinds of media (such as movies, television, and newspapers, for example) and different types of content (news and entertainment)? As the scholarly community focusing on the uses and gratifications paradigm began to expand in the late 1970s and early 1980s, a flurry of research studies attempted to more systematically map out the motives underlying the audiences' media choices (Lometti et al., 1977; Perse, 1986; Rubin, 1983, 1984, 1985; Rubin & Perse, 1987).

Alan M. Rubin is one of the most recognized scholars in the uses and gratifications paradigm. Along with his students, he was among the first to map out the area of motives and their relationship to various media uses (see Haridakis & Whitmore, 2006). In a series of studies in the early 1980s (Rubin, 1983, 1984, 1985), he found that audiences' uses for television could be divided into two broad categories. **Ritualized audiences** tended to use TV more habitually, watching in order to consume time or to be diverted from other activities. These viewers often did not particularly care what type of television programs they viewed. In contrast, **instrumental audiences** would search for specific kinds of message content, often seeking out and selecting informational material in a purposive way, suggesting greater care and selectivity over media as well as increased involvement with the programming itself. In a large-scale survey of 1,836 college students in 11 different universities around the United States, Rubin (1985) asked about levels of daytime TV soap opera viewing, along with questions about how much students identified with the characters in the soaps, how religiously they watched, how satisfied they were with their own lives, and their level of social activity. Based upon the results, these college viewers' motives for watching TV soaps were separated into four broad categories: orientation, avoidance, diversion, and social utility (see Figure 5.4). Rubin found that viewers differed on their motives for watching TV according to their levels of social activity, life satisfaction, and affinity for soap operas. For instance, those individuals who tended to watch soap operas for avoidance or social utility were also those who were more involved with soap operas. These individuals also indicated lower levels

Figure 5.4 Motivations for Watching TV Soap Operas

Viewing Motive	Definition
Orientation	Reality-exploration; seek to understand how others think and act (understand others' ideas, motives, problems, lifestyles)
Avoidance	Escapism; avoid work or life; tension release; time consumption
Diversion	Entertainment; amusement; relaxation
Social utility	Companionship; convenience; seeking to meet and spend time with others and to acquire topics for conversation

Source: Rubin, A. M. (1985). Uses of Daytime Television Soap Operas by College Students. *Journal of Broadcasting & Electronic Media, 29*(3), 241–258.

of life satisfaction. This study, like other uses and gratifications research on both news and entertainment media, draws connections between media use motives and other attitudes or behaviors. For a more recent example of this type of study, see Box 5.1.

BOX 5.1
What Motivates Social Media Use?

If you're like most undergraduate students around the world, you probably have an online profile on one or more social networking sites like Facebook, Twitter, Instagram, WeChat, Weibo, or Snapchat. In a recent survey conducted by the Pew Research Center (Smith & Anderson, 2018), 80% of young people aged 18 to 24 reported using Facebook on a regular basis. This same age group reported high rates of usage for other social media as well: 78% for Snapchat, 71% for Instagram, 45% for Twitter, and a whopping 94% for YouTube. Most Americans in this survey reported that they used at least three different social media on a regular basis. While most Americans told pollsters that it would not be difficult to give up social media, a slim majority (51%) of those 18- to 24-year-old respondents noted that it would be hard to give up social media.

So what makes these forms of online social media so compelling that young people would find modern life challenging without it? If you were a media researcher trying to understand this phenomenon, you might ask these questions: Why do so many people use Facebook and other types of social media? What do they get out of it (in other words, what *gratifications* are obtained here)? Additionally, *how* do people tend to use social media?

An early uses and gratifications study among 77 undergraduate students at a large Canadian university asked just these types of questions with regard to their Facebook usage (Quan-Haase & Young, 2010). In a survey, these users were asked questions such as "What are the different reasons why you use Facebook?" They responded on a 5-point Likert-type scale (where 1 indicated *strongly disagree* and 5 indicated *strongly agree*). What did this study reveal about how and why undergraduate students use Facebook? Why did people create Facebook accounts in the first place? The researchers found that 85% of the respondents joined Facebook because a friend suggested it. Second, what particular *gratifications* were obtained through the use of Facebook? These undergraduates reported several different types of gratifications, such as social information ("to feel involved in what's going on with other people"), sharing problems (needing someone to talk to or be with), showing affection (thanking people and showing care for others), fashion (looking stylish or fashionable), sociability (to make friends), and as a pastime (for fun, entertainment, or to kill time). What's perhaps most intriguing here is that the gratifications that people derive from Facebook are inextricably linked to their ongoing, offline friendships—Facebook is a direct outgrowth of our physical, nondigital interpersonal relationships.

Source: Quan-Haase, A., & Young, A. L. (2010). "Uses and Gratifications of Social Media: A Comparison of Facebook and Instant Messaging." *Bulletin of Science, Technology & Society, 30*(5), 350–361. https://doi.org/10.1177/0270467610380009

Expectancy-Value
Approaches to Uses and Gratifications

As Maslow's theory suggests, gratifications are critical to the understanding of needs because human beings are continually assessing whether or not their particular needs have been met. If not, then one will seek out a new source of gratification. Until the 1970s however, the focus of much of the research was on developing lists of the kinds of needs that motivated individuals to turn to media, which left open the question of whether or not (and how) these needs were gratified (see, for example, Palmgreen & Rayburn, 1982; Levy & Windahl, 1984; Rayburn, 1996). In this case, the **gratifications sought (GS)** by an individual through media use is conceptually distinct from the **gratifications obtained (GO)** from the media use. You might think of this concept whenever you find yourself at the checkout at a grocery store and the cashier asks you, "Did you find everything you were looking for?" To put it in psychological terms, this question is all about whether the needs that you brought with you to the store (your desire to purchase every-thing on your list at prices within your budget) have been gratified by the store's offerings (the items in stock). Whether or not you have gratified a particular need at a specific moment (we'll call it Time 1) can have an impact on what your needs are and how you aim to gratify those needs in the immediate future (at Time 2). If you found everything you needed at the grocery store, in sufficient quantities and at the right price, you might then be more likely to shop there again when your need for groceries arises. This builds in an *expectation* of need gratification that develops and shifts over time—in the grocery store example, you now expect that store to have your favorite cereal. It is in essence a feedback loop: once you know where and how to fully satisfy a particular need, you are likely to continue to revisit that source to gratify the need in the future. One of the key trends in the development of uses and gratifications theory through the late 1970s was a focus on this expectancy-value aspect of individual searches for gratification (Palmgreen & Rayburn, 1985).

The focus of uses and gratifications scholars on making this distinction between gratifications sought and obtained was a direct outgrowth of advances in the psychology of human motivation in the 1970s. Fishbein and Ajzen's **expectancy-value theory** directly informed this new wrinkle in the U&G paradigm (1975). Expectancy-value theory states that individuals approach new situations and infor-mation with a built-in set of beliefs and expectations and that these expectations in turn shape motivations in these new situations. Fishbein and Ajzen argued that there are three kinds of beliefs: (1) *descriptive beliefs*, which are the result of direct observation by the individual; (2) *informational beliefs*, which are formed by accept-ing information from outside sources that has not been directly observed; and (3) *inferential beliefs*, which are those beliefs based upon characteristics of objects or facts (as opposed to being directly observed) but that are developed on the basis of logic, personal experiences, or stereotyping. Based upon these classifications of beliefs, an early expectancy-value study of news gratifications among college undergraduates proposed the following model:

$$GS_i = b_i e_i$$

Here, GS_i refers to the ith gratification sought from the media, which is found by measuring the belief (b_i) that the media contains a particular attribute or behavior and the evaluative outcome of that media experience (e_i; Palmgreen & Rayburn, 1982, p. 565). In their initial study using this model, Palmgreen and Rayburn found that students' beliefs about whether or not public television news contained valuable information about current events and the importance of this news to them were reasonably good predictors for their reported public TV news viewing behaviors. This initial study sparked a number of efforts during the 1980s to calculate the correlations between GS and GO. All of these research endeavors found moderately high correlations between the two, ranging from .40 to .60 (Rayburn, 1996, p. 153). These results supported the notion that individual media use is a kind of "feedback loop," where media users will predicate their future media decisions based upon their expectations of fulfilling their needs from those choices.

The results of these GS–GO studies also raised new questions from critics about the uses and gratifications paradigm. For starters, if expectations about the gratifications we are likely to receive from media exposure figure heavily in our decisions about our media use, then why weren't the correlations observed much higher, closer to 1.0 (a perfect correlation)? Additionally, the GS-GO conceptualization envisions a closed feedback loop. What happens if the media environment itself changes dramatically, either as a result of the invention of new technologies (like satellite television or the Internet) or as a result of the influence of friends or family during media exposure? These questions motivated further research into the social origins of our media uses and needs.

Social Uses of Media

As you have no doubt noticed thus far, scholars working within the uses and gratifications tradition place heavy emphasis on the role of the individual audience members' decision-making about their media exposure. Throughout the formative period of the paradigm (the 1970s and 1980s), a number of critics took aim at this fact and at some of the other tenets of the approach. One of the recurring criticisms was that the theory focused too exclusively on the motives of the *individual*. Critics argued that needs and motives are essentially locked inside each individual's mental process and thus impossible to observe from the outside, making the uses and gratifications approach somewhat "mentalistic" (Elliott, 1974). Because U&G relies upon the self-reports of individuals, information about individuals' inner states of mind is accurate only insofar as they can readily identify their needs and can recall them. Elihu Katz, one of the earliest proponents of the uses and gratifications approach, acknowledged and agreed with many of the criticisms of the paradigm, writing in 1987 that early studies "leaned too heavily on self-reports" and were "unsophisticated about the social origin of the needs that audiences bring to the media" (Katz, 1987, p. S37).

As Katz readily acknowledged, the entire process of measuring and defining needs is potentially fraught with error. In what Elliott (1974, p. 252) called the **static-abstraction problem**, uses and gratifications theory treats individual audience members' encounters with media as isolated from other social processes. While proponents of the paradigm readily acknowledge that media compete with other sources of need satisfaction (like taking a walk or lying in the sun, both of which might satisfy a need for relaxation), critics pointed out that the theory did not build in a larger social context for our choices and desires in the first place. In order for the paradigm of uses and gratifications to effectively map onto individuals' real-world experiences with media, the social origins of individual needs and their relationship with mass media would need to be more fully explored.

With this critique in mind, a number of scholars in the late 1970s and early 1980s began to consider the question of where our needs come from and how they might relate to our social environment. For example, one of the paradigm's founders and defenders argued that individuals' social positions and demographic characteristics (such as age, gender, and occupational status) had always been envisioned as one of the factors that shaped individuals' mass media uses (Blumler, 1985). Other scholars noted that individual needs were not static, but they shifted and developed over the course of a lifetime as individual maturation and the nature of our relationships with others changed (Dimmick, McCain, & Bolton, 1979; Rubin & Rubin, 1982). The use of mass media by children and adolescents in particular may be directly influenced by their parents and peers—in households where parents regularly read a newspaper, children may be more apt to regard information surveillance of public affairs to be an important need and may turn to newspapers to satisfy this need (Adoni, 1979). The key distinction between these studies and earlier conceptualizations of uses and gratifications was that later scholars identified individual need as a fluid construct. Needs develop over time as we mature from children to adults and are subject to more longer-term influences of parents, peers, and other social groups.

But what if these shifts in individual media-related needs occur not just over extended periods of time but also in different media exposure situations? For example, it is likely that students will choose to view different kinds of movies in their dorm rooms and apartments with friends than they perhaps would at home in the presence of their parents and other family members. The notion of media uses in this example is **situational and contextual**—that is, it changes according to the particular social and situational contexts in which the media use is taking place. This also takes some of the focus away from the physical media because our uses of media arise not only from psychological needs that can be gratified from media use directly but also from the social contact and relationship maintenance that occur *around* media use (therefore, not necessarily directly connected to the medium or medium content itself).

This concentration on the social environment of media-related need gratification became a touchstone for research into the uses of television within the family. James Lull, a communication doctoral student at the University of Wisconsin–Madison, expanded the boundaries of uses and gratifications research in his dissertation by examining the uses of television *at the moment the medium was being used* (Lull, 1976). Rather than have members of the 20 families participating in the study fill out surveys about their television use, Lull visited their homes, observing their interpersonal interactions and media use over a period of 3 to 7 days, taking copious notes on the kinds of activities and behaviors that surrounded television use.

There were a number of unique aspects to Lull's research on television uses and gratifications. First, he paid careful attention to the role that the social context of the family played in individuals' uses of the television, including which programs they chose to watch (Lull, 1978). This allowed him to consider the role that social interactions and interpersonal relationships played in shaping media uses. Secondly, he addressed the perennial problem of relying on self-reports from surveys (found in most U&G research) by using **ethnographic, participant observation methods** to study use of the television within the home. This methodological technique allowed Lull to observe, in a natural, domestic setting, patterns of television-viewing behavior. From these observations, he was able to reach his own conclusions about media uses, independent from his subjects' own self-assessments.

Lull discovered that the use of television within these domestic spaces was closely intertwined with family communication patterns. For example, gender roles were an important factor in program selection—fathers generally possessed the remote control and would guide the family's viewing choices[2] (Lull, 1978, 1982). Additionally, Lull noticed that the process of gratifying needs through television often had little to do with the content of the medium! Instead, family members often used the TV to achieve other kinds of goals, which were categorized into two general groups: structural uses and relational uses (see Figure 5.5). Television use could be *structural* when family members used it as background noise or for companionship when they were alone or even when they used it to break up other activities. Lull also noticed that family members used the television for *relational* uses, such as engaging other family members in conversation or as a means to reduce conflict. You may have had this experience as well. Can you remember a time when an argument you may have had with another family member was either delayed or defused because you decided to watch TV or surf the web? Lull's ethnographic observations of family television use added two important insights to the U&G paradigm: (1) that individual uses of television could be shaped by social relationships and interactions at the point of reception and (2) that the needs being gratified by television and other forms of media sometimes have more to do with the social relationships or immediate social environment than with any kind of gratification from the television itself.

---

[2]It should be noted here that the majority of homes in the late 70s and early 80s had only one television, typically located in a central family space such as a living room or den. Given the lack of alternative viewing options for family members, therefore, conflicts over channel choice were not uncommon.

Figure 5.5 Social Uses of Television

Structural Uses	
Environmental	Background noise; companionship; entertainment
Regulative	Punctuation of time and activity; talk patterns
Relational Uses	
Communication facilitation	Experience illustration; common ground; conversational entrance; anxiety reduction; agenda for talk; value clarification
Affiliation/ avoidance	Physical, verbal contact/neglect; family solidarity; family relaxant; conflict reduction; relationship maintenance
Social learning	Decision-making; behavior modeling; problem solving; value transmission; legitimization; information dissemination; substitute schooling
Competence/ dominance	Role enactment; role reinforcement; substitute role portrayal; intellectual validation; authority exercise; gatekeeping; argument facilitation

Source: Lull, J. (1980). "The Social Uses of Television." *Human Communication Research, 6*(3), 197–209.

Lull's research on family television use within the domestic context was part of a larger renaissance in qualitative, ethnographic research methods in the 1980s. Other scholars began to use these naturalistic techniques to study the uses and gratifications among media audiences in other settings as well. For example, participant observation studies by Lemish explored the social uses of television in public locations like bars, restaurants, retail stores, and even college dormitories (1982, 1985). As a result of observing and interviewing casual participants in several public spaces where television viewing occurred, Lemish noted that watching television in these spaces "is an established phenomenon in American culture through which communication rules, in general, and specific public viewing rules in particular are created, molded, and practiced" (1982, p. 778). Specifically, she found that participant viewers in these public spaces (1) negotiated the context or physical setting in which the television was situated, (2) adjusted or attempted to "fit in" with the other viewers, (3) adjusted to the television set and reacted to it in similar ways, and finally (4) allowed themselves to be open for television-related social interaction or conversation. Like Lull's work, these studies highlighted the importance of considering the social interactions at the point of reception, since they played an important role in shaping the gratifications that individuals obtained from the media.

The Uses and Dependency Approach
•••

The concluding paragraph of Katz, Gurevitch, and Haas's 1973 Israel study included a somewhat controversial claim. They argued that "media-related needs are not, by and large, generated by the media. Most predate the emergence of the media and, properly, ought to be viewed within the wider range of human needs" (Katz et al., 1973, p. 180). This was a logical statement, given Maslow's concept of human needs. Because the core of uses and gratifications is functionalist theory, the notion that needs can be artificially manufactured or socially generated through peer pressure is all but excluded from the basic premise of the approach. In other words, according to uses and gratifications, if an individual decides to view a "junk" television program, then there must be a real need that is being satisfied by that activity. As one critic noted, "The argument that use leads to the gratification of needs is at best circular and at worst imprisons research within a stable of functional interdependencies from which there is no escape" (Elliott, 1974, p. 253). Indeed, what about the possibility that the media could mold and shape our needs? The conviction that media messages can shape human needs certainly motivates the advertising and marketing industries to invest billions each year to persuade audiences to drive a specific car or to purchase a particular brand of toothpaste. What about the concept of *effects*? Are uses and gratifications and theories of media effects incompatible?

The criticism that early U&G studies precluded the possibility of media effects catalyzed perhaps another reorientation of the uses and gratifications paradigm. This new approach, dubbed **uses and dependency** by its founders (Ball-Rokeach & DeFleur, 1976), considered media-related needs not as innate survival mechanisms, but instead as learned behaviors that are "the product of social experience" (Elliott, 1974, p. 255). Uses and dependency theory placed effects back in the center of the discussion about media, positing that any potential impacts were the result of complex interrelationships between the media, audiences, and society. In their original outline of this idea, Ball-Rokeach and DeFleur argued that individuals actively seek out media information (consistent with uses and gratifications theory), but when an individual's need satisfaction relies almost completely on the media—during times of "structural instability in the society due to conflict and change"—then media can have a more pronounced ability to alter the audience's beliefs, attitudes, and behavior (1976, p. 5).

The notion of media dependency was later formally proposed as an all-inclusive model of media uses and effects by Rubin and Windahl (1986). These scholars argued that the notion of dependency addressed many of the previous critiques of the uses and gratifications model by considering the role of gratifications obtained by the media (thereby incorporating the GS–GO perspective and the notion of time) and the role of society in shaping individual needs and desires that were obtained from the media. As you can see in Figure 5.6, Rubin and Windahl's model of uses and dependency suggests that there are numerous factors that can affect individuals' media usage over time, including the availability of alternatives

Figure 5.6   The Uses and Dependency Model of Mass Communication

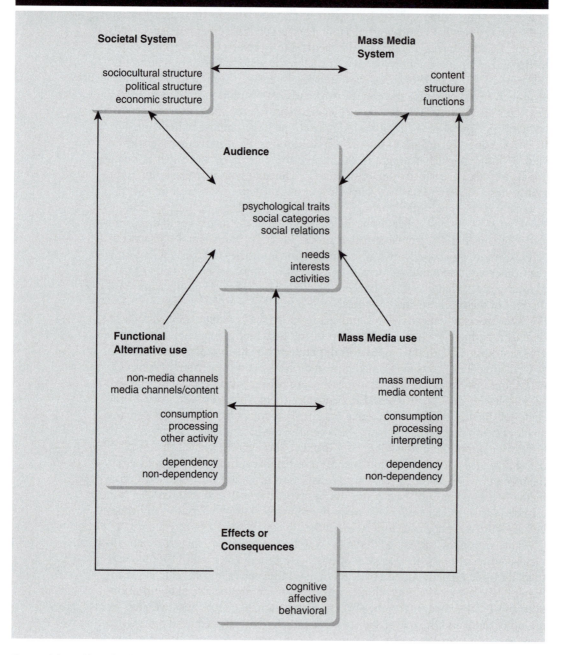

Source: Adapted from Rubin, A. M., & Windahl, S. (1986). "The Uses and Dependency Model of Mass Communication." *Critical Studies in Mass Communication, 3*(2), 184–199. Redrawn by Stephanie Plumeri Ertz.

to the media, social structure, historical events (such as a national crisis), an individual's past media use, and the degree to which that person relies upon the media for gratification. Over time, through the process of continual feedback, a particular medium or type of content can become a recurring source of need gratification so that the individual may not even consider or seek out alternative sources of gratification. Media use then becomes highly *ritualized* and *habitual*. For those who get stuck in this particular "rut," so to speak, the effects of mass media on their attitudes and behaviors may be much more pronounced than among more casual or instrumental audiences.

The uses and dependency approach merges two major perspectives with very different views of audience power: the effects paradigm, which envisions media as a force that acts upon audience members, and the uses and gratifications paradigm, which considers audiences as active decision-makers who select media choices to suit their own needs. Because the uses and dependency relationship between audiences and the media is *contingent*—that is, the potential effects of media may be quite different depending upon the degree to which individuals rely on the media to gratify their needs—the theory suggests *selective effects* of media on some people under some conditions. Although the interrelationship between uses, effects, and social contexts of media has been widely accepted in the field, there have been only a handful of studies that have empirically tested Rubin and Windahl's model. For example, a study by Sun, Chang, and Yu (2001) of Chinese newspaper readers asked respondents which newspaper they read the most, which they liked, and which newspaper they bought on a regular basis. Their results demonstrated that Chinese readers were generally dependent on the state-run newspapers because of their availability. However, as the state began to relax restrictions on the media, the researchers found that this dependency relationship diminished. Another study of college-aged Mormon undergraduates at Brigham Young University (Davies, 2007) found that those respondents who tended to strongly identify with the teachings of Mormonism (which is highly critical of violent and sexual content on television) were less likely to be dependent on television as a source of relaxation and stress relief, while those who spent more time alone and did not strongly identify themselves with Mormonism were more likely to turn to television as a source of need gratification. These results suggest some support for the uses and dependency model, though the highly particularized populations used in these studies suggest that this paradigm needs to be tested more rigorously.

Conclusion: Refocusing on Audience Power
• •

In this chapter, we have explored the numerous iterations of the uses and gratifications paradigm from the earliest research on media uses in the 1930s to the defining period of this perspective in the 1970s and 1980s. By insisting that the individual audience member, not the media, was the starting point for analysis, the uses and gratifications paradigm marked a significant change from more traditional notions of media effects. Individual needs, whether they be for information, emotional response, relating to others, strengthening our self-confidence, or escaping our daily reality, constitute the central focus of this research tradition. To shore up the potential conceptual fuzziness of the notion of "needs," scholars turned to motivation research in psychology and argued that need gratification is the central force behind our desires and actions. As this chapter has outlined, some of the critiques of the theory—its overemphasis on individual choice as the sole motivator in media selection, the absence of social factors in the shaping of those choices, and the reliance on self-reports in the data collection process—have led to important refinements. The feedback loop between gratifications sought and gratifications obtained along with Lull's research on the social uses of television and the role of contexts in shaping media uses are two important additions that have more fully captured the complexity of audiences' interactions with media.

What does this theory tell us about the relative power of the audience vis-à-vis media producers? Due to its logical outgrowth from functionalist theory in sociology, the locus of control in uses and gratifications lies squarely with the audience. Whether the audience searches for information or entertainment, members' needs are paramount in determining the role of media in their everyday lives. As we have seen in this chapter, however, the privileging of the audience's power leaves room for critique of the theory on the grounds that other social factors, such as prior media experiences, immediate social environment, and larger social forces, can also shape our needs. The uses and dependency model, while addressing some of the criticisms of uses and gratifications, also draws the possibility of media effects and long-term cultivation of attitudes back into this user-centered paradigm. If our needs are generated by forces outside of our own control, does this raise the specter of vast media power once again? Given the relatively small corpus of empirical scholarship on the uses and dependency model, more extensive research is required in order to provide a satisfactory answer to this question.

DISCUSSION ACTIVITIES

1. Construct a brief uses and gratifications survey to administer to your peers in the class. The survey will ask the participants to reflect upon what media they use for particular kinds of needs and why. Some questions might include the following:

   • What types of media have you used in the last 48 hours?

   • Were you looking for some specific kinds of content or a specific experience through your media use? If so, what were you looking for and why? If not, why did you decide to use this media?

   • Did you get what you hoped for or expected? Why or why not?

- What kind of need do you think this activity fulfilled for you?

Once you're done with this informal survey, compare your results with those of others in the class. Do you see some similarities in the types of media needs and the kinds of media that gratify those needs? What might we conclude about which needs are best served by which types of mass media?

2. Advertising attempts to persuade us to purchase certain products or services by linking the product to an audience need or desire. Randomly select an hour's worth of television programming and take a close look at the advertising you see during that hour. What kinds of product appeals are being made in these commercials? What types of *needs* are being associated with products, and are they needs that directly relate to the product itself? Use Katz, Gurevitch, and Haas's (1973) five categories of needs to help

you decide which needs are being discussed in these advertisements.

3. Audience researcher danah boyd has compiled an extensive online bibliography of research related to online social networking sites like Facebook and Twitter (http://www.danah.org/researchBibs/sns.php). Access her list and select one study to read and analyze. Once you have read the study, answer and discuss the following questions:

- What types of uses are associated with the technology? What method(s) did the scholar use to gather data on audience uses?

- What types of impacts (if any) on offline social relationships were found by the researcher in your article?

- Are the results that you found similar or different from those found by Quan-Haase and Young (Box 5.1 in this chapter)?

ADDITIONAL MATERIALS

Blumler, J. G., & Katz, E. (1974). *The uses of mass communications: Current perspectives on gratifications research.* Beverly Hills, CA: SAGE.

Boyd, D. (2012). Bibliography of research on social network sites. Available at http://www.danah.org/researchBibs/sns.php

H2G2 Online. The uses and gratifications model of the media. Available at http://h2g2.com/dna/h2g2/A770951

Matei, S. A. (2010). What can uses and gratifications theory tell us about social media? University of Purdue. Available at http://matei.org/ithink/2010/07/29/what-can-uses-and-gratifications-theory-tell-us-about-social-media/

The Media Insider. (2016). *Why do we watch TV? Uses and gratification theory explained.* Retrieved from https://www.youtube.com/watch?v=aopqPs7rb_Q

Rathnayake, C., & Winter, J. S. (2018). Carrying forward the uses and grats 2.0 agenda: An affordance-driven measure of social media uses and gratifications. *Journal of Broadcasting & Electronic Media, 62*(3), 371–389.

Rubin, A. M. (2009). The uses-and-gratifications perspective of media effects. In J. Bryant & M. B. Oliver (Eds.), *Media effects: Advances in theory and research* (3rd ed., pp. 165–184). New York, NY: Routledge.

REFERENCES

Adoni, H. (1979). The functions of mass media in the political socialization of adolescents. *Communication Research, 6*(1), 84–106.

Ball-Rokeach, S. J., & DeFleur, M. L. (1976). A dependency model of mass-media effects. *Communication Research, 3*(1), 3–21.

Berelson, B. (1954). What "missing the newspaper" means. In P. F. Lazarsfeld & F. N. Stanton (Eds.), *Communication Research 1948–1949* (pp. 111–129). New York, NY: Harper.

Berelson, B. (1959). The state of communication research. *Public Opinion Quarterly, 23*(1), 1–6.

Blumer, H. (1933). *Movies and conduct.* New York, NY: Macmillan.

Blumler, J. G. (1985). The social character of media gratifications. In K. E. Rosengren, L. A. Wenner, & P. Palmgreen (Eds.), *Media gratifications research: Current perspectives* (pp. 41–59). Beverly Hills, CA: SAGE.

Cantril, H. (1942). Professor quiz: A gratifications study. In P. F. Lazarsfeld & F. N. Stanton (Eds.), *Radio Research 1941* (pp. 34–45). New York, NY: Duell, Sloan & Pearce.

Cantril, H., & Allport, G. (1935). *The psychology of radio.* New York, NY: Harper.

Davies, J. J. (2007). Uses and dependency of entertainment television among Mormon young adults. *Journal of Media & Religion, 6*(2), 133–148.

Dimmick, J. W., McCain, T. A., & Bolton, W. T. (1979). Media use and the life span: Notes on theory and method. *American Behavioral Scientist, 23*(1), 7–31.

Elliott, P. (1974). Uses and gratifications research: A critique and a sociological alternative. In J. G. Blumler & E. Katz (Eds.), *The uses of mass communications: Current perspectives on gratifications research* (pp. 249–268). Beverly Hills, CA: SAGE.

Farquhar, L. K., & Meeds, R. (2007). Types of fantasy sports users and their motivations. *Journal of Computer-Mediated Communication, 12*(4), 1208–1228. doi:10.1111/j.1083-6101.2007.00370.x

Fishbein, M., & Ajzen, I. (1975). *Belief, attitude, intention, and behavior: An introduction to theory and research.* Reading, MA: Addison-Wesley.

Haridakis, P. M., & Whitmore, E. H. (2006). Understanding electronic media audiences: The pioneering research of Alan M. Rubin. *Journal of Broadcasting & Electronic Media, 50*(4), 766–774.

Herzog, H. (1940). Professor quiz: A gratification study. In P. F. Lazarsfeld & F. N. Stanton (Eds.), *Radio and the printed page* (pp. 64–93). New York, NY: Duell, Sloan & Pearce.

Herzog, H. (1941). On borrowed experience. *Studies in Philosophy and Social Science, 9,* 65–95.

Herzog, H. (1944). What do we really know about daytime serial listeners. In P. F. Lazarsfeld & F. N. Stanton (Eds.), *Radio Research 1942–1943* (pp. 3–33). New York, NY: Duell, Sloan & Pearce.

Jowett, G., Jarvie, I. C., & Fuller, K. H. (1996). *Children and the movies: Media influence and the Payne Fund controversy—Cambridge studies in the history of mass communications* (p. 414). New York, NY: Cambridge University Press.

Katz, E. (1959). Mass communication research and the study of popular culture: An editorial note on a possible future for this journal. *Studies in Public Communication, 2*(1), 1–6.

Katz, E. (1987). Communications research since Lazarsfeld. *The Public Opinion Quarterly, 51,* S25–S45.

Katz, E., Blumler, J. G., & Gurevitch, M. (1974). Utilization of mass communication by the individual. In J. G. Blumler & E. Katz (Eds.), *The uses of mass communications: Current perspectives on gratifications research* (pp. 19–32). Beverly Hills, CA: SAGE.

Katz, E., Gurevitch, M., & Haas, H. (1973). On the use of the mass media for important things. *American Sociological Review, 38*(2), 164–181.

Lasswell, H. D. (1948). The structure and function of communication in society. In L. Bryson (Ed.), *The communication of ideas* (pp. 37–51). New York, NY: Harper.

Lazarsfeld, P. F., & Stanton, F. N. (Eds.). (1944). *Radio Research, 1942–1943*. New York, NY: Duell, Sloan & Pearce.

Lemish, D. (1982). Rules of viewing television in public places, *Journal of Broadcasting & Electronic Media, 26*(4), 757–781.

Lemish, D. (1985). Soap opera viewing in college: A naturalistic inquiry. *Journal of Broadcasting & Electronic Media, 29*(3), 275–293.

Levy, M. R., & Windahl, S. (1984). Audience activity and gratifications: A conceptual clarification and exploration. *Communication Research, 11*(1), 51–78. doi: 10.1177/009365084011001003

Liebes, T. (2003). Herzog's "On Borrowed Experience": Its place in the debate over the active audience. In E. Katz, J. D. Peters, T. Liebes, & A. Orloff (Eds.), *Canonic texts in media research: Are there any? Should there be? How about these?* (pp. 39–54). Cambridge, United Kingdom: Polity Press.

Lometti, G. E., Reeves, B., & Bybee, C. R. (1977). Investigating the assumptions of uses and gratifications research. *Communication Research, 4*(3), 321–338.

Lull, J. (1976). *Mass media and family communication: An ethnography of audience behavior*. Doctoral dissertation, University of Wisconsin–Madison.

Lull, J. (1978). Choosing television programs by family vote. *Communication Quarterly, 26*(4), 53–57.

Lull, J. (1980). The social uses of television. *Human Communication Research, 6*(3), 197–209.

Lull, J. (1982). How families select television programs: A mass-observational study. *Journal of Broadcasting & Electronic Media, 26*, 801–811.

Maslow, A. H. (1970). *Motivation and personality* (2nd ed.). Upper Saddle River, NJ: Pearson Education.

McLeod, J. M., & Becker, L. B. (1974). Testing the validity of gratification measures through political effects analysis. In J. G. Blumler & E. Katz (Eds.), *The uses of mass communications: Current perspectives on gratifications research* (pp. 137–164). Beverly Hills, CA: SAGE.

McQuail, D., Blumler, J. G., & Brown, R. (1972). The television audience: A revised perspective. In D. McQuail (Ed.), *Sociology of Mass Communication* (pp. 135–165). London, England: Longman.

Palmgreen, P., & Rayburn, J. D. (1982). Gratifications sought and media exposure: An expectancy value model. *Communication Research, 9*(4), 561–580. doi: 10.1177/009365082009004004

Palmgreen, P., & Rayburn, J. D. (1985). An expectancy-value approach to media gratifications. In K. E. Rosengren, L. A. Wenner, & P. Palmgreen (Eds.), *Media gratifications research: Current perspectives* (pp. 61–72). Beverly Hills, CA: SAGE.

Perse, E. M. (1986). Soap opera viewing patterns of college students and cultivation. *Journal of Broadcasting & Electronic Media, 30*, 175–193.

Quan-Haase, A., & Young, A. L. (2010). Uses and gratifications of social media: A comparison of Facebook and instant messaging. *Bulletin of Science, Technology & Society, 30*(5), 350–361. https://doi.org/10.1177/0270467610380009

Rayburn, J. D. (1996). Uses and gratifications. In D. W. Stacks & M. B. Salwen (Eds.), *An integrated approach to communication theory and research* (pp. 97–119). Mahwah, NJ: Lawrence Erlbaum Associates.

Richardson, A. S. (2011, September 5). Fantasy leagues spike interest. *The Tampa Tribune*, p. 1. Tampa, FL.

Rosengren, K. E. (1974). Uses and gratifications: A paradigm outlined. In J. G. Blumler & E. Katz (Eds.), *The uses of mass communications: Current perspectives on gratifications research* (pp. 269–286). Beverly Hills, CA: SAGE.

Rubin, A. M. (1983). Television uses and gratifications: The interactions of viewing patterns and motivations. *Journal of Broadcasting & Electronic Media*, 27(1), 37–51.

Rubin, A. M. (1984). Ritualized and instrumental television viewing. *The Journal of Communication*, 34(3), 67–77.

Rubin, A. M. (1985). Uses of daytime television soap operas by college students. *Journal of Broadcasting & Electronic Media*, 29(3), 241–258.

Rubin, A. M., & Perse, E. M. (1987). Audience activity and television news gratifications. *Communication Research*, 14(1), 58–84.

Rubin, A. M., & Rubin, R. B. (1982). Contextual age and television use. *Human Communication Research*, 8(3), 228–244.

Rubin, A. M., & Windahl, S. (1986). The uses and dependency model of mass communication. *Critical Studies in Mass Communication*, 3(2), 184–199.

Schouten, F. (2011, October 18). Fantasy sports enter political arena. *USA Today*. Washington, DC. Retrieved from http://www.usatoday.com/NEWS/usaedition/2011-10-19-Fantasy-Lobbying_ST_U.htm

Smith, A., & Anderson, M. (2018). *Social media use 2018: Demographics and statistics*. Washington, DC: Pew Research Center. Retrieved from http://www.pewinternet.org/2018/03/01/social-media-use-in-2018/

Sun, T., Chang, T., & Yu, G. (2001). Social structure, media system, and audiences in China: Testing the uses and dependency model. *Mass Communication & Society*, 4(2), 199–217.

Wolfe, K. M., & Fiske, M. (1949). Why children read comics. In B. Berelson, P. F. Lazarsfeld, & F. N. Stanton (Eds.), *Communication research, 1948–1949*. New York, NY: Harper.

Wright, C. R. (1959). *Mass communication: A sociological perspective*. New York, NY: Random House.

Wright, C. R. (1960). Functional analysis and mass communication. *Public Opinion Quarterly*, 24(4), 605–620.

CHAPTER 6

Interpreting and Decoding Mass Media Texts

One of the more popular programs on the basic cable TV service The Learning Channel (TLC) in the mid-2000s was a reality TV series called *Jon & Kate Plus 8*. The program followed the day-to-day challenges of Jon and Kate Gosselin, a suburban couple whose attempts to conceive one more child following the birth of twins resulted in sextuplets. While the original premise of the show was to provide a lighthearted diary of the couple's daily life, the program became tabloid fodder in late 2008 (two seasons into the show) when the celebrity status of the parents and the daily strain of the cameras began to take a toll on the couple's marriage.[1] Soon, reports of an impending marital breakdown appeared regularly in gossip columns, in supermarket tabloids, and on entertainment news programs. When the episode documenting the couple's decision to separate was finally aired on June 22, 2009, the audience for the basic cable program spiked to a record-breaking 10.6 million viewers, the largest audience in the history of TLC (Stelter, 2009).

While the splashy tabloid covers and intense publicity surrounding this celebrity couple were certainly attention-grabbing, one fascinating aspect of this reality TV breakup was the intensity and diversity of viewers' responses. Individuals posted hundreds of messages about the episode and what they thought about it on blogs, comment sections of newspapers, and the official TLC website for the program itself:

> What a sad day for the institution of marriage and the lives of Jon, Kate and their family. Marriage is supposed to be a lifetime commitment— we all took the vow "in good times and in bad." People don't seem to remember that vow. Marriage as in life has its ups and downs, its good times and bad times. When we hit a bad patch in life do we pack it in and give up? No, we weather through it, work things out and emerge better for the experience—marriage is no different.

> This family was destroyed by the quest for fame. When Kate Gosselin started referring to traveling around the country hawking books about how "we're just a regular family" while earning untold amounts of

---

[1] In a fascinating case of history repeating itself, the breakdown of the Gosselin's marriage in the midst of a reality TV series harkens back to the first reality TV program called *An American Family*, which was a 1973 PBS program that followed the everyday lives of a suburban family in California, the Louds. During the course of the series, the Louds separated, and one of their sons, Lance, revealed on national television that he was gay (for more information, see Conan, 2009; Ruoff, 2001).

money from a TV show as "her work," and making comments about how she'd like a talk show, I knew the marriage wasn't going to work out. Her priorities are just in the wrong place.

Voyeurism and child abuse for profit.

This is VERY sad. I must say, I could see it coming, but I was hoping with all of my heart that the two of you could work things out. My parents divorced when I was a child, and it was very, very traumatic for me. Now, 15 years later, I am still dealing with the pain of it. I must admit, however, that divorce was the best option in my parents' case. The constant arguing, fighting, crying and seeing my mother SO depressed was really wearing on me. I remember I used to write her "Daily Messages" that would have something I loved about her or something silly to cheer her up. Anyways, divorce is very difficult on a family, it does have the potential to mess these kids up for the rest of their lives, or it could be a relatively easy transition. The thing that killed me the most was although my father said he would always be there, he just bailed. I never heard from him or saw him again.

Hey folks, it is what it is, watch it or not, it's what TLC wants. Drama! It's all about money, and nothing else. The kids are screwed, Jon and Kate got loads of money, and ya know what for the rest of us? Life goes on, get over it, it's entertainment either way. (Stelter, 2009)

Source: Stelter, B. (2009, June 23). "Jon and Kate" Split-Up Draws Record-Breaking Audience. *The New York Times.* Retrieved from http://mediadecoder.blogs.nytimes.com/2009/06/23/jon-and-kate-split-up-draws-record-breaking-audience/?scp=10&sq=jon%20and%20kate&st=cse

As you can see from this small sample, audience members' interpretations of the show ranged widely. Viewers were saddened by the couple's divorce, critical of either Jon or Kate as the reason for the separation, and critical of the TLC network for being voyeuristic and exploiting the personal tragedy of a family. Some people familiar with the program felt that they could relate to the trials of Jon and Kate due to experiences with divorce in their own lives, while others (see the last response) were deeply ambivalent about the entire reality show genre, dismissing it as no more than cheap exploitation of individuals' lives for viewership and profit.

How can we possibly understand these diverse and potentially conflicting audience responses to *Jon & Kate*? One might simply suggest that each individual is entitled to his or her opinion, so there will naturally be as many different interpretations of *Jon & Kate* as there are viewers. Such a conclusion, however, denies the analytical possibility that individuals' interpretations of mass media may be connected in some way. This sort of epistemological stance hardly appeals to scholars and media theorists. What if there were similarities in audiences' understandings of media content? What would account for these similarities and how could we better understand *patterns* among certain types of audiences in their reactions to mediated content? These questions are the focus of this chapter, which will provide an overview of theories of media interpretation. Like the uses and gratifications theories we explored in Chapter 5, scholars of media interpretation take as a given the notion of media audiences as actively engaged with media technologies. What distinguishes media interpretation from other uses-oriented theories of audiences is that the main concern shifts here to the *content* of the media. Rather than ask what *motivates* audiences to select media content, scholars of media interpretation look even more closely at how audiences respond to *specific aspects of media content*.

Overview of the Chapter

This chapter will focus on audience interpretations of popular media. We will begin with semiotics, the study of significant signs in society. Semiotics explores how individuals come to understand their reality through the creation and use of signs. This approach became central in the work of cultural studies scholar Stuart Hall, who focused on the process of audiences' "decoding" of media texts. As we will see in this chapter, Hall's work was the intellectual spark that launched a number of important studies in the 1980s that linked social class, gender, and race with specific media interpretations (Ang, 1985; Jhally & Lewis, 1992; Morley, 1980; Radway, 1984). The notion of audience choice and activity was pushed even further in the late 1980s, when scholars considered audience interpretation as a kind of liberation from the media text, leading some to ask whether or not the original media text even mattered anymore (Fiske, 1987). Toward the end of chapter, we will examine the legacy of these vigorous debates about the relative power of the audience to interpret media content by examining recent comparative work on popular TV programs such as *Friends, The Cosby Show, The Simpsons*, and *The Bold and the Beautiful*. We'll also consider how theories of audience interpretation are being reimagined in a digital era.

The Rise of Critical Cultural Studies

In order to contextualize the discussion about interpretation later in the chapter, it is necessary to explore the rise of critical cultural studies in the 1980s. The study of media audiences underwent two important shifts during this time period. The first was a theoretical shift toward a more **critically oriented approach to audience reception** of media. In the late 1970s and early 1980s, the rising prominence of the uses and gratifications perspective led some to question some of its basic tenets: Were media audiences truly as autonomous as the uses and gratifications perspective imagined? In an influential essay in the early 1980s titled "The Rediscovery of 'Ideology': Return of the Repressed in Media Studies," British cultural studies scholar Stuart Hall (1982) argued that a major shift was under way from a "behavioralist" paradigm (the underlying assumption of theories such as uses and gratifications) to a more critical approach to media and culture. The key drawback of the mainstream behavioralist approach, he explained, was its inextricable link to the methodological and conceptual limitations of positivistic social science. Hall reasoned that the focus on immediate, short-term effects of communication messages on individuals ignored historical shifts, questions of power and social domination, and the role of economic and other institutions on social structures. These larger issues simply did not fit into the theoretical framework of behavioralism. Additionally, since the dominant view considered communication as a process of *transmission* from a message source to a receiver, questions about specific engagements with the *content* of media texts were also left unaddressed. What if individuals made alternative and radical reinterpretations of media messages? Were only those on the margins of society engaged in this type of activity, or were challenges to the institutional authority of media a common occurrence among those receiving media content? Questions about the relative autonomy of the audience vis-à-vis the dominant ideologies found in mainstream media texts (also dubbed the "incorporation/resistance" paradigm) became the focal point for discussion and debate among critical media scholars in the 1980s (Abercrombie & Longhurst, 1998, p. 15).

The second shift was methodological: Rather than relying upon surveys and other forms of self-reporting to ascertain how audiences were digesting media, critical **media scholars began adopting the technique of *ethnography*** from the sociological and anthropological disciplines. This had two important consequences. First, researchers were freed from relying upon the self-reports of research subjects, allowing them to distance themselves from their subjects and critically analyze individuals' media consumption behaviors. In addition, the use of ethnography was also a conscious political choice for some researchers. This form of study offered audiences the opportunity to speak for themselves, instead of having their voice and sense of agency suppressed by institutional market research and scholarly investigation. Scholar Ann Gray noted that her use of qualitative observations and interviews "was often motivated by a desire to allow participants to have some say in the research agenda" (1999, p. 32). Ethnographic methods were not without their complications. Scholars' interpretation of observed audience behaviors and interview responses required them to insert themselves into the research process. This raised some interesting issues about the extent of audience autonomy from the media text.

Interpretation and Semiotics

The key to comprehending the notion of interpretation is to first understand how the process of communicating ideas and experiences takes place. We use *signs* to help us achieve understanding with one another. The systematic study of signs and their significance in society is called **semiotics**. Semiotics has also been referred to as "the study of everything that can be used for communication: words, images, traffic signs, flowers, music, medical symptoms, and much more. Semiotics studies the way such 'signs' communicate and the rules that

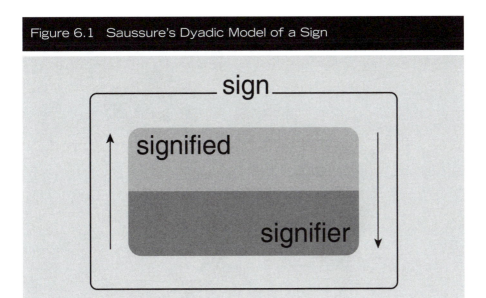

Figure 6.1   Saussure's Dyadic Model of a Sign

sign
signified
signifier

Source: Adapted from de Saussure, Ferdinand 1983): *Course in General Linguistics* (trans. Roy Harris). London: Duckworth. Found at http://www.aber.ac.uk/media/Documents/S4B/sem02.html

govern their use" (Seiter, 1992, p. 23). The foundational principles of semiotics became indispensable for media scholars in the 1970s and 1980s as they turned their attention to the strategies employed by audiences to understand their media environment.

French scholar of linguistics Ferdinand de Saussure (1857–1913) is considered to be the primary figure in the field of semiotics. De Saussure became fascinated by the building blocks of language and meaning production. He developed a *dyadic*, or two-part, model for explaining how communication takes place through all forms of linguistic communication. Saussure argued that the process of human communication is dependent upon the creation of **signs**—words, images, objects, acts. Without the transmission of signs from one person to the next, no communication is possible. Signs can be quite simple and straightforward (such as an image of a flower) or complicated (such as a chemical formula, which perhaps describes the biological makeup of one component of the flower). Signs *refer* to things that they are not. They are markers that contain vital information about the experience, object, or idea that is being referred to (see Figure 6.1). Signs are defined by the interaction between two specific elements: the **signifier**, or the form of the sign, and the **signified or referent**, which is the concept the signifier represents (De Saussure, 2000).

A short intellectual exercise can demonstrate the interplay between signifier and signified. Take a look at the image that appears in Figure 6.2 and identify it. If you are thinking that it is a frog, then you are only partially correct. Certainly,

Figure 6.2

Source: Stephanie Plumeri Ertz.

it is an *image* of a frog, but it is not the little green animal that jumps around in ponds and makes a croaking noise. Now, observe Figure 6.3 and attempt to identify that image. As you can see, it is composed of four specific letters in the English language that, when placed one right after the other in this order, spell the word *frog*. This also brings to mind a green or brown amphibian that jumps

Figure 6.3

Source: Stephanie Plumeri Ertz.

and croaks. These two figures are similar because they are both signs (or, to use de Saussure's terminology, signifiers). The thing to which these signs point (and the thing that you associated it with in your mind) is the referent. There are also differences between these two figures. You may have noticed that the first image was a pictorial representation of the frog—it more closely resembled the thing itself. In the second figure, we see a collection of words—you probably recognized only the last one, *frog*, as having any meaning. The others are the same word translated into different languages. These signs also refer to the original "thing" but this time using a complex code called language to communicate that concept. If you are not familiar with the structure or syntax of the language, then you will be unable to "decode" the sign from looking at the collection of characters on the page and form a mental picture of an actual frog in your mind.

There are two important points to emphasize about the semiotic approach. The first is that **the connection between signs and referents is not given or "natural" but is instead the result of human social relations and the rules of particular symbolic codes**. The creation, distribution, and reception of signs are at the center of ongoing shifts within societies since they are the products of those societies and not etched in stone. The second point is something of a corollary to the first: **Since the connection between signs and referents is never natural, it is therefore always changing and subject to power relations**. Those in power will inevitably attempt to assign specific meanings to signs and to identify these meanings as "common sense"—this is the function of ideology. Conversely, the tenuous connections between signs and referents also provide space for outsiders to begin to challenge the status quo through the contestation of language and meanings. The derogatory term for homosexuals, *queer*, for instance, has been profoundly altered by gay and lesbian activists, who took the term and transformed it into a marker of gay pride and social activism. The notions of societal shift and power relations link the study of interpretation of transmission of signs with political economy (see Chapter 4). As we'll see next, critical media scholars in the 1980s sought to bring Karl Marx's theories of capital and class domination back into the center of media analysis.

Ideology, Screen Theory, and the Critical Paradigm

In the 1970s, scholars began looking closely at individual media texts as a means to explore the connections between the mass media and **ideology**. The study of ideology is primarily concerned with "the ways in which meaning and power intersect . . . ways in which meaning may serve, in specific socio-historical contexts, to sustain relations of domination" (Thompson, 1988, p. 370). In the Marxist school of thought, the study of media and communications had traditionally taken a back seat to more basic critiques of capitalism such as worker alienation and income inequality. Classic Marxist theory assumed that the press and the media generally serve the interests of the ruling class, but Marx's writings did not shed any light on the mechanisms through which this might take place. In the 1930s, a group of German intellectuals formed a research collective called the **Frankfurt School** that aimed to understand the role of the media from a Marxist perspective (see Horkheimer & Adorno, 1972, 2001). They identified modern media such as radio, television, and magazines as purveyors of industrialized, standardized culture meant to lull the masses into passivity and acceptance of the economic status quo. They classified this process of manufacturing dominant ideologies as the **culture industry**. Scholars interested in pursuing a "culture industry" critique of the media were a small minority in the postwar years, largely due to the institutionalization of communication studies in the United States as primarily a positivistic, effect-oriented endeavor (see Chapter 2 for an overview of the effects tradition in audience studies). However, the publication of an influential essay by French Marxist scholar Louis Althusser in the 1970s placed ideological critiques of the media firmly back on the scholarly agenda.

Althusser's essay, "Ideology and Ideological State Apparatuses," was written in the 1960s and translated into English in 1971. The piece had a "profound impact on sections of the British academic Left" (Moores, 1993, p. 12). In this essay, Althusser (2001) addressed the issue of how the power of the state is substantiated and insulated from any possible challenge from would-be revolutionaries. According to Althusser, traditional state apparatuses such as the police, army, courts, and prisons all work to uphold the status quo through the "functions of violence." If these were the only forms of social control, he argued, then they would be easily visible to the public and quickly identified as repressive. Citizens would respond to these obvious methods of dominance, inciting protest and revolutionary change. However, nonphysical forms of ideological control engineer the consent of the governed, protecting inequities in modern industrialized societies. Althusser cited a number of these "ideological state apparatuses" (or ISAs), such as the church (or other forms of organized religion), the educational system, the family, trade unions, and forms of modern communication such as the press, radio, and television (Althusser, 2001, p. 80). In fact, he went so far as to argue that "no class can hold State power over a long period without at the same time exercising its hegemony over and in the State Ideological Apparatuses" (2001, p. 81).

Critical scholars took particular interest in Althusser's mention of the media as a focal point of the ideological domination of society and began looking closely at media texts (particularly motion pictures) for evidence of these ideological formations at work. These scholars saw themselves as the "vanguard of revolutionary struggle" (Moores, 1993, p. 12) through their analyses of the ideological functions of mainstream media. A new generation of scholars began using Althusser's Marxist analysis of culture to study the ideological underpinnings of mainstream motion picture texts. For instance, a 1974 film studies article proposed that commercial films work by "constructing an illusion of transparency" such that the film effectively "denies its own material existence as text" (Moores, 1993, p. 13). Film viewers' sense of reality, then, is essentially controlled via the "imaginary unitary," and viewers are subsequently unable to separate themselves from the film's reality because it becomes invisible and normalized. This focus on the ideological messages embedded within the structures of the film text became known as **screen theory**. Proponents of screen theory suggested that mainstream media representations also reinforce the bourgeois status quo through narrative and visual strategies, thereby forestalling any attempt by the audience to subvert the text. The antidote to these dominant messages was found in the "revolutionary" filmmaking of avant-garde filmmakers such as Sergei Eisenstein and Jean-Luc Goddard. These directors brought the machinery of the filmmaking industry to the foreground in their work, allowing the audience to observe the message creation process and obtain a critical distance from the "artificial" reality of the film.

Screen theory became a powerful force in critical media scholarship in the late 1970s, but there were several major problems with the approach. First, the theory seemed to condemn all mainstream, commercial media texts as incapable of maintaining any critical distance from the economic and social status quo. A second issue with the theory was that it seemed to advocate **textual determinism**—that is, it suggested that audiences' interpretations of mainstream media content were already predetermined by the structure of the text itself. The only interpretive option open to the viewer, then, was to respond in the way that was intended by the original producer of the message. In this way, the media served its function as an ISA.

The Birmingham School and the Encoding/Decoding Model

The very limited subject positioning offered to the audience by screen theory did not sit well with a group of critical scholars at the Birmingham University Centre for Contemporary Cultural Studies (or CCCS, for short) in England. Convinced that the reception process was more nuanced and that audiences were much more active in their interpretations of specific media texts, members of the CCCS began mapping out an alternative theoretical model of the interactions between media texts and readers. The Birmingham group argued that audiences approached media texts with a repertoire of cultural competencies and discursive experiences that would profoundly shape their understandings of messages, regardless of the meanings intended by the creator of the text. While the scholars of the CCCS recognized the power of the text to structure potential interpretations, they also imagined audiences as active decoders of media texts, leaving conceptual room for them to challenge these meanings. For Hall and others at the Birmingham Centre, social class was the primary lens through which audiences crafted their symbolic responses to media, which fit squarely within their work with youth subcultures (Murdock, 2017).

Perhaps the single-most influential essay that developed from the Birmingham group's work was "Encoding/Decoding" by Stuart Hall (1980). In this essay, Hall addressed what he perceived to be the shortcomings of two dominant paradigms in audience studies: uses and gratifications (see Chapter 5) and screen theory. As we will see later on in the chapter, Hall's essay inspired a number of important qualitative audience studies in the 1980s.

The Encoding/Decoding Model

Hall explained that there are two "determining moments" in any communication exchange: **encoding** and **decoding**. Hall's use of the term *determining* does not imply that he subscribed to a theory of textual determination, however. Instead, he saw these events as moments in which the meaning of a message or text was subject to human intervention and therefore involved power relations. The first determining moment, according to Hall, occurs when a message producer (such as a television journalist or a podcaster) successfully **encodes the message**. The creator must place an idea or event or experience in a format that will be meaningful for audiences. To transmit an event via television, it must first be transformed using "the aural-visual forms of the televisual discourse. . . . To put it paradoxically, the event must become a 'story' before it can become a *communicative event*" (emphasis in original; Hall, 1980, p. 129). This is where systems of language as well as professional codes of production and conventions of message production come into play. In the news business, for example, there are standard practices that determine (1) what types of events qualify as news and (2) how news events are designed and structured for presentation to a mass audience. This is the first part of the interpretive work involved in a communication exchange.

The second component is the reception of the message by the audience, which Hall calls the **decoding process**. Before any communication message can "'have an effect,' influence, entertain, instruct, or persuade," it must be "appropriated as a meaningful discourse and be meaningfully decoded" (Hall, 1980, p. 130). Since our goal in this text is to explore theories of the audience, the decoding process is of greatest interest to us. The encoding process transforms experiences and ideas into meaningful discourse within existing social, economic, and cultural contexts. Audiences then interpret these messages within their own contexts. Decoding is therefore both a *creative* and a *social* practice; creative because the message receiver brings to bear his or her own cognitive and associative resources to the deconstruction of a message and social because the receiver is also informed by larger-meaning structures such as language, community norms, and cultural conventions.

Media Encoding: Institutions and Production Cultures

Let's briefly discuss the factors that shape the *encoding* of media messages, which is the first half of the model. As Hall (1980) explained in his seminal essay, ideas, thoughts, or experiences need first to be expressed in terms of specific signs (signification) in order for them to be transmitted to an audience. In this sense, Hall's term *encoding* can be understood in a literal sense: Experiences are essentially translated into a specific code (language, for example) and format (speech, visual images, sounds, etc.) such that they could be understood by others. There were numerous factors that guided this encoding process. In the case of television programs, for example, Hall supposed:

> The institutional structures of broadcasting, with their practices and networks of production, their organized relations and technical infrastructures, are required to produce a programme. Using the analogy of *Capital*, this is the "labour process" in the discursive mode. Production, here, constructs the message. In one sense, then, the circuit begins here. Of course, the production process is not without its "discursive" aspect: it, too, is framed throughout by meanings and ideas: knowledge-in-use concerning the routines of production, historically defined technical skills, professional ideologies, institutional knowledge, definitions and assumptions, assumptions about the audience and so on frame the constitution of the programme through this production structure. (Hall, 1980, p. 129)

Hall is referring here to the social, economic, and political structures that guide the industrialized production of media. In this sense, Hall was building upon earlier Marxist concepts outlined by the Frankfurt School about the mass production of ideological messages via institutional control. But Hall's notion of encoding was more comprehensive and expansive than that of the Frankfurt School or Althusser's. Hall imagined a number of different types of influences on the encoding of media messages that went beyond the maintenance of the economic status quo through ideological state apparatuses.

For example, television programs are created by individuals working within large organizations. These organizations, like the British Broadcasting Corporation (BBC) in the United Kingdom or the National Broadcasting Company (NBC) in the United States, have highly skilled workers that specialize in a particular aspect of this production process, whether it be acting, scripting, camera work, editing, or working in the control room. These workers have training and are also socialized into doing their work in particular kinds of ways through organizational rules and routines. In his classic book *Deciding What's News*, for instance, scholar Herbert Gans (1980) conducted interviews with editors and journalists to discover how these individuals defined *news* (what is newsworthy) and how they translated events into a news story that was appropriate to print (and that would satisfy their editors). More recent studies of the news business have examined the impacts of the Internet and digitalization on the organizational structures and routines (see Boczkowski, 2004; Nadler, 2016). For a good example of how encoding and decoding operates within a specific news environment, see Box 6.1 on pg. 177.

Figure 6.4 Hierarchical Model of Factors Affecting the Production of Media Content

Social systems	Larger social structures; organization of media system (democratic, controlled); ideology; economic basis of media production (capitalism, state-controlled)
Social institutions	Journalism and media production norms (reliance on official sources, reliance on advertising, state control of media, public relations)
Media organizations	Expenses, revenues, ownership of media organizations, roles, structure, profitability, platform, target audience, influence from advertisers, and market competition
Routines and practices	*Journalism*: News values, objectivity, norms for newsworthiness, timeliness of stories, proximity, fact-checking *Entertainment*: Casting, hiring of talent, genres of programming, production decision-making, audience research, scheduling and distribution decisions
Individuals	Individual's professional roles, work and personal background, ethics, personal attitudes, values, beliefs

Source: Adapted from Shoemaker, P. J., & Reese, S. D. (2013). *Mediating the Message in the 21st Century: A Media Sociology Perspective* (1 edition). New York, NY: Routledge.

Todd Gitlin (1983) conducted a similar type of encoding analysis in the early 1980s when he interviewed American television executives to find out why some shows and genres were regularly approved and why some were not. The many different structural and localized influences on the industrial production of media have even spawned their own specialization within media research called production studies (Mayer, Banks, & Caldwell, 2009). Schoemaker and Reese (2013) have organized these various influences into a hierarchical model (see Figure 6.4) to demonstrate the complexity of the different types of pressures that guide the encoding of media forms.

Message Asymmetry and Multiple Levels of Meaning

Given the fact that the encoding of media messages was subject to the influence of human meaning structures outlined previously, Hall also noted that this created the likelihood (and, indeed, the inevitability) for "asymmetry" between the message producer(s) and the audience. Put another way, there is always a chance of various "degrees of understanding and misunderstanding" in any communication exchange. For Hall, symmetry of interpretation between television producers

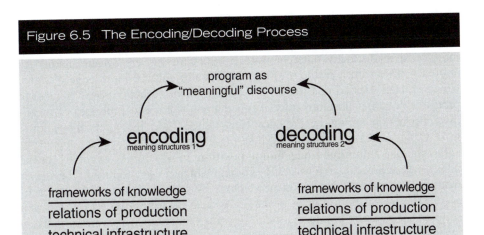

program as
"meaningful" discourse

encoding
meaning structures 1

decoding
meaning structures 2

frameworks of knowledge

relations of production

technical infrastructure

frameworks of knowledge

relations of production

technical infrastructure

Source: Adapted from Hall, S. (1980). *Encoding/Decoding.* In S. Hall, D. Hobson, A. Lowe, & P. Willis (Eds.), "Culture, Media, Language: Working Papers in Cultural Studies" (p. 130). London, England: Hutchinson. Redrawn by Stephanie Plumeri Ertz.

and viewers is a function of the "structural differences of relation and position between broadcasters and audiences, but it also has something to do with the asymmetry between the codes of 'source' and 'receiver' at the moment of transformation into and out of the discursive form" (1980, p. 131). The subject position of the audience, then, results in quite a different orientation to the message, resulting in mismatches between the producer's intended meaning and the meaning received by the audience (see Figure 6.5).

How exactly do audiences interpret communication messages? To explain this phenomenon, Hall turned to semiotics and linguistics, drawing upon the material that was outlined in the early part of this chapter. In decoding specific messages, audiences react to both the **denotative level of meaning**—the literal, "near-universal," or commonsense meaning of the sign—and the **connotative level of meaning**—or contextualized understandings of signs. This difference is similar to the disparity between what we often refer to as the "surface" meaning of an image or text and its related "subtext" (what one can *infer* from the text itself given a specific set of cultural codes and experiences). Hall described "situational ideologies" that were found at the connotative level and shaped meaning for audiences. He drew upon the work of French theorist Roland Barthes (1987), who argued that denotations are what we often learn first but that they contain ideological subject positions that guide us toward specific types of meanings (so, therefore, there is no "natural" meaning for a particular sign). Connotations, on the other hand, leave the meaning of the sign open to wider interpretations.

Polysemy and Three Subject Positions

Texts (whether print, pictorial, or televisual) are **polysemic**, capable of being interpreted in distinctly different ways by different viewers because audiences approach texts with a plethora of experiences and cultural knowledge of signs. However, Hall stressed that this empowerment of the audience vis-à-vis message producers was not absolute since it relied upon the social processes of meaning construction among the audience. Hall posited three "hypothetical positions" from which media decoding could take place. First, he argued that some viewers might take a **dominant-hegemonic position**, in which they might accept the media message exactly in terms of the code in which it was produced. The viewer would operate inside the dominant ideology by accepting the transfer of packaged meanings without a great deal of reflection, regarding the transaction as a simple dissemination of information. Hall argued that audiences were more likely to stake out what he termed a **negotiated position**. The individual would interpret the message with "a mixture of adaptive and oppositional elements" (1980, p. 137). Viewers making negotiated readings of texts relate to and understand the dominant code, but they also filter media content through the lens of their own individualized experiences and worldview. For example, a working-class person watching a television news story about a new law to restrict frivolous worker compensation lawsuits may understand and even agree with the premise of the law but would nevertheless feel entitled to file such a lawsuit should he or she become injured on the job.

Finally, Hall argued that some viewers may take a media text and "decode the message in a *globally contrary way*. He/she detotalizes the message in the preferred code in order to retotalize the message within some alternative framework of reference" (emphasis in original; 1980, pp. 137–138). These viewers occupy an **oppositional position** by focusing exclusively on the connotative meanings of the signs in order to mount an ideological struggle against the message and/or its producers. Box 6.1 outlines one example of how viewers may construct oppositional readings of mass media.

Hall's groundbreaking essay made a number of important advancements. The first one was the essay's "methodological and theoretical problematic" (Gray, 1999, p. 26). Hall was attempting to disrupt and problematize mainstream, positivistic approaches to media content and audience understanding, which presupposed a "transmission" model of communication. Instead, his model complicated the notion of a simple transmission of information when an audience member receives a mediated message. The second innovation, in Hall's own words, was essentially "political"—he argued that it was impossible for a third-party researcher to effectively determine what the ultimate meaning understood by the audience was by the application of systematic measurement techniques (this was most likely aimed specifically at critical Marxists who ascribed to the textual determinist school of thinking). Instead, Hall "insists that meaning is multi-layered/multi-referential and as such imports the then new fields semiotics and structuralism into the study of mass communication" (Gray, 1999, p. 27).

BOX 6.1

Encoding/ Decoding in Action: Reporting and Understanding News About Rape on Campus

How might social factors shape both the encoding and decoding of media messages? This was the central question posed by Worthington (2008) in her study of news about campus sexual assault and rape. A recent review of published peer-reviewed studies, reports, dissertations, and other crime statistics between 2000 and 2015 discovered that a substantial number of women are the victims of "completed forcible rape, incapacitated rape, unwanted sexual contact and sexual coercion on college campuses" (Fedina, Holmes, & Backes, 2018). Another recent nationwide survey discovered that 81% of women and 43% of men had reported experiencing some form of sexual harassment or assault in their lifetimes (Kearl, 2018). Nancy Worthington wondered what types of impacts news reports on sexual assault might have on audiences' understanding about these cases and how these reports might affect the likelihood that victims of sexual assault would report their cases to law enforcement.

For her research, Worthington focused on the reporting of a campus sexual assault at a college in the western United States. She examined a 9-minute investigative piece that aired on a local news program on November 19, 2002. Thanks to training that journalists at this local TV station had received about progressive techniques for reporting sexual assault, they incorporated a number of strategies for presenting information about this case:

(1) Story selection that reflects the types of crimes that occur (i.e., attention to assaults perpetrated by acquaintances), (2) avoidance of sexist stereotypes that either blame the victim or mitigate suspect responsibility, (3) attention to the role of social structures such as law, gender, race, and class in causing and normalizing gender violence, and (4) the inclusion of perspectives of victims and/or their advocates. (Worthington, 2008, p. 345)

Worthington began by analyzing the 9-minute news story itself, looking for dominant themes. She found that the story was built around several key elements: concern with violent crime and inadequate punishment, an institutional scandal at the college where the assault took place, and the subsequent cover-up by the college's administration.

Stuart Hall's model envisions cultural codes that structure both the production of the message (*encoding*) as well as the audience's interpretation of the message (*decoding*). While most scholars using Hall's framework tend to ignore encoding processes or achieve this via textual analysis, Worthington conducted interviews with the news story's producer and her central source for the story, the former director of the college's women's resource center. There were several important forces that shaped the encoding of the news story about this campus sexual assault. First, the central source for the story was keen to "convey the injustices done to women who had been raped on campus," and this motivation powerfully shaped the tone of the reporting. The fact that the college administration resisted requests for interviews or comments about the case, ultimately assigning a new administrator who had no direct knowledge, also shaped the

(Continued)

(Continued)

orientation of the resulting news story. The journalist was careful, however, to adhere to a traditional "news narrative" that focused more on the perceived misdeeds of the college administration in these cases rather than delving into the broader broken system of justice that prevails on college campuses when dealing with sexual assault. Worthington also found that the news station pursued its own institutional priorities and self-preservation by, for instance, deciding against running video footage of a college dean running away from a station reporter asking for comment out of concern by the station's legal department that the station might be sued by the college, which had a somewhat litigious reputation. Each of these forces powerfully shaped the encoding of the final news story.

How did news audiences interpret this story of campus sexual assault? To understand this, Worthington relied on printouts of audience responses from the television station's website the morning after the story aired. She found that a number of the respondents on the website made the "dominant or preferred" reading that the perpetrators of sexual assault are inadequately punished. One commented: "Letting the rapists off the hook is absolutely unconscionable—not only for the fact that their victims fail to receive any justice but that this is often a pattern of behavior which repeats itself." Worthington notes that this kind of dominant reading can illustrate "how progressive rape discourse in news can empower assault survivors to challenge patriarchal rape discourse" (p. 359). Some viewers posting comments created complex links between this specific case and other relevant national news stories, such as the sexual abuse scandals in the Catholic Church. These audiences added their own interpretive elements to the news story and

thereby "raised concerns about the structural nature of institutional power that transcended the story's strict adherence to narrative" (p. 360).

How about negotiated or oppositional readings to this news story? Worthington discovered evidence of those in the web comments as well. Several viewers' comments on the website essentially reproduced commonsense patriarchal discourses about female sexual assault victims, for example, by urging female students to "be careful and keep safe" when walking around campus. Another urged women to select their friends more carefully in order to avoid unsavory men who might engage in sexual violence. These alternative readings essentially amounted to a form of "victim-blaming" that the news story encoding was careful to avoid. Worthington points out that these counternarratives also tended to buy into the myth that women are at greatest risk of sexual assault from strangers, when in reality gender violence occurs overwhelmingly between acquaintances.

Worthington's study is a noteworthy example of Stuart Hall's encoding/decoding model for a number of reasons. First, through empirical data, she carefully explicated some of the encoding strategies that shape a media message. Second, her analysis of viewer responses to the news story, while based upon a convenience sample of viewers commenting on the TV station website, illustrates the dominant, negotiated, and oppositional reading strategies that audiences employ in their interpretations of media. While oppositional readings are often imagined by scholars as emancipatory, in this case the progressive reporting of campus rape by the local TV station was thwarted by some viewers' oppositional readings—readings that worked to uphold the patriarchal status quo that blames sexual assault on the victims.

Source: Based on Worthington, N. (2008). "Encoding and Decoding Rape News: How Progressive Reporting Inverts Textual Orientations." *Women's Studies in Communication, 31*(3), 344–367.

The Nationwide Audience Studies

The impact of Hall's "Encoding/Decoding" essay on the development of reader-oriented audience studies beginning in the late 1970s is difficult to overstate. Hall mapped out the theoretical territory for audience researchers but stopped short of matching up his ideas about textual decoding with observable audience data. That task was left to a number of other scholars, some of whom were active in the Birmingham group with Hall. The most well-known and influential audience study to attempt to explore Hall's ideas about audience decoding in an empirical setting was *The Nationwide Audience*, authored by sociologist and CCCS colleague David Morley (1980). The "Nationwide study," as it is more commonly known among communication scholars, documented audience responses to *Nationwide*, a weekly show produced by the BBC. *Nationwide* was a news and public affairs program that was broadcast throughout Britain, and it was one of the more heavily watched TV news broadcasts at the time. The style and format of the program were similar to other weekly TV news magazine programs in the United States such as CBS's *60 Minutes*, *Dateline NBC*, and ABC's *20/20* in that the hour-long program covered a number of topics in some depth.

Morley's 1980 book was actually the second installment of a larger research project. The first part of the series was a systematic analysis of the text of *Nationwide*, which explored the kinds of stories featured most often on the program and the show's orientations toward public policy initiatives (Brunsdon & Morley, 1978). Both Brunsdon and Morley were interested in the kinds of ideological themes that emerged in the program. They focused specifically on how particular solutions were suggested for Britain's social and economic problems. *Nationwide* was known for speaking in "commonsense" language to its audience about complex social and economic problems, with an emphasis on consensus and shared identity. The importance of common sense harkens back to notions of ideology. How was *Nationwide*'s attempt to stake out a notion of national consensus interpreted by the program's audience, many of whom might have goals that conflict and compete with some of the nation's most pressing social issues? How did the reception of some of the "commonsense" solutions offered differ between Britain's executive class and working class, for instance?

The second part of the project, and the one most remembered by scholars today, was a study of the *Nationwide* audience. The concept behind this portion of Morley's research was a direct outgrowth of Hall's essay on audience decoding. Like Hall, Morley theorized that viewers of the program would adopt one of three interpretive positions: a dominant, negotiated, or oppositional reading of the program. But who was more likely to make these readings? To answer this question, Morley turned to the work of sociologist Frank Parkin (1971), who argued that class position—which included income, type of employment, and educational level—played a profound role in shaping individuals' meaning systems, ways of culture, and views about politics and public affairs. Morley recruited individuals who were already engaged in education or training at local universities and divided them by their occupational status or trajectory. He created four groups: managers, students, apprentices, or trade unionists.

To make sure that the respondents were interpreting the same textual material, Morley selected two specific episodes of *Nationwide* to show to groups of audiences that he had recruited. The first episode, from May 1976, consisted of a report from the British Midlands, a short interview with consumer advocate Ralph Nader, and an interview with a man who was released from jail after being wrongly convicted of murder (Morley & Brunsdon, 1999, pp. 64–66). The second program was an episode from March 1977, which featured a report about the impacts of the annual budget on three individual families. Morley concentrated specifically on studying group interpretations of the program due to concern that interviews with individual viewers would be "flawed by a focus on individuals as social atoms divorced from their social context" (Morley, 1980, p. 33). In total, 29 small groups of 2–13 people from different social, economic, and educational backgrounds were recruited. Each group watched the program, then participated in a follow-up half-hour open discussion. Morley or other members of his team served as moderators. During these sessions, Morley paid special attention to the types of comments and conversations that were occurring, and he attempted to track down patterns in the viewers' responses to the program and to investigate whether or not these interpretations mapped onto the occupational categories that he had constructed.

Morley found some distinct patterns among the different occupational groups he assembled. His groups of print and bank management trainees, along with apprentices, tended to be more politically conservative in their views. These individuals generally operated within the dominant code of the *Nationwide* program (see Figure 6.6). The schoolboys (aged 14–16) tended to make dominant readings not because of any well-developed political orientation but because they found the program to be easy to understand and they had little preexisting knowledge about the topics under discussion. Teacher training groups and university arts students tended to make negotiated readings—they criticized the unsophisticated type of news offered by the program, but they did not necessarily counterargue many of the claims made. Morley discovered some distinctly oppositional decoding strategies among trade union rank-and-file members ("shop stewards"), particularly in the episode that dealt with the budget crisis. The shop stewards interpreted the program from a position of working-class consciousness. They noted that the *Nationwide* program failed to address issues from the standpoint of working-class Brits (many found the program much too sympathetic to middle management). The type of oppositional readings offered by the Black further education (FE) students differed markedly from those of the trade unionists in the sense that these students found virtually nothing redeeming about the program whatsoever. These college students "showed little interest in the text and found it extremely hard to recognize anything of themselves in the *Nationwide* image—not so much rejecting the program's preferred view of the world as refusing to read the message at all" (Moores, 1993, p. 21).

Morley's study was a turning point in audience reception studies for two reasons. First, his was the first study to look empirically and systematically at audience interpretations of television. Secondly, the study took on Hall's notion that audiences are capable of producing their own meanings from media texts outside of the structures of those texts. These interpretations are inevitably shaped by the individual's social position. It's important to note here that Morley was not simply arguing that class position and occupational status were the only factors that shaped audiences' decoding strategies. However, his use of class position as the

Figure 6.6   Audience Decodings of *Nationwide*

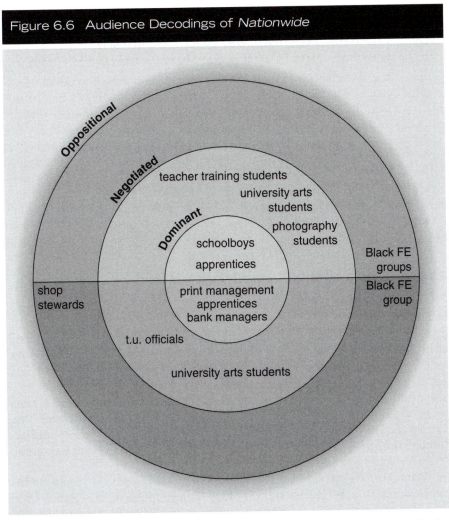

Source: Adapted from Morley, D., & Brunsdon, C. (1999). *The Nationwide Television Studies* (p. 259). London, England: Routledge. Redrawn by Stephanie Plumeri Ertz.

organizing principle of the discussion groups certainly led to this impression, and his work came under fire from critics for this oversimplification of the decoding process. When one looks at the responses of the apprentices, trade union/shop steward groups, and the Black student groups, it is clear that a number of different reading strategies can be in play even within the same class position. Nevertheless, Morley's work was seminal in its attempt to put Hall's theories of decoding into practice with real audiences, and it set the stage for more audience reception work in the 1980s and beyond.

Gender and Media Interpretation: Soap Operas, Romances, and Feminism

Despite some of the perceived shortcomings of Morley's approach to media decoding, his qualitative interview approach was groundbreaking. Morley's finding that Black students did not even engage with the *Nationwide* program because they did not perceive any connection to their own experience points to the possibility that social factors such as race and gender may play an important role in shaping an individual's interpretation of media texts. Seeking to redress earlier biases against forms of media that were popular with women, scholars in the wake of the *Nationwide* studies began to closely examine female audiences of soap operas, romance novels, and women's magazines, among other media texts. Did gender profoundly shape the decodings of these texts? Moreover, were there specifically *feminine* texts that spoke differently to women than to men?

Crossroads and the Soap Opera Viewer

In a nod to Herta Herzog's uses and gratifications studies of female radio serial listeners in the 1940s (see Chapter 6), scholars in the early 1980s returned to the genre of soap operas as a means to explore the interactions between the formal structures of popular media texts and the audiences' interpretations of this content. In particular, many of these scholars wished to understand why soap operas remained so popular with women audiences: What were they getting out of these soaps and how were they interpreting them? The focus of some of this seminal work on soap operas in the early 1980s was the popular British TV daytime serial *Crossroads*. The program, which debuted in 1964 and enjoyed a sizable audience through the 1980s, revolved around the lives of a group of working-class characters who were employed in a motel.

A number of scholars began looking closely at daytime soap operas like *Crossroads* to try to understand why they were popular with women. In an early but influential essay, Charlotte Brunsdon (who had earlier worked with Morley on the *Nationwide* project) closely examined the text of *Crossroads* and noticed that, like other soap operas, the program was broken down into small segments that featured interactions between characters. She noted that this soap opera world "is temporally and spatially fragmented, and that this fragmentation, accompanied by repetitious spatial orientation, foregrounds that dialogue of emotional and moral dilemma which makes up the action" (Brunsdon, 1981, p. 35). Moreover, she argued that the text of *Crossroads* required viewers to possess certain types of competencies in order to fully enjoy the program. This prerequisite knowledge included familiarity with the soap opera genre (generic knowledge), knowledge of specific characters and their histories (serial-specific knowledge), and knowledge of "the socially acceptable codes and conventions for the conduct of personal life (cultural knowledge)" (1981, p. 36). Because of *Crossroads*' emphasis on conversation, character development, and the intricacies of marriage, romance, and family life, Brudson argued that the program "textually implies a feminine viewer." She suggested that this textual structure is the chief form of pleasure for female viewers.

Intrigued by the notion of gender-specific programming and interpretive styles, other scholars began looking closely at the soap opera genre and how it was interpreted by female viewers. Dorothy Hobson (1982) conducted the first large-scale study of *Crossroads* audiences. Hobson had been a student at the Birmingham School along with David Morley and Charlotte Brunsdon, and she carried with her the same critical approach to social power and audience reception as was found in her peers' work on the *Nationwide* program. Unlike Morley, however, who gathered groups of viewers together in an artificial setting to show them specific episodes of *Nationwide*, Hobson went to the homes of a number of different women to watch episodes of *Crossroads* with them in order to more easily open up discussion with them about the program and to observe their television viewing in their "natural" domestic contexts. She found that many women squeezed their soap opera viewing time into small openings in their otherwise hectic daily schedules—feeding children, preparing tea, and "half-watching" the program by listening to the dialogue even when their backs were turned to the television. Hobson was keen to point out that television viewing was an integral part of these women's everyday activities and that it rarely if ever occurred in isolation from a host of other household and domestic activities. The hectic environment in which these women enjoyed *Crossroads* seemed to challenge the notion that media reception could be accurately understood without studying the physical and social contexts in which viewing occurred (see Chapter 8). Finally, Hobson found that some of her respondents were "guilty and apologetic" about watching the soap opera and "they excuse themselves for liking something which is treated in such a derogatory way by critics and sometimes by their own husbands" (1982, p. 110). The fact that these women felt that their viewing choices were devalued by the mainstream of society set up an interesting challenge for audience reception scholars: How should the gender politics in popular texts and their reception be understood? Did these women respond to the soap opera genre because they found it to resonate with their own lives or perhaps because it offered an escape from their everyday existence?

Decoding *Dallas*: The Work of Ien Ang

These questions were carried through a number of other important studies of female audience reception and interpretation in the decade following the publication of the *Crossroads* work. Ien Ang (1985), for example, conducted a study of viewers for *Dallas*, one of the most popular American prime-time dramas of the 1980s. The program was distributed worldwide to a huge international audience. Like its counterparts *Dynasty* and *Knots Landing*, *Dallas* followed the story of a wealthy family—in this case, the Ewings, who made their money from the Texas oil business. The drama followed the personal tragedies and intricacies of the family's home life, as well as the business machinations of the two competing sons, J. R. and Bobby. Ang solicited responses from women in Holland via an advertisement in a women's magazine and collected 42 letters from regular Dutch viewers of the program. Her close reading of these letters revealed a perplexing pattern: Many of these Dutch women found the trials and tribulations of the Ewing family to be similar to a great deal of the emotional challenges in their own lives. Ang wondered how a text that was so foreign to these viewers and far removed from their economic status (the Ewings lived a lavish lifestyle) could be so "realistic" and personally relevant. Her conclusion was that these women were focusing less on the *denotative* level of the program (that is, a story about a rich Texas family) and more on the *connotative* level. The women interpreted a type of what Ang termed *emotional realism* into the narrative, which spoke to their everyday roles as wives, mothers, sisters, and daughters (Ang, 1985, pp. 41–43). *Dallas* activated these women's "melodramatic imagination," which served as a focal point for their enjoyment of the text, despite the strained premise of some of the characters' actions and motives in the program.

Reading the Romance Novel Reader: Janice Radway

Ang's interpretation of women *Dallas* viewers' statements raised fascinating yet troubling questions about how scholars should understand and "read in" to viewers' responses about their own interpretive processes. These unanswered queries only multiplied after the initial publication of Janice Radway's *Reading the Romance* in 1984. Radway, an English professor at Duke University, was not aware of the previous work on decoding of soap operas that had been done by members of the Birmingham School in the early 1980s. Nevertheless, her book remains a milestone in the research on reception and interpretation of popular media and its connection to social power and feminism. The subjects of Radway's study were a small group of women (predominantly housewives) in a town she called "Smithton" (a pseudonym to hide the real name of the town) who regularly read romance novels. Radway made an initial contact with a key informant at a local bookstore, Dorothy (or "Dot" as she was known), who put the scholar in touch with some of the women who frequented the bookstore and asked for advice on which romance novels were worth reading. With the assistance of Dot, Radway gathered 42 completed questionnaires from regular romance readers. She supplemented this data with extended interviews with Dot and another longtime patron of Dot's bookstore. In the questionnaires, Radway asked about these women's romance novel reading, including how many books they regularly read and of what types, what romance novels meant to them, and what kinds of stories and characters commanded their attention. It should be noted that Radway's initial impetus was to try to find out why women would choose to read narratives that featured somewhat patriarchal notions of romance since the happiness of the female protagonists in the narratives was largely predicated on their ability to find the appreciation and affection of male characters.

In her analysis of the Smithton women's interpretations of romance novels, Radway found that the most appealing type of narrative was one in which an intelligent and dynamic heroine finds herself in a dilemma (usually at the hand of a cruel or untrustworthy male character) but then achieves resolution and peace at the end of the novel through the influence of a caring, tender, and intelligent man. These women regarded the happy ending as the absolute most important aspect of a romance novel, which "lends credence to the suggestion that romances are valued most for their ability to raise the spirits of the reader" (Radway, 1984, p. 66). Far from making alternative or oppositional readings of romance novels, Radway's respondents seemed to prefer the kind of narrative that many feminists have regarded as objectionable: that the female protagonists are at the mercy of men and must rely on them in order to achieve happiness and fulfillment within the story. Did this mean that these women were blindly complicit in their consumption of a popular text that by design reinforced a regressive notion of gender relations?

Radway argued that this, in fact, was *not* the case because of the active choices that these women made to fit romance novel reading into their busy schedules. She claimed that the stresses of everyday lives as mothers, wives, and homemakers worked to deny these women some of their personal emotional and psychological needs. In choosing to take time out from these responsibilities to read these novels, these women were carving out a critical space for the renewal of their own sense of identity and individuality:

> Romance reading, it would seem, at least for Dot and many of her customers, is a strategy with a double purpose. As an activity, it so engages their attention that it enables them to deny their physical presence in an environment associated with responsibilities that are acutely felt and occasionally experienced as too onerous to bear. Reading, in this sense, connotes a free space where they feel liberated from the need to perform duties that they otherwise willingly accept as their own. At the same time, by carefully choosing stories that make them feel particularly happy, they escape figuratively into a fairy tale where a heroine's similar needs are adequately met. As a result, they vicariously attend to their own requirements as independent individuals who require emotional sustenance and solicitude. (Radway, 1984, p. 93)

The rebellion for women in romance novels was not necessarily in the text or in its decoding but in the very act of reading. Although Radway concluded that there were some important benefits of romance novel reading for these women, she was reluctant to go too far in espousing the virtues of these books, given the limiting roles for women within the texts themselves.

The empirical work on female media audiences by Hobson, Radway, and Ang spurred more interest in the intersections between culturally devalued popular media genres (like soap operas and women's magazines) and strategies for decoding among these audiences throughout the 1990s. A study by Hermes (1995), for instance, looked at the kinds of interconnected "repertoires" of knowledge that women built up through their reading of different types of popular women's magazines. A similar study of young teen girls and their interpretations of adolescent magazines such as *Seventeen, Young & Modern, Sassy,* and *Teen* found that girls between the ages of 13 and 17 looked closely at the content of both articles and advertisements (Currie, 1999). Like Radway with romance novel readers, Currie discovered that many of these young girls internalized ideological messages about femininity and used the messages in their own lives, particularly when it came to fashion choices and advice. These studies demonstrate the tricky dynamic between the autonomy of the audience to interpret the text and the inherent structures within texts that work to narrow these interpretations into a few predefined avenues (for a recent example, see Box 6.2).

BOX 6.2
Selfies and Gender Stereotypes

Audience studies scholars often examine the close interconnections between culture and media decodings. Gender stereotypes and the resulting cultural norms (about who should work outside of the home, styles of dress, and self-representation, etc.) are built into the fabric of our media environment. In early studies of audience interpretations, audience scholars were fascinated by the ways in which women reinterpreted or reworked dominant cultural expectations about gender to suit their own needs, with varying levels of autonomy. Thanks to social media and other forms of participatory online media today, however, audiences can actively construct their own forms of identity online through their own self-representation. But are audiences using these new forms of self-representation and expression such as blogs, selfies, and Facebook posts to break down traditional gender stereotypes?

Several scholars investigated this question with regard to men and women's selfies—self-portrait photos taken with a mobile phone—that were posted to the photo-sharing platform Instagram (Döring, Reif, & Poeschl, 2016). First, to identify the dominant stereotypes in photography, the researchers looked to prior research by Goffman (1979) that identified the dominant tropes of female portrayals in advertising. Goffman found, for example, that women are portrayed in a stereotypical way through five specific visual tropes:

1. *Relative size*: Women are depicted as smaller in height and in lower positions than men.

2. *Feminine touch*: Women are typically depicted as using their hands to trace the outlines of an object or to caress its surface.

3. *Function ranking*: Men are depicted in executive roles while women are in supporting or assisting roles.

4. *Ritualization of subordination*: Women are located in lower positions in advertising than men to indicate their relative status, which includes being off-balance, lying down, or canting their heads or bodies.

5. *Licensed withdrawal*: Women appear to withdraw their gaze from the situation by not looking at the camera or by "loss of control" with expansive smiles or hiding behind objects.

Döring and colleagues wanted the answer to these questions: Would these gender stereotypes found in advertising be replicated in audiences' online selfies? Or would the inherent freedom of social media sites like Instagram provide a forum for users to actively subvert or rework these gender tropes? These questions are similar to those posed by Stuart Hall regarding the degree to which media audiences construct dominant, negotiated, or oppositional interpretations of mainstream media.

To study forms of selfie self-presentation among Instagram users, the researchers selected 500 random selfies for analysis. They found that more selfies by women tended to reproduce the "kissing pout" and "faceless portrayal" whereas the male selfies emphasized muscle presentation. Not only did women tend to reproduce some of Goffman's gender stereotypes in their own selfies, but the selfies in Döring et al.'s sample were even more gender stereotypical than a comparison sample of gender depictions in print advertising. What can we learn from this analysis? First, these results indicate that, despite the fact that young people have enormous leeway to construct and alter their self-presentations via social media, this does not necessarily mean that their self-portraits actively subvert dominant gender norms. To put this in Hall's parlance, sometimes audiences will make dominant or hegemonic interpretations of their own self-presentation. Second, how conscious were these young people of the types of images they were posting online? Although Döring et al.'s analysis was a content analysis, they note that follow-up interviews with the individuals whose selfies were used for the study would help to uncover their own self-concepts of gender and self-presentation.

Source: Döring, N., Reif, A., & Poeschl, S. (2016). How gender-stereotypical are selfies? A content analysis and comparison with magazine adverts. *Computers in Human Behavior, 55,* 955–962.

Cross-Cultural Reception of Popular Media

Given that social roles such as gender and class may be shaping audience interpretation, how do individuals from different cultural backgrounds and parts of the globe decode media texts? A number of studies, going back to the mid-1980s when the American prime-time melodrama *Dallas* was in its heyday, have examined differences in decoding strategies among audiences outside of the United States. Some are cross comparisons of audiences from different countries or cultural/ethnic backgrounds, which highlight the impacts of cultural identity on the interpretation of popular media.

Israeli Viewers of *Dallas*

In one of the first studies of its type, Liebes and Katz (1986, 1993) conducted empirical observations of Israeli viewers of *Dallas*. Interestingly, they included five different cultural subsets within their study: Israeli Arabs, recent Russian immigrants to Israel, first- and second-generation Jewish immigrants from Morocco, Israeli kibbutz members, and groups of second-generation Jews who were living in Los Angeles, California. Liebes and Katz invited a total of over 400 participants (in 66 groups of roughly six persons each) to a central location to watch an episode of *Dallas* and have an in-depth discussion following the program (reproducing the methodology used by Morley in the *Nationwide* studies). The focus on the reception of a popular American television program abroad was motivated by a desire to look for evidence of a transfer of American ideologies of consumerism and leisure to other cultures. Liebes and Katz found that the program led individuals to talk about certain types of issues that were brought up within the narrative, such as family loyalties, notions of ethics and honor, gender roles, and standards for success and wealth. Even within the groups living in Israel, cultural and ethnic differences played a role in the decoding of the program. Among the Israeli Arab and Moroccan Jewish groups, family kinship issues were reported to be the most interesting aspect of the show—these viewers used the program "referentially" by treating it as a kind of documentary that related to issues in their own lives (Liebes & Katz, 1986, p. 153). The Russian Jewish immigrants interpreted the program somewhat more "analytically" by distinguishing between the reality of the narrative (which was regarded as somewhat outsized and fictionalized) and the kinds of issues that were raised by the program, such as the ethics of money and business transactions. The cross-comparative nature and the sheer scope of Liebes and Katz's work on *Dallas* marked it as a clear milestone for scholars of media reception and interpretation.

Decoding American Soap TV in India

Since the days of *Dallas*, the expansion of cable and satellite media services has dramatically increased the ability of audiences around the globe to see

American-produced television programming. Recent research has continued the tradition of the Israeli *Dallas* study by examining the reception of American media overseas, taking note of the impacts that local cultural traditions play on audiences' interpretations of the text. For instance, the daytime soap opera *The Bold and the Beautiful* is a popular American television program in India. Rogers, Singhal, and Thombre (2004) selected a series of episodes of the program that chronicled the character Tony coming to terms with being infected with the HIV virus. How did Indian audiences interpret this plot line? Forty-two respondents in six different focus groups watched the episodes and then discussed them with a trained moderator. Many of the respondents noted that the female characters on *The Bold and the Beautiful* were particularly assertive, something that was not typically found in Indian society. Regarding the HIV storyline, messages about sexual assertiveness in the text were regarded as undesirable. In the soap narrative, the characters come to accept Tony as an HIV-infected person. However, the respondents in the sample regarded this outcome as impossible in India where there is a strong stigma attached to HIV/AIDS. Perhaps the only aspect of the program that directly impacted the lives of everyday Indians was the fashion worn by the actors in the program, which many respondents regarded as desirable.

A later comparison of American and Indian audiences' interpretations of the television sitcom *Friends* also revealed some subtle differences (Chitnis, Thombre, Rogers, Singhal, & Sengupta, 2006). Although American and Indian viewers both perceived the text of *Friends* to be somewhat transparent (meaning that they could imagine themselves in situations like the ones depicted in the program), some of the cultural experiences and lifestyle found in the program were regarded as strictly American. In particular, the strong role of women in the program and their autonomy in directing romantic and sexual encounters within the narrative were foreign to viewers in the Indian sample. As these studies demonstrate, the degree of cultural proximity assigned to media texts by audiences can play an important role in shaping not just the enjoyment of the text but also the perceived reality of the situations and characters found in those texts.

Race, Ethnicity, and Audience Decoding: Viewers Interpret *The Cosby Show*

As the previously discussed studies make clear, cultural contexts of nationality, gender, and class can play an important role in how audiences interpret media texts, especially if those texts feature characters and narratives that challenge viewers' self-concepts. In this respect, race and ethnicity emerge as equally important cultural contexts for helping us understand how audiences interpret media content. Perhaps the most important thing to understand about race and media is that mainstream media often are highly skewed when it comes to accurately representing racial and ethnic diversity in society. A 2018 study of 1,100 popular Hollywood films conducted by researchers at the Annenberg School for Communication at the University of Southern California, for example, found that only about 13% of all films released from 2007 to 2017 contained racially balanced casts (Smith, Choueiti, Pieper, Case, & Choi, 2018). Of the films they examined, roughly 70% of all roles were played by White actors, 12% of roles played by African Americans, 6.2% by Hispanics or Latinos, and 6.3% by Asians. They found that some gains had been made in representation since 2007, but those amounted to only about a 6% increase in minority representation in popular films. Consequently, when audiences of color survey the media landscape, they are first confronted with a palpable *absence* of diversity. Secondly, when minorities do appear in the media, they are often relegated to secondary or minor characters, and many of those characters are villains or antagonists. A comprehensive 20-year content analysis of the most popular American television shows from 1987 to 2009, for example, found that Latinos, Asians, and Native Americans were severely underrepresented and that these minority groups were depicted on-screen in highly stereotypical ways, which only served to strengthen racial attitudes of White audiences (Tukachinsky, Mastro, & Yarchi, 2015).

How do audiences navigate these inequalities in media? How might these television viewer's own racial identity and life experiences shape their decoding of popular media texts? In their book *Enlightened Racism*, scholars Sut Jhally and Justin Lewis (1992) set out to examine how audiences from different racial backgrounds might interpret a popular television text. They conducted 52 different focus group discussions with White, African American, and Latino/a viewers from Springfield, Massachusetts, in 1990. Each group watched an episode of the hit 1980s American situation comedy, *The Cosby Show*. The show, which followed the fictional exploits of the Huxtable family, was groundbreaking when it first appeared on American television in 1984 because it was one of the most-watched programs in history to feature a mostly all-Black cast. Additionally, in contrast to earlier depictions of African Americans as poor and uneducated, the show's main characters, Cliff and Clair Huxtable, were upwardly mobile: Cliff was a successful gynecologist and Clair was a corporate lawyer. The show was hugely popular in the United States, demonstrating that a program featuring Black actors could have a mass appeal.

Jhally and Lewis asked their focus group respondents a series of open-ended questions about the show. What did they think of the Huxtable family or the situations that were depicted in the show? What surprised the researchers initially was how much the respondents seemed to blur the distinctions between this TV family and their own social reality. They write that "many viewers were too engaged with the situations and the characters on television that they naturally read beyond the scene or program they were discussing and speculated about them as real events and characters" (Jhally & Lewis, 1992, p. 19). In fact, among the focus groups with White viewers, the researchers found that these viewers spoke mainly about the family situations and the comedy in the episode, and they did not mention the notion of race until directly questioned about it. When asked, these viewers stated that they felt that Black families in America could obtain the same kind of wealth and social status as the Huxtable family. Indeed, they felt that the TV Huxtable family was evidence of equality of opportunity in the United States. This is a strong indicator that these respondents were engaged in a dominant or hegemonic reading of the *Cosby* text.

How did African-American viewers interpret *Cosby*? Jhally and Lewis found that African-American respondents were acutely aware of racial stereotypes in the mainstream media and were correspondingly pleased and proud that *The Cosby Show* worked to counter those narratives by featuring an upper-middle-class, professional Black family. Yet while these viewers acknowledged the negative media stereotypes of Black Americans, they insisted at the same time that they knew families just like the Huxtables. Jhally and Lewis argue that this type of interpretation among Black audiences suggests that they were willing to accept the "unreality" of the Cosbys as a means of escaping racial stereotypes on prime-time television. Indeed, the need for positive Black images on American television is so strong, they argue, that African-American viewers may begin to believe that the world created by the Cosbys *is* real. This seemingly contradictory response—critiquing images of African Americans in the media while simultaneously holding on to the premise that the Cosbys represent an authentic view of economic attainment in the United States—suggests a *negotiated* approach among these audiences to *The Cosby Show*. In their conclusion, Jhally and Lewis worry that African-American audiences' need to accept the fictional Cosbys as a realistic reflection of minority life in 1990s America would instill in them the notion that such economic attainment is possible without governmental policies such as affirmative action. If African-American viewers struggle to attain the same high standard of living that they see on *The Cosby Show*, the researchers argue, they may hold themselves largely accountable for that failure rather than work to reform a society where race remains a major factor in social and economic inequality.

Open Texts and Popular Meanings

The question of how different social groupings (such as age, gender, and race) might affect the decoding of popular media was only one of the lingering uncertainties that emerged from Morley's *Nationwide* study. Another query that arose from Morley's work was who exactly was determining the difference between a dominant, negotiated, and oppositional decoding of popular television—the individuals under investigation or the researcher himself? In other words, what role does the researcher play in actually *creating* the very changes or trends that he sees in the observational data (Hartley, 1987)? This degree of unintended influence of the observer on research subjects, often simply due to the presence of an outsider among the observed community, is a long-standing concern for empirical social scientists. What if the decoding categories used by Hall and Morley were simply academic inventions that did not adequately reflect how audiences perceived their own interpretations of media texts? The research situation complicated this question because Morley brought his participants into a different setting (not the home environment where they are used to watching television), selected particular episodes for them to view, and held an in-depth discussion of the program afterward. The somewhat-artificial nature of the research setting caused some scholars to question whether audiences were giving "natural" responses to questions about their interpretations of *Nationwide*.

Open Texts: The Theories of John Fiske

These critiques of the encoding/decoding model were pushed further by John Fiske (1987, 1989), who advocated for an expansion of the theoretical role of the audience in the decoding process. For Fiske, the distinction between the text and the audience made by Hall's model was an artificial one. In fact, he argued, "There is no text, there is no audience, there are only the processes of viewing—that variety of cultural activities that take place in front of the screen which constitute the object of study" (Fiske, 1989, p. 57). The categories of text and audience should be dissolved, in essence, because without the interpretive intervention of the audience, media texts do not have existence or meaning. Texts, therefore, have fluid boundaries that are defined only by the specific audiences who create them in the process of consuming media. This takes the locus of interpretive power away from the media text itself and situates it firmly in the hands of the audience.

In his 1987 book *Television Culture*, Fiske argued that television was an "open" text due to its many gaps in narrative structure and lack of flow. The continual interruption of the serial program format and commercial breaks invites the audience to seal those gaps through their own interpretive processes (1987, p. 147). Not only was television an open text, but it was also a **polysemic text**, which means that the structure of the narrative and its presentation allow for a multitude of interpretations by different audiences. Fiske characterizes television as a "producerly" text because it "relies upon discursive competencies that the viewer already possesses, but requires that they are used in a self-interested, productive way" (1987, p. 95). Television texts become "activated" whenever audiences receive and interpret them and begin the creative process of associating meanings with the information on the screen. This creative process is pleasurable for the audience and serves as the source of television's enduring popularity. In fact, writes Fiske, the unfinished form of television itself invites the participation of the audience in completing the picture. Unlike a book, which can be read from beginning to end in a single sitting (if desired), the serial nature of television series (once per week or per day) is a continual interruption of the narrative. These breaks invite the audience to imagine what will happen in the future or to speculate about what happens to characters who are not currently on the screen. Additionally, television texts are full of what Fiske terms "semiotic excess"—cues in the message that allow viewers to construct multiple meanings, even oppositional, contrary meanings. Textual elements such as irony, jokes, contradictions, and metaphors allow for viewers to draw many of their own conclusions from the television narrative.

Intertextuality and Interpretive Communities

Another key aspect of the reception process, according to Fiske (1987), was that audiences inevitably draw outside experiences, influences, and their knowledge of other media texts into their interpretation of television. Media texts do not exist in isolation from one another, particularly in our modern era when television, the Internet, and radio are converging into one digital content stream. Audiences naturally relate texts to their own personal experiences, which includes past experiences with other media. This process of connecting our media experiences together is called **intertextuality** and can be defined as "the fundamental and inescapable interdependence of all textual meaning upon the structures of meaning proposed by other texts" (Gray, 2006, pp. 3–4). Gray's definition underscores the fact that audiences never interpret media in complete isolation from other texts. Instead, we create meanings out of our media universe by relating specific messages to others that we have seen or heard. This not only adds some greater context to the individual text in question, but it also results in a unique creative act on the part of reader/viewer. Quite often, linking the text that you are interpreting with other content or information is one of the primary pleasures derived from consuming popular texts.

The process of web surfing on the Internet demonstrates how intertextuality works in practice. On any given webpage you may be viewing, you will find hyperlinks that may direct your browser into more specific information on that topic, event, or individual. While on that new webpage, you may find more hyperlinks to more information, and pretty soon, you may be far afield from the original page that you were viewing. Similarly, while watching the latest episode of the reality TV competition series *America's Next Top Model*, you may talk with a friend about an article about Tyra Banks (the supermodel and host of the program) that you read in a gossip magazine. You might also look for some similarities in the kinds of advice Banks offers the would-be model contestants and dishes out on her daily talk show, *The Tyra Banks Show*. This kind of intertextuality is not limited just to popular films and television shows, and it is certainly not new. In fact, book audiences have been using intertextuality for centuries. As you might imagine, important foundational religious texts like the Bible, the Talmud, and the Koran are some of the most referenced texts in human societies. English playwright William Shakespeare, for example, often referenced the Bible and other important texts of Western civilization in his plays. These mentions can even be tracked in quite sophisticated ways using a Shakespeare concordance, which is essentially a large dictionary of terms and phrases found in Shakespeare's works, cross-referenced with the original source. References to Shakespeare's own original characters and plots are also found in numerous places throughout Western literature and popular culture, continuing the cycle of intertextuality. More recent incarnations of intertextual wizardry involve the selection of different aspects of popular music and "remixing" them into new creative songs that are often posted on the Internet (see Chapter 9).

Over time, certain interpretations of texts can become more permanent and consistent among audiences. Despite the "openness" of texts, groups of viewers or readers may begin to construct similar meanings based on mutual shared interests or demographic similarity (like Morley's *Nationwide* groups, for instance), social pressures, or past experiences. In this case, viewers may form what English scholar Stanley Fish (1980) called an **interpretive community**. Like Fiske, Fish proposed that authors and texts themselves exist only insofar as they are experienced by readers, such that "the reader's response is not *to* the meaning; it *is* the meaning" (emphasis in original; 1980, p. 3). This means that different groups of readers or audiences will develop interpretations that coincide with their interests and experiences with a text or collection of texts. For example, literary or media critics will sometimes come to interpretive conclusions about a text that will conflict with those of casual audiences or fans of that text. Fish emphasizes that these interpretive strategies "exist prior to the act of reading and therefore determine the shape of what is read rather than, as is usually assumed, the other way around" (1980, p. 171). This formulation places the power of defining and, indeed, of *creating* meaning out of the formal properties of texts firmly in the hands of readers and viewers. Just as interpretations of texts can shift, so too can interpretive communities because they are

> not natural or universal, but learned. . . . The only stability, then, inheres in the fact (at least in [Fish's] model) that interpretive strategies are always being deployed, and this means that communication is a much more chancy affair than we are accustomed to think of it. (Fish, 1980, p. 172)

In other words, interpretive communities come into being only through the actions of their members and are subject to shifts over time. One of the more interesting recent investigations of complex interactions between popular texts and interpretive communities is Jonathan Gray's work on the hit Fox animated series *The Simpsons* (see Box 6.3).

BOX 6.3
D'oh! Parody, Irony, and Audiences for *The Simpsons*

Fox Television's animated family comedy *The Simpsons* premiered as a regular series on American screens in January 1990 and is currently the longest-running prime-time television series in U.S. history (Hudson, 2009). The program

follows the exploits of the Simpson family in the fictional town of Springfield, USA (the state is unknown), but its cultural resonance has been felt worldwide. One of the most interesting and thorough recent analyses of the interpretive interactions between texts and readers is Jonathan Gray's 2006 book, *Watching With the Simpsons*.

Gray writes that not only is the show popular around the globe, but it has also ushered in a new type of "ironically distanced and distancing humor" as a narrative style (Gray, 2006, p. 6). The show parodies current political, social, and religious debates while casting an ironic gaze on the media itself, making the program a densely layered and highly intertextual text. Gray writes:

> Much of its humor is deeply transitive, pointing outside the borders of *The Simpsons* to all manner of other genres, texts, and discourses. To laugh at these jokes is frequently to read those other genres, texts, and discourses as much as it is to read *The Simpsons*. (2006, p. 10)

The critical and popular success of *The Simpsons* owes much to this complex interplay of textual knowledge, inviting viewers to appreciate multiple levels of humor depending upon the initial level of awareness of popular culture, television, current events, and the history of the series itself. What do such regular viewers make of the program?

In 2001 and 2002, Gray interviewed 35 regular *Simpsons* viewers who lived in the central London area. Gray's respondents ranged in age from 22 to 38 years old. The average age was 27, which reflects the somewhat younger age demographic for the program as a whole (Gray, 2006, p. 120). Gray asked viewers about their favorite or least favorite characters on the program,

what they thought about the quality of the show (whether it was getting better or worse), what was funny about *The Simpsons*, and whether the show has any particular "politics" or point of view, among other things.

He found that *The Simpsons* was the kind of program that brought people together and formed an initial social bond of mutual interest and appreciation of the show's wry, ironic humor and deft parody of celebrities and modern popular media. Viewers who watched the show together found that it served as a tool to connect to others through *Simpsons*-related conversation. Some who did not watch the show regularly even found themselves somewhat cut off from their friends who did. How did these viewers interpret the show's relentless parody and ironic take on the media, celebrities, and current events? Many of Gray's respondents described the program as "clever" or "witty" or even "smart but funny," noting that the show's humor works on a surface level as well as on a deeper level of social commentary and satire. Viewers noted that *The Simpsons* often took critical aim at big issues such as capitalism, consumerism, the television industry (even the show's parent, the Fox TV network), suburban life, and the notion of TV sitcoms themselves. As one respondent put it, "Everyone and everything is fair game. Including themselves" (Gray, 2006, p. 147). Ultimately, these viewers found the intertextuality of *The Simpsons* to be a prime source of interpretive pleasure. However, Gray warns that the end result of the program's relentless parody may be a cynical detachment from the types of social problems and human foibles that are so mercilessly parodied in every episode.

Source: Gray, J. (2006). *Watching With The Simpsons: Television: Parody, and Intertextuality.* London, England: Routledge.

Revisiting Encoding/ Decoding in the 21st Century

The classical theories of audience interpretation outlined in this chapter were conceived in a pre-Internet era. It's clear that the arrival of the Internet in the 1990s and the explosion of user-generated content via blogs, YouTube, and social media has radically reoriented the media landscape (which will be the central focus of Chapter 10). A media environment that was once dominated by industrialized, formalized systems of production and distribution has now expanded and diversified to incorporate a rising tide of mediated content, much of which is generated by individual media users (the erstwhile "audience"). Stuart Hall and a number of his contemporaries sought to decenter the role of the text as a dominating force in meaning production by highlighting audiences' abilities to sometimes reinscribe or reimagine the meaning of the text. For Hall, the key to unlocking oppositional readings of the text were found in cultural competencies that were linked to sociodemographic categories such as class, race, and gender. Hall's notion of oppositional readings and the realization that texts were "open" (to use Fiske's term) seemed to offer audiences a pathway to liberate themselves from media texts to inscribe meaning into media, thereby completing the "circuit" of communication between the message producer and the audience. Was Hall potentially overstating the power of the audience, however? Several scholars in early 2000s pointed to some potential weaknesses in Hall's model and offered revisions.

Reimagining Audience Decoding: Carolyn Michelle's Modes of Interpretation

One major restructuring of Hall's model was offered by Carolyn Michelle (2007). She argued that the encoding/decoding model essentially conflates two different dimensions of audience interpretation: their understanding of the *form and structure* of a media text and the *content* (and potential ideological meanings) of the text. When respondents in Hall's *Nationwide* study were responding to the program in what Hall identified as an oppositional reading, were they responding to the ideological subtext of the news program (as Hall concluded), or were they reacting critically instead to the formal elements of the program (the denotative aspect of the message), such as the news program's low production values? Michelle argues that, in fact, the kind of counterideological interpretations imagined by Hall are much rarer than scholars might think. By separating audience interpretations of message from its content, Michelle finds that "the only form of critical reading that is seriously capable of resisting or opposing the semantic or ideological content of a text is one which challenges that content directly in terms of its ideological or discursive grounding" (2007, p. 192).

In place of the three interpretive reading strategies outlined by Hall—dominant, negotiated, and oppositional—Michelle proposes four modes of audience engagement with media texts (see Figure 6.7 for a visual of the model). The first three

Figure 6.7 Michelle's (2007) Multidimensional Model of Audience Interpretation

DENOTATIVE LEVEL OF MEANING

Transparent Mode:

Text _as_ life

- *Non-fiction texts:* perceived as a "mirror" of reality
- *Fiction texts:* "suspension of disbelief"
- Ideological/discursive content is *implicitly* read "straight" → dominant/preferred decoding

Referential Mode:

Text as _like_ life

Comparative sources potentially drawn on:

i) Personal experience/individual biography

ii) Immediate life world experience

iii) Experience and knowledge of the wider social/political/economic/cultural/national/international context of production or reception

Mediated Mode:

Text as a _production_

Heightened attunement to:

i) Textual aesthetics

ii) Generic form

iii) Intentionality
- Textual
- Generic
- Professional/Industry-based

CONNOTATIVE LEVEL OF MEANING

Discursive Mode: Text as a *message*

i) *Analytical* (Comprehension of message)
- Identification
- Motivation
- Implication

ii) *Positional* (Response to that message)

Dominant/Preferred   *Negotiated*   *Oppositional*

EVALUATION

Hegemonic Reading   *Contesting Reading*   *Counterhegemonic Reading*

Close/ Subjective ←   → **Distant / Objective**

(Relationship between text and viewer)

Source: Adapted from Michelle, C. (2007). "Modes of Reception: A Consolidated Analytical Framework." *Communication Review, 10*(3), 181–222.

reception modes are all focused on the denotative level of meaning or the formal and structural elements of the media message (such as the script, the camera angles, the writing, characters, plot, etc.). The first mode of reception is "transparent" and occurs when audiences perceive nonfiction texts as a mirror to reality. For fiction, this occurs when audiences suspend their disbelief to engage directly with the story and characters in a narrative. Michelle notes that this type of interpretation effectively leads to a dominant or preferred reading of the media text that Hall's model outlines. The second decoding strategy is what Michelle describes as the "referential" mode, wherein audiences connect media texts to their own personal experiences or real-world knowledge. The third reading strategy, called the "mediated" mode, occurs when audiences focus their attention on the aesthetics or form of the text itself, bringing to the fore their awareness of the institutions or structures that guide the production of media messages. So, for example, a film viewer using the mediated reception mode may decide that she is largely unimpressed by actor Tom Cruise's performance in the hit film *Mission Impossible: Rogue Nation*, but at the same time, she may draw upon her knowledge that Cruise's production company has bankrolled the film, so there likely was no real choice about who would play the lead male character.

The fourth reception mode shifts from the formal aspects of the text (the denotative level of meaning) and considers the content of the message (the connotative level). Called the "discursive" mode, this occurs when audiences "specifically address the text's propositional or 'message' content—i.e., its ideological connotations" (Michelle, 2007, p. 206). This reading mode is perhaps most similar to the analytical categories originally proposed by Stuart Hall. This reception mode is identified by an "analytical" dimension—whereby viewers "may identify (comprehend) the message that is explicitly articulated within the text, and perhaps analyze it further in terms of its motivations or implications" or by reflecting on "the viewer's *position* in relation to textual connotations" (Michelle, 2007, p. 208). This reception mode requires that audiences engage directly with the content of the material presented to them and is a prerequisite for kinds of oppositional readings imagined by Hall. The final category of Michelle's model is called "evaluation." Once an individual audience member's response to a text is ascertained via the four criteria, their descriptive responses to those criteria are then evaluated according to whether these interpretations constitute *hegemonic, contesting*, or *counterhegemonic* readings. These three evaluative criteria—so central to the encoding/decoding mode—are preserved but are anchored in a more nuanced understanding of audiences' reaction to media texts at the denotative level.

Let's take a closer look at how Michelle's audience interpretation framework can apply to a specific example. Granelli and Zenor (2016) studied audience reactions to the crime drama and mystery television series *Dexter*, which aired on the Showtime cable network from 2006 to 2013. The series centers on the character Dexter Morgan who is a forensic technician specializing in blood splatter analysis for the Miami Metro Police Department. By day, Dexter is employed by the police, but in his off hours, he leads a parallel life as a vigilante serial killer who hunts down and murders individuals who have previously escaped justice. Granelli and Zenor wanted to know this: How do audiences interpret and reconcile the conflicting norms of morality in this program? To study this question, they evaluated professional and amateur published reviews of the first season of the program and identified 59 specific dominant themes in the responses. Then they recruited 62 respondents from a midsize public university in the U.S. Northeast and asked them to sort these statements into two piles: those they agreed with and those they disagreed with. After the sorting was complete, open-ended interviews with the respondents were conducted to explore the reasoning behind their sorts.

Their results revealed several distinct interpretation modes among *Dexter* viewers. One interpretive scheme, which Granelli and Zenor dubbed "justified vigilante," perceived the Dexter character to be a hero because he used his impulses for good and not for gratuitous revenge. They identified this interpretive strategy as the "transparent" mode in Michelle's (2007) framework because these viewers lost themselves in the text and its moral universe. Other respondents approached the program with an alternative interpretation, which focused on the ways in which the program depicted the complexities of human morality. These individuals were working in a "referential" mode of engagement because they had some empathy for the lead character while also noting that their own actions and moral compass were quite different. The third interpretive strategy, dubbed "gratuitous violence" by Granelli and Zenor, was repulsed by Dexter's violent vigilantism. As one respondent replied, "Do I think killing is wrong and unjust? No matter what? Yes." These viewers operated in a "discursive" mode because they dealt primarily with the connotative level of meaning and explicitly rejected the program's premise that violent criminals can have sympathetic qualities. The last interpretive strategy used by the respondents recognized that the program was fictionalized yet enjoyable because it depicted a type of "deviant escapism" found only in popular culture. Because these individuals made clear distinctions between reality and the fantasy environment of the program, they were interpreting the program through a "mediated" form of engagement in Michelle's (2007) framework. This example demonstrates the degree of nuance that audiences bring to media texts, particularly those that explore complex themes and morally ambiguous protagonists. Granelli and Zenor's study also revealed that respondents were more likely to center their interpretations on the *form* of the text (the denotative level of meaning) as opposed to the *content* (connotative meaning), consistent with Michelle's model.

Online, Digital Media, and Audience Decoding

Theories of audience interpretation have historically examined audiences' reactions to popular media since these texts are both widely available and are based upon the broadcast model: Media messages flow oneway from institutionalized message producers (television, radio, film, etc.) to audiences. Think about our current media environment, much of which is mediated via the Internet. The lines between producers and audiences have been considerably blurred, thanks to a host of user-generated content such as personal websites, blogs, wikis, podcasts, and social media, just to mention a few. Can models of audience interpretation from the 20th century be effectively mapped onto our media experiences in the 21st century?

A number of scholars have argued that, yes, in fact, Hall's encoding/decoding model and the model's careful consideration of the connection between culture and audience interpretations can be valuable for analyzing today's media environment. How might scholars understand something like video games within the context of audience interpretations, for example? Video games scholar Adrienne Shaw (2017) has wrestled with this question, noting that Hall's notion of decoding doesn't necessarily take into account the kind of active engagement with the text that is a basic requirement of digital games. She writes:

> Audience activity with digital media does not simply demonstrate the resistive agency of audience members, as in much of digital, contemporary media it is largely a requirement for using these media. A video game, for example, simply cannot function without a measure of activity and involvement beyond that which is required in other media. This makes video games activities as much as they are texts. The interactive properties of the texts, however, do not define the experience of game play. Understanding their reception, thus, must interrogate what actions these texts invite and how players actually use them. (Shaw, 2017, p. 597)

As Shaw makes clear, audiences are increasingly called upon to engage actively with media. She advocates for the use of the concept of *affordances* to help scholars apply encoding/decoding to 21st-century media. Affordances essentially refers both to the structural features of a particular technology, application, or text (its environment), as well as the universe of potential applications for that thing (something that is called "imagined affordances" by Nagy & Neff, 2015). So, for example, a dominant or hegemonic use of a text/technology like video games might involve following the rules and doing what the text/technology imagines. An oppositional use might involve subverting that text/technology by changing the design parameters (by hacking or modding the games, for example) or by employing cheats or other tools to jump ahead of other players. These alterations of the encoding/decoding model could assist scholars in applying Hall's theoretical framework to a range of new, interactive technologies and texts that dominate our media world today.

Conclusion: Interpretation and Audience Power

In this chapter, we have explored the idea of audience interpretation, beginning with the notion that audiences not only select specific media content but also bring to it a range of intellectual competencies that profoundly shape their understandings of media. The 1980s saw a shift in the paradigm for studying audiences away from a transmission model and toward a process model that examined the specific interactions between individual viewers and media texts. Theories of media interpretation that were developed in the 1970s and 1980s rested upon the foundation of semiotics, or the production and circulation of signs in society. The theories of Althusser were used to reintroduce Marxist concerns with ideology and resistance into the field of media interpretation. The potential for audience liberation from the ideological constraints of mainstream media was the key theoretical antecedent to Stuart Hall's groundbreaking "Encoding/Decoding" essay. Hall's work, in turn, encouraged a new generation of scholars such as David Morley, Charlotte Brunsdon, Dorothy Hobson, Ien Ang, Carolyn Michelle and Adrienne Shaw (among others) to incorporate qualitative observational and interview methods to explore how viewers actually understood their media environment. While Morley relied heavily on class distinctions as one of the more powerful determinants of audience decoding style, others focused on gender, race, and cultural context key influences in audiences' interpretations of media. Scholars such as John Fiske went even further in questioning the relevance of the text/audience distinction by arguing that media texts themselves exist only insofar as they are created by the interpretive activities of the audience.

One of the critical questions that remained unanswered from Morley's *Nationwide* study was the extent to which the somewhat artificial research setting created by the study itself created the very responses that Morley recorded and analyzed. Could audiences provide their "true" and natural responses to a researcher in a viewing setting that was contrived to produce research results? The same critique could be leveled at Ang's study of *Dallas* viewers and Radway's research on romance novel readers: What role did the reception context *itself* play in the interpretation of media texts? Hobson's *Crossroads* study spearheaded a new direction for reception scholars: to engage audiences and their media consumption in individual, domestic contexts to investigate whether and how reception settings might play a role in textual interpretation. To that end, the next chapter returns to the 1980s to explore the growing interest in social and situational contexts and their role in shaping audience experiences with the media.

DISCUSSION ACTIVITIES

1. Select a film or television program of your choice (it could be a fictional program or even a sporting event). Sit down to watch the program and, as you do, keep a running diary of your thoughts and interpretations in a stream-of-consciousness style. Alternatively, you can ask someone else not familiar with the theories in this chapter to do this exercise. Then, once you have completed the freewrite, look back on your response and think about the following questions:

   - What kinds of meanings or interpretations were you making of this program?

   - Were any other texts or experiences talked about in the freewrite? Cite some examples of intertextuality in the response.

- Do you see any evidence of negotiated or oppositional readings in your response? If so, what examples can you cite? If not, think about what might constitute a negotiated or oppositional reading (in Hall's terminology) to the media text you viewed and make some notes about this to share with the class.

2. Select a news program (either an evening newscast or a newsmagazine program such as *20/20, Dateline*, or PBS's *Frontline*) and closely examine a particular news story within the program. What issues or problems were addressed in the program? What type of argument, if any, is being made about the possible solution to the issue or how the issue may develop in the future? Make notes on the dominant or ideological messages that you see at either a denotative or connotative level. Next, show your news story to family, to friends, or to classmates and ask them what their responses or reactions are to the program. Do you see any evidence of dominant, negotiated, or oppositional readings here?

3. Watch the video *Representation and the Media*. It is an extended lecture by scholar Stuart Hall and was produced by the Media Education Foundation (http://www.mediaed.org/cgi-bin/commerce.cgi?preadd=action&key=409). Once you have done so, answer the following questions:

- What kinds of meanings are embedded within popular cultural texts, according to Hall? In what ways are some of Hall's ideas similar to those of screen theory and Louis Althusser?

- How do language and other "signification practices" work to create and fix meanings of media texts? How is ideology at work here?

- What is the role of the audience in this process, according to Stuart Hall? Do audiences have the power to combat media stereotypes and make oppositional readings? How might this be accomplished?

ADDITIONAL MATERIALS

Abercrombie, N., & Longhurst, B. (1998). Changing audiences, changing paradigms of research. *Audiences: A sociological theory of performance and imagination* (pp. 3–37). London, England: SAGE.

Akomfrah, J. (2013). *The Stuart Hall project*. Retrieved from http://www.imdb.com/title/tt2578290/

Alasuutari, P. (1999). Introduction: Three phases of reception studies. In P. Alasuutari (Ed.), *Rethinking the media audience: The new agenda* (pp. 1–21). London, England: SAGE.

BBC audio programs honoring the life and work of Stuart Hall following his death in 2014 (https://www.bbc.co.uk/programmes/p01s49fk).

Hall, S. (1980). Encoding/decoding. In S. Hall, D. Hobson, A. Lowe, & P. Willis (Eds.), *Culture, media, language: Working papers in cultural studies* (pp. 128–138). London, England: Hutchinson.

Livingstone, S., & Das, R. (2013). Interpretation/reception [Data set]. In P. Moy (Ed.), *Oxford bibliographies online: Communication*. Oxford, United Kingdom: Oxford University Press. Available at http://eprints.lse.ac.uk/62649/1/Interpretation_reception.pdf

Moores, S. (1993). *Interpreting audiences: The ethnography of media consumption*. London, England: SAGE.

Murdock, G. (2017). Encoding and decoding. In P. Rössler, C. Hoffner, & L. van Zoonen (Eds.), *The international encyclopedia of media effects* (pp. 1–11). London, England: John Wiley & Sons. https://doi .org/10.1002/9781118783764.wbieme0113

Sender, K. (1998). *Off the straight & narrow: Lesbians, gays, bisexuals & television, 1967–1998.* Media Education Foundation [Video documentary].

Available at http://www.mediaed.org/cgi-bin/ commerce.cgi?preadd=action&key=207

Sender, K. (2006). *Further off the straight & narrow: New gay visibility on television, 1998–2006.* Media Education Foundation [Video documentary]. Available at http://www.mediaed.org/cgi-bin/ commerce.cgi?preadd=action&key=225

REFERENCES

Abercrombie, N., & Longhurst, B. (1998). *Audiences: A sociological theory of performance and imagination.* London, England: SAGE.

Althusser, L. (2001). Ideology and ideological state apparatuses (notes towards an investigation). In M. G. Durham & D. M. Kellner (Eds.), *Media and cultural studies: keyworks* (pp. 79–88). London, England: Blackwell.

Ang, I. (1985). *Watching* Dallas: *Soap opera and the melodramatic imagination.* London, England: Methuen.

Barthes, R. (1987). *Mythologies.* New York, NY: Hill and Wang.

Boczkowski, P. J. (2004). *Digitizing the news: Innovation in online newspapers.* Cambridge, MA: MIT Press.

Brunsdon, C. (1981). "Crossroads": Notes on soap opera. *Screen, 22*(4), 32–37.

Brunsdon, C., & Morley, D. (1978). *Everyday television: Nationwide.* London, England: British Film Institute.

Chitnis, K. S., Thombre, A., Rogers, E. M., Singhal, A., & Sengupta, A. (2006). (Dis)similar readings: Indian and American audiences' interpretation of Friends. *International Communication Gazette, 68*(2), 131–145.

Conan, N. (2009, July 1). Loud family paved way for reality TV. *Talk of the Nation.* National Public Radio. Retrieved from http://www.npr.org/templates/story/ story.php?storyId=106161851

Currie, D. (1999). *Girl talk: Adolescent magazines and their readers.* Toronto, Ontario: University of Toronto Press.

de Saussure, F. (2000). *Course in general linguistics.* (R. Harris, Trans.). Peru, IL: Open Court.

Döring, N., Reif, A., & Poeschl, S. (2016). How gender-stereotypical are selfies? A content analysis and comparison with magazine adverts. *Computers in Human Behavior, 55,* 955–962.

Fedina, L., Holmes, J. L., & Backes, B. L. (2018). Campus sexual assault: A systematic review of prevalence research from 2000 to 2015. *Trauma, Violence, & Abuse, 19*(1), 76–93. https://doi .org/10.1177/1524838016631129

Fish, S. (1980). *Is there a text in this class? The authority of interpretive communities.* Cambridge, MA: Harvard University Press.

Fiske, J. (1987). *Television culture.* London, England: Methuen.

Fiske, J. (1989). Moments of television: Neither the text nor the audience. In E. Seiter, H. Borchers, G. Kreutzner, & E.-M. Warth (Eds.), *Remote control: Television, audiences, and cultural power* (pp. 56–78). London, England: Routledge.

Gans, H. J. (1980). *Deciding what's news: A study of CBS Evening News, NBC Nightly News, Newsweek, and Time*. New York, NY: Vintage Books.

Gitlin, T. (1983). *Inside prime time*. New York, NY: Pantheon Books.

Goffman, E. (1979). *Gender advertisements*. New York, NY: Harper & Row.

Granelli, S., & Zenor, J. (2016). Decoding "The Code": Reception theory and moral judgment of *Dexter. International Journal of Communication*, *10*, 5056–5078.

Gray, A. (1999). Audience and reception research in retrospect: The trouble with audiences. In P. Alasuutari (Ed.), *Rethinking the media audience: The new agenda* (pp. 22–37). London: SAGE.

Gray, J. (2006). *Watching with the Simpsons: Television, parody, and intertextuality*. London, England: Routledge.

Hall, S. (1980). Encoding/decoding. In S. Hall, D. Hobson, A. Lowe, & P. Willis (Eds.), *Culture, media, language: Working papers in cultural studies* (pp. 128–138). London, England: Hutchinson.

Hall, S. (1982). The rediscovery of "ideology": Return of the repressed in media studies. In M. Gurevitch, T. Bennett, J. Curran, & J. Woollacott (Eds.), *Culture, society and the media* (pp. 56–90). London, England: Methuen.

Hartley, J. (1987). Invisible fictions: Television audiences, paedocracy, pleasure. *Textual Practice*, *1*(2), 121–138.

Hermes, J. (1995). *Reading women's magazines: An analysis of everyday media use*. Cambridge, United Kingdom: Polity Press.

Hobson, D. (1982). *Crossroads: The drama of a soap opera*. London, England: Methuen.

Horkheimer, M., & Adorno, T. W. (1972). *Dialectic of enlightenment*. New York, NY: Herder and Herder.

Horkheimer, M., & Adorno, T. W. (2001). The culture industry: Enlightenment as mass deception. In M. G. Durham & D. M. Kellner (Eds.), *Media and cultural studies: Keyworks* (pp. 41–72). London, England: Blackwell.

Hudson, J. (2009). *Fox renews hit animated series The Simpsons for two additional seasons* [Press release]. Los Angeles, CA: Fox Broadcasting. Retrieved from http://www.foxflash.com/div.php/main/page?aID=1z 2z2z175z17z8&ID=4786

Jhally, S., & Lewis, J. (1992). *Enlightened racism: The Cosby Show, audiences, and the myth of the American dream*. Boulder, CO: Westview Press.

Kearl, H. (2018). The facts behind the #metoo movement: A national study on sexual harassment and assault. *Stop street harassment*. http://www .stopstreetharassment.org/wp-content/ uploads/2018/01/Full-Report-2018-National-Study-on-Sexual-Harassment-and-Assault.pdf

Liebes, T., & Katz, E. (1986). Patterns of involvement in television fiction: A comparative analysis. *European Journal of Communication*, *1*(2), 151–171.

Liebes, T., & Katz, E. (1993). *The export of meaning: Cross-cultural readings of* Dallas. London, England: Polity Press.

Mayer, V., Banks, M. J., & Caldwell, J. T. (2009). *Production studies: Cultural studies of media industries*. London, England: Routledge.

Michelle, C. (2007). Modes of reception: A consolidated analytical framework. *Communication Review*, *10*(3), 181–222.

Moores, S. (1993). *Interpreting audiences: The ethnography of media consumption*. London, England: SAGE.

Morley, D. (1980). *The Nationwide audience: Structure and decoding*. London, England: British Film Institute.

Morley, D., & Brunsdon, C. (1999). *The Nationwide television studies*. London, England: Routledge.

Murdock, G. (2017). Encoding and decoding. In P. Rössler, C. Hoffner, & L. van Zoonen (Eds.), *The international encyclopedia of media effects* (pp. 1–11). London, England: John Wiley & Sons. https://doi .org/10.1002/9781118783764.wbieme0113

Nadler, A. M. (2016). *Making the news popular: Mobilizing U.S. news audiences*. Urbana: University of Illinois Press.

Nagy, P., & Neff, G. (2015). Imagined affordance: Reconstructing a keyword for communication theory. *Social Media + Society*, *1*(2), 1–9.

Parkin, F. (1971). *Class inequality and political order*. New York, NY: Praeger.

Radway, J. A. (1984). *Reading the romance: Women, patriarchy, and popular literature*. Chapel Hill: University of North Carolina Press.

Rogers, E. M., Singhal, A., & Thombre, A. (2004). Indian audience interpretations of health-related content in *The Bold and the Beautiful*. *Gazette*, *66*(5), 437–458.

Ruoff, J. (2001). *An American family: A televised life*. Minneapolis: University of Minnesota Press.

Seiter, E. (1992). Semiotics, structuralism, and television. *Channels of discourse, reassembled* (pp. 23–51). London, England: Routledge.

Shaw, A. (2017). Encoding and decoding affordances: Stuart Hall and interactive media technologies. *Media, Culture & Society*, *39*(4), 592–602.

Shoemaker, P. J., & Reese, S. D. (2013). *Mediating the message in the 21st century: A media sociology perspective*. New York, NY: Routledge.

Smith, S. L., Choueiti, M., Pieper, K., Case, A., & Choi, A. (2018). *Inequality in 1,100 popular films: Examining portrayals of gender, race/ethnicity, LGBT, & disability from 2007 to 2017*. Annenberg School for Communication at USC. Retrieved from http://assets .uscannenberg.org/docs/inequality-in-1100-popular-films.pdf

Stelter, B. (2009, June 23). *Jon and Kate split-up draws record-breaking audience. The New York Times*. Retrieved from http://mediadecoder.blogs.nytimes .com/2009/06/23/jon-and-kate-split-up-draws-record-breaking-audience/?scp=10&sq=jon%20 and%20kate&st=cse

Thompson, J. B. (1988). Mass communication and modern culture: Contribution to a critical theory of ideology. *Sociology*, *22*(3), 359–383.

Tukachinsky, R., Mastro, D., & Yarchis, M. (2015). Documenting portrayals of race/ethnicity on prime-time television over a 20-year span and their association with national-level racial/ethnic attitudes. *Journal of Social Issues*, *71*(1), 17–38.

Worthington, N. (2008). Encoding and decoding rape news: How progressive reporting inverts textual orientations. *Women's Studies in Communication*, *31*(3), 344–367.

Reception Contexts and Media Rituals

Stop for a moment and think about your everyday morning routine: Think about when you usually awaken; what you do as soon as you roll out of bed (or even before then); when you eat meals; when you watch television, surf the web, or check your Facebook and Twitter accounts (or other social networking sites); and when you send text messages to friends and family on your cell phone. If you mapped out precisely how much time you spend with forms of mass media, how many minutes or hours might you log for your media use in a single day, week, or year? In what kinds of situations do you find yourself being a part of an audience for some media technology? Do you generally access these technologies while you are alone or in the company of others? The answers to these questions may reveal how closely ingrained our media use has become in our daily lives and how the instantaneous availability of these technologies has begun to slowly yet radically alter the ways in which we engage with others.

Take the case of the Gude family from East Lansing, Michigan (Stone, 2009). In years past, Mr. and Mrs. Gude and their two sons, Cole and Erik, would have breakfast together before heading out the front door to work and school, respectively. Today, Mr. Gude wakes up at 6:00 a.m. in order to have sufficient time to check his work e-mail. Instead of waking his two sons, Mr. Gude simply sends a text message to their cell phones. "We use texting as an in-house intercom," he said. "I could just walk upstairs, but they always answer their texts." After being awakened by this "alarm," the two boys begin their morning by checking their text messages, playing video games, and updating their Facebook accounts. Initially, Mrs. Gude complained that media technologies were usurping valuable family time at the dinner table, but even she began using her laptop to check e-mail during the breakfast routine. Now the Gude family is actively trying to reclaim some of this lost interaction time by forcibly shutting down their electronic devices on the weekends. Does this scenario sound at all familiar to you? As the example of the Gude family illustrates, media technologies have burrowed themselves deeply into our everyday lives, permeating even our most private moments and spaces. Therefore, a full accounting of audience reception of television and other mass media is incomplete without specific attention to the "situatedness" (for lack of a better term) of these media in our routines and habits.

How can scholars study audience reception of television and other media in a way that does justice to the ingrained character of our media experiences? Since the consumption of media takes place largely in the private, domestic sphere, the picture that scholars have of actual reception behavior is naturally limited and incomplete. How, then, can researchers glean some insight into how audiences consume media in these private settings? One way is to rely on individuals' self-reports of their media-viewing behaviors, as uses and gratifications scholars have done (see Chapter 5), but this methodology is limited by its reliance on respondents' recollections of their media exposure and choices. Individuals have an inherent tendency to underestimate the time that they spend doing specific tasks (such as watching television or surfing the web), and they rarely pay close attention to the physical and social settings in which media exposure takes place. These shortcomings led reception theorists in the early 1980s to begin to develop ethnographic, anthropological techniques for observing audience behaviors to more accurately capture these contextual aspects of media use.

Overview of the Chapter

In this chapter, we focus on research into forms of **media reception**, the study of audience interpretation of media that occurs in specific contexts. Our media experiences occur during specific times and in particular physical spaces, and these contexts can play a powerful role in shaping our understandings of media content. The first part of the chapter looks at how the technology of television radically altered the physical and social environments of American homes beginning in the 1950s. We will then explore research by David Morley and other media reception scholars in the 1980s that examined the role that television has played in family communication patterns. This domestic focus will be expanded to encompass media technologies themselves and how their embeddedness in our everyday routines structures our sense of reality. We will see how technology links the private sphere of the home with the public events and outside personalities transmitted through our walls. Finally, we will continue the contextual approach to audiences by considering how media reception experiences themselves become intertwined with rituals. Both our everyday habits and those special occasions that interrupt these daily rituals call our attention and focus to the media and thereby offer us a moment to reflect on social practices and power relations.

While examining some classic studies of media reception within the family context, it is important to note that the media landscape that confronts us as audiences has transformed significantly in the past 25 years. Many of the social settings that scholars encountered in homes in the 1980s (such as single television set homes and centralized family use of television and other media) are now antiquated. An even more critical change comes from media that were not in existence in the 1980s but are now used on a daily basis by many individuals, such as satellite TV, the Internet, iPods, and smartphones. It is easy to see how the increasing ubiquity and portability of media have transformed both the physical and time contexts for media reception. We can be in contact with media messages almost anytime and anywhere, and we have almost complete control over *when* we view media content due to the sophistication of time-shifting. Therefore, we have more access to media than at any other time in our history. This chapter will provide an overview of the classic studies of media reception, while noting that the landscape has changed significantly. Toward the end of the chapter, I'll point to some research on the consequences of these changes for media audiences.

Media in Context: Notions of Space and Time

The focus of critical reception scholars beginning in the 1980s was centered on the local, situated, and *contextual* aspects of media use. The word **context** is used here to mean the specific environments in which media consumption occurs. Moores (1993, p. 32) refers to contexts as "everyday micro-settings" or "the routine physical locations and interpersonal relations of reception." It is important to understand that **contexts refer both to a *place* and a *web of interpersonal relationships and interactions that occur within that space***. The notion of **time** is also a part of this definition since we engage with media at specific moments during our day—sometimes planned, sometimes opportunistic. These three elements (space, social environment, and time) situate our media reception experiences and shape their meanings for us. This is not to say that the kinds of macrosocial contexts of class, race, gender, and cultural environment that we explored in Chapter 6 do not shape individual interpretations. However, we must also emphasize the specific microsocial situational and social contexts that play a role in audiences' reception.

Social and Situational Contexts

Whenever we encounter media texts, we are engaged with them in a particular moment and space. The unique interactions between those two elements can play an outsized role in (1) how we receive those texts (whether we are distracted or interacting with others, for example) and (2) how we interpret those texts. First, media consumption always takes place within a particular **spatial or physical context**—that is, the concrete, physical dimensions of the location. You may be watching an episode of the television series *American Idol* in your dorm room with a friend, in your living room at home with parents and siblings, or alone with your headphones plugged in to your portable media device (such as an iPod or MP4 player). Although you are viewing the same content in each of these examples, the experience that you are having as a viewer can be radically different because of the dimensions of the technology (a tiny 3-inch screen versus a large 50-inch screen) and because of the other people who regularly inhabit those spaces with you. For example, in your dorm room you may be continually interrupted or distracted by friends popping by, Snapchat messages flashing on your computer, or the essay for your communication class that sits half written on your computer screen. The influence of spatial context on reception of media is inseparable from the role of

social contexts in our media experiences. Reception spaces are partially defined by the people and relationships that are found there. Your home, for example, is not simply a physical structure with living spaces, bedrooms, and bathrooms; it is a dynamic, multifaceted space that encompasses people (family and loved ones), relationships, and vivid memories of past experiences. Often, the physical and social centrality of media in these spaces means that accounts of reception must recognize and acknowledge the deeply interconnected nature of these contexts for audiences (see Figure 7.1).

Figure 7.1 Group Viewing in Public Places Can Alter the Television Experience

Source: Stephanie Plumeri Ertz.

The introduction of television into America's living rooms in the early 1950s provides a fascinating example of how spatial and social contexts surrounding mass media are inextricably linked. The early days of television, which coincided with suburbanization and the postwar housing boom, made the introduction of the device seem all-the-more natural. New homeowners began outfitting their new spaces with all of the latest gadgets of convenience and leisure, including TV sets. However, the sheer newness of the medium challenged existing notions of space within the home. In 1949, as the first television sets began to appear in American homes, lifestyle magazines such as *Better Homes & Gardens* asked the pressing question: "Where does the receiver go?" By 1954, images of living rooms found in magazine articles and advertisements began to prominently feature TV sets (Spigel, 1992). As Lynn Spigel argues in *Make Room for TV* (her history of television in the postwar years), advertising images in the early 1950s "presented the television set as the new family hearth through which love and affection might be rekindled" (1992, p. 38). As the 1951 DuMont television advertisement in Figure 7.2 depicts, television was marketed as a technology that would bring the family together. The scene is straight out of a Norman Rockwell painting, and this advertisement is notable because the drawing of the family was done by none other than Rockwell himself. As Spigel notes in her analysis of popular home magazines from the period, pianos began to slowly disappear from images of living areas in American homes, replaced by televisions and other entertainment centers. In *Electronic Hearth*, Cecelia Tichi (1991) argues that television also became part of the gendered division of space within the home. Images in advertising and popular magazines invariably depicted the male head of household reclining in an easy chair in front of the TV, while women were shown preparing food for family members or guests. Tichi (1991, p. 7) states that "no matter how strikingly new a technology may be, once introduced into society it becomes deeply enmeshed in long-term cultural traditions and conflicts." In these insightful historical analyses, we see that the introduction of television sparked profound shifts in the organization of living spaces in American homes and disrupted existing family communication patterns by introducing a new focal point for family attention and activity within the domestic environment.

Time and Media Use

The third important context for our media reception is **time**. The concept of time has multiple dimensions. First, there are our daily schedule and routines. Media reception always occurs at specific moments in our day, whether it is listening to radio in the car on the way to work during rush hour or watching a rerun of an old television show late at night, right before we go to bed. We fit media exposure into the busy structure of our day (by filling in gaps with media use—when we are tired, waiting for someone or something, or simply taking a short break). We also use media to structure our day into discrete time segments (called time "punctuation"). During the 1980s, when some of the first landmark

Figure 7.2 1951 DuMont Television Advertisement

Source: Allan D. Dumont Laboratories, © 1958. Public Domain.

work on qualitative television reception was conducted, audiences were observed to "appointment view" their favorite programs. In other words, they adapted their activities to be able to consume a TV program at the specific time it was broadcast. However, with the rise of digital video recorder (DVR) technologies such as TiVo (the successor to the popular videocassette recorder, or VCR, from the 1980s) and web-based forms of television and film distribution such as Hulu.com and YouTube, audiences are more frequently **time-shifting** their media exposure. Viewers can choose to watch their favorite shows at more convenient times and on a variety of media platforms such as computers, videogame players, iPods, iPads, Kindles, and more.

Exactly how much time do individuals spend with media on a given day? In *Time for Life* (1997), sociologist John Robinson used surveys to track how much free time Americans had in their schedules and how they allocated that time. He found that over a 20-year period from 1965 to 1985, Americans' nonsleeping, noneating, and nonworking time slowly increased to about one hundred hours per week. About forty of those 100 hours could be characterized as "leisure time." The good news was that Americans had a significant amount of time in their week for nonwork activities. The bad news was that respondents reportedly devoted about half of this leisure time to watching television. As political scientist Robert Putnam (2000) argued in his seminal book *Bowling Alone*, these time-use data coupled with other historical trends suggested that Americans were abandoning civic organizations and other community activities in favor of watching television in the home. More recent data from the Bureau of Labor Statistics (see Figure 7.3)

Figure 7.3 How Americans Use Their Free Time (2007)

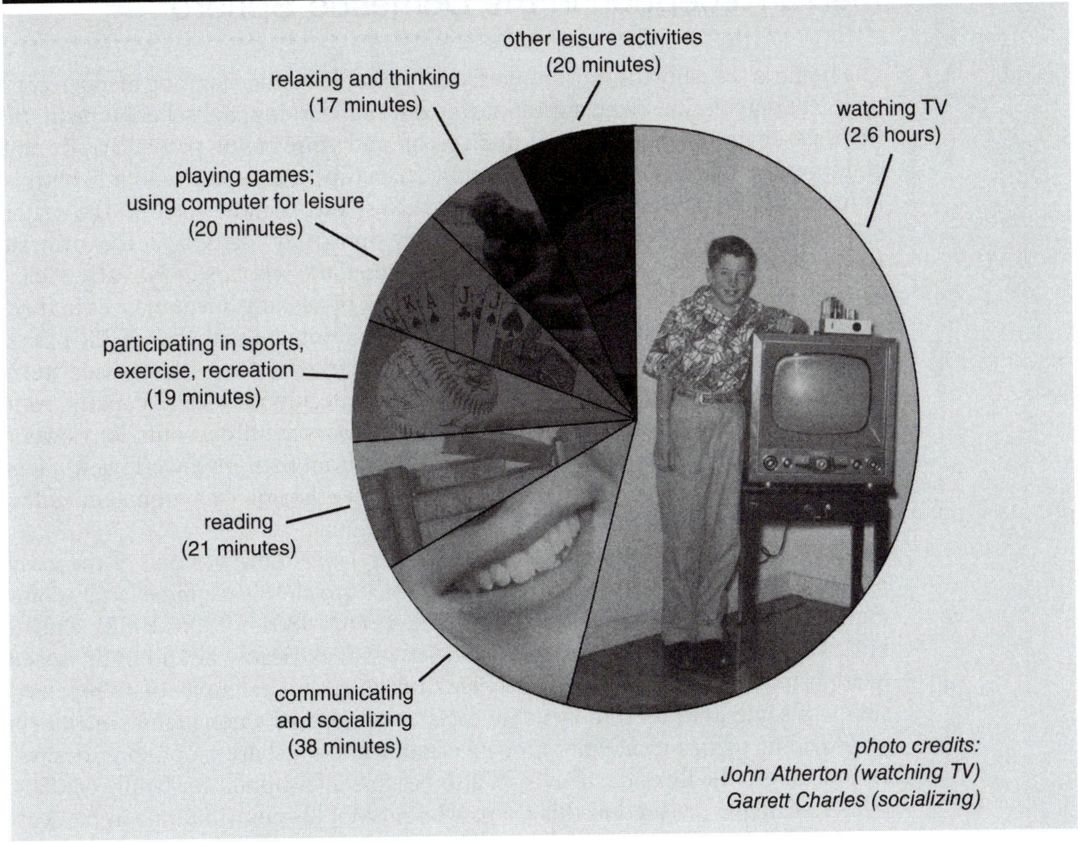

other leisure activities
(20 minutes)

relaxing and thinking
(17 minutes)

watching TV
(2.6 hours)

playing games;
using computer for leisure
(20 minutes)

participating in sports,
exercise, recreation
(19 minutes)

reading
(21 minutes)

communicating
and socializing
(38 minutes)

photo credits:
John Atherton (watching TV)
Garrett Charles (socializing)

Source: Based on Bureau of Labor Statistics, Time Use Survey. Images compiled by Stephanie Plumeri Ertz.

suggests that television and other forms of media continue to dominate our free time. The overwhelming presence of television in our daily rituals is an important context for understanding media reception.

In addition to the discrete, quantitative measurement of how many seconds, minutes, or hours we spend consuming media texts, the context of time can also be thought of in terms of a specific historical era. The experience of watching television in the early years of the 21st century is qualitatively different than the type of interactions that 1950s audiences had with the medium. Given the portability of media, digitalization, and the rise of computers as entertainment-oriented video devices, today's audiences are never more than a few seconds away from a media experience. The proliferation of technology has caused many of us to "squeeze" our media exposure into the short lulls during our daily activities. This too creates new environments for media consumption, altering our interpretive frameworks for these media.

Media Reception in the Domestic Sphere

The home is arguably the most importance "space" for understanding media reception. Not only do we spend a great deal of our nonworking, nonschool time in the domestic environment, but our outlook on life and sense of self, particularly during childhood and adolescence, is profoundly shaped by the people who inhabit this intimate space (parents, siblings, close relatives, and friends). One of the major criticisms leveled at Morley's *Nationwide* television study focused on the artificial reception context (see Chapter 6 for a full discussion). Scholars in the early 1980s began building on Morley's groundbreaking work by seeking out audiences in their natural viewing habitats, bringing the research environment to those specific places where audiences engage with media texts. This marked a more "naturalistic" turn in the study of audiences. Ethnographic research techniques such as participant observation and in-depth interviewing were used to more fully account for viewers' experiences with media, in their own words, and from their own worldviews. It is no accident, then, that scholars turned their focus to the home environment and to the *family* as the most critical audience reception unit.

As we saw in Chapter 5, American scholar James Lull was one of the early pioneers in using naturalistic observation methods to closely examine family communication patterns and television use (Lull, 1978, 1980a, 1980b, 1982). One of Lull's key findings was that the television set was inextricably bound in the social relationships that surrounded its use. He discovered, for example, that the television was sometimes used to facilitate social relationships among family members by providing them a focal point for conversation and for sharing opinions, desires, and ideas. On the flip side, television also became a flashpoint for family conflict. Lull's research is revisited in this chapter because of his contributions in pioneering the use of qualitative methods in the study of media reception in the context of the home environment. Although Lull's work has a methodological connection to that of British cultural studies scholars, his theoretical outlook is quite different. The unit of analysis is one key difference between the "social uses" of media he catalogued and the work of reception theorists outlined in this chapter. In much of Lull's research and more generally in the uses and gratifications paradigm, the unit of analysis is the individual and the psychological motivations that underlie decision-making regarding media exposure. For reception theorists interested in the social and situational contexts of media use, however, the unit of analysis is the family. Reception theorists in the 1980s explored how the routines and relationship maintenance within the household profoundly shaped the kinds of media consumption and interpretation behaviors that occurred there. Cultural studies were also more attentive to larger issues of gender disparity and power relations, as these social forces played themselves out within the family context. As Moores (1993) explains,

> What [Lull] was prevented from doing—as a direct consequence of the intellectual baggage he inherited—was explaining those power relations with reference to, say, a theory of patriarchy or a feminist critique of the family. Cultural studies insist on making such connections. (p. 35)

In other words, Lull introduced notions of social "rules" without specifically tying those rules to larger issues of social power, demographics, or other social variables. For this reason, Lull's family television research fits more closely within the more individualized, positivistic framework of uses and gratifications than with the critical cultural studies work on family television reception.

Housewives and Mass Media

One of the key aspects of qualitative audience studies in the field of British cultural studies was developing a theory of power relationships within the family environment. An early forerunner of this type of family reception research was a study of housewives and their use of media within the home conducted by Dorothy Hobson (1980). Hobson, an active member of the Women's Study Group at the Center for Contemporary Cultural Studies (CCCS), conducted interviews with working-class British housewives in their homes as part of a larger project on the culture of stay-at-home mothers with small children. Hobson's interviews with these women, in combination with her own position as a feminist scholar, led her to identify these working-class households as places of subordination and isolation for housewives and mothers. Many of the women she interviewed made a special point to listen to specific radio programs during their morning routines, which involved child care, cleaning, and other domestic responsibilities. Listening to music and entertainment-oriented radio programs was a vital lifeline to the outside world and helped these women to alleviate feelings of isolation. In addition, the women actively avoided listening to news on the radio or watching it on television. Hobson noted this as a distinction made by her subjects between "masculine" and "feminine" programming. Along with the methodology of in-depth interviewing and observation within the home environment, Hobson's study can also be identified as an early forerunner of audience reception research because of her critical look at working-class gender roles. Her work demonstrated how popular media texts helped these women carve out a notion of aesthetic pleasure and leisure within the strict societal constraints of their roles as housewives and mothers.

Morley's *Nationwide* Follow-Up: Family Television

Sociologist David Morley's (1980) seminal work in *The Nationwide Audience* opened the doors for audience scholars to examine specific interpretations of media texts and to associate those meanings with social categories. As outlined in Chapter 6, one of the primary critiques of Morley's methodology (acknowledged by Morley himself) was the artificiality of the research setting that he chose—inviting participants into a classroom setting and showing them specific programs, followed by a guided discussion. Morley's next large-scale research endeavor addressed this potential validity problem by venturing into the context of family homes to elicit more naturalistic responses from audiences about their television use. In *Family Television*, published in 1986, Morley turned his attention away from individual interpretations of a specific television text and focused on "the social processes within which television viewing is enclosed" (G. Turner, 2003, p. 144). Morley's main thesis was that "the changing patterns of television viewing could only be understood in the overall context of family leisure activity" (1986, p. 13). To study the intersections between family social interactions and television viewing, Morley recruited 18 families to be interviewed for one to two hours in their homes in the spring of 1985.

What became immediately clear in Morley's discussions with these families was the discrepancy between the definition of the *home* for women and men. For men, the home was a space of leisure, a respite from the "industrial time" that was spent in the workplace. Meanwhile, women found the home to be a sphere of work in which television viewing was seen more as a guilty pleasure than as a source of relaxation. This domestic gender division was evidenced in a number of ways. For example, the male head of household typically controlled the choice of program on the television and would invariably retain possession of the remote control during the evening hours (Morley, 1986, pp. 148–150). Interestingly, the pattern of male-dominated program choice was fairly consistent, except in cases where the male head of household was unemployed. This suggested that the strict gendered construction of the "breadwinner" within the domestic context was a fragile one. Morley's respondents also reported stark differences in channel choices and viewing style. The men in this sample noted preferences for "factual" programs such as news and documentaries, while women tended to enjoy more fictional programs. Men preferred "viewing attentively, in silence, without interruption 'in order not to miss anything,'" while women used the television as a social tool for conversations with other family members or to monitor peripherally while doing other things.

A number of women expressed the opinion that viewing television was a waste of time and that they felt guilty if they were not somehow engaged in another household chore during their screen time. *Family Television* demonstrated that patterns of audience reception within the home were tied closely to the operation of gender expectations and patterns of family communication, revealing fascinating intersections of class, gender, and localized contextual factors in the experience of television viewing.

Television and "Gendered" Technologies in the Home

As Hobson's and Morley's work revealed, the home is potentially quite a different type of space for men and for women—the former finds it a place of solace and rest, while the latter associates it with isolation, work, and subjugation. Ann Gray (1987, 1992) expanded this critical feminist approach to media reception in a large-scale ethnographic analysis of videocassette recorder (VCR) use within the home in the mid-1980s. After securing an initial contact at a video rental store, Gray employed a snowball sampling technique to recruit 30 women from Yorkshire, England, all of whom had a VCR in the home. Gray was interested exclusively in these women's use of and reactions to a specific media technology. However, to Gray's initial consternation, the women she interviewed spoke much more expansively about their life experiences, their everyday routines, and other background information about their lives. This information actually turned out to be quite useful in contextualizing their VCR use in the home environment. For most of these women, the breakdown of labor within the home was quite traditional, with the women taking on responsibility for child care, much of the shopping and cooking, and all sorts of basic household maintenance, despite the fact that some of the women in her sample had university degrees. Although her initial response to these wide-ranging conversations was one of frustration at their off-topic nature, Gray eventually came to realize and appreciate that, as Hobson's previous research had demonstrated, domestic technologies like televisions and VCRs were inextricably bound with gender roles and social power. Gray argued that it was necessary to understand the VCR as a *socially situated object*.

In an effort to make the gendered meanings of the home a bit more concrete, Gray asked the women in her sample to go around the house and rate activities and technologies on a scale from *pink* to *blue* (for either feminine or masculine). She found that the VCR had to be broken down into specific "modes" in order to parse the gender relationships associated with the technology (see Figure 7.4). She wrote that "the 'record,' 'rewind' and 'play' modes are usually lilac, but the timer switch is nearly always blue, with the women having to depend on their male partners or their children to set the timer for them" (Gray, 1992, p. 42). Her female respondents expressed a sense of inadequacy when it came to programming the timer on the VCR. It is important to note that there are not inherently "masculine" and "feminine" technologies but that technologies can become gendered through their social construction within the home environment. Alternatively, these expressions of ignorance or laziness by these women regarding some of the technological features of VCRs can also be read as a subtle sign of resistance. When asked if she was willing to learn how to program the VCR, one woman remarked, "No, I'm not going to try. No. Once I learned how to put a plug on, now there's nobody else puts a plug in this house but me . . . so [laugh] there's a method in my madness, oh yes" (Gray, 1992, p. 168). As this quote suggests, these women's refusal to engage with the timer feature may have been a kind of calculated ignorance. If they had become proficient with the timer feature, the burden of programming the VCR would have fallen to them, adding yet another task to their list of household duties.

Domestic Media Reception in the 1990s and Beyond

These early forays into audience reception in the domestic context uncovered important connections between social forces such as gender roles and daily interactions with media technologies. However, the landscape of media use in the home has been dramatically transformed since the 1980s. One-television-set households are now the exception rather than the norm. Most children growing up today have extraordinary access to media technologies—television sets in their bedrooms, broadband Internet access, smartphones, and tablet computing

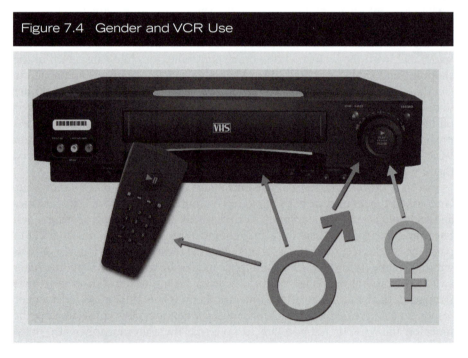

Figure 7.4   Gender and VCR Use

Source: Stephanie Plumeri Ertz.

devices. American homes have become elaborate electronic menageries. How have these changes reshaped the type of research that scholars have conducted on media reception? Are the types of firm gender hierarchies uncovered by Morley, Gray, and Hobson still visible in the patterns of media reception in the 21st-century private, domestic sphere?

Although there is now a glut of electronic media in modern households, one trend remains constant: Television continues to be the most important and widely used media technology in the domestic context. Looking back over 40 years of time diaries of household activities in the United States and a number of other countries, Robinson and Martin (2009, p. 78) concluded that the amount of television viewing has remained surprisingly constant: "No matter whether the programming was in a capitalist or socialist country, whether the broadcast day was almost full-time or confined to evening 'prime-time' hours, viewing time for set owners averaged an hour and a half per day." They also note that "TV has not been greatly displaced by the Internet and other new information technologies" (Robinson & Martin, 2009, p. 85). Recent time-diary studies of families revealed that television use continues to dominate children's free time at home as well, accounting for an average of 14.5 hours per week (or more than 2 hours per day on average; Bianchi, Robinson, & Milkie, 2006, p. 146). The introduction of new media technologies has not fundamentally altered the *amount* of television use in the home. However, there have been some significant changes since the mid-1990s in *how* television and other forms of electronic media are experienced in the domestic context.

Social Versus Individualized Viewing Behaviors

Recent research underscores the fact that television viewing has become (a) more ubiquitous given the proliferation of small-screen TV viewing via mobile phones, computers, and MP4 players and (b) more individualized. In their most recent analysis of time-use audience data, Robinson and Martin (2009) argue that since

> more sets in the home became available and more people live alone,
> more viewing is *done alone*—producing a more "individualized"
> experience, akin to that presumably fostered by the arrival of print
> media centuries earlier. It also means that TV has become less of a social
> experience, in which others can participate at the same time. (p. 83)

Respondents to time-use surveys have also revealed that the act of watching TV is often accompanied by a "secondary activity" such as housework or child care (Robinson & Martin, 2009, p. 83). Multitasking while viewing television has become a standard feature of the audience experience.

Audience scholar Sonia Livingstone (2002, 2007, 2009) has been tracking some of the shifts in media use in the home environment for some time, particularly among young people. In 1997, as part of a larger *Young People, New Media* project, she interviewed and surveyed children and adolescents (aged 6–17) and their parents in the United Kingdom about their media use in the home. The results of these interviews revealed two central trends that are permanently altering the character of the home and the use of media within the domestic space. First, she discovered that "there has been a gradual shift from children's leisure time spent outside (in the streets, woods or countryside) to that spent primarily at home, both reflecting and shaping cultural conceptions of childhood over the past half century" (Livingstone, 2007, p. 304). The second trend was marked by "continual multiplication of media goods at home, fostering a shift in media use from that of 'family television' to that of individualized media styles and, for children and young people, of 'bedroom culture'" (p. 304). Not only are children spending more time indoors with media, but they are also increasingly spending their screen time in isolation, in their own rooms or other segmented spaces within the household (what Livingstone referred to as **bedroom culture**). The phenomenon of families experiencing television or other media together, which was commonly observed in the audience reception studies of the 1980s, was not present in this research. Instead, Livingstone and her coauthors charted "a discernible shift away from shared toward privatized viewing," and that "this shift is more evident for thirteen- and fourteen-year-olds than for ten- and eleven-year olds" (2009, p. 156). As the example of the Gude family at the beginning of this chapter demonstrates, the trend toward increasing privatization of media usage poses new challenges for scholars looking to observe media audiences within the home environment.

The Internet and New Media in the Home

Although time spent online still pales in comparison with the amount of time spent with television, the Internet is nevertheless slowly shifting individuals' media use away from TV and toward more individualized media forms like computers, mobile phones, and iPods (Kraut, Kiesler, Boneva, & Shklovski, 2006). How might the introductions of these interactive technologies reshape the family dynamic, given the expanding availability of television outlined above? Though research in this area is still ongoing, a few studies have already hinted at some of the changes. For example, in 1998 and 1999 Bakardjieva (2006) conducted in-depth interviews and house visits with 20 different families with Internet access living around Vancouver, Canada. She found that these families had purchased a computer and signed up for Internet service either because they were curious about having access to the Internet or as the result of fear that their children would be left behind at school if they could not use the Internet at home. While Bakardjieva's subjects initially relied upon "Internet-savvy" relatives and close friends to help them get connected, these tight social bonds loosened as these subjects became more familiar with the technology and began building their own online networks of "e-friends."

Another recent ethnographic study by Mackay and Ivey (2004) explored the use of multiple media technologies in 10 households in Wales, United Kingdom, in 2001 to 2002. True to the spirit of Morley's earlier research in *Family Television*,

MacKay and Ivey described in detail the physical surroundings of each of the 10 households they observed and closely monitored the social environment within each home. Through in-depth qualitative interviews and observations, they discovered that media technologies "shape the daily routines of households" and mold into the free time available to household members. Media technologies such as video game consoles were often found in the living room or other common spaces. However, Mackay and Ivey documented an increasing privatization of media spaces, with family members retreating to their own spaces within the home, similar to Sonia Livingstone's findings. These private spaces were often equipped with televisions, thereby individualizing the media experience. The scholars found fewer mothers and older women who were interested in using digital television or the Internet, leaving those activities for the children and male head of household. In this sense, the gender-technology divide uncovered by Morley, Gray, and others 25 years ago was still evident in some modern multimedia households. Although the sample size of this study was quite small and limited to a specific location (Wales), the results suggest that perhaps a generational shift is well under way. Younger audiences are adapting to the greater intrusion of more media technologies within the home, and their experiences with these technologies are becoming increasingly individualized and privatized.

Media and Everyday Life in the Domestic Context

As the previous section illustrated, social and situational contexts play an important role in understanding audience experiences with media texts. Our media choices and interpretations can be shaped by our immediate physical and social environment. Let's further extend the notion of context a bit further for a moment. What if there were some contexts of audience reception that stretched beyond our immediate experiences with the media? In the aftermath of his research on television interpretation in *Family Television*, David Morley and colleague Roger Silverstone began exploring the meanings that audiences make of *the technology of television itself*, as opposed to the messages that are carried by it. As many of the scholars I'll discuss in this section argue, we cannot understand audiences' interpretations of media texts without acknowledging their specific interactions and expectations of the medium itself. Television, in particular, occupies a very specific niche in our everyday lives. The technology is situated in the heart of the private, domestic space. This dimension of our media shapes audience reception because of the privileged position of television in our lives.

In the late 1980s, British audience researchers David Morley, Roger Silverstone, and others who had been both directly and peripherally involved in the Birmingham School began to outline a new orientation to audience reception research. This new perspective would properly situate television and other electronic media within the social and situational contexts of the household while simultaneously linking those interactions to larger, external social forces. Rather than taking the everyday nature of media use for granted, the perceived normalcy and omnipresence of media in our daily lives became the focus for a more complete, holistic understanding of technology's role in modern society. The researchers gained inspiration from German sociologist Hermann Bausinger (1984, p. 343), who urged scholars to focus on the "culture of the everyday," which often masks itself as "common sense" and is therefore somewhat insulated from direct analysis. Bausinger argued that our sense of reality and our understanding of ourselves are inextricably bound with the electronic media with which we interact almost continually during our daily routines. The key for scholars was to recognize and explore the embedded nature of media technologies.

In the wake of Bausinger's conclusion, Morley and Silverstone proposed a reshaping of audience reception research to take into account the embeddedness of electronic media in our everyday lives. In a 1990 essay outlining this new approach, they wrote that studying television "requires a study of the domestic context within which an audience's activities in relation to it are articulated and constrained" (Morley & Silverstone, 1990, p. 34). The crucial component of Morley and Silverstone's argument was the connection of technology use within the domestic environment to external social, economic, political, and cultural trends. To understand audiences' experiences with television in the early 1990s, scholars would need to consider not only family relationship dynamics and gender roles but also the ways in which daily television usage rearranged the situational contexts within the home. They also had to contemplate the manner in which the content of the medium (whether it be news or entertainment) connected audiences with the larger economic and social realities outside of the home. They emphasized that "an understanding of the place of television both in society and in the household cannot ignore its contextualization by the market, technology, or culture" (p. 35).

The Blending of Public and Private Spaces: Modernity and Time–Space Distanciation

One of the primary goals in considering the role of television and other media technologies in our everyday lives was to acknowledge several fundamental shifts in how human beings engage with one another in modern societies. Morley and Silverstone, along with other reception theorists, looked to the ideas of British social theorist Anthony Giddens to conceptualize some of these fundamental changes. In his 1990 book *The Consequences of Modernity*, Giddens argued that one of the hallmarks of modern societies is the breakdown in the traditional notion of "place" as a specific physical location—something he called **"time-space distanciation."** He explained that "modernity increasingly tears space away from place by fostering relations between 'absent' others, locationally distant from any given situation of face-to-face interaction" (Giddens, 1990, p. 18). Put another way, our actions have become increasingly shaped by forces that are far away from our everyday physical and situational localities. Morning TV talk shows, for instance, demonstrate this aspect of our modern existence by addressing us informally, as if we were close friends. When hosts begin the broadcasts with "Hi there, how are you this morning?" they are engaging a distant and invisible audience in what appears to be a casual and ongoing conversation (Moores, 1995).

This expansion of notions of place also calls into question the distinction between the realms of public and private. Television and other media technologies are more than simply everyday household objects like toasters and microwave ovens. Like their kitchen counterparts, communication and information technologies serve specific purposes. However, as Silverstone, Hirsch, and Morley (1992) argue, these devices are unique because they provide instantaneous links between our private, domestic world and the world outside. British cultural theorist Raymond Williams coined the term **mobile privatization** to describe how television had historically served both a "mobile and home-centered way of living" (Williams, 1975, p. 26). Similarly, in his classic book *No Sense of Place*, scholar Joshua Meyrowitz (1985, p. 6) argued that electronic media fostered "a blurring of many formerly distinct social roles," changing the "situational geography" of social life.

Media Technology and the Home

In order to capture the multiple intersecting realities surrounding television use by audiences in the home, Morley, Silverstone, and their colleagues embarked on a new project called the Household Uses of Information and Communication Technologies (HICT). Supported by a grant from the U.K. Economic and Social Research Council, the HICT project employed qualitative observational research techniques to map how domestic households were "conceived as part of a transactional system of economic and social relations within the formal or more objective economy and society of the public sphere" (Silverstone et al., 1992, p. 16). Silverstone and colleagues argued that the home is part of what they termed a **moral economy** in the sense that the household is "both an economic unit, which is involved, through the productive and consumptive activities of its members, in the public economy, and at the same time it is a complex economic unit in its own terms" (Silverstone et al., 1992, p. 18). The prominence and importance of television as a media technology in the home, along with the complex ways in which it both shapes and is shaped by this social environment, invite closer scrutiny.

Silverstone and his coauthors outlined four elements of the **transactional system** in which the moral economy of the household is expressed. First is *appropriation*, when the family takes possession of the communication technology itself (whether it is a television, video game console, or computer, for instance) and the device becomes a part of the home environment. Next, *objectification* takes place when the technology object is displayed or organized in the home—when it is incorporated within the spatial environment of the household. This process is visible when families rearrange furniture to maximize viewing of a new TV or place it within an aesthetically attractive media center. Third, *incorporation* encompasses the ways in which these technologies are used by those in the household. This element brings research by Morley on gendered uses of the television and Gray's observations about different levels of expertise with VCR programming to the forefront. Lastly, *conversion* occurs when the information that is carried via communication technology becomes part of everyday social interactions and builds social capital outside of the home. The plot twists of a favorite soap opera or news about a tragic event witnessed in the private setting of TV viewing become part of conversations with others in the public realm. This final process solidifies the communication technology's role as a cultural touchstone. Silverstone later expanded upon this outline to formulate a program of research that would consider the complexities of the domestic sphere, which itself is "the product of a historically defined and constantly shifting relationship between public and private spaces and cultures, a shifting relationship to which television itself contributes" (1994, p. 25).

Media Spaces in the 21st Century

Silverstone's call for what some regarded as a radical contextualization of audience reception certainly set the bar rather high (too high, some believed) for scholars to observe and connect every facet of individuals' lives both inside and outside the home environment in order to grasp the meaning of audience reception. Scholars such as Ien Ang (1996) argued that Silverstone's suggestions had inadvertently paralyzed audience researchers. Some of these scholars may have decided that in order to study some aspect of audience reception, they had to study literally *everything* about the domestic, neighborhood, regional, and national contexts. Despite the seemingly overwhelming effort needed to properly contextualize audience reception, a number of recent studies have taken on the methodological challenge represented by Silverstone's work (see Box 7.1).

Another recent volume, by Couldry and McCarthy (2004), addresses recent shifts in electronic technologies and the temporal and spatial reorganizations that have accompanied the introduction of these devices into the household. The falling cost of computers has increased their ubiquity within the home environment. One of the chief purposes of home computing has been to connect to the Internet. Perhaps more than any other form of electronic media (save for television), the Internet blurs the traditional boundaries between private and public spaces in the ways that Silverstone (1994) and Meyrowitz (1985) describe. Through chat groups, Facebook posts, online games, and other forms of social interaction, the Internet has allowed for widespread social interaction among complete (and often anonymous) strangers. When we are online chatting with faceless others via our computers, are individual users transported to a different, "virtual" space and reality? Shaun Moores (2004) argues that our "presence" in the virtual space of the online world exists side by side with our physical presence in another space—whether it be at home, in an Internet-enabled café, or at work. Moores argues that we are instead experiencing a "doubling" of space. Instead of removing individuals from their current situational contexts, these new media allow them to inhabit two

BOX 7.1
Everyday Cultures of TV Living

Inspired by Silverstone and other audience reception theorists, David Gauntlett and Annette Hill (1999) aimed to capture the role of television in peoples' everyday lives with a 5-year longitudinal study of TV audiences in the United Kingdom from 1991 to 1996. They distributed diaries to families in the United Kingdom (with an extensive questionnaire about their use of television in the home). The surveys included both closed- and open-ended questions. The latter queries were designed to elicit more detailed responses about these families' use of television and to understand how family communication patterns might be affected by technology use. In total, 427 respondents completed the 5-year study. It should be noted that no observation of these individuals within the domestic context actually took place—all contextual details were inferred from the open-ended diary responses.

In looking at 5 years' worth of diary data, Gauntlett and Hill found a good deal of regularity in the responses. As Morley and Silverstone's research suggested, television viewing was fully integrated into individuals' daily habits, and their activities were often scheduled around particular programs that were important to them. They also noted that their subjects were particularly attentive to the notion of *time*, reporting the time structures of their day in often startling detail—how much time they spent watching particular TV programs and how this consumption waxed and waned according to other shifts in their lives, such as periods of depression or grief, starting or concluding a relationship, or becoming busy with other activities.

Gauntlett and Hill also noted that the more traditional gender distinctions in television and VCR use observed by David Morley and others in the 1980s had begun to break down. In the 1990s study sample, women were reportedly as adept as men at operating video recorders, and news programming was of continued interest to both men and women. Respondents generally regarded the television as a seductive drain on their time, rather than as a legitimate leisure activity. They reportedly regulated their own television exposure as a means to control what would otherwise be a strong desire to watch more on a regular basis. Finally, Gauntlett and Hill noted some shifts *over time* in television use toward more individualized programming that fit specific interests of the respondents. Rather than simply watching what was on, respondents either "appointment" viewed, time-shifted specific programs to watch later, or tuned in to more cable programming with niche content. This suggests the beginning of a trend toward the kind of individualization of viewing that Sonia Livingstone and others have begun to chart in audience reception.

Source: Gauntlett, D., & Hill, A. (1999). *TV Living: Television, culture, and everyday life*. London, England: Routledge in association with the British Film Institute.

specific spatial contexts (one local, the other one possibly quite distant) at the same time. This simultaneous presence in two distinct locational universes has become a regular feature of our technology-saturated lives.

Computer webcams also demonstrate this phenomenon. Marc Andrejevic (2004a, 2004b) has recently examined increasing use of Internet webcams to document and broadcast the private spaces of individual to the globe. Now that millions of "netizens" can be instantly present for one another on their computer screens, "we can all gain access to the means for production by migrating into the undifferentiated, liberating realm of cyberspace" (Andrejevic, 2004a, p. 194). However, Andrejevic argues that the new virtual public spaces created by online webcam users are far from a media utopia. The new "locations" exist primarily to market products and services to audiences who freely surrender their most intimate and personal details. He writes that "the dedifferentiation of spaces of consumption and production achieved by new media serves as a form of spatial enclosure: a technology for enfolding previously unmonitored activities within the monitoring gaze of marketers" (Andrejevic, 2004a, p. 195). Andrejevic argues that audiences engage in a process of "self-commodification" by expending their own labor in order to allow themselves to be marketed to by advertisers and external corporate forces (see Chapter 9). These recent analyses point to some of the major shifts in the audience experience thanks to time-space distanciation and the collapse of public and private space in our modern society.

Media Rituals: Another Reception Context
••

As Bausinger, Silverstone, and other scholars have noted, the presence of the television within the domestic environment needs to be considered within a much broader sociohistorical context to better understand the role of media within that everyday physical and social space. What about specific types of *content* carried by media technologies, such as television, and their connections with the social structure of family and community life? Turning again to anthropological theory, scholars of media reception have grappled with the powerful role that television in particular plays during times of national crisis and forms of traditional observance by focusing on **media rituals**.

Defining Rituals

The concept of **ritual** is important in anthropology because it is a significant tool for understanding the meaning behind everyday human behaviors in different cultural contexts around the globe. In one sense, ritual can simply mean your regular, habitual activities—you may make it a "ritual" to eat your dinner in front of the television and watch the 6:00 news every evening. While this may be important to you as an individual, it probably does not have a great deal of larger symbolic meaning in society. Anthropologists are most interested in the types of rituals that include formalized actions that occur with regularity in cultures and communities around the globe. For example, the manner in which you arrange your silverware and plates at the table is the type of customary behavior that reveals something about the larger culture. Ceremonies such as weddings, funerals, or Holy Communion in the Christian church (just to name a few) are good examples of ritualistic behaviors that reveal widely held core beliefs and reinforce larger social values and morals for those who participate in these activities. Not only do these ceremonial activities follow a carefully planned script and pattern, but they are also transformative for those who participate in them. Wedding ceremonies mark a significant transition for individuals. The wedding couple undergoes a symbolic transformation from two separate individual beings to one, symbolized in Western cultures by the exchange of rings, the binding of hands, and other ritualistic acts.

These ideas about the fundamental importance of rituals to understanding human societies were first explored by French sociologist Emile Durkheim (1858–1917). The influence of Durkheim's work on the development of the discipline of sociology was far-reaching. For the purposes of our current discussion, we will focus on his writings about how ritual works to shape human societies and give them cohesion. This was the primary topic of Durkheim's *Elementary Forms of the Religious Life*, in which he defined *religion* as "first and foremost a system of ideas by means of which individuals imagine the society of which they are members and the obscure yet intimate relations they have with it" (Durkheim, 1995, p. 227). Religion, in Durkheim's estimation, was not something cosmic or fantastical. Instead, it was a series of social practices and beliefs that bonded people together as members of a group. Anthropologist Arnold van Gennep (1960) was first to note that the types of rituals Durkheim was discussing were also **"liminal."** Van Gennep was referring to a whole range of social activities that occur outside the framework of normal social interactions and that traditionally mark rites of passage for individuals. These rituals carry transcendent meanings and are often carried out in spaces that have been demarcated as having special significance, such as a sacred shrine, a church, or hallowed ground. Within these spaces, human beings undergo transformative activities that link them to a higher moral or spiritual purpose or design. Anthropologist Victor Turner (1969) expanded the use of liminality to include activities even outside ritualistic behavior such as those following times of social crisis or conflict, when social order is eventually restored and fundamental values are reaffirmed. By closely examining liminal events, anthropologists and sociologists can better understand how a society sees itself and how it polices certain kinds of behaviors or beliefs.

Media Events: Creating Television's "High Holidays"

Dayan and Katz turned their attention to the importance of rituals surrounding the media in their 1992 book *Media Events: The Live Broadcasting of History*. Their work explored a particular subgenre of television programming: live, unscripted, but preplanned events that command the attention of huge audiences and also serve the same kind of social integrative function that Durkheim identified with religious rituals. Dayan and Katz examined the kinds of audience reception activities that surrounded key historical events as they played out on television screens, such as the coronation of Queen Elizabeth II in Britain or the funeral of John F. Kennedy in the United States (see Figure 7.5). It is important to note that breaking news stories that have consequences for history, such as the news of President Kennedy's assassination or the September 11, 2001, attacks in New York, Pennsylvania, and Washington, would not fit Dayan and Katz's definition because they were not preplanned and known to the television audience in advance. They argued that the point of these media events is to bring audiences together to reflect on the nature of society as a whole and ultimately to "invite reexamination of the status quo" (Dayan & Katz, 1992, p. 20). In effect, media events offer a kind of modern-day civil religion because of their power to interrupt the patterns of everyday life, making these experiences "reminiscent of holy days" (p. 16). Dayan and Katz pointed to a dual meaning of the notion of ritual. First, the television set acts as a conduit to transmit images of ritualistic acts to large

Figure 7.5 The Funeral of President John F. Kennedy (1963)

Source: Abbie Rowe White House Photographs.

numbers of people. Secondly, the act of watching these events unfold on television is itself a type of ritualistic behavior that is centered on media use within the home environment. Audiences interrupt daily schedules and may even wear different clothing or host family and friends in a celebration of the televised happening. They also noted that media events emphasize reconciliation instead of conflict. These preplanned events function to remind audiences of their affiliation with a larger community or sets of values by modeling the appropriate responses to those events through television. On-air news anchors and announcers act as "chiefs of protocol," modeling for audiences how to think about and respond to these events. Dayan and Katz argued that these ritualistic aspects of our media environment periodically dominate our television experiences and shape our understandings of both the medium and ourselves.

In a more recent critique and reimagining of the notion of media events, British scholar Nick Couldry (2003) looked back at Dayan and Katz's seminal book and explored some of the deeper complexities of media events for audiences. Couldry was skeptical of the largely functionalist interpretation offered by Dayan and Katz, arguing instead that the deep integration of media into our everyday lives is fundamentally connected to issues of power. Instead of being cultural rallying points for social unity, Couldry argued that "media events, then, are privileged moments, not because they reveal society's underlying solidarity, but because they reveal the mythical construction of the mediated center at its most intense" (2003, p. 56). For Couldry, media events such as state funerals and coronations offer only the *appearance* of cultural or social unification. It is an attempt by those in power to create the very kind of social cohesion that the media event seeks to portray.

What about these media events would serve the ideological or hegemonic interests of the state or the cultural status quo? Couldry stated that Dayan and Katz's strict and limited definition of media events "help[s] to ensure that media events for them always have positive, hegemonic effects" (2003, p. 63). In this sense, Dayan and Katz's reading of these media rituals looks back to Durkheim's notion that rituals serve to bring communities and societies together into a cohesive whole. Couldry's critique took a decidedly post-Durkheimian stance, arguing that there are any number of media events that do not necessarily help to integrate society. The continual coverage of the aftermath of the attacks of September 11, 2001, is an example of the kinds of "disaster coverage" that attract huge television audiences. Additionally, how applicable are the assumptions of Dayan and Katz's model of the importance of media events on a global scale? Would the funeral of Princess Diana of Wales in 1997 have the same social integrative effect in Tanzania or Venezuela as it might have in Britain? The likelihood of this is somewhat suspect. Context therefore is critical when considering the importance of media events to notions of ritual.

In place of the functionalism of Dayan and Katz, Couldry offered that media events are "large-scale event-based media-focused narratives where the claims associated with the myth of the mediated center are particularly intense" (Couldry, 2003, p. 67). Rather than revealing anything necessarily universal or unifying about a society, these events point to times in which the "symbolic work of ritualization" can be seen. This process is notable and well worth understanding. For example, a standard aspect of ritualistic or religious dogma is the concept of a "pilgrimage," wherein an individual travels to a specific space that has a deeper theological or mystical meaning. By making the journey and experiencing that space firsthand, audience members are transformed. Couldry traced the increasing proliferation of "media pilgrimages" in which audience members travel to exterior locations, streets, or buildings that have been used in television programs and movies as a means of more deeply experiencing those media texts. In particular, Couldry recalled his amazement at audience behaviors on a tour of the NBC Television Studios in New York City, where attendees gasped in awe at the studio soundstage for the *Rosie O'Donnell Show* (then a popular daytime talk show). Members of the tour group wanted to know exactly where the host sat and placed themselves on the stage as if they too were appearing on the program. Similarly, the historic city of Salzberg in the Austrian Alps regularly organizes tours of some of the locations featured in the film *The Sound of Music*. Audiences are transported around the city to personally witness a number of locations where the 1965 Hollywood musical starring Julie Andrews and Christopher Plummer was filmed. This type of ritualistic behavior by audiences solidifies the power of the media as society's primary storyteller. The ritual mythologizes the texts that producers create for audiences, making the media a permanent part of our cultural fabric.

Conclusion: Audiences in Context

In this chapter, we have explored the idea of context within audience reception studies. Since the 1980s, notions of time, spatial relations, and social environment have been important to scholars in order to better grasp the motivations for viewing television and the pleasures that audiences obtain from it. Research in the late 1980s captured a growing interest in the dynamics of family life and how television influenced and was in turn shaped by those interactions. Morley's later collaborations with Roger Silverstone and others affiliated with the Birmingham School trained a careful eye on the technology of television itself. These studies examined the role that the device plays in the spatial context of the home, as well as the connections between the public realm of events and ideas and private realm of household consumption that are facilitated by television. More recent work on media contexts has stressed the steady shift away from group reception of media toward more private, individualized media environments within the home. Technologies such as computers, iPods, mobile phones, and portable media players have enabled children and parents to carve out personalized media environments for themselves within the same physical space, often to the detriment of family time and face-to-face relationships. Instead of communicating with one another, we are increasingly engaged with people, events, and ideas outside the four walls of the home. Sociologist Anthony Giddens argues that this effective collapse between the public and private realms is one of the hallmarks of our modern way of living. However, it also poses new challenges to traditional notions of privacy, safety, and security offered by the very notion of "home."

Finally, we considered the notion of ritual as another context that shapes media reception. As Dayan and Katz argued in their 1992 book on media rituals, some events and information transmitted via technologies such as television transcend our everyday experiences with media. These liminal moments, such as political funerals, may serve to crystallize or reinforce certain cultural myths in our society. While some recent scholarship has actively questioned the functional role played by media in creating a mythical center, the notion that certain media forms can link individuals and create "imagined communities" through shared media experiences is one that continues to excite the scholarly imagination.

DISCUSSION ACTIVITIES

1. Take out a blank sheet of paper and draw an outline of the room where you do a large share of your media viewing (which may include a television, computer, stereo system or all of these). Sketch out an outline of the room, drawing in the outlines of the location of all of your media technologies, including the outlines of the furniture and other large objects in the room. Once you've done this, swap your room diagram with a classmate and take a look at the organization of the room itself and think about the following questions:

   • What can you say about the physical context in which media viewing takes place?

   • What is the orientation of the furniture?

   • How might the space either encourage or discourage various types of social interactions? What might the answers to these questions tell you about the impact of *context* on media reception and social interaction?

2. Take a moment and write down some recollections about an important event that you saw on television—the event in question should have been carried live, and it should be one that you also witnessed as it was happening (see the chapter for a detailed discussion of Dayan and Katz's definition of *media events*). Now, on your sheet provide as much detail as you can in answer to the following questions:

   • What was the event, and where were you when you witnessed it?

   • Were other people with you when you witnessed this event on television? If so, who were they, and do you recall how their presence may have shaped your reaction to the event?

   • How did your regular routines change, if at all, as a result of this event? What was different about your day as a result of watching this event unfold on television?

Once you're done making these reflections, pair up with a classmate or a small group of your classmates and compare notes: Are the events you recalled similar at all? Did your social activities during this media event differ from routine patterns of interaction surrounding television? Develop a list of similarities between the responses of your classmates to their media events: What generalizations, if any, might we be able to make about how society responds to live media events on television? Are your observations at all similar to those offered by Dayan and Katz, for instance?

3. Log on and watch the first two chapters of a 2008 PBS *Frontline* documentary called *Growing Up Online* (http://www.pbs.org/wgbh/pages/frontline/kidsonline/view/). As you watch this documentary about the role of the Internet, computers, and video games

in the lives of young people, answer the following questions:

- How are new forms of technology shaping kids' spatial and social relationships with other members of the family, particularly their relationships with their parents?

- Do you see any similarities between the young people described in the video and those investigated by Sonia Livingstone in her *Young People, New Media* project? What are they?

- Can you personally relate to some of the experiences described in the video? Which parts of the video do you find most relevant to your own experience and why?

ADDITIONAL MATERIALS

Couldry, N. (2003). *Media rituals: A critical approach.* London, England: Routledge.

Dretzin, R., & Maggio, J. (2008). Growing up online [Video documentary]. *Frontline.* WGBH Boston: PBS. More information at http://www.pbs.org/wgbh/pages/frontline/kidsonline/

Livingstone, S. M. (2007). From family television to bedroom culture: Young people's media at home. In E. Devereux (Ed.), *Media studies: Key issues and debates* (pp. 302–321). Thousand Oaks, CA: SAGE.

MacQueen, A. (1995). *People's century: Picture power—Television captivates the world.* WGBH Boston. More information at http://www.pbs.org/wgbh/peoples-century/episodes/picturepower/

Morley, D. (1986). *Family television: Cultural power and domestic leisure.* London, England: Comedia.

Professor Sonia Livingstone describes how families have adapted to new forms of privatized media within the home: https://www.youtube.com/watch?v=weN-fYhD6new

Silverstone, R. (1994). *Television and everyday life.* London, England: Routledge.

REFERENCES

Andrejevic, M. (Ed.). (2004a). The webcam subculture and the digital enclosure. In *MediaSpace: Place, scale, and culture in a media age, Comedia* (pp. 193–208). London, England: Routledge.

Andrejevic, M. (2004b). *Reality TV: The work of being watched—Critical media studies.* Lanham, MD: Rowman & Littlefield.

Ang, I. (1996). *Living room wars: Rethinking media audiences for a postmodern world.* London, England: Routledge.

Bakardjieva, M. (2006). The consumption junction revisited: Networks and contexts. In R. E. Kraut, M. Brynin, & S. Kiesler (Eds.), *Computers, phones, and the Internet: Domesticating information technology—Oxford* series in human-technology interaction (pp. 97–108). Oxford, England: Oxford University Press.

Bausinger, H. (1984). Media, technology and daily life (L. Jaddou & J. Williams, Trans.). *Media, Culture & Society*, 6(4), 343–351. doi:10.1177/016344378 400600403

Bianchi, S. M., Robinson, J. P., & Milkie, M. A. (2006). *Changing rhythms of American family life*. New York, NY: Russell Sage Foundation.

Couldry, N. (2003). *Media rituals: A critical approach*. London, England: Routledge.

Couldry, N., & McCarthy, A. (Eds.). (2004). *MediaSpace: Place, scale, and culture in a media age—Comedia*. London, England: Routledge.

Dayan, D., & Katz, E. (1992). *Media events: The live broadcasting of history*. Cambridge, MA: Harvard University Press.

Durkheim, E. (1995). *The elementary forms of religious life* (K. E. Fields, Tran.). New York, NY: Free Press.

Gauntlett, D., & Hill, A. (1999). *TV living: Television, culture, and everyday life*. London, England: Routledge in association with the British Film Institute.

Giddens, A. (1990). *The consequences of modernity*. Stanford, CA: Stanford University Press.

Gray, A. (1987). Behind closed doors: Video recorders in the home. In H. Baehr & G. Dyer (Eds.), *Boxed in: Women and television* (pp. 38–54). London, England: Pandora Press.

Gray, A. (1992). *Video playtime: The gendering of a leisure technology*. London, England: Routledge.

Hobson, D. (1980). Housewives and the mass media. In S. Hall, D. Hobson, A. Lowe, & P. Willis (Eds.), *Culture, media, language: Working papers in cultural studies, 1972–1979* (pp. 105–114). London, England: Hutchinson.

Kraut, R., Kiesler, S., Boneva, B. S., & Shklovski, I. (2006). Examining the effect of Internet use on television viewing: Details make a difference. In R. E. Kraut, M. Brynin, & S. Kiesler (Eds.), *Computers, phones, and the Internet: Domesticating information technology—Oxford series in human-technology interaction* (pp. 70–83). Oxford, England: Oxford University Press.

Livingstone, S. M. (2002). *Young people and new media: Childhood and the changing media environment*. London, England: SAGE.

Livingstone, S. M. (2007). From family television to bedroom culture: Young people's media at home. In E. Devereux (Ed.), *Media studies: Key issues and debates* (pp. 302–321). Thousand Oaks, CA: SAGE.

Livingstone, S. (2009). Half a century of television in the lives of our children. *The ANNALS of the American Academy of Political and Social Science*, 625(1), 151–163. doi:10.1177/0002716209338572

Lull, J. (1978). Choosing television programs by family vote. *Communication Quarterly*, 26(4), 53–57.

Lull, J. (1980a). Family communication patterns and the social uses of television. *Communication Research*, 7(3), 319–333.

Lull, J. (1980b). The social uses of television. *Human Communication Research*, 6(3), 197–209.

Lull, J. (1982). How families select television programs: A mass-observational study. *Journal of Broadcasting & Electronic Media*, 26, 801–811.

Mackay, H., & Ivey, D. (2004). *Modern media in the home: An ethnographic study*. Rome, Italy: John Libbey.

Meyrowitz, J. (1985). *No sense of place: The impact of electronic media on social behavior*. New York, NY: Oxford University Press.

Moores, S. (1993). *Interpreting audiences: The ethnography of media consumption*. London, England: SAGE.

Moores, S. (1995). TV discourse and 'time-space distanciation': On mediated interaction in modern society. *Time and Society*, 4(3), 329–344. doi:10.117 7/0961463X95004003004

Moores, S. (Ed.). (2004). The doubling of place: Electronic media, time-space arrangements and social relationships. In *MediaSpace: Place, Scale, and Culture in a Media Age—Comedia* (pp. 21–36). London, England: Routledge.

Morley, D. (1980). *The Nationwide audience: Structure and decoding*. London, England: British Film Institute.

Morley, D. (1986). *Family television: Cultural power and domestic leisure*. London, England: Comedia.

Morley, D., & Silverstone, R. (1990). Domestic communication—technologies and meanings. *Media, Culture & Society, 12*(1), 31–55.

Putnam, R. D. (2000). *Bowling alone: The collapse and revival of American community*. New York, NY: Simon & Schuster.

Robinson, J. P. (1997). *Time for life: The surprising ways Americans use their time*. University Park: Pennsylvania State University Press.

Robinson, J. P., & Martin, S. (2009). Of time and television. *The ANNALS of the American Academy of Political and Social Science, 625*(1), 74–86. doi:10.1177/0002716209339275

Silverstone, R. (1994). *Television and everyday life*. London, England: Routledge.

Silverstone, R., Hirsch, E., & Morley, D. (1992). Information and communication technologies and the moral economy of the household. In *Consuming technologies: Media and information in domestic spaces* (pp. 15–31). London, England: Routledge.

Spigel, L. (1992). *Make room for TV: Television and the family ideal in postwar America*. Chicago, IL: University of Chicago Press.

Stone, B. (2009, August 10). Breakfast can wait. The day's first stop is online. *The New York Times*. Retrieved from http://www.nytimes.com/2009/08/10/technology/10morning.html?hpw

Tichi, C. (1991). *Electronic hearth: Creating an American television culture*. Oxford, England: Oxford University Press.

Turner, G. (2003). *British cultural studies: An introduction* (3rd ed.). London, England: Routledge.

Turner, V. W. (1969). *The ritual process: Structure and anti-structure*. Chicago, IL: Aldine.

Van Gennep, A. (1960). *The rites of passage*. London, England: Routledge & Paul.

Williams, R. (1975). *Television: Technology and cultural form*. New York, NY: Schocken Books.

Audiences as Producers and Subcultures

As the previous section illustrated, research beginning in the 1940s began to break from the dominant model of the audience as object to consider the ways in which audiences make deliberate choices about their media consumption. In part, this shift toward audience uses was a consequence of the lack of strong evidence in support of the persuasive effects of media messages during the World War II era (Chapter 2). The theory of uses and gratifications (Chapter 5) provided an alternative framework to imagine audiences: as active choosers of media. Critical and cultural studies–oriented audience research beginning in the 1980s expanded the notion of active audiences still further to consider how media reception reflected existing social and spatial relationships (Chapter 7).

This fourth and final section of the text explores recent scholarship that understands audiences as **media producers and subcultures**. Beginning in the late 1980s, a number of scholars began to consider some of the ways in which media fandom represented a new category of audience interpretive activity. Rather than simply selecting media content to fulfill their individual or social needs, enthusiasts for a particular television program, film, or other media event invested a great deal of time and intellectual energy into media texts. These fans collected artifacts related to their favorite texts, sought out social connections with similarly minded individuals, and even marked themselves as fans to outsiders (through distinctive clothing, bumper stickers, or even tattoos, for example). Moreover, some fans engaged creatively with their favorite media texts by reworking the original narratives to fashion new ones. Fan audiences transcended their traditional role as consumers to become media producers themselves. Scholars began to take note, and the field of "fan studies" was born. Chapter 8 takes a close look at fan studies to consider how media fandom can expand our understanding of audience uses and interpretations.

Thanks to digitalization, mass computerization, and the rise of the Internet, the ability of modern audiences to select, consume, and remix media content has become greater than ever. Chapter 9 focuses on the expansion of audience autonomy in the 21st century. It considers how networked media forms such as YouTube, Facebook, and the online role-playing game *World of Warcraft* are creating new opportunities for audiences to contribute their own creative ideas to media texts. In fact, audience input is so vital to these new online platforms that the traditional distinction between producers and audiences has been blurred. The chapters in this section of the text privilege the study of audience *agency* in a networked media world. However, this new audience agency exists within the context of *structure* as well. As we'll see, traditional media corporations have attempted to dramatically circumscribe the ability of the audience to rework existing media narratives through legal, technological, and social means.

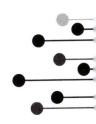

CHAPTER 8

Media Fandom and Audience Subcultures

On April Fool's Day in 1976 at the Waverly Theater in Greenwich Village, New York City, a new film opened to audiences at a special midnight screening. *The Rocky Horror Picture Show* (*RHPS*) was a motion picture version of a low-budget science fiction/horror musical. The stage show had been successful in London and had been brought to the United States for a theatrical run in Los Angeles. The musical theater production featured a campy, cabaret-style narrative in which an innocent, conservative suburban couple is stranded in a haunted house full of cross-dressing transvestites, aliens, and a Frankenstein-style mad scientist. The initial rollout of the film in the United States was far from auspicious. Critics in Los Angeles had widely panned the stage version. Influential New York commentator Rex Reed, for example, wrote that "the rock score is beneath contempt, the acting is a disgrace, and the entire evening gave me a headache for which suicide seemed the only possible relief" (Hoberman & Rosenbaum, 1983, p. 11). The movie version attracted sizable crowds in Los Angeles when it opened in September 1975, most likely due to the press surrounding the stage performance. However, the film was bombing everywhere else that it appeared around the country. Local theater exhibitors complained to 20th Century Fox (the distributor of *Rocky Horror*) that perhaps only 50 seats out of 800 were occupied for each showing of the film. Fox, already nervous about the negative reviews and wary of the film's campy transgressions of gender roles, yanked the film from nationwide circulation. That might have been the end of the story for *Rocky Horror*, but it wasn't.

Movie theater owners failed to realize that the consistently small audiences for the film were made up of largely the *same* 50 people, who attended the screenings again and again. A young publicist named Bill Quigley, who worked for a theater chain in New York City, noticed this trend and convinced Fox to release the film in one theater at a time as a midnight movie in order to slowly build an audience (Weinstock, 2007, p. 18). What happened following the film's midnight opening in Manhattan was startling. Groups of young people in their 20s attended the movie in droves, many of them paying to see the film repeatedly. The viewing experience began to play a large role in the film's appeal. A dedicated core of regular viewers began dressing up as the characters in the film, interacting with the film by shouting out raunchy lines of dialogue (which they knew by heart), throwing rice at the screen during a wedding scene, and dancing in the aisles during key musical sequences. A scholarly study of *Rocky Horror* audiences conducted in Rochester, New York, found that roughly two thirds of the people waiting in line to see the film had already seen it once. The research also noted that the biggest draw for repeat viewings, aside from the film itself, was the audience participation that occurred in the theater (Austin, 1981). Fan clubs dedicated to *RHPS* began sprouting up all over the country, educating new fans about the etiquette of audience response to various scenes in the film (see Figure 8.1 for a list of expected interactive practices for each showing of *RHPS*). The film became a "cult" phenomenon through midnight showings in the United States and around the world, grossing over $100 million thus far. The primary draw for fans continues to be the social experience of the film, which allows participants to interact with the screen and with each other. The unique social environment surrounding *Rocky Horror* points to some of the fascinating ways in which fandom

Figure 8.1   Forms of Expected Audience Participation for *The Rocky Horror Picture Show*

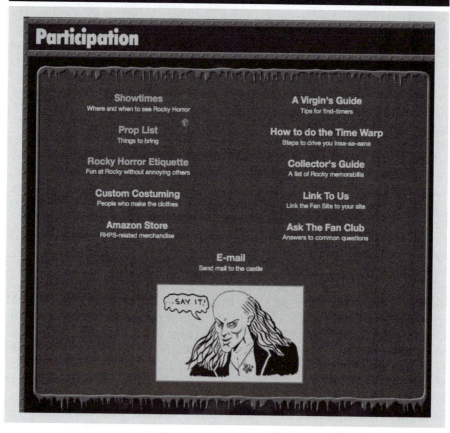

Source: *The Rocky Horror Picture Show* Official Fan Site. http://www.rockyhorror.com/participation.

alters and even creates new cultural experiences out of popular media texts. These unique interactions between fans and media place theories of fandom squarely in the sights of audience scholars.

As we explored in Chapter 6, audiences actively interpret media content by producing meaning out of the signs and symbols that make up the media text. These interpretations are also closely connected to both the immediate and larger social contexts of audiences. The "transaction" (for lack of a better term) between the medium and the audience goes beyond a single interaction with a television program, movie, or book. Imagine that you have just finished reading a fiction book that you have found fascinating or inspiring. You might subsequently turn on your computer and find a fan website dedicated to the book or perhaps an online chat room frequented by other readers who are as enthusiastic about the book as you are. On one of these websites, you may even find that some fans enjoyed the narrative so much that they inserted its characters into their own "fan fiction" writings. These short stories would be posted on online bulletin boards and websites for other fans to read and discuss. This hypothetical but common scenario demonstrates that our interactions with media texts today rarely have any clear boundaries. The expansive, malleable nature of the Internet and the declining cost of computers have allowed audiences to easily extend their media experiences beyond the reception of the original text. Texts can be reinterpreted in many new and contrary ways: through connections to other audiences online, creation of new media texts based upon the source material, and—thanks to the power of inexpensive computers to achieve professional-quality video and audio editing—even alteration of the original media text. As we will see later in Chapter 10, the latter activity often runs afoul of copyright law and can pit even the most ardent media fans against the creators and media organizations that produced the media product in the first place.

Overview of the Chapter

This chapter builds upon the audience interpretation and decoding theories presented in Chapter 7 and explores the ways in which media audiences use their interpretive power to actively subvert, distort, and even reimagine mainstream media content to suit their own needs and desires. We begin with the concept of media fandom: exploring how fan communities extend their interactions with media texts by logging on to discussions on the Internet, collecting artifacts associated with their media interests, and even by participating in fan conventions and other related social activities. Fans are emotionally invested in their favorite media by thinking deeply about the plots, characters, and messages of those texts. They also reach out to other fans to discuss their mutual objects of affection, building "interpretive communities" around a particular media program. Beyond activities designed to more fully appreciate the original texts (a television program or a film, for instance), some fans go even further by modifying their favorite texts to suit their needs and interests. Fans of science fiction television programs such as

Star Trek, Star Wars, and *Battlestar Galactica* have even translated their enthusiasm into elaborate social and textual subcultures, producing their own media texts and challenging the interpretive authority of media institutions in the process. Although there are numerous examples of these kinds of fan activities in relation to soap operas, mystery novels, and musical artists (just to name a few), this chapter explores previous research primarily on science fiction television programs. Do all of these fan activities mean that the balance of power between media and the audience has been tipped in the favor of individual audience members who can reinterpret and even alter media texts to suit themselves? At the conclusion of the chapter, we will explore more recent scholarship on fandom, which revisits the concept of a "fan" and calls into question the emancipation of audiences from media and cultural hierarchies in our society.

Defining Fan Cultures
....

What is a *fan?* You might call yourself a fan of something such as a TV program, a sports team, a particular book, or a popular music group. We use the term in everyday parlance, but what does it really mean? Images of fans are ubiquitous in our popular media and often reveal a conflicting picture of the fan. For instance, there is the image of the geeky, socially challenged, but ultimately benign and lovable fan. We see this common stereotype in recent Hollywood films such as 2005's *Fever Pitch* (with Jimmy Fallon portraying an obsessed but ultimately reformed Red Sox fan) and in the fictionalizations of science fiction fandom such as 1999's *GalaxyQuest* (centered on fans of a pseudo–*Star Trek* television program) and 2008's *Fanboys* (the fictionalized exploits of a group of hard-core *Star Wars* fans and their adventures in pursuing an advance screening of *Star Wars I: The Phantom Menace*). This notion of the sweet but socially awkward fan exists alongside a much darker view offered in films such as *The Fan* (1996), in which a baseball player is stalked and threatened by a violent sports enthusiast. Negative fan connotations are also associated with figures in the news such as Mark David Chapman (a Beatles fan who murdered singer John Lennon in 1980, which some suggest was an outgrowth of his fanatical devotion to J.D. Salinger's book *The Catcher in the Rye*) and John Hinckley Jr. (who attempted to murder President Ronald Reagan in 1981, reportedly in a bid to impress movie actress Jodie Foster).

This somewhat shadowy, sinister image of **the fan** captures a fair amount of the essence of the original etymology of the word. Short for *fanatic*, the term originally referred to religious membership "of or belonging to the temple, a temple servant, a devotee" (Jenkins, 1992, p. 12). It later turned toward much more negative connotations. Beginning in the 17th century, the word described "an action or speech: Such as might result from possession by a deity or demon; frantic, furious" and later "characterized, influenced, or prompted by excessive and mistaken enthusiasm, especially in religious matters" (Oxford English Dictionary Online, 2000). The connections between fandom and religion are particularly notable, as the usage of *fanatic* generally referred to an unwavering, uncritical belief in (usually religious) dogma. In Britain, the term *cult media* is often used to describe media fan cultures. *Cult* also conjures up religious imagery in an extreme and negative sense of the word. The Oxford English Dictionary describes *cult* as "a relatively small group of people having religious beliefs or practices regarded by others as strange or sinister" (2000). The etymological roots of the word *fanatic*, particularly the connections to religious fundamentalism, fueled early negative stereotypes about fandom, portraying individuals as misguided at best and delusional at worst.

Fan Stereotypes

Negative notions of fans, seen through the lens of extremism and psychopathology, dominated the popular consciousness when scholars began to examine the phenomenon of fandom. In the early 1990s, media scholars such as Henry Jenkins (1992) and Camille Bacon-Smith (1992) attempted to correct this imbalance with their own ethnographic research into fans of the popular 1960s television series *Star Trek*. Jenkins, himself an avowed *Trek* fan, knew from his own experiences with other fans that the negative stereotypes with which they were associated were gross distortions of their attitudes and behaviors. For example, media fans are often portrayed as brainless consumers, willing to buy anything with a logo or image of their favorite media program or star. The popular cultural materials that fans tend to spend their time thinking carefully about are also seen by many to be culturally worthless or simply there for entertainment purposes. Jenkins also discovered that media fans were often tagged as social misfits, intellectually immature, and feminized. Concern has also been raised about the inability of fans to separate the fantasy of media texts from the reality of their everyday lives. In his 1992 touchstone book *Textual Poachers*, Jenkins looked beyond the popular stereotypes of fans by letting fans speak for themselves, conducting interviews, and examining fan textual productions. The range of fan activities and interpretations uncovered by Jenkins and later scholars demonstrates that fan audiences are deeply engaged in their favorite media texts. Fans often reinterpret media content and create their own cultural productions in response.

Defining Fan Studies: Why Study Fans?

Before launching into any research project, scholars must define the subject under consideration, and studies of fandom are no different. However, the definition of *fandom* has been disputed among researchers who approached the field with competing agendas. Early fan studies set out explicitly to debunk many of the negative stereotypes that had been associated with fan activities. For example, John Fiske noted that fandom is "associated with the cultural tastes of subordinated formations of the people, particularly those disempowered by any combination of gender, age, class, and race (1992, p. 30). Following the same line of reasoning that he presented in *Television Culture* (1987, see Chapter 6 for a full discussion), Fiske claimed that fans resisted their negative characterizations in popular culture by establishing a sense of ownership over their favorite media texts and engaging in interpretive play with those texts. The fact that fandom appealed to "subordinated" groups transformed fan participation into a kind of political resistance. Early scholars of media fandom were drawn to this notion because it challenged the idea of the "commodity audience" that we explored in Chapter 4. Instead of audiences' viewing choices being totally determined by institutional constructions, fans develop their own sense of self-identity around their media consumption. This challenges the perceived negative stereotypes of the passive, unimaginative, or uneducated mass audience. The activities of media fans were envisioned as a corrective to the seemingly bleak top-down picture of media power that emerged out of the political economic critique of audiences. Fandom was more than simple enthusiasm for a TV program or film; it was a form of collective interpretation of popular culture that created a powerful sense of group cohesion. Fan studies for these scholars "therefore constituted a purposeful political intervention that sided with the tactics of fan audiences in their evasion of dominant ideologies, and that set out to rigorously defend fan communities against their ridicule in the mass media and by nonfans" (Gray, Sandvoss, & Harrington, 2007, p. 2).

Scholars in the later, so-called second wave of fan studies questioned the normative conceptualization of fandom because it seemed to be at odds with a great deal of mainstream enthusiasm across different sociodemographic groups for television programs, movies, and popular music. The category of "fan" has dramatically expanded as a result of the even smaller niche media products and platforms available today (such as smartphone games and media, cable and satellite television channels, YouTube channels, and other forms of micromedia). Abercrombie and Longhurst (1998, p. 141), recognizing that there are perhaps different levels of passion and involvement in fan activities, developed a continuum of audience experiences. Levels of engagement with popular media ranged from "consumer" on one end to "petty producer" (people who turn their fan activity into a profession and market their productions back to fans) on the other, with "enthusiast" and "fan" as levels of fan involvement in the middle of the continuum (see Figure 8.2). Sandvoss offered a more inclusive definition of *fandom*, taking into account both dedicated and casual fans:

> The regular, emotionally involved consumption of a given popular
> narrative or text in the form of books, television shows, films, or music,
> as well as popular texts in a broader sense such as sports teams and
> popular icons and stars ranging from athletes and musicians to actors.
> (2005, p. 8)

As Sandvoss's definition demonstrates, we are all fans of something in today's media-saturated environment, which makes the cultural and sociological study of fandom all the more important for understanding media audiences.

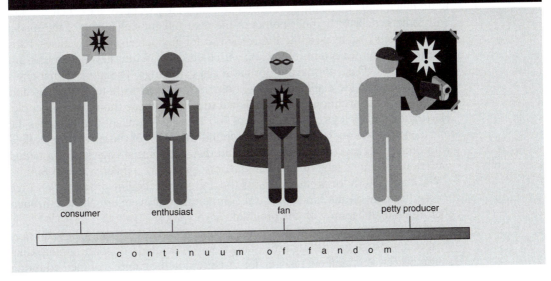

Figure 8.2   Continuum of Fandom

consumer   enthusiast   fan   petty producer

c o n t i n u u m   o f   f a n d o m

Source: Stephanie Plumeri Ertz.

Fan Cultures and Interpretive Activity

Although all audiences bring their own interpretive frameworks to popular media, the deep interest and involvement in media content demonstrated specifically by fans has attracted the close attention of scholars. Two aspects of media fandom have emerged as central to theorists in this tradition. The first element is the **social aspect**, where media fans band together in either informal or more formally structured groups (such as fan clubs) to share their mutual interest with others. Second, fans act as interpreters and producers of media content, which we will call the **interpretive aspect** of media fandom. In this section of the chapter, we will explore some of the early systematic analyses of media fans, focusing on the social and interpretive aspects of fan cultures.

The Social Aspect of Media Fandom: Developing Communities and Subcultures

Fans occupy an interesting position in society. They participate in many of the same types of social and textual activities that most media audiences engage in, but they have traditionally existed more on the fringe of mainstream culture. Fan-related activities are built largely around a close affiliation with the popular texts at the center of the enthusiasm. Fans of popular television programs, movies, or books will often spend a great deal of time with their favorite texts, reading them closely and often repeatedly, looking for greater nuance and detail. However, audiences who are initially quite enthusiastic about their chosen media text want to do much more than simply consume the text. They want to share their passion with others, debate the finer points of the text, integrate elements of the media text into their own lives, and critique the text for any perceived deficiencies. Fans spread their enthusiasm by interacting with their peers in Internet chat groups, fan websites, and even informal and formal social gatherings. The more formal types of gathering include elaborate conventions of fans held in hotel ballrooms and (increasingly) convention centers designed to accommodate thousands of people. Harrington and Bielby's (1995) survey of 706 TV soap opera fans demonstrates the prevalence of this social element. They found that 96% of those surveyed talked with other soap fans on a regular basis and that 37% of that large segment talked with four or more fans about their favorite program. Similarly, Bacon-Smith's (1992) early study of women fans of the TV science fiction program *Star Trek* focused heavily on the kinds of social community that were established through their mutual affiliation with the program.

The emergence of social groupings around a particular interest or activity is quite common. What distinguishes fans from other kinds of social groups (like stamp collectors or golf enthusiasts, for instance) are the subjects of their admiring gaze. Fans are not maligned due to the type of individual and collective activities in which they engage (after all, sports fans are by and large celebrated in our popular media). Rather, negative perceptions arise because the materials that fans have selected to rally around are typically found on the low end of the **cultural hierarchy.** Therefore, the "'scandal' stems from the perceived merits and cultural status of these particular works rather than anything intrinsic to the fans' behavior" (Jenkins, 1992, p. 53). The selection and fan internalization of these mainstream cultural materials into their own personal lives (by dressing up as characters from their favorite TV shows or decorating their homes or places of work with paraphernalia from popular texts) distinguishes these individuals as a unique **subculture.** Fans who outwardly and proudly claim their affiliation with their favorite popular culture texts, particularly when those media are generally considered to be "fluff" or mindless distractions from reality, may be challenging the status quo through their activities.

The notion of subcultures came into academic vogue following the 1979 publication of Dick Hebdige's book *Subculture: The Meaning of Style.* Hebdige argued that communities of punks, mods, hipsters, Rastafarians, and other groups dedicated to the specific musical genres were distinctive cultural entities unto themselves. These groups challenged the authority of traditional mainstream British culture—not through any overt political demonstrations or violent clashes with authority, per se, but through their clothing, pierced ears and noses, and other publicly visible signs (their *style*). These signs were ultimately unsettling and disruptive to the status quo. Hebdige noted that these symbolic transgressions "briefly expose the arbitrary nature of the codes which underlie and shape all forms of discourse" (1979, pp. 90–91). Media fans are members of subcultures in the sense that they adopt their own linguistic codes (specialized ways of talk, unique forms of greeting and address, and the use of codenames or titles, for example) and symbolic forms (including styles of dress) that delineate them from the rest of the population. For Hebdige and other British scholars who observed and analyzed subcultural groups in Britain (McRobbie & Nava, 1984; Willis, 1981), such forms of cultural expression not only established a sense of self-identity for these groups but also functioned as acts of emancipation from traditional authority. Early scholars of media fandom suggested that fans, while not necessarily posing the kind of threat to traditional cultural authority that punk music did in the 1970s and '80s, still challenge existing hierarchies by redeeming "trashy" cultural forms like TV soap operas, science fiction programs, horror films, and mystery novels.

Fan Activism: Challenging Institutional Producers

As Hebdige's analysis suggests, the function of social interaction among fans is not merely to spur a deeper appreciation of the original text. Close-knit communities of fans can also offer direct challenges to existing authority. Fans can be mobilized to press producers and media corporations for change (or, as is more often the case, to prevent changes from coming about in a favorite media text). This kind of activism often serves as a rallying point for fan movements. The groups solidify a sense of mission and purpose for themselves, which can have the mutually reinforcing effect of expanding their ranks. One of the clearest examples of fan activism centered on the 1960s science fiction television series *Star Trek*. The original *Star Trek* television series, which premiered on NBC on September 8, 1966, followed the exploits of the crew aboard a quasi-military spaceship called the *Enterprise*. The series, conceived by creator Gene Roddenberry, was designed to be a kind of Western in space (Roddenberry once claimed that the program was designed to be a "*Wagon Train* to the stars," referencing the title of a popular Western program on NBC at the time) with a moral message at the end of each show. Although the program dealt with interesting groundbreaking themes and won accolades among some science fiction audiences, it was in danger of cancellation almost from the outset due to lackluster ratings.

The threat of cancellation of this new outer-space TV series galvanized what was to become one of the largest and most enduring media fan movements in the world. When word of the impending cancellation of the series leaked in 1967, both Roddenberry and a group of science fiction fans began to organize an extensive letter-writing campaign to help save the program. Two fans, John and Bjo Trimble, even wrote an advice sheet for would-be fan petitioners called "How to Write Effective Letters to Save *Star Trek*." They directed fans to send these letters to the president of NBC, to NBC affiliate TV stations, to TV columnists, and to *TV Guide* (Messenger-Davies & Pearson, 2007, p. 218). According to an NBC press release, the network received over 115,893 letters in response to the cancellation announcement—a surprisingly large response for such a small program—and NBC renewed the program for a third season. The fans were elated, with Bjo Trimble proclaiming, "And so a major triumph of the consumer public over the network and over the stupid Nielsen ratings was accomplished through advocacy letter-writing" (Trimble, 1982, p. 36). However, the fans' victory was short-lived.

In January 1969, a 50% drop-off in viewer ratings led NBC to again cancel the program, this time for good.

Despite the disappearance of the original media text from American television screens (and, indeed, because of it), the community of fans devoted to Roddenberry's space adventure series expanded dramatically in the years following its cancellation. In February 1972, fans organized the first formal convention of *Star Trek* enthusiasts in the ballroom of New York's Statler-Hilton Hotel. They expected several hundred attendees but were astonished when more than 3,000 actually showed up to see many of the original cast members from the now-defunct series in person (Tulloch & Jenkins, 1995, pp. 10–11). More than 6,000 people attended the New York convention the following year, and many similar *Star Trek* conventions emerged in other cities around the country (p. 11). The success of the fan-as-activist model in the case of *Star Trek* spurred passionate followers of other television programs, including soap operas (see, for example, Baym, 2000; Harrington & Bielby, 1995; Scardaville, 2005), to form fan organizations in response to the threat of cancellation due to a program's lack of commercial viability. Perhaps the most successful of these campaigns in the 21st century was the extensive Kickstarter crowdfunding campaign mounted by fans of the UPN television series *Veronica Mars* (2004–2007) in 2009, which raised over $5 million to partially fund a follow-up film with the original actors (Navar-Gill, 2018). Despite these successes, however, most attempts to alter media producers' decision-making have been failures. For this reason, Tulloch and Jenkins refer to fans as a "powerless elite." This phrase defines fans as "structurally situated between producers they have little control over and the 'wider public' whose continued following of the show can never be assured, but on whom the survival of the show depends" (1995, p. 145).

Fans and Media Texts: Protecting Continuity and Canon

When fans connect to other enthusiasts through face-to-face or online interactions, they immediately share a common bond of fascination with, and knowledge of, a particular media text. Fans abandon any sort of critical distance from their favorite media. They experience these texts in a much deeper way by integrating them into their lives.[1] As Jenkins (1992, p. 56) notes, "The difference between watching a [television] series and becoming a fan lies in the intensity of their emotional and intellectual involvement." Through close interpretation and rereading of the text and spirited debates and discussions with others, fans develop an extensive repertoire of knowledge about their favorite media. Although these "trivia" details

---

[1]There is much discussion among scholars of media fandom about what degree of involvement with media texts constitutes a "fan" of a particular text. As Hills (2002) and Sandvoss (2005) have argued, for example, the category of *fan* should be expanded to include those more casual enthusiasts for particular media. Those casual fans, while not nearly as invested as the fans Jenkins (1992) outlined, nevertheless comprise the dominant share of the fan audience for popular media texts.

about popular media are not necessary for casual audiences to obtain entertainment from popular media, the utilization and trading of these extensive volumes of knowledge about popular texts are key sources of fan pleasure. Fan audiences may feel so connected to the narrative that they revere that they develop a sense of *ownership* over the text. This places these audience members on a head-on collision course with the producers and copyright holders, who have a vested interest in developing the characters and story lines in particular ways. When the interests of fans and media creators diverge, controversy and struggle emerge as important aspects of the media–audience relationship.

Fan audiences pay special attention to the details and nuances of their favorite texts, dissecting them with care and discussing them at length with other fans. Science fiction television, in particular, demands from viewers a willingness to understand and accept how a particular universe operates (whether it is futuristic or in another part of the galaxy with alien species) and how the characters in that universe interact with one another. Fans revel in the details of the workings of the fictional world and amass a storehouse of knowledge about the program. This information is collected from external sources like fan magazines, general interest media, blogs, chat rooms, and fan websites. Viewing favorite television programs over and over again is therefore an important aspect of fan cultures. It helps not only to internalize details about the narrative but allows individuals to experience the thrill of seeing the narrative for the first time all over again. It also allows those viewers to discuss ideas about the narrative with other fans. As Jenkins notes, "Rereading is central to the fan's aesthetic pleasure. Much of fan culture facilitates repeated encounters with favored texts" (1992, p. 69).

The result of intense fan interest in popular television shows is that the producers of those programs have to tread carefully whenever they decide to alter the fundamental outlines of the narrative or to develop characters in specific ways. An awareness of the character and plot development of a particular program is called **continuity**. Whenever the narrative introduces a new plot or character element that is somehow inconsistent with earlier stories, fans' ire is inevitably raised. This is mostly because "the fans' particular competence is their intimate and detailed knowledge of the show; consequently, any producer or script editor who needlessly breaches the continuity and coherence of that knowledge is 'insulting their intelligence'" (Tulloch & Jenkins, 1995, p. 147). In their research on fans of the long-running British science fiction series *Doctor Who*, Tulloch and Jenkins found that avid viewers were particularly critical of one episode of the program titled "Destiny of the Daleks," in which a Time Lord character named Romana changes her form ("regenerates") six different times before deciding upon a new body. This regeneration of the character was prompted by a sudden shift in the casting of the program: The previous actress to play Romana had quit the production suddenly, and the producers had to scramble to find her replacement. As one fan commented,

> I could never forgive Graham Williams [the executive producer] for
> the regeneration scene. . . . It has been clearly established that a Time
> Lord can only have twelve regenerations, clearly established. In many

stories that fact has been stated. So how can they have some supposedly responsible female Time Lord in the TARDIS trying on about six different faces before she decides which one she wants?—which is obviously wasting six regenerations. It is just ludicrous. (Tulloch & Jenkins, 1995, p. 148)

In this case, fans' close attention to the detail of the program quickly revealed the inconsistency in the narrative, resulting in a fan backlash against the producers of the program (see Box 8.1 for another example of fan–producer conflict due to continuity issues). Conversely, television episodes that pay homage to earlier ones or make reference to earlier plots or character histories are particularly rewarding for fans. These types of narratives encourage fans to use their extensive knowledge of the program to extract extra meaning from the text, which for them is a source of particular satisfaction and pleasure.

BOX 8.1
The Battle for *Battlestar Galactica*: A Producer–Fan Continuity Struggle

The importance of narrative continuity for fans is readily apparent in the story of the recent resurrection of the 1978 science fiction television series *Battlestar Galactica*. *Battlestar* premiered in the shadow of *Star Wars*. It was generally panned by critics at the time as an imitator, designed to benefit from the gargantuan profits being generated by the *Star Wars* franchise. The series followed the exploits of a group of human galactic wanderers who were fleeing from hostile robots called Cylons that they had themselves created. Although the premiere of the show drew a huge audience of 65 million viewers, its popularity quickly waned, and it was canceled after only 8 months on the air.

As with the series demise of the original *Star Trek*, the cancellation of *Battlestar Galactica* catalyzed the creation of fan clubs and an entire fan convention (dubbed "Galacticon") dedicated to the program, though the size and scale of these fan efforts paled in comparison to the much-larger communities connected with *Trek* and with *Star Wars*. Richard Hatch, an actor who played one of the lead roles on the series, attended his first fan convention in 1995 and was astonished by the warm reception he received from fans there. Hatch became the public face of a fan-centered movement to return *Battlestar* to the small screen. Using roughly $30,000 of his own money and the help of other actors and cinematographers he knew (as well as some fans), he created a short promotional called *Battlestar Galactica: The Second Coming*. The film was meant to spark interest among television producers for a continuation of the 1970s series. The short film, featuring Hatch reprising his role as Lee Adama, premiered to wide acclaim at the 1999 Comic Convention in San Diego. Two separate productions were begun on a continuation series, but both failed to materialize, much to Hatch's dismay.

What Hatch and the *Battlestar* fans did not know was that Universal Studios had commissioned former *Star Trek: The Next Generation* writer Ron Moore to draft a completely new concept for the series in preparation for a *Battlestar* miniseries that would be broadcast on cable's SyFy Channel. The fans' triumph about the show's return was overshadowed by their gall at the fact that Richard Hatch had not been asked to participate in the project. Even worse, one of the key roles in the original series (a hot-shot, womanizing star pilot named "Starbuck") was being recast as a woman.

Fans were outraged that the characters they knew and loved from the old series were being radically redrawn by Moore and his writing staff. One New York fan started an Internet chat group called "Ron Moore Sucks," and fans participating in the forum insisted on referring to him as "MooreRon." In 2003, shortly before the premiere of the miniseries, Moore was invited to appear at the 25th Anniversary Galacticon convention to talk about the new program. Surprisingly, he accepted the invitation, and the stage was set for a public showdown with the fans. According to reports, a tense and angry crowd began to boo and hiss when Moore was introduced and took the stage. They calmed only when Hatch himself stood up and praised Moore for the courage to defend his vision of the program and address fans' concerns. Eventually, Hatch accepted an invitation from Moore to appear as a recurring character on the new incarnation of *Battlestar Galactica*. Fittingly, Hatch played a former terrorist who clashes with the crew.

Source: Hodgman, J. (2005, July17). "Ron Moore's Deep Space Journey," *The New York Times Magazine*, 32.

The notion of a **canon** is closely related to the concept of continuity. *Canon* is a term used in the study of literature to describe a group of texts that are considered significant or valuable. These works are deemed worthy due to their level of quality or because they are part of a larger corpus of work from a respected author or artist. The word was originally associated with religion, referring to a "collection or list of books of the Bible accepted by the Christian Church as genuine and inspired" (Oxford English Dictionary). Which authors, artists, and musicians should be included in the "canon" of culturally valued material? The definition of *canon* is subject to debate and alteration by scholars and experts. Author and literary critic Harold Bloom generated controversy over the notion of *canon* when he published *The Western Canon* (1994). In this work, Bloom created a list of the most significant literary works from antiquity to the present day. Similar to scholars of historical literature and art historians, media fans engage in lively debates over which texts should be included in a canon. Fans demonstrate types of attention to detail and logic similar to that of their academic counterparts; the only difference is that fans focus on popular culture.

Canon Wars: *Star Wars* Fans Define the Popular Text

The case of fan discussions about *Star Wars*, the successful multibillion-dollar science fiction film franchise, demonstrates the importance of canon to those devotees. The explosion of fan enthusiasm for director George Lucas's space saga *Star Wars* began almost immediately following the release of the first film (subtitled *A New Hope*) in 1977. As fan-turned-academic Will Brooker notes in his analysis of the *Star Wars* fan phenomenon (2002), the question of what counts as "official" or canonic *Star Wars* texts is sometimes a thorny one. Clearly, he argues, the films themselves (beginning with Episodes 4, 5, and 6 in the 1980s and continuing with the prequels in 1999) represent the official texts, against which all other films should be compared. The films form the backbone of George Lucas's vision for the *Star Wars* universe. However, the films represent only one aspect of the larger *Star Wars* textual universe. They are supplemented by "authorized" book adaptations of the films (called "novelizations"), a series of radio dramas broadcast on NPR in the 1980s (featuring actors from the films reprising their roles), a TV special featuring the lovable furry Ewok creatures (introduced in *Return of the Jedi*), and many new novels featuring many of the same characters and situations from the films but written by outside authors (these are called the "Expanded Universe" of *Star Wars*, or EU for short). Which of these media texts, all commercially available to fans, represents the "true" story of Luke Skywalker and his intrepid band of rebels as they battle against galactic domination by the Empire? More importantly, why would fans care to answer this question?

Brooker's analysis of online discussions among *Star Wars* fans demonstrates the importance of canon in their ongoing interpretations of the text. The specific online fan debate that Brooker examines concerns what to outsiders might seem a trivial point: Some fans wonder who coined the name of the Imperial planet-city Coruscant that appears in the *Star Wars* prequel films. Was it the brainchild of *Star Wars* creator George Lucas, or did Timothy Zahn (science fiction writer and author of the 1991 *Star Wars*–themed novel *Heir to the Empire*, a part of the EU) use the name first? Fans posting to the online forums that Brooker studies take the debate quite seriously because the original creator of this story detail matters. The fact that George Lucas did not dream up "Coruscant," if true, would imply that the name of the city might have been coined by an EU author (with no connection to the production of the films themselves) and subsequently featured in a film created by Lucas. This would in turn necessitate the elevation of Zahn's novel to the level of canon equal to that the films. The debate about the origin of the name was finally settled when one fan cited an extract from a book *Star Wars: The Annotated Screenplays* (Bouzereau, 1997) that featured a quote from Lucas himself:

> Of course I had a million different names for the home planet
> of the Empire, but Coruscant came out of publishing. Definitive
> proof . . . what does this say? That Coruscant was not George Lucas's
> name for the Imperial Homeworld? Who created the name Coruscant?
> Timothy Zahn! Sorry, guys, I know you take every shot you can at
> the EU, but you really should think before you post. (Brooker,
> 2002, p. 110)

This exchange among *Star Wars* fans on an online bulletin board demonstrates the critical importance of both continuity and canon to media fans. First, these fans demand continuity from the *Star Wars* narrative in its many textual forms by assuming that the Imperial home planet has one official name. If there was a discrepancy in the name between the books and the films, that continuity error would certainly be a cause for reflection and debate. The issue of canon here is important because George Lucas is regarded as the most important creative force in the larger group of texts. Therefore, his input about the series trumps all others'. Clearly, fan communities thrive on interaction, discussion, and close attention to the nuances of the text itself. These interpretive activities clearly distinguish fans from more casual viewers of the *Star Wars* films.

Fans and Textual Productions

The previous section outlined two important aspects of media fandom. First, fan audiences gather together to form communities based upon mutual interest and appreciation of their favorite media texts. Secondly, fans employ a number of deeper interpretive strategies while engaging with their favorite texts, paying close attention to continuity details in the narrative and protecting the original canon of the program against unauthorized encroachment and alteration. Many fans, however, go beyond even the close reading and interpretation of the original text. As Jenkins and many other fan culture scholars have uncovered, some audience members become inspired enough to create their own media texts using situations, settings, and characters provided by their favorite TV shows, movies, and books.

De Certeau and Textual Poaching

Early fan scholars (particularly Jenkins, 1992; Bacon-Smith, 1992) were fascinated not only by the complex ways in which fans interpret their favorite media texts but also by the ability of these audiences to become textually *productive* in their reception practices. This productivity comes in the form of both close readings of the primary text and the material production of creative texts that use the original as "raw material" for brand-new narratives. These fans begin to transcend the traditional boundary between media production and consumption, the classic binary that distinguishes the creator or originator of a media message (the producer) from the receiver of the message (the audience).

Jenkins's early work on *Star Trek* fans used the theories of French scholar Michel de Certeau. In his book *The Practice of Everyday Life* (1984), de Certeau argued that the act of reading a book or other literary work was akin to the practice of **poaching**. Readers temporarily inhabit the intellectual space of whatever text they are encountering, making that space their own for that brief moment. De Certeau explained that when a reader encounters a book narrative, he

> insinuates into another person's text the ruses of pleasure and appropriation: he poaches on it, is transported into it, pluralizes himself in it like the internal rumblings of one's body. . . . A different world (the reader's) slips into the author's place. This mutation makes the text habitable, like a rented apartment. It transforms another person's property into a space borrowed for a moment by a transient. . . . Reading thus introduces an "art" which is anything but passive. (1984, p. xxi–xxii)

Like John Fiske's notion of semiotic productivity, de Certeau's conceptualization of the act of reading is as an inherently creative and imaginative process, full of play and "invention" within the mind of the reader. Additionally, de Certeau argued that readers are essentially "nomads" who move from one idea or text to another, continually appropriating the information and synthesizing it into new meanings. Media fans, argued Jenkins (1992, p. 37), also look across different media to construct their own creative understandings of their favorite texts since "their pleasure comes through the particular juxtapositions that they create between specific program content and other cultural materials." For example, fans of a popular television soap opera may not limit their textual engagement to watching the program religiously every week. They might also read ancillary magazines, such as *Soap Opera Digest* or *People* magazine, for insights on the characters and the actors or even log on to chat groups and websites for more in-depth information about the show. All of these actions contribute to a deeper and more sophisticated understanding of the original text.

In his initial fan-based study, *Textual Poachers*, Jenkins (1992) also sympathized with de Certeau's insistence that the cultural practices of one's everyday life—including our encounters with and interpretations of popular media—could be active sites of resistance to the dominant linguistic codes built into the message. Audiences of popular texts are at an inherent disadvantage vis-à-vis institutional producers. Fans have neither access to the funds and technical resources for professional media production nor the legal control over the narratives and characters that are near and dear to their hearts (due to the often fierce protection of copyrights by producers). As Jenkins noted, "Like the poachers of old, fans operate from a position of cultural marginality and social weakness" (1992, p. 26). The repossession of the text by fans from the producers allows members of the former party to explore their own self-identities and to play with many of the textual elements found in their favorite popular narratives. This creates a new avenue for expanded audience autonomy vis-à-vis media texts. As Jenkins argued, fans "possess not simply borrowed remnants snatched from mass culture, but their own culture built from the semiotic raw materials the media provides" (1992, p. 49).

Fanzines, Fanfic, and Filking: Textual Poaching in Action

The textual poaching of media fans takes many different forms. Fans in the pre-Internet age kept themselves updated on the latest developments in their media texts by producing newsletters or magazines (called "fanzines") that were mailed by subscription to fan club members. Most of these early fanzines were primitive by today's standards. They were typically typeset using typewriters and then photocopied and stapled together. These makeshift periodicals contained a variety of different types of content, including updates on the activities of fan organizations, news, and other information about the original fan media text (whether it be a television program, film, or music group, to name a few), profiles of people connected with the media text, interviews, fan-created artwork, and even original fictional stories written by fans themselves. Today, these paper-and-ink fan connections have been largely supplanted by the Internet, which allows individual fans and fan organizations to easily create websites with news, information, creative content, and links to a myriad of other content choices related to the primary media text.

One aspect of fans' creativity that scholars find most interesting is the original stories written by fans about their favorite media texts. Called **fan fiction or fanfic**, these short stories often feature existing characters from favorite fan texts or are written in the creative universe of the original text. There are numerous fanfic genres, all of which are extensions of the original. For example, some fans choose to "fill in" existing gaps in the narrative of their favorite TV shows or movies by writing extensive backstories of characters or describing encounters between characters that were not seen on the screen. Alternatively, some fanfic expands the timeline of the original text by suggesting what happened to some of the main characters before or after the events that transpired within the existing narrative. Fans enjoy expanding the plot or rewriting endings of their favorite media texts, particularly when they are dissatisfied with the choices of the official writers or producers of the text (Jenkins, 1992, pp. 164–165; see Figure 8.3 for a complete list of narrative styles in fan fiction).

Two genres of fan fiction exist on the margins of fan communities due to their rather controversial nature. First, some fans enjoy breaking down the wall between the narrative and the audience by inserting themselves (or a character who is clearly similar to the fan-author) into the story to interact with figures from the popular text. In her research on women *Star Trek* fans in the 1980s, Bacon-Smith (1992) described these fanfics as **"Mary Sue" stories**:

> A very young heroine, often in her teens and possessing genius,
> intelligence, great beauty, and a charmingly impish personality, joins
> the heroes either on the bridge of the starship or on the streets with
> the spies or police. She generally resolves the conflict of the story,
> saves the lives of the protagonists who have grown to love her, but dies
> heroically in the process. (p. 53)

Although these types of personalized stories fulfill fan desires, this particular fanfic genre has been the subject of fierce backlash within fan communities, who consider these writings to be hackneyed and juvenile. Even more controversial is **"slash" fiction**, or fan stories that explore sexual relationships among the main characters that fall well beyond the purview of mainstream popular cultural texts. In the *Star Trek* fan universe, "slash" fiction refers to stories that detail an intense emotional and sexual relationship between the two primary male characters in the program, Captain James Kirk and Vulcan Science Officer Spock. These Kirk/Spock romances (or "K/S" for short) are written largely by women for women audiences. "Slash" fiction such as K/S stories challenge the existing gender boundaries of the popular text itself by introducing the notion of homosexuality into a mainstream, heterosexual narrative.

Another common form of fan textual production is **filking**, the process of fan music-making. Fans write poems or lyrics, which are then either left in textual form or set to original music. The subjects of filk music are similar to the narrative styles of fanfic outlined in Figure 8.3, with many lyrics expanding the narrative timeline or focusing on minor characters of the existing text. Jenkins (1992) describes filking sessions at *Star Trek* conventions in which fans perform original songs for one another. The *Star Trek* fans also sing together "classic" filk tunes that have achieved renown within the fan community and form the basis of a shared filking culture. Following performances, filk singers may ask the audience if the lyrics need to be explained, thereby cementing the role of filking as both an individual creative and community-building fan activity.

The purposes of fanfic and filking are not simply to allow fans to expand their experiences with their favorite texts beyond the initial reception. Rather, the circulation of stories between fan authors allows them to give supportive feedback and critiques to one another, cementing a strong sense of community. The goal of writing original fan stories and music is altogether distinct from mainstream publishing. Instead of selling stories to audiences (something anathema within fan cultures), fans freely distribute their creative efforts to others in order to (1) support the larger fan community and (2) to exercise their own imaginations regarding their favorite characters and situations from media texts. Bacon-Smith (1992), writing about groups of women *Star Trek* fans who circulate stories among themselves, noted that traditional notions of proprietary authorship found in literary communities are not operative among these fan groups. Instead, she argued, these women fan-writers "value their workmanship in the community but place little or no emphasis on the concept of 'auteur' as solitary creator of an aesthetically unique piece of art. In the fan community, fiction creates the community" (Bacon-Smith, 1992, p. 57). In this sense, popular cultural texts allow fans not only to exchange ideas and explore alternative character and narrative developments, but they also develop a unique sense of community around the distribution and consumption of these texts. The women that Bacon-Smith interviewed in her research reported that the expressive potential of their fan productions also gave them an increased sense of autonomy in a society that often pushes concerns of women to

Figure 8.3 Narrative Styles in Fan Fiction

Fan Fiction Type	Definition
1. Recontextualization	Short stories or "missing scenes" that fill in gaps in the existing media text (TV program, film, etc.)
2. Expanding the series timeline	Exploring characters' backgrounds or rewriting unpopular endings to the existing media narrative
3. Refocalization	Shifting the focus away from central characters to focus on secondary, minor, or one-off characters (often women and minorities)
4. Moral realignment	Inverting the moral universe of the original narrative; villains are transformed into protagonists with their own narratives
5. Genre shifting	Changing the primary genre of the narrative (transforming science fiction into mystery or romance, for example)
6. Crossovers	Blurring boundaries between distinct media texts; introducing characters from one media narrative into another
7. Character dislocation	Removing main characters from their original situations and giving them alternative names, identities, and milieus
8. Personalization	Fan writers writing themselves into their favorite media narratives; "Mary Sue" stories
9. Emotional intensification	Exploring psychological motivations of main characters, focusing on moments of crisis; "hurt-comfort" stories
10. Eroticization	Exploring characters' sexuality and sexual encounters not seen in the primary narrative; K/S stories or "slash" fiction

Source: Adapted from Jenkins, H. (1992). *Textual Poachers: Television Fans and Participatory Culture*. London, England: Routledge.

the margins. As we can see from the numerous examples in this section, the first wave of fan studies catalogued and celebrated the potential of fan production to transcend existing social hierarchies and boundaries.

Fans and Cultural Hierarchy: The Limits of Textual Reinterpretation

Let's pause for a moment and take stock of the various notions of fandom that we have been exploring thus far in this chapter. First, fans are distinguished from the rest of the audience through their intense interest and dedication to specific popular media. Fans expend extra time and interpretive energy on popular or "throwaway" media and seek out others who are like them to form social bonds of community via their shared enthusiasm for a particular television program, film, music group, or sport. Scholarship on fans in the late 1980s and early 1990s made special note of the ways in which fans turned their media consumption into the creative *production* of new texts, based upon audience members' intense admiration for popular media. Scholars such as Henry Jenkins and Camille Bacon-Smith discovered that fans of popular TV programs like *Star Trek* were far from being passive consumers of media. These active individuals produced their own newsletters, fictional stories, artwork, poems, and songs and shared them with other fans at local meet-ups, conventions, and other social gatherings. These scholars viewed fan participation as more than a simple pastime or hobby; it was a kind of liberation from the traditionally passive role played by the audience. This overview of fan audiences can be described as the first wave of fan scholarship.

The second wave of fan studies in the late 1990s looked back somewhat critically at initial claims by Jenkins, Bacon-Smith, Fiske, and other scholars that deep engagement with popular culture constituted a fundamental challenge to the existing status quo. These early scholars, themselves fans of specific popular cultural forms, were intent on rehabilitating the notion of fandom from negative stereotypes by aesthetic "elites." However, scholars in the mid-1990s began to train a critical eye back on the notion of fandom itself, looking specifically at the ways in which the attitudes and behaviors of fans may be unwittingly reproducing many of the same cultural, gender, and economic hierarchies that they were attempting to escape from in the mainstream. The second wave moved beyond the "incorporation/resistance" dichotomy and focused more on the "sociology of consumption" of popular texts by audiences (Gray et al., 2007, p. 6).

Pierre Bourdieu and the Sociology of Cultural Consumption

The theoretical touchstone for many of these scholars was the work of French sociologist Pierre Bourdieu. In his most well-known work, titled *Distinction* (translated into English in 1984), Bourdieu played on the notion of his book's title to make a specific argument about class positions in modern societies. Bourdieu (1984) observed that class "distinctions" among individuals were linked not only to their economic capital (as Marxist scholars had argued), but they were also connected to their social, educational, and cultural capital. Individuals place their class status on display, he wrote, via their *taste* or consumption patterns (in essence, what makes us individually "distinct" from other individuals in society). Taste, in turn, is a function of the **habitus**, which is a complex function of an individual's social, cultural, and economic capital.

> [The habitus] includes the notion of a habitat, the habitants and the processes of inhabiting it, and the habituating ways of thinking that go with it. It encompasses our position within the social space, the

ways of living that go with it and what Bourdieu calls the associated "dispositions" of mind, cultural tastes and ways of thinking and feeling. (Fiske, 1992, p. 32)

For instance, a college-educated, middle-class individual might purchase tickets to the opera rather than a vaudeville show because doing so is a clear distinct reminder of that person's social status. It serves as a tool of self-identity and also provides a visible indicator to others of one's place in the social hierarchy. Bourdieu (1984) proposed that consumption behaviors, rather than constituting a statement of emancipation from social norms, were inextricably linked to the habitus. Bourdieu sought to connect those sociological variables to the consumption of specific cultural products (such as styles of furniture or types of music).

How might Bourdieu's theories map onto our discussion of fans and their activities? The second wave of fan research used Bourdieu's analysis as the theoretical backbone to understand the specific cultural consumption patterns of popular media fans and to explore the extent to which those patterns challenged or reaffirmed existing cultural hierarchies in society. Early studies of fans detailed the ways in which fan celebrations of popular media were potentially liberating, in that these activities distanced fans from the more commercial aspects of popular culture. Rather than regarding the TV program *Bewitched* (for example) as filler fluff to keep viewers tuned in between commercial breaks, fans treated TV texts with the same level of interpretive thoughtfulness and reverence that one might assign to a Proust novel or the plays of Shakespeare. However, as second-wave fan scholars argue, enthusiasm for popular media is not universal. Fans actively choose and discriminate (in the neutral sense of the term) among and between different types of popular media. These audience subsets can be some of the harshest critics of their favorite programs and movies, particularly when they are disappointed by a popular text or its creators. Questions asked by second-wave fan studies scholars address the social positioning of fans vis-à-vis mainstream or "official" culture and whether the potential of fan cultures to challenge the existing status quo is realized in specific settings.

Second-Wave Fan Studies: The Reproduction of Economic and Social Hierarchies

The enthusiasm and care with which fans interpret popular texts suggest a challenge to the consumer-oriented nature of TV shows, movies, and music. How much do fans truly extricate themselves from the capitalist orientation of popular media through their interpretive activities? Recent fan scholarship has reexamined fan practices in light of Bourdieu's theories. Contrary to earlier fan research, later studies have found some close parallels between the distinct cultural world of fans and those of mainstream or "official" culture. Although popular media fans may occupy the lower end of the economic capital spectrum, these individuals may nevertheless mimic aspects of official culture by adopting many similar practices. As Fiske (1992) notes,

> Capitalist societies are built upon accumulation and investment, and this is as true of their cultural as well as financial economies. The shadow economy of fan culture in many ways parallels the workings of the official culture, but it adapts them to the habitus of the subordinate. (p. 45)

Collecting, for example, is a prominent pastime for both wealthy art patrons and comic book aficionados. The primary difference is that oil paintings are quite expensive and valued according to the perceived talents of the artist (hence, uniqueness and originality are key), while popular cultural materials are comparatively cheap to procure and are not valued for their uniqueness. You might imagine that fan collecting is all about amassing the largest possible collection, rather than focusing on the distinctiveness of each piece (Fiske, 1992).

The case of comic book collectors demonstrates the partial falsehood of the "more-is-better" theory of fan collectors. In a 1997 in-depth study of comic book collectors, Jeffrey Brown discovered that these individuals had a highly sophisticated system for "valuing" comic books that often directly mimicked the appraisal practices found among official or "high-culture" art critics. Rather than wantonly purchasing as many comic books as their pocketbooks would allow, serious comic book collectors developed the "ability to distinguish between objects of worth and worthlessness, a knowledge of important canonical features, and a substantiation of 'good taste'" (Brown, 1997, p. 23). For comic book fans, acquiring a taste for "good" comics involved discriminating between individual authors, comic artists, and characters (and different versions of the characters), as well as developing an awareness of the history of a specific character or title. Serious collectors also made it a point to acquire "canonical texts," or rare and significant comic strips such as the first issue of *Action Comics* (in which the character of Superman was introduced). This particular issue has been recently valued at $100,000 or more, which shows how the economic hierarchies of comic fandom can closely mirror those of official or "high" cultural artifacts like painting or sculpture. Comic collectors also perform the role of "experts" in their field and distinguish among themselves according to both their level of knowledge about comics and their personal collections of rare and unique comic books. This again calls into question the independence of fan cultures from existing economic hierarchies in society.

Another key aspect of fan cultures outlined in the early research of Jenkins and Bacon-Smith was the sense of camaraderie and cohesion among groups of fans. Brought together by their common interests in a TV program or music group, fan communities were viewed as socially "safe" spaces where individuals could celebrate culturally devalued texts without fear of social reprisals or ridicule. No fan at a *Star Trek* convention would raise an eyebrow at another fan who chose to dress in a costume from the program or to spend time writing fan fiction for the consumption of only a small circle of interested readers. However, as the traditional boundaries of media fandom expanded dramatically with the rise of the Internet in the 1990s, scholars began to "explode" the definition of a fan to include a wide variety of activities that occupy a much larger proportion of the population (see, for example, Hills, 2002; Sandvoss, 2005). Far from the image of the socially awkward, marginalized *Star Trek* fans of the late 1980s, 21st-century fandom is becoming a much more common phenomenon.[2] The new age of audience engagement and enthusiasm requires a scholarly analysis to take a somewhat different approach. While Bourdieu isolated class as the central dividing line between different strata of the population (and thus, their habitus and cultural consumption habits), some scholars have questioned this premise, arguing that notions of gender, race (Fiske, 1992), and social network (Erickson, 1996) play a more central role in structuring fans' social position in society.

More recent fan scholarship, pushing aside the sense of community that early fan scholars found so compelling, takes note of the darker side of **fan identity and group cohesion**. A group will create exclusivity and difference in order to enhance its self-definition and to give it purpose and coherence. In this respect, fan cultures are no different from the mainstream in the sense that fan groups will often create clear boundaries between casual fans or enthusiasts and "real" fans. As Fiske (1992, p. 35) noted, "Textual and social discrimination are part and parcel of the same cultural activity." Jancovich (2002), for example, focused on cult film fans, closely examining their self-identity in contrast to the mainstream. He found that the

> subcultural identity which underpins cult movies fandom not only celebrates the unwatchable and/or unobtainable—that which is by definition usually unpleasurable or inaccessible to most viewers—but how this emerges from a need to produce and protect a sense of rarity and exclusivity. (Jancovich, 2002, p. 309)

By creating an artificial boundary and castigating others who chose to spend their time watching mainstream Hollywood films, cult film fans carved out a specific group identity for themselves. Sarah Thornton (1996) noticed in her influential study of club culture in the early 1990s that even among members of the young "counterculture" who frequented raves and other dance clubs, those with higher discretionary incomes (often identified as "hip" or "authentic" due to the specific styles of clothing they were wearing) more easily gained entrée into these establishments. The club scene was not immune to racial hierarchies and discrimination either. Some clubs, for example, made it a consistent practice to limit the

---

[2]Indeed, it is likely you may consider yourself a "fan" of multiple types of popular culture, whether it be a musical group, a sports team, a TV show, or a particular actor or actress. The phrase "being a fan of . . ." has even been integrated into the prominent social networking website Facebook, which allows users to publicly display their fandom(s) for each of their online friends.

number of Black males that were allowed in. As these second-wave fan scholars have demonstrated, "escaping" into the world of popular media often does not mean that individuals are escaping the systems of discrimination and power that define the society at large. Instead, these systems of hierarchy are re-created or reconstituted in slightly different forms by fan cultures.

Conclusion: Fans, Creativity, and Cultural Hierarchy
....

In this chapter, we have extended the notion of audience interpretations of media to focus on fan cultures. Unlike more casual audiences for popular media, fans invest extraordinary amounts of time and interpretive energy in their media consumption. In doing so, they blur the traditional boundary between media producers and audiences. Fans of science fiction television programs and movies like *Star Trek* and *Star Wars* carefully interpret the original texts in the same way as a scholar might examine ancient manuscripts for nuance and detail, take possession of the texts, and integrate them into their own lives. For some scholars, the very act of taking television, movies, and popular music seriously is evidence that fan cultures are challenging the dominant message of the original text by liberating themselves from the commercial nature of mass culture. Fans also develop social networks through their mutual interest in popular media and become involved in their own cultural productions such as newsletters, fan fiction writing, online websites, and other types of creativity. This suggests a level of intelligence and playfulness with popular media that belies the passivity that is often associated with media audiences.

We have also explored some of the scholarly debates about the role of popular media fans in our understanding of the mass media audience. Early fan research centered on legitimizing both the scholarship of fandom and fandom itself by destigmatizing fans' activities and emphasizing the autonomy of fans over the popular media. The second wave of research critically examined these initial assumptions. As one scholar argued recently, "Cultural analyses of fandom may have erred in too readily accepting fans' individualist self-conception as the price to be paid for dislodging prevailing negative stereotypes and for establishing fandom as a legitimate topic for academic inquiry" (Murray, 2004, p. 20). The second wave used the theories of Pierre Bourdieu to focus on the ways in which fan cultures mimic or reproduce existing class, gender, racial, and cultural hierarchies that exist in mainstream culture. Although these debates continue in scholarly circles, it is clear that the Internet and newer forms of technology are rapidly altering the landscape for media audiences by expanding their ability to interact both with popular texts and one another. In the next chapter, we will concentrate on the future of media audiences in a world where continual, recursive forms of feedback have become commonplace. In this new online, interactive world, where does the text end and the audience begin?

DISCUSSION ACTIVITIES

1. To get an up-close look at fan communities, you need look no further than the Internet. Try logging on to one or more of the fan-based forums and chat groups listed here. As you read through the bulletin board postings from users, think about the following questions:

   - Do you see examples of fan textual interpretations here? (Think about continuity, canon, reinterpretations of the content, or expressions of textual competency.)

   - Do you see examples of the integration of popular texts into fans' everyday lives? (Think about meeting for fan conventions, group meetings, website development, or even fan fiction.)

   - Do you see evidence of any discussions that touch upon social hierarchies or issues of race, gender, or class?

     Star Trek Fan Forums: https://www.trekbbs.com

     http://www.fanforum.com/f89/

     Star Wars Fan Forums: http://boards.theforce.net/

2. To access another good source of fan discourse, tune in to a local sports talk radio station in your community or log on to a website that allows fans to play fantasy football or fantasy baseball. In the discourse among sports fans, do you hear or see any similarities to or differences from what you read in this chapter about fans of science fiction television? Write down some of your observations and discuss them with the class.

3. As the chapter outlined, comic book fans sometimes reproduce cultural and economic hierarchies through their comic book collecting activities. Head down to a local comic book store and take a look at the types of comics being sold, paying special attention to those comic book issues that may be found behind locked glass window cases. You might also engage the proprietor or owner of the store in conversation about why certain issues of a comic book are more expensive than others. What kinds of fan knowledge about comic books are on display, and how is the business of comic collecting similar to the collecting of other artifacts in society?

ADDITIONAL MATERIALS

Booth, P. (Ed.). (2018). *A companion to media fandom and fan studies*. Hoboken, NJ: Wiley-Blackwell.

Brooker, W. (2002). *Using the force: Creativity, community and Star Wars fans*. New York, NY: Continuum.

Click, M. A., & Scott, S. (Eds.). (2017). *The Routledge companion to media fandom*. New York: Routledge.

Cordova, C. (2005). *Ringers: Lord of the fans* [Documentary film]. Sony Pictures Home Entertainment. More information at http://www.imdb.com/title/tt0379473/

Gray, J., Sandvoss, C., & Harrington, C. L. (Eds.). (2017). *Fandom: Identities and communities in a mediated world* (2nd ed.). New York: New York University Press.

Hesmondhalgh, D. (2006). Bourdieu, the media and cultural production. *Media Culture & Society, 28*(2), 211–231.

Nygard, R. C. (1999). *Trekkies* [Documentary film]. Paramount Pictures. More information at http://www.trekdoc.com/

Sandvoss, C. (2005). *Fans: The mirror of consumption*. Cambridge, United Kingdom: Polity Press.

REFERENCES

Abercrombie, N., & Longhurst, B. (1998). *Audiences: A sociological theory of performance and imagination.* London, England: SAGE.

Austin, B. A. (1981). Portrait of a cult film audience: *The Rocky Horror Picture Show. The Journal of Communication, 31*(2), 43–54.

Bacon-Smith, C. (1992). *Enterprising women: Television fandom and the creation of popular myth.* Philadelphia: University of Pennsylvania Press.

Baym, N. K. (2000). *Tune in, log on: Soaps, fandom, and online community.* Thousand Oaks, CA: SAGE.

Bloom, H. (1994). *The Western canon: The books and school of the ages.* New York, NY: Harcourt Brace.

Bourdieu, P. (1984). *Distinction: A social critique of the judgment of taste* (R. Nice, Trans.). Cambridge, MA: Harvard University Press.

Bouzereau, L. (1997). *Star Wars: The annotated screenplays.* New York, NY: Del Rey.

Brooker, W. (2002). *Using the force: Creativity, community and Star Wars fans.* New York, NY: Continuum.

Brown, J. A. (1997). Comic book fandom and cultural capital. *Journal of Popular Culture, 30*(4), 13–31.

De Certeau, M. (1984). *The practice of everyday life.* Berkeley: University of California Press.

Erickson, B. H. (1996). Culture, class, and connections. *The American Journal of Sociology, 102*(1), 217–251.

Fiske, J. (1987). *Television culture.* London, England: Methuen.

Fiske, J. (1992). The cultural economy of fandom. *The adoring audience: Fan culture and popular media* (pp. 30–49). London, England: Routledge.

Gray, J., Sandvoss, C., & Harrington, C. L. (2007). Introduction: Why study fans? In J. Gray, C. Sandvoss, & C. L. Harrington (Eds.), *Fandom:*

Identities and communities in a mediated world (pp. 1–16). New York: New York University Press.

Harrington, C. L., & Bielby, D. D. (1995). *Soap fans: Pursuing pleasure and making meaning in everyday life.* Philadelphia, PA: Temple University Press.

Hebdige, D. (1979). *Subculture: The meaning of style.* London, England: Methuen.

Hills, M. (2002). *Fan cultures.* London, England: Routledge.

Hoberman, J., & Rosenbaum, J. (1983). *Midnight movies.* New York, NY: Harper & Row.

Hodgman, J. (2005, July 17). Ron Moore's deep space journey. *New York Times Magazine* on p. 249. Retrieved from http://www.nytimes.com/2005/07/17/magazine/17GALACTICA.html

Jancovich, M. (2002). Cult fictions: Cult movies, subcultural capital and the production of cultural distinctions. *Cultural Studies, 16*(2), 306–322.

Jenkins, H. (1992). *Textual poachers: Television fans and participatory culture.* London, England: Routledge.

McRobbie, A., & Nava, M. (Eds.). (1984). *Gender and generation.* Hampshire, United Kingdom: Macmillan.

Messenger-Davies, M., & Pearson, R. (2007). The little program that could: The relationship between NBC and *Star Trek*. In M. Hilmes & M. L. Henry (Eds.), *NBC: America's network* (pp. 209–223). Berkeley: University of California Press.

Murray, S. (2004). "Celebrating the story the way it is": Cultural studies, corporate media and the contested utility of fandom. *Continuum: Journal of Media & Cultural Studies, 18*(1), 7–25.

Navar-Gill, A. (2018). The Fan/Creator Alliance: Social Media, Audience Mandates, and the Rebalancing of Power in Studio–Showrunner Disputes. *Media Industries Journal, 5*(2).

Oxford English Dictionary Online. (2000). Oxford University Press. Retrieved from http://dictionary.oed.com/cgi/entry/50082098

Sandvoss, C. (2005). *Fans: The mirror of consumption*. Cambridge, United Kingdom: Polity Press.

Scardaville, M. C. (2005). Accidental activists: Fan activism in the soap opera community. *American Behavioral Scientist, 48*(7), 881–901.

Thornton, S. (1996). *Club cultures: Music, media, and subcultural capital*. Middletown, CT: Wesleyan University Press.

Trimble, B. (1982). *On the good ship* Enterprise: *My 15 years with Star Trek*. Norfolk/Virginia Beach, VA: Donning.

Tulloch, J., & Jenkins, H. (1995). *Science fiction audiences: Watching Doctor Who and Star Trek*. London, England: Routledge.

Weinstock, J. A. (2007). *The Rocky Horror Picture Show*. London, England: Wallflower Press.

Willis, P. E. (1981). *Learning to labor: How working class kids get working class jobs*. New York, NY: Columbia University Press.

Online, Interactive Audiences in a Digital Media World

On February 10, 2011, a young woman named Rebecca Black uploaded a quasi-homemade music video to YouTube, the free online service that dramatically simplifies the distribution of audiovisual material on the Internet. No doubt thousands of users were uploading their own videos at that moment as well, but what made Rebecca's unique was the fact that it "went viral" to become an Internet sensation, attracting more than 30 million views over the next month. These 30 million viewers were drawn to Black's music video via links through social networking sites like Twitter and Facebook, via numerous blogs and entertainment media websites, and finally via the traditional television and cable media that began reporting on this 13-year-old singing phenom because of the outsized attention she was attracting on the Internet. The source of this intense interest was Black's song "Friday"—a rather formulaic techno-pop song with lyrics that reflected her morning routine as she eats and gets ready for school ("Gotta get down to the bus stop / Gotta catch my bus / I see my friends"). The lyrics of the song communicated the singer's excitement about the end of the school week and the start of the weekend. The song was actually written by a company called Ark Music Factory, which offers aspiring singers the opportunity to record a song written by the company for $2,000.

Black's song and accompanying video (which starred her and some of her friends) were widely panned in the media and in the comments on the YouTube website, with some music critics calling it the "worst video ever." However, because of the high traffic to her video on YouTube, sales of her single at online music stores like iTunes and Amazon Music began to take off. *Forbes* (Barth, 2011) estimated that Black and Ark Music Factory could have earned as much as $20,000 on YouTube page views alone (a 1000% return on investment). When she released the song as an audio file, it debuted at No. 57 on Apple's iTunes service, with 37,000 downloads in its first week (Caulfield, 2011). The song spurred numerous online YouTube parodies and remixes and was eventually covered by the cast of the hit television program *Glee*.

Here's another case to consider: Amanda Hocking was a typical, if troubled, teenager living in Austin, Minnesota (Saroyan, 2011). An avid fan of science fiction and fantasy television programs, at age 11 she began writing fictional stories based on her favorite TV characters when her parents gave her a computer for her birthday. By age 17, she had completed her first full-length novel, which she sent to roughly 50 traditional publishers, all of which rejected her with form letters. By the time she was 24, she decided to turn her writing hobby into a full-time endeavor, churning out romance novels that featured paranormal and fantasy themes (with characters such as vampires and trolls as central parts of the narrative). She was frustrated time and time again, however, by rejections from traditional book publishers. After receiving her last form rejection letter in February 2010, Amanda resolved to find another way to reach potential readers. She decided to upload her vampire romance novel *My Blood Approves* to Amazon.com, which allows authors to easily upload and sell their books directly to consumers. A month later, she uploaded her book to Smashwords, an online direct-to-consumer bookseller that releases books in an electronic format compatible with Barnes & Noble's Nook e-reader. At first she sold a few books per day, but then, after uploading another book, she began selling 30 to 40 books per day. Her readers began spreading the word about her books via social networking sites such as Facebook and Twitter. By July 2010, Amanda was selling over 10,000 books per day: She was a bona fide Internet superstar. Hocking now has a contract with St. Martin's Press for her new books and is negotiating with Hollywood agents to sell her existing stories to major studios for film adaptations.

What are we to make of cultural phenomena like Rebecca Black's "Friday" and Amanda Hocking's self-produced novels? Both of these stories carry all the hallmarks of a classic, appealing "rags-to-riches" narrative, but I'd like you to focus for a moment on the larger picture of what the experiences of these two young women tell us about the state of media and audiences today. What's remarkable about these examples is the relative ease with which unknown artists can create their own cultural materials and circulate them to millions of people at a time via the web, effectively bypassing the institutional gatekeepers in the traditional media. In Black's case, a small company (Ark Music Factory) offered her and other music listeners the opportunity to transform themselves into widely recognized recording artists without ever having to deal directly with a talent agent, a record label, MTV, or any other entity. Had it been up to decision-makers in these media organizations, Rebecca Black would likely have never recorded "Friday." Instead, a vast network of always-on, plugged-in Internet users catapulted her into online infamy in a very short time without being blessed by official music industry insiders and critics. The once-dominant traditional media of television and radio had to play catch-up by reporting after the fact about Black's burgeoning celebrity. The same storyline aptly describes Amanda Hocking's strategy for success: She transformed her fandom for fantasy books into a new career as a successful romance–fantasy writer in a relatively short period of time.

Something profound has changed about our media landscape. The relatively low cost of microprocessing technology has made computers ubiquitous in industrialized societies. Simultaneously, the dramatic expansion of the Internet, beginning in the 1990s, meant that individuals could access and process information faster and more efficiently than ever before. Scholar Yochai Benkler (2006) argues that we are witnessing a unique tipping point in human society, where the ubiquity of networked computing in the most advanced economies of the world is creating a new mode of production by transforming passive information receivers into engaged information producers. The result, he writes, is that "a good deal more that human beings value can now be done by individuals, who interact with each other socially, as human beings and as social beings, rather than as market actors through the price system" (Benkler, 2006, p. 6). Instead of being information consumers, 21st-century audiences have transformed themselves into "prosumers." Futurist Alvin Toffler explains that the "producer and consumer, divorced by the Industrial Revolution, are reunited in the cycle of wealth creation, with the customer contributing not just the money but market and design information vital for the production process" (Toffler, 1990, p. 239). Scholar Axel Bruns describes this new breed of audiences as "produsers," a term similar to Toffler's but meant to underscore "the communities which engage in the collaborative creation and extension of information and knowledge" (2008, p. 2). Jay Rosen has even gone so far as to pronounce this new group of engaged information producers as "the people formerly known as the audience," a new cadre of citizen activists who are leveraging online media such as blogs (which he calls "First Amendment machines") to extend the freedom of the press to more people every day (2006). The changing dynamic between media producers and audiences has been noticed by the mainstream media as well. In 2006, the cover of *Time* magazine proclaimed that the Person of the Year was the audience ("You"), which—the magazine claimed—was responsible for revolutionizing media production through websites like YouTube, Wikipedia, and Tumblr. Clearly, something fundamental has shifted in our media experience: The challenge is to identify what those shifts are and how best to understand them in the broader context of our existing scholarly notions of audiences.

This text has offered an overview of theories and notions of the audience, both historically and through the lens of scholarly research. Despite the best efforts of academics to observe and understand the experiences of individuals with mass media, the scholarly study of audiences often struggles to keep up with the pace of change in the media landscape. The convergence of media technologies into forms of portable digital media with interchangeable content has greatly complicated the study of audience "effects" or even the hitherto straightforward definition of *medium*. For instance, if someone watches episodes of a television drama on YouTube or downloads them from a peer-to-peer file sharing network to watch on their mobile telephone, is that individual still "watching television" according to our 20th-century notion of that experience? Furthermore, the digitization of media has also meant that audiences have been free to directly interact with content producers and distributors in a fashion that would have been impossible even 15 years ago. In fact, media audiences today have come to *expect* the ability to provide instant feedback to media producers and to other audiences. In this type of interactive media environment, where do media producers end and the audience begin? In an era of mobile phones and social media, is it even appropriate to speak of the "audience" as a distinct entity anymore?

Overview of the Chapter

This chapter will look toward the future of media audiences by considering some of the newest forms of online, interactive media and how they complicate our understanding of media audiences. As we traverse this new territory in audience studies, I will be drawing on many of the theories that have been discussed in previous chapters, including notions of effects, audience reception and interpretation, audience measurements, and political economy. First, we'll focus on some of the key trends that are driving this shift in the audience, such as media fragmentation, platformization, and new forms of audience autonomy. Second, we'll consider the metrics that have been developed to measure forms of online audience activity, including social media. Third, we'll consider how a new type of audience agency and creativity is evidenced in current online media forms such as YouTube multiuser dungeon games (or MUDs) such as *World of Warcraft*. In particular, we'll examine the practices of audio and video "remixing" and consider how these forms of audience activity add new interpretive layers to existing mass media products. Online media such as wikis and blogs are also leveraging the power of individual audience members via "crowdsourcing" to create sophisticated information products and services that were hitherto created only by large, centralized media organizations. We'll consider how these new forms of networked creativity may be changing journalism and other forms of media production.

These new online media have certainly shifted the media producer–consumer power dynamic, but other scholars have argued that claims about the dramatic expansion of audience autonomy can only go so far. In this vein, we'll return to debates about audience power vis-à-vis media producers by exploring recent scholarship, chiefly from a political economic perspective, that identifies serious concerns with the rise of digital platforms, such as privacy, notions of the self, and unwaged digital labor.

Digitalization, Fragmentation, Platforms, and the Rise of Audience Autonomy

To understand what's happening with media audiences today, we need to first grapple with several important transformations in our media. The first major shift is, of course, the rapid digitalization that has occurred in the media over the past 15 years. **Digitalization** refers to the standards by which media images and sounds are recorded and transmitted. According to Havens and Lotz, digital media

> are those media that translate the content of media—be it images or sound—into digital code, a language of ones and zeroes. This digital language has many advantages, particularly that it uses space efficiently, maintains quality, and operates as a common language that allows different types of machines to speak to one another. (2011, p. 204)

The release of music, movies, and television programs on digital media such as compact discs and DVDs means that those formats are now compatible with technologies besides dedicated music and video players. This process, called **convergence**, allows media content to be displayed on any number of different devices, but it has also enabled the simple reproduction of these media into computer file formats that can be easily distributed via the Internet, leading to widespread piracy of copyrighted material. Jenkins notes that convergence is much more than a technological phenomenon, however. Instead, he argues that convergence also "represents a cultural shift as consumers are encouraged to seek out new information and make connections among dispersed media content" (2006a, p. 3).

Spurred by widespread digitalization, Napoli (2011) cites two more important trends that are shifting the orientation of media institutions to audiences—specifically, **audience fragmentation** and **audience autonomy** (p. 5). First, media audiences have been continually fragmented into smaller and smaller groups, thanks to the dramatic expansion in media channels (cable and satellite, for instance) and media platforms (including the Internet, handheld media devices such as iPods and tablet computers, and media-capable smartphones). Increasingly, this type of fragmentation is threatening to make traditional forms of audience measurement obsolete. The problem stems from the fact that audiences are now scattered across so many different media channels and technologies that obtaining a representative snapshot of these individuals would require larger and larger samples, making audience measurement much slower and costlier.

The other key trend that has dramatically reshaped media audiences in the 21st century is what Napoli calls "audience autonomy." This term describes "how contemporary characteristics of the media environment, ranging from interactivity to mobility to on-demand functionality to the increased capacity for user-generated content, all serve to enhance the extent to which audiences have control over the process of media consumption" (Napoli, 2011, p. 8). On one level, media audiences are retaining more control over their media consumption by time-shifting programming via digital video recorders (DVRs), by streaming their video on-demand via companies like Netflix (see Chapter 4), or by circumventing media producers and distributors altogether via peer-to-peer computer file transfers over the Internet. Audiences' independence from more traditional forms of media distribution such as over-the-air television and radio has further complicated the already arduous process of locating these individuals in time and space for the purpose of advertising to them.

But this autonomy has been extended much further through the transformative nature of **user-generated content (UGC)**. Think about massively multiplayer online role-playing games (MMORPGs) such as *World of Warcraft* (*WoW*), for instance—something we will explore in detail later on in the chapter. The gaming environment was designed by Blizzard Entertainment (2011), a gaming software company, and sold to computer users for their enjoyment. But what makes *WoW* so popular is the fact that players are interacting with one another in a virtual space and creating their *own* experiences within that environment. The media product itself would not exist outside of the inputs from tens of thousands of users, something entirely new yet increasingly commonplace in our media environment today. The smash hit of 2018 was Epic Games' *Fortnite*, which—like *World of Warcraft*—features millions of players interacting and cooperating online in real time to complete tasks and gain experience points (Statt, 2018).

This new model—whereby media corporations are providing consumers the means to create, store, and distribute content that is designed by users themselves—serves as the operating principle behind some of the most popular online services today such as YouTube, Facebook, Twitter, and Wikipedia, just to name a few. This proliferation of these types of services is the result of a shift in the technological structure of the Internet, known as **Web 2.0**. This term reportedly originated with DiNucci (1999), who predicted that the static, didactic nature of web pages that characterized the early Internet would change dramatically:

> The Web we know now, which loads into a browser window in essentially static screenfulls, is only an embryo of the Web to come. The first glimmerings of Web 2.0 are beginning to appear, and we are just starting to see how that embryo might develop. The Web will be understood not as screenfulls of text and graphics but as a transport mechanism, the ether through which interactivity happens. (DiNucci, 1999, p. 32)

Technology book publisher Tim O'Reilly (2005) offered a more concrete definition of the Web 2.0 concept, describing it as "the network as platform, spanning all connected devices" (para. 1). He went on, "Web 2.0 applications are those that make the most of the intrinsic advantages of that platform . . . creating network effects through an 'architecture of participation,' and going beyond the page metaphor of Web 1.0 to deliver rich user experiences" (2005, para. 1). O'Reilly was pointing to two specific aspects of the Internet as we know it today. The first aspect is technological: Because the Internet exists as a series of interconnected servers that are continually exchanging data, they become a uniquely powerful platform for users to pass along information to others (and to modify this information as well). This means that any number of devices, such as computers, handheld tablets, mobile telephones, and other Internet-capable devices, can easily access and exchange information in the same way. The second aspect is social: Because the technology allows for easy information exchange, users will begin to leverage the technology to interact with one another in ways that mimic traditional forms of conversation and cooperation found in the "offline" world. Unlike the offline world, however, the Internet empowers thousands of individuals working in far-flung places to easily collaborate on projects that would otherwise be quite expensive and time-consuming. This allows users to harness the ability to engage in large-scale cultural productions without having to bother with the burdensome creation of an institutional infrastructure (the implications of this for crowdsourcing will be discussed later in the chapter).

This explosion of UGC on the web has been fueled by the emergence of online infrastructures that connect users together to allow them to easily create, distribute, store, and edit creative content. Most of these services exist in **the cloud**, in which web servers not only store files but also host applications and services that allow for millions of users to interact with media content (and each other) at any one time (see Mosco, 2014). These online cloud services, such as video sharing, wikis, photo sharing, social media, ridesharing, and social gaming (among many others), are commonly referred to as **platforms**. Platforms can be understood at their most basic level as "digital infrastructures that enable two or more groups to interact" (Srnicek, 2016, p. 43). These infrastructures act as intermediaries between different types of users, including customers, suppliers, producers, service providers, suppliers, and advertisers. Gillespie (2018, p. 254) offers a similar definition, noting that platforms can be understood as "sites and services that host public expression, store it on and serve it up from the cloud, organize access to it through search and recommendation, or install it onto mobile devices." The centralized organization of platforms allows for a shared space that affords users the "opportunity to communicate, interact or sell" (Gillespie, 2010, p. 351). Widely used digital media such as social media (e.g., Facebook, Twitter, Snapchat), online shopping (e.g., Amazon, Overstock.com), and video sharing sites (e.g., YouTube, Vimeo) are some of the most common examples.

Platforms shape much of our experiences with the Internet today, enabling users to easily create new information, share it with others, and react or respond to the content of others. The most widely used platforms today can be categorized as **social media**. Social media are essentially "web-based services that allow individuals, communities, and organizations to collaborate, connect, interact, and build community by enabling them to create, co-create, modify, share, and engage with user-generated content that is easily accessible" (McCay-Peet & Quan-Haase, 2016, p. 17). Some prominent social media platforms, such as YouTube and Facebook, are widely used by large segments of the population, while others such as Instagram, Snapchat, Pinterest, and Twitter are popular with different demographic segments (see Figure 9.1). In fact, the term *social media* encompasses a wide range of online services that structure our online interactions today (see Figure 9.2 for a list).

Because online platforms eliminate technical barriers for users to create and store media messages, they have sparked a new "sharing economy" by turning media consumers into users and creators, argues Bruns (2008). Instead of "passive" receivers of media (an assumption that has of course been challenged in semiotics and cultural studies of media), Bruns asserts that 21st-century audiences

> become much more actively involved in shaping their own media and network usage. Provided suitable tools and frameworks . . . what the network model makes possible is the existence of a distributed but coordinated community, organized not according to the directions of a central authority to which all other nodes in the network are subordinate, but by the community's own protocols of interaction. (2008, p. 15)

Figure 9.1   U.S. Adults Who Use Social Media

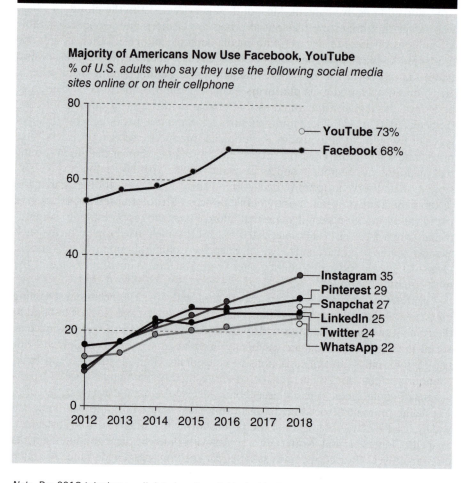

Majority of Americans Now Use Facebook, YouTube
% of U.S. adults who say they use the following social media sites online or on their cellphone

Note: Pre-2018 telephone poll data is not available for YouTube, Snapchat, or WhatsApp.

Source: Pew Research Center, Aaron Smith and Monica Anderson. Licensed via CC BY-SA 4.0 (https://creativecommons.org/licenses/by-sa/4.0).

Despite some of the excited rhetoric about the dawning of a new era of audience cultural creation, Napoli (2011) observes that the power to *generate* media content in today's online media environment is not necessarily all that new. Instead, the extraordinary power to *distribute* these original media productions—along with pirated or altered traditional media content—represents perhaps the most revolutionary and disruptive feature of the Internet.

Figure 9.2 Types of Social Media

Type of Social Media	Examples	Definition
Social networking	Facebook, LinkedIn	Users create profiles and connect with others
Bookmarking	Delicious, StumbleUpon	Users Share resources and links
Microblogging	Twitter, Tumblr	Provide short, ongoing updates to subscribers
Blogs and forums	LiveJournal, Wordpress	Users engage in Ongoing conversations and long-form messages among subscribers
Media sharing	YouTube, Pinterest, Flickr, Twitch.TV	Allows for sharing of media (photos, video) as well as commenting
Social news	Digg, Reddit	Allows users to post news items and vote them up or down (social visibility)
Collaborative authoring	Wikipedia, Google Docs	Web-based services that allow multiple users to create and edit textual content
Web conferencing	Skype, GotoMeeting, Zoom, Facetime, Google Hangouts	Online services that facilitate face-to-face audiovisual meetings
Geo-location sites	Foursquare, Tinder, Waze	Allows users to exchange information about their location
Scheduling and meeting	Doodle, Google calendar	Web-based services that allow for group decision-making
Gaming	World of Warcraft, Fortnite, Player's Unknown Battlegrounds (PUBG)	Online, interactive real-time game play

Sources: Adapted from McCay-Peet and Quan-Haase (2016) and Kaplan and Haenlein (2010).

Big Data and Online Audience Metrics

The centrality of the Internet in our media lives today has also brought on some major changes in the ways that audiences are measured and understood. Since social media and other Web 2.0 services are hosted in the cloud, users' online activities are passively monitored and recorded by those web servers, by search portals like Google and Yahoo, and by major social media platforms like Facebook and Twitter.

The data that we as Internet users generate simply by clicking links or visiting our newsfeeds have become ubiquitous and are a major driving force behind the online economy today. This is the era of **big data**. Mosco (2014, p. 177) describes big data as "the movement to analyze the increasingly vast amounts of information stored in multiple locations, but mainly online and primarily in the cloud." In their book outlining the virtues of this new phenomenon, Mayer-Schönberger and Cukier (2014, p. 17) noted that "the preponderance of things that could never be measured, stored, analyzed, and shared before is becoming datafied." The type of data that are now more readily available are quite powerful because they are generally *more exhaustive* in scope (they monitor and record all activities of human beings or systems) and are very *fine-grained in their detail* or resolution. Big data are also *relational*, meaning that multiple large datasets are used in conjunction with one another to generate analytical insights that would not be possible without exploring those interconnections, and *flexible* in the sense that they can be deployed in multiple contexts with relative speed (Kitchin, 2017). For example, mobile phones record multiple types of information about their owners, such as geolocation data, app data, browsing activity, and even profile information. Once these forms of data are combined, they can create a fairly detailed picture of a single user or even of large populations.

The impacts of this new explosion of data are far-reaching, argue Mayer-Schönberger and Cukier, because "big data is poised to shake up everything from businesses and the sciences to healthcare, government, education, economics, the humanities, and every other aspect of society" (2014, p. 11). *Forbes* magazine opined that the key to the future success of media companies was contingent upon their ability "to get better at sifting through it and blending together the multiple streams of data—some from new digital sources, others from reliable analog ones—to understand what their audiences like so they can deliver more of it" (Bain Insights, 2014). Lurking beneath these supposed benefits of datafication, of course, are downsides such as rising social and economic inequality, environmental degradation, and a vast expansion of the surveillance state (Fuchs, 2017; Mosco, 2014; see later in this chapter for more details).

The emergence of big data as a major player in our concept of the audience has wrought major changes in audience measurement as well. These changes fall into three broad categories. First, whereas traditional audience measurement (outlined in Chapter 4) requires careful planning, organization, and cost, today's **consumers now passively generate much of the data** that are used in efforts to reach them with advertising (whether they have consciously consented to this practice or not). The second major shift in the past decade has been the **importance of automated, server-side audience metrics**. Of course, major audience measurement corporations like Nielsen, comScore, and Rentrak, along with a host of other companies, are still very much in the business of measuring audience responses to media, analyzing those data, and distributing insights about their findings to their main clients (typically program providers and advertisers). But major platform services with billions of users that are owned by companies such as Google, Amazon, Facebook, and Twitter have amassed huge troves of user data on their servers, which they use to sell highly targeted advertising messages to consumers who use their services. Since these online platforms gather and analyze user data using sophisticated, automated computer algorithms that work in the background all the time, they are also able to deliver insights on audiences on a moment-by-moment basis.

The third major shift is the **democratization of audience analytics**. Major platform services operated by Google, Twitter, Apple, and Facebook have begun providing audience data to individuals or organizations wishing to track visitors to their websites, measure the "likes" or shares to their content on social media, or to calculate the "return on investment" (ROI) of particular marketing messages that are distributed online. For example, Google has made its ubiquitous Google Analytics service available to anyone by providing computer code for websites to track the number of unique visitors, the location of those visitors, the amount of time each visitor has spent on the website (a potential measure of engagement), and whether those visitors were "converted" to subscribers or customers. Google even provides a free step-by-step online guide called "Google Analytics Academy" (https://analytics .google.com/analytics/academy/course/6) that teaches users how to install the service on websites and blogs and how to analyze the results. In 2017, Apple launched a similar initiative by allowing people who had a podcast listed in their directory to access a page with statistics on the number of downloads per episode, the pace of those downloads, and location information about those users (Webster, 2017). Facebook offers its users a service called Facebook Insights (https://www.facebook.com/ business/a/page/page-insights) that tracks user interactions with specific Facebook pages, while the Twitter Analytics service allows for tracking likes, followers, retweets, and click-throughs via links (https://analytics.twitter.com/about). These efforts have created an environment that encourages the widespread use of online-based metrics by media producers, advertisers, scholars, and audiences alike.

While I argue that audience metrics have been democratized via their mainstream availability at low cost, this is not to say that social media sites have allowed full, unfettered, and transparent access to user data. In fact, social media sites like Facebook and Twitter still maintain a firm grip on their data and allow outsiders, including researchers, only limited access to these data. This often places academics in a precarious position if they rely too heavily on these sources for audience data (Burgess & Bruns, 2012). Thanks to the massive data-gathering practices and sophisticated sorting algorithms employed by cloud-based media sites, there is still a huge information asymmetry between these services and the public when it comes to the provision of audience data (see Andrejevic, 2014). In the wake of scandal about the misuse of user data, in 2018 Facebook announced that it was severely limiting the types of access to outside parties in the future, creating a backlash from scholars around the globe who relied on these data for legitimate research about important social issues (Smee, 2018).

Web-Based Audience Metrics

The logic surrounding the measurement of online audiences is similar to that of television and radio audiences in that the ultimate goal is to match a specific advertising impression or exposure to a single individual. Unlike television and radio, however, there are numerous techniques available to audience measurement firms for generating these data. The enormous array of online data that are harvested for analysis makes for a dizzying and chaotic situation. As Webster, Phalen, and Lichty (2014) have noted,

> There is so much data that analysts parse in so many ways that the industry is awash in metrics. . . . There are too many metrics with too little standardization. The result can be confusion about what the numbers mean and disagreement about which of them to use. (pp. 125–126)

For instance, Internet webpages keep logs of every visitor to access that page, and these records, called **server logs**, allow for passive monitoring of the online audience. This passive method has limits, however, because it cannot identify an individual user, so its utility is limited to counting the amount of traffic to an individual website. Server logs record the date and time of access, what page referred the user to that page, "cookies" stored in the web browser software (identification files), and the IP (internet protocol) address of that user, which provides general location information (Bermejo, 2007, pp. 120–121). Every time you land on a web page, that is registered as a **pageview** or a **view**. Another passive measure, called a **click**, is registered when you click on a button or hyperlink and go to another website (Webster et. al., 2014). When advertisers embed their messages in banners or on in-between content, they want to know when a user has the opportunity to see their advertisement, whether they interact with it (by clicking it) or not. This is called an **impression** and is a widely used metric to calculate important numbers like CPMs (or cost per thousand users) for online audiences.

More active methods of online audience measurement include online surveys, though these techniques often attract individuals who seek them out, thus potentially skewing the sample. The most accurate metrics of online media usage are found in **electronic measurement panels**, which provide a mixture of active surveys and passive online metering. Just as with the Nielsen household sample, individuals are recruited randomly to participate in these panels in exchange for a small sum of money. Software that precisely tracks panelists' online movements and communicates this information to the measurement company is installed (Bermejo, 2007, p. 155). Using this technique, companies such as Media Metrix, NetRatings, and NetValue can match online viewing behaviors with specific individuals. Thanks to the randomness of the sample, these results can also be generalized to the larger population as well.

Social Media Metrics

The techniques described have been adopted widely for measuring the consumption of online information that is accessed via web browsers, both on desktop computers and smartphones. But what about media content that is filtered through platform services like social media where audiences spend a good amount of time? How are social media audiences measured, and how do those measurements differ from traditional web-based metrics? Platform-based services like social media have typically developed their own particular audience usage metrics based upon the particularities of their sites. Since users of services like Facebook, Twitter, and Snapchat agree to have their online activities monitored as a condition of creating an account, social media companies have access to an impressive array of data about their users. Each social media site offers slightly different metrics for audience usage, though they typically fall into one of two categories. The first is based upon measures of exposure (similar to page views or clicks), and the second is based upon both quantitative and qualitative measures of engagement.

Similar to web analytics, all forms of social media have built-in **measures of exposure** to help identify how many users have accessed specific items of web content, whether it be a Facebook post, a tweet, or an Instagram story. Each social media service offers its own **dashboard**, which is a web screen that provides the user with an array of options to see how many times other users on the platform interacted with a specific piece of content. On Twitter Analytics, for example, an individual can investigate the number of times a specific tweet was viewed (an impression), replied to, and retweeted by other Twitter users (see Figure 9.3 for an example of the Twitter dashboard). Twitter also allows individuals to track impressions over time, which allows those individuals to track trends, and to compare the performance of one tweet over another. Marketers can also find out about the **reach** of their social media posts by examining the number of times a message was shared or retweeted by others to their own followers. A YouTube video or tweet that is shared with millions of users within a short period of time is known as a **viral post**. Facebook Insights offers a similar array of data by allowing its users to see the number of times a specific Facebook page was accessed, the location of those who accessed it, and how much time they spent on the page before moving on (another measure of exposure). Facebook's enormous value to advertisers—and the major source of its billions in annual advertising revenue—comes from its ability to match these exposure data to other forms of information contained in user profiles. So, for example, if an average of 20% of the 10,000 impressions for my Facebook posts have "liked" M&M candies, then I can pursue an advertising sponsorship relationship with Mars, the maker of M&Ms. Basic demographic targeting, a mainstay of traditional surveys and audience panels, are also possible by connecting exposure metrics to user profile data.

Social media have become extremely valuable for marketers and advertisers because they offer more than just measures of exposure. As Napoli (2012, p. 88) argues, online advertising is increasingly moving away from exposure models and more toward engagement models—something he terms the **post-exposure audience marketplace**—since advertisers want to see that consumers have done something to indicate their acceptance or interest in a particular advertising message. Web 2.0 services like social media are extremely "sticky" in the sense that they enable users to directly engage with mediated content and to provide instantaneous reactions to posts and pages. These activities are known as **measures of**

Figure 9.3   Twitter Analytics Dashboard

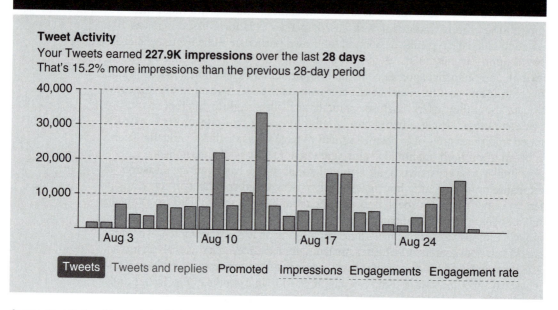

Tweet Activity

Your Tweets earned **227.9K impressions** over the last **28 days**
That's 15.2% more impressions than the previous 28-day period

Source: Ned Potter. Licensed via CC BY 2.0 (https://creativecommons.org/licenses/by/2.0/). Available at: https://www
.flickr.com/photos/thewikiman/14884955408.

engagement. Twitter, for example, is often used as a means to alert social media users about content that has been updated on an external website, and it creates a hypertext link from the tweet to its web content (where it may have banner or other types of advertising). Twitter's data analytics will keep track of the "click-through-rate" (CTR) to measure the number of times that Twitter users clicked on a link to send them to an external website. Click-throughs to external web pages can also be used as a metric for **conversions**, or the number of users who take a specific type of action in relation to a social media post (see Kaushik, 2009). Google Analytics can also provide information about how long a user spends on a particular website or watching a particular YouTube video, which serves as another indicator of user engagement.

The emergence of these new online metrics and their relative ubiquity in the audience marketplace has transformed advertisers' and marketers' expectations with regard to audience feedback. More than ever before, advertisers expect to pay for only a narrow slice of the audience that matches specific demographic and engagement dimensions. These type of data-driven advertiser demands have placed new pressure on media producers to deliver these new targets, which has folded back upon the media production and consumption processes (see Box 9.1). Widespread datafication has also led to a rapid diversification of companies and services offering data analytics services, making for a messy and chaotic landscape of 21st-century audience measurement.

BOX 9.1
Online Analytics and Digital Journalism: Changing Patterns of Production and Consumption

The increasing importance of web-based and social media metrics is changing the ways that institutional media producers approach their own strategies for content creation. Audience datafication has had a powerful effect on how journalists make editorial decisions. Since the 1970s and particularly after the popularization of the Internet in the 1990s, major print news outlets have closely tracked declining subscription rates and leveraged market research to identify and maintain a solid base of readers (see Nadler, 2016). Since the 2010s, however, the type of online analytics described in this chapter have been deeply integrated into the process of creating news. A 2015 study sponsored by the Tow Center for Digital Journalism and the John S. and James L. Knight Foundation examined the impacts of audience metrics on news production.

Scholar Caitlin Petre conducted ethnographic observations of Chartbeat, a dominant metrics vendor; Gawker Media, an online news source; and *The New York Times*, a legacy news outlet. Petre found that the two news organizations' use of audience metrics had some powerful effects on the journalists. For one, journalists described feeling stressed and anxious about how many readers would access or share their online news stories. Petre writes,

> As Chartbeat and other analytics tools become more common and influential in newsrooms, journalists' sense of dignity, pride, and self-worth are increasingly tied up in

their traffic numbers. Metrics have earned a reputation as ego-busters, as journalists discover that their readership is considerably smaller and less engaged than they imagined. (2015, p. 29)

One journalist at Gawker, for example, struggled with the emotional roller coaster that came with the ups and downs associated with a reliance on online metrics to judge the success of reporting, remarking,

> When traffic is just average or low, or if we have a really spikey period and it goes down to what it was pre-spike, I get upset. I feel like I'm not good at my job . . . I notice it all the time. (Petre, 2015, p. 36)

Journalists also became fixated on the metrics that ranked their stories, often using them as proxies for quality instead of considering more substantive criteria. This led to more short-term decision-making among journalists and editors, she argued, which could potentially damage the long-term strategic vision of the news service.

Online audience metrics have been shown to affect how *readers* consume news as well. A 2017 study by Chung asked 202 randomly assigned research subjects to read a news story about an E. coli outbreak. One version of the news story was identified as coming from a "high-credibility" source and the other source was identified as "low credibility." Additionally,

(Continued)

(Continued)

one version of the news story displayed three social media metrics in the corner (number of recommendations, likes, and shares on social media), while another did not. Chung found that, like source credibility, the mere presence of social media metrics on one version of the news story led to respondents identifying that story as higher quality than the nonmetrics version, even though the text of the article in all four conditions was exactly the same. The presence of social media metrics also moderated the differences between high- and low-credibility sources. In other words, respondents with no social media metrics rated the high-credibility source as much higher quality than the low-credibility source, but those differences were much smaller when social media metrics were included. Chung argues that online audience metrics (likes and shares) may be emerging as a new type of *two-step flow* (see Chapter 2) that can affect how audiences evaluate the quality of online news. These two studies demonstrate that the adoption of online metrics has important consequences for both news production and consumption.

Sources: Chung, M. (2017). Not just numbers: The role of social media metrics in online news evaluations. *Computers in Human Behavior, 75,* 949–957; Petre, C. (2015). *The traffic factories: Metrics at Chartbeat, Gawker Media, and* The New York Times. New York, NY: Tow Center for Digital Journalism. Retrieved from https://towcenter.org/research/traffic-factories/

Audience Agency, Creativity, and Democratic Participation

One of the recurring themes throughout the book has been the struggle for material and interpretive control between institutional media producers and the mass audience. As Ien Ang put it in Chapter 4, the audience is like a "fugitive" that global media conglomerates want to control and carefully monitor at all times. As the previous chapter on fans demonstrated, audiences are fully engaged in producing complex alternative meanings to popular media. If modern media audiences are fugitives in the eyes of media corporations, you might also say that these fugitives are "armed and dangerous." In the 21st century, audiences are "armed" with new forms of video and computer technologies that make the (re)production, distribution, and consumption of popular media easier than ever before. These new textually savvy and engaged audiences are even more "dangerous" to traditional media because of several potential threats to established media business models, such as (1) piracy of popular music and video via online peer-to-peer file-sharing networks, (2) instantaneous feedback about media materials that often short-circuits media corporations' slick and expensive public relations and marketing initiatives, and (3) an increased sense of audience empowerment and consumer sovereignty developed via online social networking.

The Rise of Participatory Culture

As noted, changes in technology are enabling new forms of collaboration and creativity among media audiences. Henry Jenkins, who has written extensively about how fans of popular culture have historically resisted their roles as passive consumers (see Chapter 8 for a full discussion), has argued that the Internet has empowered audiences to create a new **"participatory culture"** in which "fans and other consumers are invited to actively participate in the creation and circulation of new content" (2006a, p. 290). He explains that this participatory culture is occurring at the intersection of three important trends: (1) new technologies that enable audiences to "archive, annotate, appropriate, and recirculate media content"; (2) the rise of subcultures of DIY media production; and (3) "economic trends favoring the horizontal media conglomerates to encourage the flow of images, ideas, and narratives across multiple media channels and demand more active modes of spectatorship" (Jenkins, 2006b, pp. 135–136). This claim has been echoed by Benkler (2006, p. 15), who argues that new technologies are enabling the emergence of a "new folk culture . . . where many more of us participate actively in making cultural moves and finding meaning in the world around us." Since media audiences now routinely practice their own content production by capturing and editing audio, pictures, and video, he writes, these activities make them "better 'readers' of their own culture and more self-reflective and critical of the culture they occupy, thereby enabling them to become more self-reflective participants in conversations within that culture." These notions of extending audience autonomy into full-scale media production are the logical extension of the theories of active audience interpretation and creation found in cultural studies research in the 1990s. Some have even argued that we are now approaching the kind of "semiotic democracy" described by John Fiske (1987) long before the rise of the Internet and mass computerization. In this section, we'll consider some of the most important new media tools for audience agency and creativity.

YouTube as a Site for Participatory Culture

Perhaps the single-most important online tool for empowering audiences in the 21st century has been the video-sharing website YouTube. Launched with little fanfare in June 2005, the original concept behind YouTube was a simple one: It was one of a number of competing online services designed to allow users with no technical knowledge to be able to upload and share video clips with other users, even those with slow connections to the Internet. What set YouTube apart from its competitors and vaulted it to success, according to one of the site's cofounders, was the implementation of four key features of the site: video recommendations via a "related videos" list, an e-mail link to share links to YouTube content, comments from other users, and a video player that was embedded into the website (Gannes, 2006). In other words, the social features—those that allowed users to talk to one another about the videos, to comment on them, and to respond to them—were the ones that may have enabled YouTube to become a cultural touchstone for a new generation. Realizing the business potential of YouTube, technology giant Google acquired it for $1.65 billion in October 2006 (Burgess & Green, 2009, p. 1). Clearly, Google recognized the potential power of YouTube to serve as a critical new distribution outlet for mainstream mass media. As Burgess and Green (2009) explain, YouTube has been traditionally viewed through one of two specific frameworks: as an online extension of the traditional mass media or as a "site of vernacular creativity and lawless distribution" of these media. In contrast, they argue that we should view YouTube as a "coordinating mechanism between individual and collective creativity and meaning production; and as a mediator between various competing industry-oriented discourses and ideologies and various audience- or user-oriented ones" (p. 37). YouTube becomes a fascinating nexus point, then, where 20th-century media corporations are coming to grips with a force of newly empowered social and creative 21st-century audiences.

To be sure, many videos posted on YouTube are direct reproductions of copyrighted material: full-length television programs or films, music videos, or documentaries. Media conglomerates like Viacom, Time-Warner, and Disney frequently complain that YouTube is violating the law by distributing their copyrighted content for free. Viacom even sued YouTube for $1 billion in 2007 for distributing its copyrighted content (BBC News, 2007). Despite the undeniable appeal of easy online access to mainstream films and television, the majority of the "most favorite" and "most viewed" uploads to YouTube are amateur videos made by YouTube community members (see Figure 9.4). Burgess and Green (2009, p. 52) found that a good number of these user-created videos focused on the video technology itself, using video "tricks" such as green screens, split screens, or reversed footage to achieve a novel or comic effect. The advent of built-in camcorders on many computers has led to another user-led video innovation on YouTube: the *vlog* (or video log). **Vlogs** feature an individual speaking directly into the camera (a talking head) with some minimal editing. YouTube users upload numerous variations to the vlog format, including comments on other YouTube entries, musical performances, diary entries (also known as "life-blogging"), stand-up comedy, and more.

YouTubers have found ways to meld their own individual playfulness with popular media by selecting small portions of existing, copyrighted media material and combining them in new and interesting ways. This process, called **remixing**, has emerged as a major new form of creativity that has blossomed on YouTube and in other online venues (see Box 9.2). For example, fans of the CW Television Network's *Gossip Girls* have uploaded numerous fan videos, known as *vids*, to YouTube. These vids contain clips from the program (often focusing on one or two specific characters) arranged in different configurations and often featuring popular music in the background (Burwell, 2010, p. 389). Others radically reimagine the narrative of the program by skillfully reediting scenes to suggest same-sex

Figure 9.4 Most Popular YouTube Content

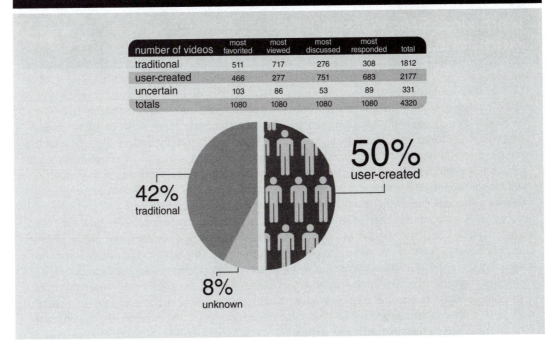

number of videos	most favorited	most viewed	most discussed	most responded	total
traditional	511	717	276	308	1812
user-created	466	277	751	683	2177
uncertain	103	86	53	89	331
totals	1080	1080	1080	1080	4320

50% user-created

42% traditional

8% unknown

Source: Adapted from Burgess, J., & Green, J. (2009). *YouTube: Online Video and Participatory Culture* (p. 42). Cambridge, MA: Polity. Redrawn by Stephanie Plumeri Ertz.

relationships in *Gossip Girl* that are not evident in the original program. Fans of Japanese anime animation have invented their own subgenre of remix vids by reediting their favorite anime clips and adding popular musical tracks. There have been so many of these vids flooding YouTube, in fact, that they have offloaded many of these into their own dedicated website (animemusicvideos.org).

Legal scholar Larry Lessig (2004, 2008) has written expansively and enthusiastically about the possibilities of remixing for reworking popular culture in ways that help us to critically reflect on that culture. He argues that these new tools are allowing us to transform our "read-only" (RO) culture—in which a small group of professionals produces culture for the masses—into a "read-write" (RW) culture, in which the public is free to produce, interact with, change, and influence their own culture. Since making and distributing audiovisual material has become so commonplace in our culture today, you might ask, Why don't audiences simply produce their own content? Why rely at all on traditional, mass-produced media, particularly since most of it is covered by copyright restrictions that severely restrict what audiences can legally do with it? Lessig's response is that mediated culture is all around us—to ignore it or to bracket it off as a realm devoid of comment or reflection would

BOX 9.2
Remixing *Star Wars*—
Additions, Deletions, and New Creations

One audience constituency that has embraced video remixing, in particular, is fans of popular media. As we explored in Chapter 8, media fans have long held a strong interest in exploring their favorite situations and characters in ways that expand well beyond the confines of the original text itself. In the pre-Internet era, this was accomplished by relatively primitive means: the informal exchange of videotapes, the production and distribution via print of original fan stories ("fanfic"), and the production of other forms of artistic works (paintings, sketches, T-shirts, etc.). The advent of powerful home computing and the digitalization of media have allowed fans to become full-fledged media producers in their own right, sometimes challenging the primacy of the original text.

Star Wars fans once again provide a fascinating window into this world. In 2003, with director and creator George Lucas's official blessing, AtomFilms launched an official *Star Wars* fan film contest. It received more than 250 entries (Jenkins, 2006a, p. 131). The winning submissions that year put on display both the dedication of fans as well as the creative and technical sophistication of their entries. The winner of the Audience Choice Award was a short, animated film by Thomas Lee called *Star Wars Gangsta Rap* (https://www.youtube.com/watch?v=tEeAjy-05OI). It featured a rap beat with clever lyrics describing the action in the *Star Wars* films accompanied by broadcast-quality original animation. Another winning entry that year was *Troops*, directed by Kevin Rubio (https://www.youtube.com/watch?v=t-coZBDIPDP8). Rubio's live-action short film

was a spoof film, a comedic meld of the original *Star Wars* movie and the reality television program *Cops* (where viewers follow police officers on their daily duties). With believable storm-trooper costumes and green-screen special effects, Rubio's effort was widely admired by Lucas and others in Hollywood, leading to job offers from several studios.

Other fan remixes, however, have not been so welcomed by Lucasfilm, the owner of the copyrights to the *Star Wars* franchise. Some fans were stunned when other highly regarded fan films such as *Dark Redemption* were not even eligible for entry in the contest. The reason? The film was set 2 days before the beginning of the original *Star Wars* film, thereby potentially adding new plot and character material to the existing story line (something out of bounds and in violation of copyright, according to Lucas). Another fan and freelance film editor, Mike Nichols, decided that the 1999 prequel to the franchise, *Star Wars I: The Phantom Menace*, would have been much better without the introduction of a much-maligned character, Jar-Jar Binks. Once the film was released on DVD, Nichols burned a digital copy to his computer and reedited film to cut out roughly 20 minutes of the original film, including almost all of the scenes with Jar-Jar. He rereleased the film as an online download called *Star Wars 1.1: The Phantom Edit*, and it quickly became an Internet sensation. Lucasfilm responded by threatening lawsuits against websites that hosted the edited film, and it quickly went underground. More recently, a group of fans deeply disappointed by *Star Wars: The Last Jedi* (2017) launched a crowdfunding campaign to remake the film's story lines to better suit fans' tastes. These *Star Wars* fan responses demonstrate both the creative potential of remix as well as the danger that this type of audience activity holds for traditional media producers.

Sources: Burton, B. (2018, June 21). *Star Wars* fans start campaign to remake *The Last Jedi*. *CNET*. Retrieved from https://www.cnet.com/news/star-wars-fans-start-campaign-to-remake-the-last-jedi/; Harmon, A. (2002, April 28). *Star Wars* fan films come tumbling back to Earth. *The New York Times*. Retrieved from http://www.nytimes.com/2002/04/28/movies/film-star-wars-fan-films-come-tumbling-back-to-earth.html; Jenkins, H. (2006a). Quentin Tarantino's *Star Wars?* Grassroots creativity meets the media industry. *Convergence culture: Where old and new media collide* (pp. 131–168). New York: New York University Press.

be denying an essential part of ourselves. In fact, he argues, the process of juxtaposing different sorts of media images and sounds with one another is a legitimate and valuable form of critical and creative thinking. The meaning of the resulting remix "comes not from the content of what they say; it comes from the reference, which is expressible only if it is the original that gets used. Images or sounds collected from real-world examples become 'paint on a palette'" (Lessig, 2008, p. 74).

World of Warcraft as Creative Playground and Social Center

Along with the potential for remixing, the expansion of online, digitalized media has also encouraged the growth new kinds of interactive media experiences that leverage the networked, social aspects of the web, such as online gaming. *World of Warcraft* (or *WoW*, as it is known) is the most popular massively multi-player online role-playing game (MMORPG) on the market, attracting more than 11 million online players in North America, Europe, and Asia by December 2008 (Bainbridge, 2010, p. 4). *WoW* currently has just under 12 million users worldwide (Blizzard Entertainment, 2011). The game features a fantasy role-playing environment in which users create their own characters to interact within a virtual space. Players interact in real time with other players, cooperate with them, and engage in "quests" where groups of characters travel and achieve goals within the *WoW* universe, which allows them to gather experience and progress to higher levels of skill. What has aroused the most interest among scholars about MMORPGs is that they allow and even encourage users to become active participants in *defining* the actual game they are playing. For *WoW*, Blizzard Entertainment provides the framework for the action, but what keeps the millions of players coming back again and again is the ability to compete against and interact with millions of other game players in real time. Additionally, the fact that players can largely dictate their own movements and goals within the virtual environment means that MMORPGs like *World of Warcraft* have transcended the traditional media/producer–audience/consumer dynamic to place the audience in the role of cocreator.

This process begins when a user creates a fantasy character (or avatar) in the *WoW* universe. Users can experiment with multiple identities via the process of character creation that is built into the game. Users also adopt different types of roles via their interactions with other users online. Bainbridge (2010) conducted an online ethnographic study of *World of Warcraft* from January 2007 to December 2008. Along with learning the basics of the game, he describes in detail how the elements of social interaction and cooperation emerged as major facets of both success and enjoyment in the game. Identity also plays a major role in the game since users can choose to role-play different types of characters, especially those of different races, genders, and sexualities.

A number of scholars have begun to ask some important questions about the audiences for these types of interactive online games. For instance, what attracts players to these types of games? What types of play do they engage in online, and how might these choices reflect users' underlying goals for seeking out these games? Adopting a uses and gratifications perspective (see Chapter 5 for a full discussion), scholars have surveyed thousands of online participants in MMORPGs such as *World of Warcraft* and *Second Life* with the goal of organizing players' motivations into typologies for further analysis. In an early analysis of online game-playing motivations in MUDs (or multiuser dungeons), long before *WoW* emerged, Bartle (1996) conducted extensive observations and found that online players could be organized into four distinct types, including socializers (chatting and interacting with other users), achievers (looking for treasure within the game), explorers (interested in the inner workings of the game), and killers (those whose interest simply revolved around imposing their own will on others). Yee (2006) set out to test Bartle's player types by surveying over 3,000 regular MMORPG players via online surveys. Instead of four distinct play types, Yee discovered a rich complexity of interrelated factors that motivated MMORPG users, such as the desire for advancement and power (achievement component), a desire for meaningful relationships (social component) and the desire to role-play a fictional character (immersion component). While men were more likely than women to cite achievement as their motivation for game play and women conversely more likely to pursue social interactions, Yee (2006, p. 774) found that differences in motivation were "better explained by age than gender." Bates (2009) identified at least five different identity types that shape *WoW* users' roles online such as gamers, role-players, and independents. More recently, a study of Finnish MMORPG players found at least nine major "mentalities" among gamers, which were organized into three categories: (1) the "intensity of gaming"; (2) the "sociability in gaming"; and (3) the "games played," or the importance of playing games for the sake of playing games (Kallio, Mäyrä, & Kaipainen, 2011, p. 339). Despite their differences, these various uses and gratifications–based studies all point to two important conclusions. First, online game players are seeking out these experiences to *engage actively* with the game, thereby transcending their role as passive consumers of media. Secondly, the ability to *interact with other audiences and engage in social relationships online* is another strong draw for players.

Crowdsourcing Media Production: Wikis and Blogs

We explored in the last section how some audiences have leveraged the power of modern computers to create, remix, and distribute their own media via the Internet. Modern audiences have also become accustomed to a high level of inter-activity online—with each other and with traditional content producers—such that traditional one-way media like television, radio, and film have begun to lose some of their allure. In short, there are millions of audience members that *want to be engaged* as well as informed, entertained, and outraged by their media today. In the case of YouTube and MMORPGs like *World of Warcraft*, the quality of the experience largely depends on the collective contributions of each audience member. More than ever, individual media users are transforming their interests and free time into a new, collective resource—something Clay Shirky (2010) calls a "cognitive surplus." This surplus of audience activity has enabled Internet users to accomplish some tasks that would prove daunting for each individual alone. Collectively, however, knowledgeable and talented yet geographically dispersed individuals can pool their resources in real time to create media and solve prob-lems quickly and efficiently. For example, in June 2011 *The New York Times* was presented with a World War II–era photo album by a 72-year-old garment indus-try executive wishing to establish its worth. The album, which featured images of Nazi soldiers, Jewish prisoners of war, and even a photo of Adolf Hitler, was unsigned, with no captions to identify either the photo subjects or the photogra-pher. The *Times* digitized and posted the photos on its website, and within 3 *hours*, thanks to over 7 million page views and social media, the photographer was iden-tified and the photos' approximate dates and locations were clearly established (Barron & Dunlap, 2011).

The key to this new phenomenon is **crowdsourcing**. Crowdsourcing refers to "the act of a company or institution taking a function once performed by employ-ees and outsourcing it to an undefined (and generally large) network of people in the form of an open call" (Howe, 2006). Instead of outsourcing the labor required to make cultural materials to other countries with cheap labor, crowdsourcing essentially transforms media audiences into an ersatz labor force by encouraging individuals to help create a product or to solve a thorny problem (see Howe, 2008; Von Hippel, 2005). For example, in 2009 *Star Wars* fan Casey Pugh embarked on a massive project to re-create the entire original 1977 film—except that the film would be produced by hundreds of similar fans, each of which was assigned a 15-second scene to shoot (Paul, 2010, p. 38). Fans uploaded their scenes by the thousands—including some new live action sequences, others animated, and others using Legos and Kenner action figures. The end result was *Star Wars Uncut*, an entirely crowdsourced fan project (see Figure 9.5). Projects like these rely heavily on the power of the Internet to "aggregat[e] millions of disparate, inde-pendent ideas in the way markets and intelligent voting systems do" (Brabham, 2008, p. 80). Crowdsourced projects take advantage of a new kind of "collective intelligence"—since everyone knows something potentially useful, the Internet can bring all of these bits of knowledge together to create a "far-flung genius" (Levy, 1997, p. 13).

Wikis and the Crowdsourcing of Audience Knowledge

Another type of online media that has leveraged the "wisdom of crowds" is **wikis**. The core technology of this collaborative service is something called WikiWikiWeb—a computer programming protocol that allows anyone browsing on the Internet to click a button marked *Edit* and begin changing the information displayed on a webpage (Lih, 2009, p. 44). The most prominent wiki site is, of course, Wikipedia, an online encyclopedia that allows anyone who accesses the site to edit entries on different topics, with no prior screening of that individual's level of knowledge or expertise about that topic. In theory, the easy editing capability of wikis makes it "easy to correct mistakes, rather than making it difficult to make them" (Quiggin, 2006, p. 484).

Figure 9.5 A Montage of Scenes From *Star Wars Uncut* (2010)

Source: http://www.starwarsuncut.com. Images compiled by Stephanie Plumeri Ertz.

Wikipedia combines both aspects of the Web 2.0 experience that have made YouTube so successful: an openness to all for participation and a lowering of the technical barriers to such participation. Over time, Wikipedians (as Wikipedia users and editors are known) have developed their own sets of rules and conventions for making appropriate edits to pages, developing what Bruns (2008, p. 108) calls "fluid hierarchies organized through ad hoc meritocratic governance." These kinds of "adhocracies" (Konieczny, 2010) are meant to be self-correcting since "any knowledge that gets posted can and most likely will be revised and corrected by other readers" (Jenkins, 2006a, p. 255). Despite some of these conventions, Wikipedia has at times become a cultural battleground, particularly regarding topics and individuals who command public attention. In August of 2008, for example, the Wikipedia entry for then-Alaska governor Sarah Palin was significantly altered with much more flattering information fewer than 24 hours before Republican presidential nominee John McCain announced her selection to be his vice-presidential running mate. This episode of "wikiscrubbing" demonstrates the power of anonymous users to alter this public resource. However, it also calls into question the ultimate utility of Wikipedia as a trustworthy source of information for users.

Blogs and Citizen Journalism

The power of crowdsourcing has extended beyond the realm of entertainment to incorporate how news is gathered and relayed to the public. This trend is evident in the growing importance of **weblogs or *blogs***—daily or regularly-updated online websites that appear in journal format. Blogging began to expand dramatically in 1998 and 1999 when a number of different online tools, such as OpenDiary and LiveJournal, became available to web users. In 1999, the website Blogger.com was launched, allowing anyone to create his or her own blog website within seconds. Like YouTube and Wikipedia, websites like Blogger.com opened up the process of creating and maintaining a website relatively simple for everyone, particularly those with no knowledge of computer programming languages like HTML or Java. A study by the Pew Internet and American Life Project (Lenhart & Fox, 2006) in 2006 found that there were more than 118 million unique blogs being tracked by technorati.com and that these blogs were visited by over 57 million adults in the United States alone. By 2010, however, blogging activity had dropped off among teens, who began turning more to social media such as Facebook and Twitter to record their daily experiences and observations (Lenhart, Purcell, Smith, & Zickuhr, 2010). By 2017, blogs had largely fallen off the radar of national surveys to be supplanted by social media like Facebook, Instagram, and Snapchat (Poushter, 2017). Blogs are typically (though not always) sole-authored and focus on a particular topic or theme. Examples of blog themes include gardenblogging, babyblogging, photoblogging, and carblogging, just to name a few. Other important elements of blogs include the capacity for readers to comment, post links to other blogs, and praise or critique blog posts. Most online bloggers also "locate themselves within a larger community through the device of a 'blogroll,' that is, a sidebar with a list of permanent links to other blogs likely to be of interest to readers" (Quiggin, 2006, p. 483). Just as we saw with YouTube and wikis, the interactive nature of blogs emerges as a central feature of their popularity.

Increasingly, the practice of blogging has expanded beyond individuals' daily journals to include news commentary and original news reporting. In fact, blogging has now become semiprofessionalized, as journalists and commentators have turned to blogging as a full-time career. In one of the few studies of the extent and nature of the "blogosphere," Karpf (2008) distinguishes among four different types of blogs found online today: (1) classic blogs, or those that serve as a platform for commentary on individuals' daily lives; (2) community blogs, or those that serve an interest community regarding a particular activity or topic; (3) institutional blogs, or blogs that are professionally designed and maintained by large institutions such as newspapers, political parties, and nongovernmental organizations, for instance; and (4) **bridge blogs**, an emerging phenomenon that combines a daily news feature with an engaged participation focus found on community blogs (such as Huffingtonpost.com or Townhall.com).

A number of popular blog websites that fall into Karpf's last category, bridge blogs, are beginning to act as alternatives to the mainstream news media. These websites are able to crowdsource the practice of journalism by accessing, editing, and uploading documents, photographs, and other materials that can quickly provide readers with a vast wealth of information about a particular topic. This practice potentially decenters the traditional news media (such as newspapers and television news outlets) as the de facto source for detailed information about political leaders and their policies. Instead, educated and informed blog readers, through their comments and contributions to these blogs, become **citizen journalists** who act as watchdogs on political elites as well as on the mainstream press itself. The New York City–based news blog talkingpointsmemo.com (TPM), for instance, leveraged the powerful resource of its 400,000 daily readers by soliciting their help in tracking down leads on a developing story in 2007. Tipped off by one of its readers that the Bush administration had fired eight U.S. attorneys in the state of Arkansas, Joshua Marshall, the editor of TPM, posted a call on the website asking readers to inform them of any potential U.S. attorney firings in their own states (Muthukumaraswamy, 2010, p. 52). Later when the Department of Justice released thousands of pages of documents related to the attorney-firing scandal, TPM was one of the first news organizations to offer a concise summary of the most important pieces of information from the documents, mainly because it had enlisted its readers' help in reading and summarizing the voluminous material (McDermott, 2007). As the TPM example illustrates, citizen journalism "has become increasingly powerful in its own right and has begun to pursue its own stories independent of the coverage of the mainstream news outlets" (Bruns, 2008, p. 87). As news and political blogs become more independent, traditional news media outlets are actually using these blogs and other forms of social media as sources for their own news stories, further blurring the distinction between the two.

Questioning Audience Power in the Networked Information Society: Issues of Media Ownership, Surveillance, and Labor Exploitation

....

As the previous section outlined, the new power of media users to not only reinterpret and discuss but to essentially *create, remake, and mass distribute* mainstream media products heralds a new era of audience engagement and potential liberation from the hegemonic control of the text. In this sense, the arrival of Web 2.0 may mark the end of any meaningful distinction between traditional media producers and audiences. These new forms of audience engagement do not exist in a vacuum, however. Instead, these social practices are inscribed within broader social, economic, and cultural contexts. It's when we pull back to consider these various contexts that the liberating potential of today's online, interactive media environments becomes murkier. In this section, we'll explore some contemporary scholars who have openly questioned the claim that the balance of power between media producers and audiences has definitively shifted in favor of the audience. These scholars approach this new networked information environment from a critical or political economic perspective (see Chapter 4 for a complete review of political economy), arguing that issues of media ownership, intellectual property rights, and excessive online surveillance complicate claims about the reemergence of a grassroots, folk culture on the web. Additionally, these scholars argue that the labor involved in creating and distributing our own media products is in danger of being exploited by the same online services that make the Internet such a fascinating place to inhabit.

Audience-Produced Media: The Question of Intellectual Property

The increasingly important role of audiences in actually *creating* content that is then hosted online by private, for-profit media corporations raises thorny and fascinating questions about the role of intellectual property in today's digitized media environment. In past decades, the line between media corporations and the audience was clearly marked: Media companies hired writers, actors, directors, and thousands of other skilled media professionals to produce creative content for distribution via one-way technologies while audiences consumed these products in private spaces. With the rise of digitalization and the Internet, the possibility for interactivity between audiences and media producers began to blur this line. Thus, the *Star Trek* fans that Henry Jenkins analyzed in the late 1980s were truly "poaching" on the original text by reworking the story to include new plots, characters, and settings and sharing those creative works with other interested fans. However, the very notion of poaching seems to lose its relevance in an era when the nature of the media product itself is defined by, and increasingly reliant upon, audience involvement (Holmes, 2004). The appeal of reality TV programming like *American Idol*, for instance, is its involvement of the audience in the most critical aspect of the program: selecting a new pop singer.

Though a novelty at first, the interactive nature of today's digital media has become a taken-for-granted aspect of any new media production. Whether it comes in the form of allowing viewers or fans to chat about a new TV program on forums hosted by a media production company or whether the participation of the audience becomes an actual feature of the production of the content itself (in the case of the audience voting on *American Idol* or the programs that report on the "top-trending" stories on social media, for instance), audience participation has become an integral part of media productions today. In the most extreme examples on websites such as YouTube, Instagram, Tumblr, or Facebook, media corporations act merely as *distributors* of content that is created by the users. Without the audience to create the media content and without the interest of other audience members in accessing this content (which allows the corporate owner to sell advertising), these Internet media businesses would not be economically viable.

You might imagine that this new state of affairs produces a win–win situation for audiences and for media companies. While audience members are empowered to create their own media for themselves and others, media corporations are able to widely distribute this user-created content, thus saving themselves millions of dollars in up-front production costs. But this new producer–audience cooperation creates some new dilemmas for the ever-shifting power dynamics of the new media world. Perhaps the most important question here is, Who *owns* the content that is now generating millions of dollars in advertising revenue for Twitter, Facebook, and Google (which owns YouTube)? Who is empowered to shape the cultural meanings surrounding this content? These questions raise important issues about a new area of struggle between traditional, mass media producers and 21st-century audiences over the ownership of cultural products.

There is an irony that surrounds the boom in new technologies that allows for easy production, reproduction, and distribution of media content: While audiences have been busily exploring these new tools, media corporations have successfully lobbied government for ever-tighter restrictions on copyright and intellectual property. Because the cost of reproducing media content has collapsed toward zero, media companies have successfully argued to the federal government that the Internet threat is dangerous enough to warrant a dramatic expansion of copyright law. Through new laws in the United States like the Digital Millennium Copyright Act of 1998 and the Sonny Bono Copyright Term Extension Act (CTEA) of 1998 (which extended the term of copyright to the life of the author plus 70 years), existing protective rights have been extended to digital forms of media, the term of rights has been extended, penalties have been increased, and noncommercial illicit copying has become a crime (Boyle, 2008, p. 61).

Even seemingly innocent use of copyrighted media content has been threat-ened by infringement lawsuits. For instance, on the Google blog in 2007, YouTube's product manager announced the release of a "content identification" tool that would attempt to locate and disable videos that may contain copy-righted material. One group of music fans called The Living Room Rock Gods (LRRG) continued to post their videos, many of which featured them playing musical accompaniment to their favorite rock songs (Jenkins, 2009). They chan-neled their displeasure into a loose resistance movement called "Tribute Is Not Theft" (http://tributeisnottheft.blogspot.com/), which attempted to counter the stereotype of wanton copyright Internet piracy. In another example, once Warner Brothers had purchased the film rights to the Harry Potter book series, the stu-dio began seeking out Internet domain names that used copyrighted or trade-marked phrases from the books (most of which were fan-oriented websites) and threatened those websites with legal action if they did not change the domain or agree to hand over the rights of the content to Time-Warner (Jenkins, 2006a, pp. 185–186).

Corporate clampdowns on amateur media production are just one side of the coin, however. In order to achieve a measure of folk authenticity to asso-ciate with their products and services, corporations will often place corporate public relations and marketing information online in the guise of amateur, user-generated content. **Flogs**, for instance, are fake blogs, or blogs that seem to be written by an individual, but are instead authored by a company for the sole purpose of promoting the products and services of that company (Deuze, 2008, p. 34). **Splogs**, or spam blogs, are another recent variation on this theme. Splogs also masquerade as individual blog sites, but their purpose is simply to promote affiliate websites or to increase the search engine rankings of those sites. These examples demonstrate that the creative freedom to remix and explore commercial popular culture is being severely challenged by new and more restrictive legal and corporate regimes.

Social Media and Audience Surveillance in a Networked Environment

As more and more audiences turn to online media for information, enter-tainment, and creative participation, marketers and advertisers have attempted to follow audiences into these new, networked spaces. The introduction of powerful computing in the 1990s and 2000s not only expanded the ability of individuals to produce new media, but it also enabled the sophisticated, large-scale storage and classification of consumer data. With these data, adver-tisers and marketers began to target their messages to specific subsections of the audience with greater and greater accuracy (Gandy, 1993; Turow, 1997, 2006). Social networking platforms such as Facebook, Twitter, and Instagram have made the process of interacting with peers exceedingly easy, but they have simultaneously generated an online treasure trove of private data that has been mined and resold to advertisers. Long before the Internet or online social networking tools, Mark Poster (1990, p. 93) argued that new technologies had the ability to create a "superpanoptic" environment that would not only condition audiences to constant, intrusive surveillance by the state and the market, but it would actively encourage individuals to participate in this process of their own accord. Albrechtslund (2008) finds that online social networking sites have achieved much of what Poster warned against in the pre-Internet era. Indeed, services such as Facebook and Twitter are uniquely designed to facilitate **lateral surveillance** or "peer-to-peer monitoring," which Andrejevic (2005, p. 488) describes as "the use of surveillance tools by individuals, rather than by agents of institutions public or private, to keep track of one another, [and it] covers (but is not limited to) three main categories: romantic interests, family, and friends or acquaintances." If we become accustomed to routinely spying on our friends, family, and neighbors, we will be less likely to protest when corporations and government agencies monitor our own social profiles online. This type of active monitoring of social networking sites is not just a paranoid delusion, either—it is already widespread (Andrejevic, 2007; Turow, 2005).

Audience Creativity and Labor Exploitation

As noted earlier in the chapter, today's online audiences are productive in the sense that they are regularly creating and distributing their own media materials via the Internet. With traditional mass media audiences beginning to dwindle in favor of online media, companies have raced to be the first to offer web services that will attract the attention and devotion of web-savvy audiences. Online media forms like MMORPGs, YouTube, and Facebook have created a new form of entertainment enterprise: one that relies on the participation of the audience to actually shape and define the enterprise itself. To put this in economic terms, **the audience becomes an integral part of the media production apparatus itself,** without which the product would cease to have value in the market. Indeed, the main reason for the stellar financial success of companies such as Facebook and Twitter is that they routinely sell the individual data placed online by their users to interested parties, a practice that is spelled out only in the fine print in the "terms of service" to which each user must agree before signing in to use these services. Lauer (2008) uses Marxist theory to describe how our own personal information (name, address, zip code, credit history, hobbies, etc.) has become commodified into a product that is bought and sold in the digital economy, often without our knowledge or consent. The act of creating one's own self-identity profile online is a productive activity, argues Lauer, but one that simply generates "surplus value" for companies like Facebook.

Much as scholars such as Dallas Smythe and Eileen Meehan argued back in the 1980s, contemporary audiences generate huge profits for media firms by essentially donating their time, attention, and creative productions. On the one hand, the free exchange of ideas, information, and creativity is part of the larger "gift economy" of the Internet. On the other hand, this freely distributed creativity has become increasingly monetized by corporations, transforming it into essentially **free labor**. Terranova (2000, p. 37) writes that "free labor is the moment where this knowledgeable consumption of culture is translated into productive activities that are pleasurably embraced and at the same time often shamelessly exploited." There are plenty of examples that demonstrate the value of audience labor to corporate media owners (see Box 9.3 for one of them). In a game such as *World of Warcraft*, players spend countless hours creating their in-game avatars and guiding them through quests and adventures in order to gain experience points. The value of that time and effort has created a secondary

BOX 9.3
Managing Digital
Participation in *The Colbert Report*

As noted in an earlier chapter, Comedy Central's satirical faux news and commentary program, *The Colbert Report*, was one of the more popular programs among young people in the early 2000s. One of the reasons cited for the show's popularity with this age demographic was the fact that it continually taps into its audience's desire to participate with host and satirist-in-chief Stephen Colbert, writes Catherine Burwell (2010). In a 2006 segment of the program devoted to Marin County, California, home to *Star Wars* creator George Lucas, Colbert was shown wielding a light saber against a green screen. The next day, fans had already remixed the green screen clip with various background images and posted them to YouTube. Seeking to exploit this online remixing, *Colbert Report* producers issued an on-air challenge to viewers to remix the footage, making the best entries available on the official website for the program, *The Colbert Nation*.

Burwell observes that "not only did this centralization strategy bring more viewers to the program's official site; it also kept videos from being uploaded to YouTube, where attention—and thus profits—would migrate to YouTube's owner Google" (2010, p. 393). Along with the free promotion for *The Colbert Report*, writes Burwell, the video submissions themselves fit into a very narrow creative vision. Most of the videos featured the same images and narratives of the original program itself. Finally, in order for these fan-created videos to be hosted on the program's website, uploaders had to agree to the "terms of use" of *The Colbert Nation* website, which demanded that all content was "perpetually and indefinitely" the intellectual property of Viacom, the corporate owner of the Comedy Central network. This move to consolidate control of the labor of fan audiences calls into question the potentially liberating potential of new technologies.

Source: Burwell, C. (2010). Rewriting the script: Toward a politics of young people's digital media participation. *Review of Education, Pedagogy & Cultural Studies, 32*(4/5), 382–402.

market for those avatars. So-called gold farmers are digital information workers who play *WoW* 12 to 18 hours a day in order to build experience points and then resell their characters via eBay and other online trading sites (Dibbell, 2007). This has raised some tricky but fascinating questions about intellectual property ownership in a new, networked information economy. Who owns the characters created in the game? Grimes (2006) argues that *WoW* players actively construct these characters as their own property, even though Blizzard Entertainment claims that any activity that takes place on their web servers is their intellectual property, a claim bolstered by the End User License Agreement (EULA) that every *WoW* player must sign in order to log on and play. As you can see, issues of labor exploitation and intellectual property are closely intertwined.

Conclusion: Networked Creativity Meets Undercompensated Labor

In this chapter, I have briefly outlined some of the recent scholarship on networked, online audiences. The rise of online platforms like social media has led to an explosion in the amount of data gathered about audiences. This has led, in turn, to new forms of audience metrics for capturing exposure and engagement with web content, with important consequences for media production and consumption. Despite the creative potential of new media technologies, there is considerable debate about the implications of these media for audiences and their relative power vis-à-vis media producers. On the one hand, as Henry Jenkins and others have argued, new forms of media offer an unprecedented level of control over the media experience. Audiences can now easily produce and distribute media content, some of which rivals traditional mass media in its technical and creative sophistication. Digitalization of the media has also enabled audiences to actually alter the original media text itself, remixing it with other forms to create a new kind of assemblage art form. The networked infrastructure of the Internet has also made collaboration quite easy, allowing audiences to leverage the power of the crowd to assemble a vast online encyclopedia (Wikipedia) as well as a rapid-response information network that can challenge existing traditional news outlets (via blogs and wikis).

On the other hand, the democratic and liberating potential of these new media is also being potentially stifled by the extension of the logic of capital accumulation into these new media realms. By extending our analysis from the individual uses and motivations behind audience media production to the broader economic and political contexts, we see that these online media have become battlegrounds for the control and interpretation of popular culture. In the concluding chapter, we'll draw together some of the threads in the book to make some observations about the future direction of audience studies in an era of networked information production.

DISCUSSION ACTIVITIES

1. As individuals or in groups, click on the links at the end of this question to find a list of the top 10 YouTube videos, according to their usage statistics, in the last several years. Select a year and watch each of the 10 videos in that year while taking notes on them and recording your observations of the following criteria:

   - Theme of the video

   - Main subject (who or what is featured in the video)

   - Production value (amateur or professionally produced video)

   - Intended purpose (humorous, serious, social message, etc.)

   - Responses/comments (number of comments, types of comments)

   - Response videos (number and types of video responses)

   Now, compare your notes with your classmates about what they observed. What similarities do you find across all of these videos? What do you think accounts for their enormous popularity among YouTube users?

   Top 10 YouTube Videos of 2018: https://www.fastcompany.com/90277300/youtubes-top-10-videos-of-the-year-are-the-2018-diversions-we-deserved

   Top 10 YouTube Videos of 2017: https://mashable.com/2017/12/06/top-youtube-videos-2017-most-watched/#CRr1sf7NbOqJ

2. Look at these remix videos online and then think about what specific meanings or interpretations you make of them. What types of cultural materials are they using and how? What new meanings are these videos exploring through the use of these traditional media? Are these meanings critical of the original text or merely celebratory of that text? Why do you say this?

   Remix video examples:

   - Charlie Rose by Samuel Beckett: http://www.youtube.com/watch?v=LFE2CCfAP1o

   - George Bush/Tony Blair-My Endless Love: https://www.youtube.com/watch?v=UtEH6wZXPA4

   - Bert and Ernie Try Gangsta Rap by stianhafstad: http://www.youtube.com/watch?v=21OH0wlkfbc

   - Quentin Tarantino's *Star Wars* by Evan Mather: https://www.youtube.com/watch?v=OTmvYmGdkJc

3. Conduct a web search for the Terms of Service or End User License Agreement (EULA) for one of the following websites: YouTube, Facebook, Twitter, Pinterest, or *World of Warcraft*. Once you have found it, print it out and read through it carefully and answer the following questions:

   - Is there any mention made of privacy of personal data online? If so, what is this service's policy on the privacy of personal data?

   - Who owns personal data or images uploaded to the site, according to the terms of service?

   - How might personal information be used by the website?

   - How does this service manage the ownership of sounds, images, or other data that are uploaded and stored on the site?

- What do you think about these terms of service? Do you think these policy terms are fair to the users of these services? Why or why not?

4. Watch the video documentary *Generation Like* (https://www.pbs.org/wgbh/frontline/film/generation-like/), produced by the PBS investigative television series *Frontline* in 2014. As you watch the documentary, answer the following questions about the use of online audience metrics:

- How are teen social media audiences characterized by *Frontline* correspondent Douglas Rushkoff? Are they characterized by what Philip Napoli calls "audience autonomy"? Why or why not?

- According to the documentary, how important are social media outlets to marketers and advertisers today? Give some examples.

- How are Twitter followers, YouTube channel subscriptions, and Facebook "likes" monetized by advertisers and corporate marketing firms?

- How do companies such as TVGLA and Mondelez, Intl. use research and social media data to market and sell brands to the audience?

- What strategies do the news media use to report on public opinion? Do the news media accurately reflect public concerns as expressed through polls? Why or why not?

- What are some of the implications of these new types of data gathering and social marketing for personal privacy in the digital era?

ADDITIONAL MATERIALS

Albarran, A. B. (Ed.). (2013). *The social media industries*. New York, NY: Routledge.

Bainbridge, W. S. (2010). *The Warcraft civilization: Social science in a virtual world*. Cambridge, MA: The MIT Press.

Burgess, J., & Green, J. (2018). *YouTube: Online video and participatory culture* (2nd ed.). Cambridge, United Kingdom: Polity.

Confessions of an aca-fan: An online blog by Henry Jenkins. Available at http://henryjenkins.org/index.html

Digitally mediated surveillance blog: http://www.digitallymediatedsurveillance.ca/

Fuchs, C. (2017). *Social media: A critical introduction* (2nd ed.). Los Angeles, CA: SAGE.

Gaylor, B. (2009). *Rip: A remix manifesto* [Video documentary]. Available at http://www.archive.org/details/RipRemixManifesto

Jenkins, H. (2006). *Convergence culture: Where old and new media collide*. New York: New York University Press.

Koughan, F., & Rushkoff, D. (Producers). (2014). *Generation like* [Video documentary]. PBS *Frontline*. Available at https://www.pbs.org/wgbh/frontline/film/generation-like/

Napoli, P. M. (2011). *Audience evolution: New technologies and the transformation of media audiences*. New York, NY: Columbia University Press.

Star Wars Uncut website: http://www.starwarsuncut.com/

YouTube Trends. Available at http://youtube-trends.blogspot.com/

REFERENCES

Albrechtslund, A. (2008). Online social networking as participatory surveillance. *First Monday*, *13*(3), 3.

Andrejevic, M. (2005). The work of watching one another: Lateral surveillance, risk, and governance. *Surveillance & Society*, *2*(4), 479–497.

Andrejevic, M. (2007). *iSpy: Surveillance and power in the interactive era*. Lawrence: University Press of Kansas.

Andrejevic, M. (2014). The big data divide. *International Journal of Communication*, *8*, 1673–1689.

Ang, I. (1991). *Desperately Seeking the Audience*. London: Routledge.

Bain Insights. (2014, September 18). Big data: Media's blockbuster business tool. *Forbes*. Retrieved from https://www.forbes.com/sites/baininsights/2014/09/18/big-data-medias-blockbuster-business-tool/

Bainbridge, W. S. (2010). *The warcraft civilization: Social science in a virtual world*. Cambridge, MA: The MIT Press.

Barron, J., & Dunlap, D. W. (2011, June 24). Mystery of a Nazi photographer solved by online readers. *The New York Times*. Retrieved from https://www.nytimes.com/2011/06/25/arts/design/mystery-of-a-nazi-photographer-solved-by-online-readers.html?_r=2&hp=&adxnnl=1&adxnnlx=1309001304-KDejbdx+oevJhn8J%205P6Lng

Barth, C. (2011, March 21). Mock Rebecca Black all you want, she's laughing to the bank. Forbes.com. Retrieved from http://blogs.forbes.com/chrisbarth/2011/03/21/mock-rebecca-black-all-you-want-shes-laughing-to-the-bank/

Bartle, R. (1996). Hearts, clubs, diamonds, spades: Players who suit MUDs. Available at http://www.mud.co.uk/richard/hcds.htm

Bates, M. C. (2009). Persistent rhetoric for persistent worlds: The mutability of the self in massively multiplayer online role-playing games. *Quarterly Review of Film & Video*, *26*(2), 102–117.

BBC News. (2007, March 13). Viacom will sue YouTube for $1bn. *BBC News*. Retrieved from http://news.bbc.co.uk/2/hi/business/6446193.stm

Benkler, Y. (2006). *The wealth of networks: How social production transforms markets and freedom*. New Haven, CN: Yale University Press.

Bermejo, F. (2007). *The Internet audience: Constitution and measurement*. New York, NY: Peter Lang.

Blizzard Entertainment. (2011, January 10). *World of Warcraft: Cataclysm one-month sales top 4.7 million*. Retrieved from http://us.blizzard.com/en-us/company/press/pressreleases.html?id=2847887

Boyle, J. (2008). *The public domain: Enclosing the commons of the mind*. New Haven, CN: Yale University Press.

Brabham, D. C. (2008). Crowdsourcing as a model for problem solving. *Convergence: The International Journal of Research into New Media Technologies*, *14*(1), 75–90.

Bruns, A. (2008). *Blogs, Wikipedia, second life, and beyond*. New York, NY: Peter Lang.

Burgess, J., & Bruns, A. (2012). Twitter archives and the challenges of "big social data" for media and communication research. *M/C Journal*, *15*(5). Retrieved from http://journal.media-culture.org.au/index.php/mcjournal/article/view/561

Burgess, J., & Green, J. (2009). *YouTube: Online video and participatory culture*. Cambridge, United Kingdom: Polity.

Burton, B. (2018, June 21). *Star Wars* fans start campaign to remake *The Last Jedi*. *CNET*. Retrieved from https://www.cnet.com/news/star-wars-fans-start-campaign-to-remake-the-last-jedi/

Burwell, C. (2010). Rewriting the script: Toward a politics of young people's digital media participation. *Review* of Education, Pedagogy & Cultural Studies, 32(4/5), 382–402. doi:10.1080/10714413.2010.510354

Caulfield, K. (2011, March 23). Glee's original songs, Rebecca Black, Nate Dogg debut on digital songs chart. Billboard.com. Retrieved from http://www.billboard.com/#/news/glee-s-original-songs-rebecca-black-nate-1005086782.story

Chung, M. (2017). Not just numbers: The role of social media metrics in online news evaluations. Computers in Human Behavior, 75, 949–957.

Deuze, M. (2008). Corporate appropriation of participatory culture. In B. De Cleen & N. Carpentier (Eds.), Participation and media production: Critical reflections on content creation (pp. 27–40). Cambridge, United Kingdom: Cambridge Scholars.

Dibbell, J. (2007, June 17). The life of the Chinese gold farmer. The New York Times. New York, NY. Retrieved from https://www.nytimes.com/2007/06/17/magazine/17lootfarmers-t.html?adxnnl=1&adxnnlx=1313440939-uqePzPxS45CTbfEoBUlxiw

DiNucci, D. (1999). Fragmented future. Print, 53(4), 32.

Fiske, J. (1987). Television culture. London, England: Methuen.

Fuchs, C. (2017). Social media: A critical introduction (2nd ed.). Los Angeles, CA: SAGE.

Gandy, O. H. (1993). The panoptic sort: A political economy of personal information. Boulder, CO: Westview Press.

Gannes, L. (2006, October 26). Jawed Karim: How YouTube took off. Gigaom. Retrieved from http://gigaom.com/2006/10/26/jawed-karim-how-you-tube-took-off/

Gillespie, T. (2010). The politics of "platforms." New Media & Society, 12(3), 347–364.

Gillespie, T. (2018). Governance of and by platforms. In J. Burgess, A. E. Marwick, & T. Poell (Eds.), The SAGE handbook of social media (pp. 254–278). Thousand Oaks, CA: SAGE.

Grimes, S. M. (2006). Online multiplayer games: A virtual space for intellectual property debates? New Media & Society, 8(6), 969–990. doi: 10.1177/1461444806069651

Harmon, A. (2002, April 28). Star Wars fan films come tumbling back to Earth. The New York Times. Retrieved from http://www.nytimes.com/2002/04/28/movies/film-star-wars-fan-films-come-tumbling-back-to-earth.html

Havens, T., & Lotz, A. (2011). Understanding media industries. New York, NY: Oxford University Press.

Holmes, S. (2004). "But this time you choose!": Approaching the "interactive" audience in reality TV. International Journal of Cultural Studies, 7(2), 213–231. doi: 10.1177/1367877904043238

Howe, J. (2006, June 2). Crowdsourcing: A definition. Weblog. Retrieved from http://crowdsourcing.type-pad.com/cs/2006/06/crowdsourcing_a.html

Howe, J. (2008). Crowdsourcing: Why the power of the crowd is driving the future of business. New York, NY: Three Rivers Press.

Jenkins, H. (2006a). Convergence culture: Where old and new media collide. New York: New York University Press.

Jenkins, H. (2006b). Fans, bloggers, and gamers: Exploring participatory culture. New York: New York University Press.

Jenkins, H. (2009, March 13). Locating fair use in the space between fandom and the art world (part two). Confessions of an aca-fan. Retrieved from http://www.henryjenkins.org/2009/03/locating_fair_use_in_the_space_1.html

Kallio, K. P., Mäyrä, F., & Kaipainen, K. (2011). At least nine ways to play: Approaching gamer mentalities. Games and Culture, 6(4). 327–353. doi:10.1177/1555412010391089

Kaplan, A. M., & Haenlein, M. (2010). Users of the world, unite! The challenges and opportunities of social media. Business Horizons, 53(1), 59–68.

Karpf, D. (2008). Understanding blogspace. *Journal of Information Technology & Politics*, 5(4), 369–385.

Kaushik, A. (2009). *Web analytics 2.0: The art of online accountability and science of customer centricity*. Indianapolis, IN: Sybex.

Kitchin, R. (2017). Big data: Hype or revolution? In L. Sloan & A. Quan-Haase (Eds.), *The SAGE handbook of social media research methods* (pp. 27–39). London, England: SAGE.

Konieczny, P. (2010). Adhocratic governance in the Internet age: A case of Wikipedia. *Journal of Information Technology & Politics*, 7(4), 263–283. doi:10.1080/19331681.2010.489408

Lauer, J. (2008). Alienation in the information economy: Toward a Marxist critique of consumer surveillance. In B. De Cleen & N. Carpentier (Eds.), *Participation and media production: Critical reflections on content creation* (pp. 41–53). Cambridge, United Kingdom: Cambridge Scholars.

Lenhart, A., & Fox, S. (2006). *Bloggers: A portrait of the Internet's new storytellers*. Pew Internet and American Life Project. Washington, DC: The Pew Charitable Trusts. Retrieved from http://www.pewtrusts.org/our_work_report_detail.aspx?id=21106

Lenhart, A., Purcell, K., Smith, A., & Zickuhr, K. (2010). *Social media and young adults*. Pew Research Center's Internet & American Life Project. Washington, DC: The Pew Charitable Trusts. Retrieved from http://pewinternet.org/Reports/2010/Social-Media-and-Young-Adults.aspx

Lessig, L. (2004). *Free culture: How big media uses technology and the law to lock down culture and control creativity*. New York, NY: Penguin Press.

Lessig, L. (2008). *Remix: Making art and commerce thrive in the hybrid economy*. New York, NY: Penguin Press.

Levy, P. (1997). *Collective intelligence: Mankind's emerging world in cyberspace*. Cambridge, MA: Helix Books.

Lih, A. (2009). *The Wikipedia revolution: How a bunch of nobodies created the world's greatest encyclopedia*. New York, NY: Hyperion.

Mayer-Schönberger, V., & Cukier, K. (2014). *Big data: A revolution that will transform how we live, work, and think* (Reprint edition). Boston, MA: Eamon Dolan/Mariner Books.

McCay-Peet, L., & Quan-Haase, A. (2016). What is social media and what questions can social media research help us answer? In L. Sloan, & A. Quan-Haase (Eds.), *The SAGE handbook of social media research methods* (pp. 13–26). London, England: SAGE.

McDermott, T. (2007, March 17). Blogs can top the presses. *The Los Angeles Times*. Los Angeles, CA. Retrieved from http://articles.latimes.com/2007/mar/17/nation/na-blogs17

Mosco, V. (2014). *To the cloud: Big data in a turbulent world*. Boulder, CO: Paradigm.

Muthukumaraswamy, K. (2010). When the media meet crowds of wisdom. *Journalism Practice*, 4(1), 48–65.

Nadler, A. M. (2016). *Making the news popular: Mobilizing U.S. news audiences*. Urbana: University of Illinois Press.

Napoli, P. M. (2011). *Audience evolution: New technologies and the transformation of media audiences*. New York, NY: Columbia University Press.

Napoli, P. M. (2012). Audience evolution and the future of audience research. *JMM: The International Journal on Media Management*, 14(2), 79–97.

O'Reilly, T. (2005, October 1). Web 2.0: Compact definition? *O'Reilly Radar*. Retrieved from http://radar.oreilly.com/2005/10/web-20-compact-definition.html

Paul, B. (2010). *Digital fandom*. New York, NY: Peter Lang.

Petre, C. (2015). *The traffic factories: Metrics at Chartbeat, Gawker Media, and* The New York Times. New York, NY: Tow Center for Digital Journalism. Retrieved from https://towcenter.org/research/traffic-factories/

Poster, M. (1990). *The mode of information: Poststructuralism and social context*. Chicago, IL: University of Chicago Press.

Poushter, J. (2017, April 20). Not everyone in advanced countries uses social media. Retrieved from http://www.pewresearch.org/fact-tank/2017/04/20/not-everyone-in-advanced-economies-is-using-social-media/

Quiggin, J. (2006). Blogs, wikis and creative innovation. *International Journal of Cultural Studies*, 9(4), 481–496. doi: 10.1177/1367877906069897

Rosen, J. (2006, June 27). The people formerly known as the audience. *PressThink*. Retrieved from http://archive.pressthink.org/2006/06/27/ppl_frmr.html

Saroyan, S. (2011, June 17). Amanda Hocking, storyseller. *The New York Times*. Retrieved from http://www.nytimes.com/2011/06/19/magazine/amanda-hocking-storyseller.html?_r=1&scp=1&sq=storyseller&st=Search

Shirky, C. (2010). *Cognitive surplus: Creativity and generosity in a connected age*. New York, NY: Penguin Press.

Smee, B. (2018, April 25). Facebook's data changes will hamper research and oversight, academics warn. *The Guardian*. Retrieved from https://www.theguardian.com/technology/2018/apr/25/facebooks-data-changes-will-hamper-research-and-oversight-academics-warn

Srnicek, N. (2016). *Platform capitalism*. Cambridge, United Kingdom: Polity.

Statt, N. (2018, May 6). Fortnite is the biggest game on the planet right now because it's a living, breathing world. *The Verge*. Retrieved from https://www.theverge.com/2018/5/6/17321172/fortnite-epic-games-biggest-game-living-breathing-world-mmo-rpg-battle-royale

Terranova, T. (2000). Free labor: Producing culture for the digital economy. *Social Text*, 18(2), 33–58. doi: 10.1215/01642472-18-2_63-33

Toffler, A. (1990). *Powershift: Knowledge, wealth, and violence at the edge of the 21st century*. New York, NY: Bantam Books.

Turow, J. (1997). *Breaking up America: Advertisers and the new media world*. Chicago, IL: University of Chicago Press.

Turow, J. (2005). Audience construction and culture production: Marketing surveillance in the digital age. *The ANNALS of the American Academy of Political and Social Science*, 597(1), 103–121. doi: 10.1177/0002716204270469

Turow, J. (2006). *Niche envy: Marketing discrimination in the digital age*. Cambridge, MA: MIT Press.

Von Hippel, E. (2005). *Democratizing innovation*. Cambridge, MA: MIT Press.

Webster, J. G., Phalen, P. F., & Lichty, L. W. (2014). *Ratings analysis: Audience measurement and analytics* (4th ed.). New York, NY: Routledge.

Webster, T. (2017, June 18). The partially-filled glass of Apple's new podcast statistics. Retrieved from https://medium.com/@webby2001/the-partially-filled-glass-of-apples-new-podcast-statistics-7bc8e273bf9b

Yee, N. (2006). Motivations for play in online games. *CyberPsychology & Behavior*, 9(6), 772–775. doi:10.1089/cpb.2006.9.772

Conclusion: Audience Studies in an Era of Datafication

In this text, we have explored the concept of media audiences from multiple perspectives: as objects of media influence, as quantified constructions of institutions, as active users, and as subcultures and media producers. By now, it should be clear that the definition of the term *audience* has been contested throughout its history. In fact, the struggle over its definition often mirrors the social and economic conflicts in our society. As Chapter 9 outlined, there are numerous shifts under way in our media environment that challenge the traditional distinctions between the media text and the audience. In an era of Internet-enabled computers, smartphones, and iPads, we are able to instantaneously engage with media at any point during our day. This has given audiences unprecedented levels of control over their media exposure and has empowered them to become media producers as well. At the same time, media corporations and advertisers have adapted their business practices in a bid to retain their ability to track and measure media exposure. In the past 10 years, platforms like social media have emerged as key components of users' online experiences. Platforms such as Facebook, Twitter, LinkedIn, and Snapchat enjoy widespread adoption in part because they streamline the process of creating and sharing information. However, as we explored in Chapter 9, these platforms also structure our experiences with the Internet in powerful ways, which has introduced a number of challenges for audiences.

The rise of social media has changed the nature of the audience marketplace as well since content producers and advertisers have sought to maximize their own revenues by harnessing the productive activities of engaged audiences within these interactive environments. For example, on October 28, 2011, Hyperion Books (owned by the Walt Disney Corporation)—the publisher of a series of popular children's picture books by author Mo Willems—hosted an event at the Magnolia Bakery on the Upper West Side of Manhattan to launch a new iPad, iPhone, and iPad application called "Don't Let the Pigeon Run This App!" The application was an interactive word search and drawing game based upon Willem's series of children's books about an inquisitive pigeon. A number of guests were invited (their travel expenses were covered by the publisher) to meet the author and to test the new application. These invited guests were not journalists, technology reviewers, or public relations executives, however. Instead, they were a group of stay-at-home mothers who hosted their own online blogs about parenting. These so-called mommybloggers brought their children to the event to meet Willems, to take pictures with him, and to explore the new app. After returning home, many of the moms who attended the event blogged about the experience, raving about Mo Willems and the new iOS application (Coast 2 Coast Mom, 2011; Feliciano, 2011; Harper, 2011).

This event is notable because it clearly illustrated some of the recent shifts in the audience experience. First, the focus of the event was an interactive media application designed for mobile media platforms, an important new aspect to our media environment. Second, this application was connected to a children's print book series, acting as an extension of that series. This type of cross-platform narrative experience is typical of *transmedia production*, something we will explore in this chapter. Finally, the invited guests for this product-marketing event were amateur bloggers who were members of the target audience. Disney's strategy to use these moms as volunteer labor in their marketing efforts demonstrated the company's recognition of the important role that contemporary audiences play in the media production process. These women were enlisted as erstwhile *opinion leaders*, and Disney was banking on the likelihood that the blog entries would seem more authentic and credible to other potential customers than a slickly produced advertising campaign. These days, the line between media producers and the audience has become increasingly blurred.

This blurriness between producers and audiences is even more striking when we consider that billions of Internet users are continually and actively involved as media producers via their contributions to online social media platforms such as Facebook, Instagram, Snapchat, and YouTube, just to name a few. At the same time, users' thoughts, ideas, and creative outputs are being fed back into a media system that is continually hungry for original content. The "mommybloggers" described earlier were caught up in a system that took their labor and creative energies, appropriated them, and marketed them back to them and other consumers as an authentic expression of culture. How can audience studies help us understand this?

Overview of the Chapter

In this final chapter, we will return to some of the major themes of the book, including individual agency, institutional constructions of audiences, and shifts in the media landscape that are shaping our interactions with information and entertainment today. We'll start by extending the analysis in Chapter 9 to consider the impact of transmedia experiences and the miniaturization of video screens on our understanding of contemporary audiences. Next, we return to the institutional construction of audiences to explore how audience fragmentation is catalyzing some important shifts in the audience-measurement industry. In the last section of the chapter, we will examine recent audience research that points the way to the future of the field. Although the audience theories have been arranged in different chapters throughout this text, there is a good deal of conceptual overlap among these theories. In order to grasp the complexity of the audience experience in today's media environment, we will draw upon multiple theoretical traditions. The goal of this concluding chapter is not to offer a single, unified theory of audience engagement and response to the media. Rather, we will draw together some of the theoretical threads from across the previous chapters to consider how the field of audience studies is changing in the 21st century.

The Rise of Mobile, Transmedia Experiences in the Post-Network Era

Our understanding of media audiences has undergone substantial shifts throughout history, in part due to shifts in the technologies for creating and distributing media content. At each stage in the evolution of media technologies, access to information and entertainment has expanded or simplified, thereby creating new opportunities for audience engagement. As outlined in Chapter 9, our current media moment is characterized by two interrelated trends: digitalization of content and convergence of media technologies. These trends have in many ways reshaped the structural features of the audience landscape. A quick look at the television and motion picture industries demonstrates the extent of these changes. Technologies such as the VCR, digital video recorders (DVRs), cable and satellite television, and online video streaming have enabled audiences to time-shift their viewing such that most of our media exposure today occurs "on demand." Since audiences are no longer constrained by network television schedules, we are now living in a "post-network" era (Lotz, 2009). The rise of online video access has had similarly profound effects on the motion picture industry. According to recent estimates, Americans are seeing more films than ever before, but 57% of this viewing is in the form of online streaming through services like Hulu and Netflix, which generate $1.72 billion in revenue (Fritz, 2012). By contrast, sales of DVD and Blu-ray discs generated $11.1 billion in 2011.

These shifts in the business of creating and distributing information and entertainment are also reorganizing audience expectations. The Magnolia Bakery episode with the mommybloggers represents a small microcosm of a larger trend toward what scholars and practitioners have called **transmedia production**. The term, coined by scholar Henry Jenkins (2002, 2011), refers to the coordinated use of multiple media platforms (or technologies) to craft a narrative. Unlike traditional storytelling in a single medium such as television, film, or books, transmedia narratives open up the possibility for audience participation and dialogue with media producers. An early example was independent filmmaker Lance Weiler's 1997 production *The Last Broadcast*, which encouraged audiences to help solve a mystery in the story by logging on to the film's website (http://www.thelastbroadcastmovie .com/). On the website, audiences could listen to fake 911 calls and could search through the classifieds of actual newspapers for more clues. Industry insiders have been buzzing about the potential of transmedia narratives to lure back their lost audiences (DeMartino, 2011). According to one public relations executive,

"Transmedia storytelling is the future of marketing. And those who can span across formats and share their expertise will stand out in an age of digital relativity" (Rubel, 2010). In the Internet era, audiences have become equally enthusiastic about the ability to engage more directly with media texts. For example, Yoo (2011) discovered that the expectation of interactivity has become a new type of gratification that is obtained from media exposure. Another recent study of online fans found that the most popular programs are those that encourage audiences to stretch their imaginations and cultural assumptions (Costello & Moore, 2007). Today's television audiences "want to create their own venues for sharing their views; they even want to influence the development of the program" (2007, p. 140).

The rise of transmedia reinforces an important truth about our contemporary popular culture: that the boundaries between media texts are becoming more fluid. Jonathan Gray (2010) argues that modern audiences have also become avid consumers of **paratexts**, or textual material that surrounds media narratives and informs us about them. For example, before we make a decision to see a feature film in the theater, we have likely seen trailers, advertisements, posters, information about merchandising tie-ins, parodies, entertainment news stories about the actors in the film, and any number of other messages that comment on or extend the film itself. Thus, by the time that we actually view the film "we have already begun to decode it and to preview its meanings and effects" (Gray, 2010, p. 3). Studies of audience interpretation must therefore take into account the interplay between texts and paratexts.

Another important shift in the audience landscape has been the dramatic expansion of portable media-capable technologies. The proliferation of devices such tablets and smartphones has multiplied the number of video screens available to us. A recent study by the Pew Research Center found that almost all Americans (95%) now own a smartphone (Pew Research Center, 2018). A recent report by the Nielsen Company revealed that Americans spent an average of 2 hours and 19 minutes on their smartphones per day (Nielsen Media Research, 2018). A 2012 report from Nielsen also coined the term *Generation C* to describe the new cohort of 18- to 34-year-old audiences (Nielsen Media Research, 2012). While these audiences make up 23% of the U.S. population, according to the 2010 census, they represent an outsized percentage of consumers who watch online video (27%), visit social networking sites and blogs (27%), own tablets (33%), and use smartphones (39%). Nielsen argues that these new consumers are uniquely accessible to advertisers because of their connectedness to digital media, but thus far, mobile advertising has not proven to be anywhere near as successful as television or traditional web advertising (Meadows, 2010).

Thanks to the ubiquity of transmedia and portable screening devices like smartphones and tablets, media reception now occurs in multiple locations, on different media technologies, and with a variety of textual materials. David Croteau (2006, p. 343) has argued that this dramatically complicates the efforts of researchers to fully understand audience activity in the 21st century. He cautions that "media scholars will need to devise new ways to assess content trends across these new production platforms." New forms of analysis should also recognize the situated aspects of the audience experience. The contexts of our media experiences are continually changing as we move from place to place during our day. In the studies of television reception in the 1980s, scholars like James Lull and David Morley could isolate the home as the primary site for media exposure. As the technologies for displaying media have diversified and miniaturized, the number of possible reception contexts have mushroomed, making the task of understanding them all quite daunting.

One project that addresses these complexities is *Transmedia Television* by Elizabeth Evans (2011). Evans recruited 118 viewers of the television programs *Spooks* and *24* from northeast England and investigated their interpretations of these programs via surveys, diaries completed by the participants, and focus group discussions. Her research began in 2005 and was completed in early 2007. In those intervening years, Evans's participants revealed that their television viewing experiences were shifting markedly, thanks to the ability to engage with their favorite programs via mobile technologies. These audiences enjoyed the immersive experience of their favorite programs, but they also made repeated use of other related transmedia texts, such as online alternative-reality games (ARGs), Internet fan websites, and chat rooms. Evans found that transmedia narratives extended audiences' knowledge of their favorite programs and fueled their deeper engagement with the original television text. This deeper engagement was encouraged in part by the constant accessibility of online media. Evans's research is instructive for current audience scholars because of her sensitivity to the shifting nature of audience reception in an era of technological change.

The New Economics of Audience Aggregation

Thanks to the expansion of media texts and technological platforms, the independence of the audience from content providers is greater than ever before. In the 21st century, audiences can access media whenever and wherever they desire, provided that they have broadband Internet access. This ubiquity of information has democratized access to information and freed audiences from the need to adjust their schedules and viewing habits to meet the demands of content providers and advertisers. Does this mean that the power dynamic between media institutions and individuals has shifted irreversibly in the direction of the audience? The evidence doesn't seem to support this conclusion. In fact, there are plenty of signs that media producers and distributors have begun to effectively adapt to the shifts in our media consumption habits. In this section, we'll return to notions of political economy from Chapter 4 to examine the impact of fragmentation on the measurement of audience attention.

To understand the shifts in the business of audience measurement, it's important first to consider the impacts of audience fragmentation on the market. The most influential and popularized discussion of these impacts was provided by

Wired magazine editor Chris Anderson in an article (2004) that later became a bestselling book (2006). Anderson described the mathematical pattern of the **long tail** (see Figure 10.1), which demonstrates the result of fragmentation. Most audiences focus their viewing on a few very popular media products or hit programs (the head), but the rest of viewer attention is spread out across a larger group of much smaller, niche content options (the tail). In today's media environment, Anderson (2006) noted that the tail is getting longer so that the size of the combined audience attention along the tail will eventually rival the large audiences for products in the head. He urged companies to focus more attention on the revenue potential of the smaller, niche media options since these represented the best opportunity for future growth. For example, online streaming video services such as Hulu, Netflix, Popcornflix, and others can provide instant access to many lesser-known films and television programs for relatively little cost, making it possible to cater to a selective group of viewers who might be interested in these films.

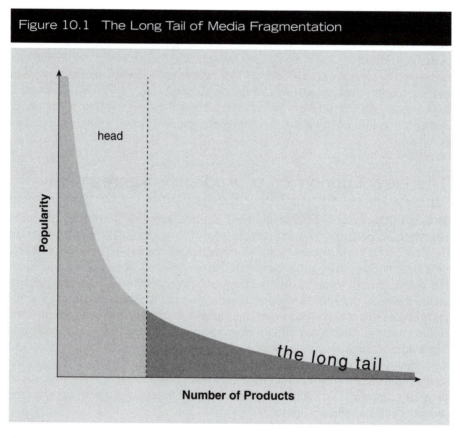

Figure 10.1   The Long Tail of Media Fragmentation

Source: Chris Anderson, http://www.longtail.com/the_long_tail/about.html. Redrawn by Stephanie Plumeri Ertz.

Some scholars have argued that fragmentation of our media landscape is also leading to **audience polarization** because individuals are beginning to avoid media content that they find distasteful or offensive (Sunstein, 2007; Turow, 1997). This could have serious long-term sociological consequences by isolating us from one another and thereby decreasing the public's tolerance for diversity, cooperation, and mutual respect. The U.K. Brexit debate and the 2016 U.S. presidential election demonstrated that forms of media can indeed have a polarizing impact on audience (see Chapter 3). Finding more concrete empirical evidence of such polarization has been difficult, however. In a secondary analysis of Nielsen data, for example, Webster (2005) found that the evidence of audience polarization was quite modest. A follow-up study revealed that there was substantial overlap in audience viewing across a number of cable, satellite, and network television stations, which also challenged the polarization hypothesis (Webster & Ksiazek, 2012).

How will the long tail force a change in the methods of institutional audience measurement? McDonald (2008) argues that the shift of audience away from the head and toward the tail will begin to challenge the monopoly power of audience measurement firms like Nielsen and Nielsen Audio. Because it is not "economically viable to apply conventional random sampling methods to the measurement of increasingly minute audiences," the smaller niche media options will likely go unmeasured (McDonald, 2008, p. 316). This would be sustainable only as long as the popular media options remained highly profitable and attractive to advertisers. Once advertisers shift their attention to niche audiences in the tail of the graph, McDonald suggests that nonsample-based measurements will be needed. As Chapter 9 explored, our fragmented media environment and increased reliance on online platforms to access news and entertainment has spurred an arms race among advertisers and marketers for ever-increasingly detailed personal information about audiences.

Given all of the potential media options from which to choose, the media landscape today can be somewhat bewildering to audiences. In this seemingly abundant environment of media options, how do we navigate all of the potential choices? Often we turn to web-based search and recommendation systems such as Google, Yahoo, Bing, and others. Webster (2010) has called these "user information systems." While these technologies help us to locate media materials on the Internet, these tools are also bundled with intrusive forms of surveillance to more precisely track what we are watching and when. Despite the fragmentation of the audience into thousands of tiny media outlets and experiences, content providers and advertisers have sought to reconstitute the mass audience through other means. For example, we are accustomed to thinking of the web search giant Google as a partner and guide in our travels on the Internet. However, Google is not a disinterested party in the expansion of online media consumption since it generates billions of dollars in revenue from online advertising. As discussed in Chapter 9, platform companies like Google do not require an outside research company like A. C. Nielsen to measure online consumer behavior because the company has a variety of means to do this already. Google, for example, monitors users' search queries and Gmail messages for specific keywords and then instantly exposes users to relevant, targeted advertising. Therefore "the user interests that are analyzed by Google are much more precise than television program rating systems" (Kang & McAllister, 2011, p. 148). In early 2012, Google revamped its privacy policy to allow the sharing of user data across all of its online services, such as Gmail, Search, Google Docs, Google Maps, and YouTube, which is owned by Google (Grobart, 2012). In another bid to aggregate user data for easier measurement, YouTube changed its layout to better feature content that looks more similar to professionally produced content. By bundling amateur and produced content in easy-to-find locations, YouTube is adopting a standardized broadcast model to canalize user attention into more narrow portals for better user predictability and easier surveillance (Sisario, 2012).

Despite the freedom of audiences to roam the Internet for media content, recent trends in audience measurement indicate that the agency of audiences continues to be circumscribed by the measurement demands of the market system. Of course, public opinion polls and commercial ratings systems remain critical tools of audience measurement. Alongside these traditional metrics, however, online media distributors and web portals like Google are developing more sophisticated techniques for maximizing surveillance of the audience online. What is most troubling about these newer forms of audience measurement is that they are relatively hidden from public scrutiny because they are deeply embedded into the very technologies that allow us to navigate the Internet. As Turow and Couldry (2018) have recently argued, one cannot understand our communications landscape today without grasping the pervasive power of online platforms to extract, sort, analyze, and commodify user data. The sophisticated analysis of these data by media corporation enables them to tailor their messages to each individual customer, which accelerates the process of media and social fragmentation. This has fueled the insatiable desire of corporate media for ever-more-specific audience data in order to further target marketing claims to consumers, something Zuboff (2015) has termed *surveillance capitalism*. Turow and Couldry note,

> We now are entering a quite different age of mobile personalization. In it, individuals, wherever they are, are (a) continuous targets of personally-adapted messages and content; (b) potential producers of content and so, in some sense, personalizers of the media environment; and (c) the subjects of continuous tracking and profiling, with (a) and (b) generating the incentives that drive (c). It is (c), our subjection to continuous tracking and profiling via media platforms, which makes surveillance capitalism possible. (2018, p. 417)

As this quote makes clear, the myriad benefits of online platforms for enabling easy creation and sharing of knowledge has exacted a price: our personal data. Why would audiences be willing to give up their privacy in order to use these services? Most users are victims of "involuntary co-option of their data" because they have unconsciously agreed to give away such data by agreeing to the terms of service for these services (Stehling, Vesnic-Alujvic, Jorge, & Maropo, 2018). As Stehling and colleagues (2018) argue further, even forms of crowdsourced audience creativity—something that is celebrated as emancipatory by some scholars—can be exploited and commodified by media corporations looking to capitalize on audiences as a source of free labor. These developments point to the continuing relevance of critical and political economic approaches to the study of media audiences (see Napoli, 2010).

Rediscovering Media Audiences in the 21st Century

The trends outlined tell us some of the challenges for scholars wishing to study media audiences in the 21st century. In the 20th century, there was a clear distinction between producers and audiences, making the study of audiences clear-cut: Media institutions produced information and entertainment content that was consumed remotely by audiences. But in our current environment, whereby users actively engage with media content, produce, share, and remix it via online platforms, what does this suggest about the meaning of the term *audience*? Indeed, the semantic shift from talking about "audiences" in the 20th century to considering the role of online media "users" (or "produsers," as noted in Chapter 9) in the 21st century suggests that we take a more instrumental and active role in our own media environment today. How might notions of agency and structure inform our understanding of audiences in an Internet age? Given the independence of individuals from "institutional communicators" such as TV networks and newspapers (Napoli, 2010), does the concept of "audience" still have relevance in today's media environment? I would argue that the concept is more important than ever but that scholars should pay careful attention to the shifting boundaries between media texts and the audience. What central questions should occupy audience scholars? This section considers some unanswered questions about our media consumption and explores some recent research that attempts to address these questions.

Let's return for a moment to the problem of definitions. This text has charted some of the important shifts in the audience concept throughout history, beginning with egalitarian notions of citizen participation and shifting toward concerns about the vulnerability of the crowd. The rise of motion pictures and radio in the early 20th century cemented the view that audiences were relatively powerless to defend themselves against media influence. The later shift toward the concept of the active audience beginning in the 1970s can be seen partially as a reaction to the idea of this "audience as victim" model that pervaded the dominant effects tradition throughout the 20th century. Is the concept of the active audience still relevant? How should we understand the nature of audiences in today's fragmented, interactive media environment? In general, the distinctions between media producers and audiences have become much less clear. Hermes (2009, p. 112) laments that "we appear to have lost both the audience as identifiable entity, and reception of particular genres or texts as researchable media practice." Therefore, Grindstaff and Turow (2006, p. 120) argue that scholars should consider the ways in which audiences form "video cultures" around the texts that they consume, circulate, and produce. Along these lines, Hermes (2009) argues that the recent focus on fandom may have shifted scholars' attention away from the ordinariness of everyday media exposure. She advocates a renewed focus on all manner of audience activity, including the most temporary and fleeting incidents when individuals encounter texts and then promptly forget about them. David Morley has advocated a similar holistic approach to audience experiences, remarking that "the current claims for the specificity of the realm of interactive media can thus be seen as woefully exaggerated" (2006, p. 116). The key here is that our identities as audiences are continually shifting and adapting as we interact with new technologies in different social and situational contexts.

How, then, can scholars incorporate this new contextual sensitivity into their research? In a speech made at the Versailles International Conference on the Future of Audience Research in 2003, University of Wales (Aberystwyth) Professor Martin Barker (2006) mapped out some specific goals for the field in the new century. He first argued that Stuart Hall's "Encoding/Decoding" 1980 essay had initially opened new avenues for the conceptualization of media audiences but that the model had unfortunately hamstrung and narrowly defined the field ever since. In particular, Barker noted that the study of the interactions between texts and audiences since 1980 had not developed into a coherent paradigm with its own set of conceptual and methodological tools. Barker outlined a number of "ambitions" for the field of audience studies (pp. 129–131):

- Making the concept of interpretive communities "measurable and testable" using empirical observation techniques

- Exploring the relations among Hall's different reading positions (dominant or preferred, negotiated, and oppositional)

- Exploring how interpretive communities are formed and how they make sense of multiple texts, including paratexts

- Stating "with sufficient precision" the conditions in which an audience member can be said to experience a positive cultural encounter with a media text

- Developing consistent methods to study these aspects of the audience experience to allow scholars to compare their findings

The deficiencies outlined by Barker here highlight the lack of coherence in the field due to the unique aspects of each audience study. In a retrospective look at the field of audience studies, David Morley (2006) acknowledged that one of the central problems facing the field was its post-1980 adherence to qualitative and ethnographic methods (part of a revolution in the field that was catalyzed by his groundbreaking work on *Nationwide*). However, the two scholars fundamentally disagreed about the impact of the encoding/decoding model. While Barker claimed that Hall's conceptualization had little to offer modern studies of audiences, Morley argued that Hall's essay offered a valuable "working model" that had encouraged a wide variety of innovative research.

A number of studies have closely examined the situated nature of audience experiences in a digital age, thereby pointing the way to a new agenda for audience research. For example, Barker (2006) examined the audience experience of *The Lord of the Rings* films that were released between 2001 and 2003. His research incorporated an analysis of paratexts relating to the film (promotional materials, merchandise tie-ins, online teaser trailers, etc.), a quantitative survey of audiences about their interpretations, and follow-up qualitative interviews with selected respondents about how they have integrated film fantasy into their own lives. Another innovative study by Das (2011) explored how audiences navigate social networking sites like Facebook and Twitter. Das conducted hour-long interviews with 15 young people aged 17 to 23. Each interviewee sat at a computer with Internet access and responded to questions as they navigated their online social networking presence, narrating their thoughts and interpretations of this new technology. They were then asked to express through any means what social networking sites meant to them. The result was a rich collection of visual and narrative imagery that revealed an ongoing process of interpretation and meaning production surrounding online tools like Facebook. Müller and Hermes (2010) also incorporated multiple methods in their study of *WestSide*, a multicultural Dutch soap opera. Their research included street interviews, focus group discussions, in-depth interviews, and an analysis of fan discussions on the official *WestSide* website. They discovered that the program could encourage "the performance of cultural citizenship," though this occurred only when audiences were confronted with issues of cultural diversity in their own lives.

How should audience studies confront the new realities of our datafied media landscape? What role might audience studies play in an environment where individuals' autonomy is seemingly bound and heavily circumscribed by the structures of online platforms like Facebook, Twitter, and YouTube? Livingstone and Das (2013) argue that recent scholarship on the operations of online platforms and datafication has seemed to render obsolete the distinction between texts and audiences. Does this new reality allow theoretical space for audience studies? Indeed, Livingstone and Das (2013) argue that audience studies are still relevant to our media environment today. They call for a refocus on the question of the "legibility" of online media when it comes to situating the audience concept within an era of online media. Returning to Hall's (1980) notion of encoding and decoding, how are various enablements or affordances built into forms of technology, and how are those forms navigated and understood by individual users? Moreover, in what ways do audiences bring their own goals, aspirations, and notions of digital and political citizenship to their digital media environments? By focusing scholarly attention on how the "microtactics of appropriation reshape and remediate media texts and technologies," classic concepts from the field of audience studies can be leveraged to help us understand the role of the individual and society in our current datafied media environment.

Charting a Course for
Audience Studies: The 2030 Agenda

The question of how best to reimagine audience studies in an online era motivated a group of 29 audience researchers from 14 different countries to form a study group in 2015 called the Consortium on Emerging Directions in Audience Research, or CEDAR (www.sites.google.com/site/audiencescedar/). The consortium undertook a year-long analysis of emerging themes and trends in audience research over the 2004 to 2014 decade. These scholars wanted to know this: How had audience studies research grappled with the technological and social transformations of the decade? How might this analysis help create a road map for audience studies moving into the next decade? This year-long effort culminated in a final report, *Audiences, Towards 2030: Priorities for Audience Analysis*, coedited by Brita Ytre-Arne and Ranjana Das (2017). In a follow-up article in a recent issue of the journal *Television & New Media* dedicated to media audiences, Ytre-Arne and Das (2019) outlined a five-point agenda for audience studies for the next decade. This agenda acknowledges the centrality of online platforms, computer algorithms, and big data in the lives of media consumers, but it seeks to carve out theoretical spaces for rich inquiry into the lived experiences of audiences. This effort is the largest and most comprehensive look at the field to date, and its careful consideration of the intersections between our mobile, interactive media environment and classic concepts of audiences merits close attention. Each point of this agenda is outlined and explained briefly as follows:

Agenda Item #1: Audience studies should seek to understand audiences' critical literacies surrounding increasingly intrusive, individualized, and tightly connected technological experiences.

Online platforms, especially social media, create environments for social interactivity over which end users have little to no control. These platforms, like Facebook, have hidden, proprietary mechanisms and algorithms that silently and ceaselessly harvest user activity, emotion, and creation and use it to sell to advertisers as evidence of user "engagement." Because audiences have no choice but to accept these platform environments as a condition for engaging meaningfully with one another through these services, their negotiated responses to these "intrusive" digital structures is an area ripe for investigation. As Mollen and Dhaenens argue,

From an audience studies perspective, the intrusiveness of digital media interfaces then requires an analysis that not only takes into account meanings that providers associate with their media. Instead, it also becomes pertinent to address at the same time the possible divergent meanings and coping practices that people in their practices of use establish with regard to them. (2018, p. 46)

One of the goals, then, of audiences studies should be to uncover how audiences—through either self-management or technology management—negotiate and even resist the intrusive nature of these platforms. In ethnographic interviews with teens, for example, Marwick and boyd (2014) discovered that Facebook's "one-size-fits-all" privacy model created tensions between them and their peers, families, and even outsiders because sharing some information with everyone in their friend group resulted in "context collapse." Some teens negotiated these problems by trying to fine-tune Facebook's privacy settings to meet their needs. Others, like Mikalah, an 18-year-old African-American woman who was a ward of the state, prevented unwanted surveillance by social workers by deactivating her Facebook account every night so that her interactions with her friends could not be monitored (Marwick & boyd, 2014). Mikalah's creative negotiation of Facebook to meet her own privacy needs speaks to the "critical data literacies" that are evidenced by audiences in an era of platform dominance (Ytre-Arne & Das, 2019).

Agenda Item #2: Audience studies should foreground the political aspects of audiences' reactions to intrusive technologies, particularly forms of resistance.

In a recent essay, audience studies scholar Sonia Livingstone (2018) argues that the recent focus of scholars on the power of online platforms runs the risk of returning to the era of moral panics surrounding the powerful effects of media that dominated the field in the early half of the 20th century (see Chapter 2). She writes,

In today's heady climate of media panics—over so-called fake news, election hacking, Internet and smartphone addiction, the algorithmic amplification of hate speech, viral scams, filter bubbles and echo chambers, discriminatory data profiling and data breaches, the crisis in quality journalism, the demise of face-to-face conversation, and a host of digital anxieties about youth—fears about audience gullibility, ignorance, and exploitation are again heightened in popular and academic debate. (Livingstone, 2018, p. 2)

How should audience studies respond to this current moral panic? Ytre-Arne and Das (2019) argue that scholars should explore audience responses to the increasingly pervasive nature of online surveillance. This can and should include explorations of political protest and organized resistance to the status quo. U.S. citizen activism in support of net neutrality (Crawford, 2013; MacKinnon, 2013) as well as the recent European Union regulations in support of data privacy (Zarsky, 2016) are but two examples of this type of organized activism on behalf of online audiences.

Agenda Item #3: Audience studies should renew its commitment to researching fundamental audience experiences such as reading, viewing, listening, and interpreting as well as producing media.

Ytre-Arne and Das (2019) point here to an imbalance in the research of online forms of media. While much of the literature on these new forms focuses on the ability of audiences to transcend their role as passive consumers and to become media producers and contributors to a broader "convergence culture," to use the phrase coined by Henry Jenkins (see Chapters 8 and 9), these forms of audience activity make up only a small fraction of the audience experience. The study of audiences can engage with its roots, Ytre-Arne and Das argue, by recommitting itself to qualitative interview and ethnographic research methods to uncover the "small acts of engagement" such as clicking, liking, commenting, voting, debating, endorsing, sharing, and other platform-enabled moves that work to create social communities online. This also refocuses audience research on processes of meaning-making that distinguished the field in the 1970s and 1980s (see Chapter 6).

Agenda Item #4: Audience studies should investigate the "co-option of and commercial interest in audiences' attention, data, and productive work."

This specific agenda suggestion for audience research hearkens back to the political economic analysis of Dallas Smythe and Sut Jhally on the nature of the audience as a commodity (see Chapter 4). Here, Ytre-Arne and Das argue for the continued relevance of political economy for our understanding of how audiences are harnessed by media providers as a source of surplus value for the purpose of commodification. For example, in 2011 Facebook launched a type of premium advertising called "sponsored stories." Sponsored stories were essentially corporate brand advertising that were appended onto an individual user's organic Facebook post, which was then seen in the newsfeed of that individual's friends. Fisher (2015) explores how sponsored stories turned posts with mundane information such as a specific café one visited into a "commodified social communication" by adding a logo for Starbucks at the end of such a post. If a Facebook friend replied to such a post, their responses would also be tagged with the Starbucks logo and communicated to their friends as well. By leveraging and updating Dallas Smythe's arguments about the audience commodity from the 20th century, Fisher's analysis demonstrates how "the audience on social media is a commodity sold to advertisers, labour power that produces attention to ads as well as data which feeds into the production of ads, and a medium through which targeted messages are propagated" (2015, p. 65). Moving forward, audience studies should continue to explore the co-optation of audiences' engagements via online media.

Agenda Item #5: Audience studies should engage in research that serves the interest of audiences in diverse global, cultural, political, and scholarly contexts.

Here, Ytre-Arne and Das speak to the need for audience studies to continue to investigate audience experiences around the globe, taking note of the influences of local contexts in the shaping of audiences experiences with media. In an era of datafication, many scholars will be tempted to rely widely on social media metrics and other forms of online measurement as sources of insight into audience behaviors. As Livingstone (2018, p. 7) argues, "Attention to empirical audiences is easily displaced by a fascination with the data traces they leave, deliberately or inadvertently, in the digital record." The ubiquity of online audience data draws scholarly interest, but this may unfortunately preclude the desire to engage audiences in conversation about their own media use. This is a methodological shortcoming, notes Livingstone, which can be addressed only by returning to a focus on the lived experiences as the focal point for audience studies. "Indeed," she writes, "including *the people* in a mediated, perhaps mediatized, increasingly datafied age—that's the task in front of us" (2018, p. 11).

These five agendas for audience research provide a valuable road map for audience studies into the future. As you can see from the descriptions of each agenda item, they build upon the rich history and traditions of audience research yet also point to a renewed relevance of the concept of the audience even within a media landscape dominated by interactive, online media.

Conclusion
· ·

As we have explored throughout this text, our roles as audiences are the result of a complex interplay of agency and structure. Audience scholarship during the 20th century tended to overemphasize one side or the other of this agency–structure dynamic, but the recent explosion of interactive media has forced scholars to concede that audience power exists on a continuum. Every media encounter represents a subtle renegotiation between the text and the audience. The key is to start with our *everyday, lived experiences* as the departure point for deeper analysis of the audience experience. We need to keep asking how technology, social relationships, and physical contexts can shape our identities as individuals, consumers, and citizens. These are exciting times to be studying audiences, and the hope is that this text has provided you with the tools to think more deeply about your own media use in a rapidly changing world.

ADDITIONAL MATERIALS

Anderson, C. (2006). *The long tail: Why the future of business is selling less of more.* New York, NY: Hyperion Books.

Consortium on emerging directions in audience research. Available at https://sites.google.com/site/audiencescedar/

Das, R., & Ytre-Arne, B. (Eds.). (2018). *The future of audiences: A foresight analysis of interfaces and engagement.* Cham, Switzerland: Palgrave Macmillan.

Evans, E. (2011). *Transmedia television: Audiences, new media, and daily life.* New York, NY: Routledge.

Hermes, J. (2009). Audience Studies 2.0. On the theory, politics and method of qualitative audience research. *Interactions: Studies in Communication & Culture, 1*(1), 111–127.

Jenkins, H. (2007, March 22). Transmedia storytelling 101. *Confessions of an Aca/Fan.* Available at http://www.henryjenkins.org/2007/03/transmedia_storytelling_101.html

Livingstone, S. (2018). Audiences in an age of datafication: Critical questions for media research. *Television & New Media*, 1–14.

Morley, D. (2006). Unanswered questions in audience research. *Communication Review, 9*(2), 101–121.

Weiler, L. (2010). Transmedia keynote presentation, DarkLight Festival 2010, October 29, 2010 [Video presentation]. Available at https://www.youtube.com/watch?v=8Gzo6gel2mo

Ytre-Arne, B., & Das, R. (2017). *Audiences, towards 2030: Priorities for audience analysis.* Surrey, United Kingdom: CEDAR. Retrieved from http://epubs.surrey.ac.uk/842403/7/For%20web%20CEDAR-report.pdf

REFERENCES

Anderson, C. (2004, October 1). The long tail. *Wired, 12*(10). Retrieved from http://www.wired.com/wired/archive/12.10/tail.html

Anderson, C. (2006). *The long tail: Why the future of business is selling less of more.* New York, NY: Hyperion Books.

Barker, M. (2006). I have seen the future and it is not here yet . . . ; or, on being ambitious for audience research. *Communication Review, 9*(2), 123–141. doi:10.1080/10714420600663310

Coast 2 Coast Mom. (2011, November 2). Don't let the pigeon run this app by Mo Willems launches from Disney. *Coast 2 Coast Mom.* Retrieved from http://www.coast2coastmom.com/2011/11/dont-let-the-pigeon-app-launches-lunch-with-mo-willems.html

Costello, V., & Moore, B. (2007). Cultural outlaws: An examination of audience activity and online television fandom. *Television & New Media, 8*(2), 124–143. doi:10.1177/1527476406299112

Crawford, S. P. (2013). *Captive audience: The telecom industry and monopoly power in the new gilded age.* New Haven, CT: Yale University Press.

Croteau, D. (2006). The growth of self-produced media content and the challenge to media studies. *Critical Studies in Media Communication, 23*(4), 340–344. doi:10.1080/07393180600933170

Das, R. (2011). Converging perspectives in audience studies and digital literacies: Youthful interpretations of an online genre. *European Journal of Communication, 26*(4), 343–360. doi:10.1177/0267323111423379

DeMartino, N. (2011, July 5). Why transmedia is catching on (part 1). TribecaFilm.com. Retrieved from http://www.tribecafilm.com/tribecaonline/future-of-film/124727224.html#.T2vWk47YnKc

Evans, E. (2011). *Transmedia television: Audiences, new media, and daily life—Comedia*. New York, NY: Routledge.

Feliciano, N. (2011, November 13). Mo Willems launches "don't let the pigeon run this app!" *Momtrends*. Retrieved from http://www.mom trends .com/2011/11/mo-willems-launches-dont-let-the-pigeon-run-this-app/

Fisher, E. (2015). 'You media': Audiencing as marketing in social media. *Media, Culture & Society*, 37(1), 50–67.

Fritz, B. (2012, March 23). Internet to surpass DVD in movie consumption, not revenue. *Los Angeles Times*. Los Angeles, CA. Retrieved from http://latimesblogs .latimes.com/entertainmentnewsbuzz/2012/03/internet-to-surpass-dvd-in-movie-consumption-not-revenue.html

Gray, J. (2010). *Show sold separately: Promos, spoilers, and other media paratexts*. New York, NY: NYU Press.

Grindstaff, L., & Turow, J. (2006). Video cultures: Television sociology in the "new TV" age. *Annual Review of Sociology*, 32(1), 103–125. doi:10.1146/annurev.soc.32.061604.143122

Grobart, S. (2012, March 1). Google's new privacy policy: What to do. *Gadgetwise Blog*. Retrieved from http://gadgetwise.blogs.nytimes.com/2012/03/01/googles-new-privacy-policy-what-to-do/

Hall, S. (1980). Encoding/decoding. In S. Hall, D. Hobson, A. Lowe, & P. Willis (Eds.), *Culture, media, language: Working papers in cultural studies* (pp. 128–138). London, England: Hutchinson.

Harper, A. (2011, November 1). Mo Willems, a pigeon (or two), and Aiden's birthday celebration. *Mommy delicious*. Retrieved from http://www .mommydelicious.com/2011/11/mo-willems-pigeon-or-two-and-aidens.html

Hermes, J. (2009). Audience studies 2.0. On the theory, politics and method of qualitative audience research. *Interactions: Studies in communication & culture*, 1(1), 111–127. doi:10.1386/iscc.1.1.111/1

Jenkins, H. (2002). Interactive audiences. In D. Harries (Ed.), *The new media book* (pp. 157–170). London, England: BFI.

Jenkins, H. (2011, April 8). Seven myths about transmedia storytelling debunked. *Fast Company*. Retrieved from http://www.fastcompany .com/1745746/seven-myths-about-transmedia-storytelling-debunked

Kang, H., & McAllister, M. P. (2011). Selling you and your clicks: Examining the audience commodification of Google. *TripleC (cognition, communication, co-operation): Open Access Journal for a Global Sustainable Information Society*, 9(2), 141–153.

Livingstone, S. (2018). Audiences in an age of datafication: Critical questions for media research. *Television & New Media*, 1–14.

Livingstone, S., & Das, R. (2013). Interpretation/reception [Data set]. In P. Moy (Ed.), *Oxford bibliographies online: Communication*. Oxford, United Kingdom: Oxford University Press. Available at http://eprints.lse.ac.uk/62649/1/Interpretation_reception.pdf

Lotz, A. D. (2009). What is U.S. television now? *The ANNALS of the American Academy of Political and Social Science*, 625(1), 49–59. doi:10.1177/0002716209338366

MacKinnon, R. (2013). *Consent of the networked: The worldwide struggle for internet freedom*. New York, NY: Basic Books.

Marwick, A. E., & boyd, d. (2014). Networked privacy: How teenagers negotiate context in social media. *New Media & Society*, 1–17.

McDonald, S. (2008). The long tail and its implications for media audience measurement. *Journal of Advertising Research*, 48(3), 313–319. doi:10.2501/S0021849908080379

Meadows, J. (2010). Broadcast and cable on the third screen: Moving television content to mobile devices. In J. A. Hendricks (Ed.), *The twenty-first-century media industry: Economic and managerial implications in the age of new media—Studies in new media* (pp. 173–190). Lanham, MD: Lexington Books.

Mollen, A., & Dhaenens, F. (2018). Audiences' coping practices with intrusive interfaces: Researching audiences in algorithmic, datafied, platform societies. In R. Das & B. Ytre-Arne (Eds.). *The future of audiences* (pp. 43–60). Cham, Switzerland: Palgrave Macmillan.

Morley, D. (2006). Unanswered questions in audience research. *Communication Review, 9*(2), 101–121. doi:10.1080/10714420600663286

Müller, F., & Hermes, J. (2010). The performance of cultural citizenship: Audiences and the politics of multicultural television drama. *Critical Studies in Media Communication, 27*(2), 193–208. doi:10.1080/15295030903550993

Napoli, P. M. (2010). Revisiting "mass communication" and the "work" of the audience in the new media environment. *Media, Culture & Society, 32*(3), 505–516. doi:10.1177/0163443710361658

Nielsen Media Research. (2012). *State of the media: U.S. digital consumer report, Q3–Q4 2011*. Retrieved from http://www.nielsen.com/us/en/insights/reports-downloads/2012/us-digital-consumer-report.html

Nielsen Media Research. (2018). *The Nielsen Total Audience Report Q2 2018*. New York: Nielsen. Retrieved from https://www.nielsen.com/us/en/insights/reports/2018/q2-2018-total-audience-report.html

Pew Research Center. (2018, February 5). Mobile fact sheet. Retrieved from http://www.pewinternet.org/fact-sheet/mobile/

Rubel, S. (2010, October 11). The rise of the corporate transmedia storyteller. Forbes.com. Retrieved from http://www.forbes.com/2010/10/11/google-eric-schmidt-bieber-facebook-social-networking-storytelling-steve-rubel-cmo-net work.html

Sisario, B. (2012, March 11).YouTube channels seek advertisers and audiences. *The New York Times*. Retrieved from https://www.nytimes.com/2012/03/12/technology/youtube-channels-seek -advertisers-and-audiences.html

Stehling, M., Vesnic-Alujvic, L., Jorge, A., & Maropo, L. (2018). In R. Das & A. Ytre-Arne (Eds.), *The future of audiences: A foresight analysis of interfaces and engagement* (pp. 79–99). Cham, Switzerland: Palgrave Macmillan.

Sunstein, C. R. (2007). *Republic.com 2.0*. Princeton, NJ: Princeton University Press.

Turow, J. (1997). *Breaking up America: Advertisers and the new media world*. Chicago, IL: University of Chicago Press.

Turow, J., & Couldry, N. (2018). Media as data extraction: Towards a new map of a transformed communications field. *Journal of Communication, 68*(2), 415–423.

Webster, J. G. (2005). Beneath the veneer of fragmentation: Television audience polarization in a multichannel world. *Journal of Communication, 55*(2), 366–382.

Webster, J. G. (2010). User information regimes: How social media shape patterns of consumption. *Northwestern University Law Review, 104*(2), 593–612.

Webster, J. G., & Ksiazek, T. B. (2012). The dynamics of audience fragmentation: Public attention in an age of digital media. *Journal of Communication, 62*(1), 39–56. doi:10.1111/j.1460-2466.2011.01616.x

Weiler, L., & Avalos, S. (Directors). (1997). *The last broadcast* [Motion picture]. United States: Ventura Distribution.

Yoo, C. Y. (2011). Modeling audience interactivity as the gratification-seeking process in online newspapers. *Communication Theory, 21*(1), 67–89.

Ytre-Arne, B., & Das, R. (2017). *Audiences, towards 2030: Priorities for audience analysis.* Surrey, United Kingdom: CEDAR. Retrieved from http://epubs.surrey.ac.uk/842403/7/For%20web%20CEDAR-report.pdf

Ytre-Arne, B., & Das, R. (2019). *An agenda in the interest of audiences: Facing the challenges of intrusive media technologies, 20* (2), 184–198.

Zarsky, T. Z. (2016). Incompatible: The GDPR in the age of big data. *Seton Hall Law Review, 47,* 995–1020.

Zuboff, S. (2015). Big other: Surveillance capitalism and the prospects of an information civilization. *Journal of Information Technology, 30*(1), 75–89.

Index

Claritas, 116

Class, 259. *See also* Cultural hierarchy
advertising and, 121
audiences linked to, 14–17
concerns about, 18
distinctions of, 256–257
interpretation and, 171, 179–182
ISAs and, 170
motion pictures and, 32
notion of public and, 72–73

Class domination, 169

Click, 276

Clinton, Hillary, 67, 82, 84, 90

Cloud computing, 271

Club culture, 259–260

Coalition for Innovative Media Measurement, 119

Cocreator, audience as, 285–286. *See also* Producers, audiences as

Coffeehouse, 72–73

Cognitive consistency, 46

Cognitive dissonance, 46

Cohen, Stanley, 34

Colbert, Stephen, 47 (box), 295 (box)

Colbert Report, The (television series), 47 (box), 295 (box)

Collecting, 258

Collective will of public, 74

College-aged audiences, 111 (box), 112 (figure)

Comet Ping Pong pizzeria, 90

Comey, James, 29

Comic book collectors, 258

Commercial-based ratings, 118–119

Commercials, 104. *See also* Advertising; Marketing

Committee on Public Information (CPI), 41–43

Commodity audience, 103–106, 316

Common sense, 21

Communication
Cooley's description of, 31
general model of, 4 (figure)
meaning-based view of, 3
oral, 9
transmission view of, 3

Community and Society (Tönnies), 34–35

Computers. *See* Mobile media; Producer-audience relationship; Producers, audiences as

Computers, media landscape and, 266–267

ComScore, 119

Conceptual error, 111

Connotative level of meaning, 175, 184, 198, 199

Consequences of Modernity, The (Giddens), 222

Consistency theory, 46

Consolidation of media, 101–102

Consortium on Emerging Directions in Audience Research (CEDAR), 314

Conspiracy theories, 90

Constructing Public Opinion (Lewis), 83 (box)

Constructionism, 6–7

Consumer behavior, 99

Consumer information, 99, 100, 275. *See also* Data

Consumption, media
selectivity of, 88–89
self-identity and, 242

Contesting readings, 198

Context
audiences experiences and, 317
interpretation and, 183
reception and, 209–214
use of term, 209

Continuity, 247–249, 248–249 (box), 251

Convergence, 269

Converse, Philip, 82

Conversion, 224, 278

Cooley, Charles Horton, 31

Cooper, E., 47 (box)

Copyright, 239, 282, 284 (box). *See also* Intellectual property; Ownership

Correlation, 147

Cosby Show, The (television series), 190–191

Cost per point (CPP), 117 (box), 118

Cost per thousand users (CPMs), 117 (box), 118, 122 (box), 276

Couldry, N., 224, 229–230, 310

Counterhegemonic readings, 198

CPMs (cost per thousand users), 117 (box), 118, 122 (box), 276

CPP (cost per point), 117 (box), 118

Creators. *See* Producers; Senders

Credibility, source, 46, 279–280 (box)

Creel, George, 41–43

Critical cultural studies, 164–166

Critical data literacies, 315

Crossroads (soap opera), 182–183

Cross-sectional surveys, 77

Croteau, David, 306

Crowd, 14–17, 18, 27, 30–31

culture and, 186, 186–187 (box), 188–191, 200

encoding/decoding model, 172–178, 175 (figure), 192, 196, 200

gender and, 182–186

Hall on, 175

influences on, 192, 193

interplay between texts and paratexts, 306

interpretive community, 194

Michelle's model of, 196–199

multidimensional model of, 196, 197 (figure), 198–199

multiple, 192

race and, 181, 182

Reading the Romance, 184–186

semiotics and, 166–169

subject positions, 176

textual determinism, 171

in 21st Century, 196–200

Interpretive community, 194

Intertextuality, 193, 195 (box)

Intrusive technologies, 315–316. *See also* Surveillance

ISAs (ideological state apparatuses), 170, 171

Ivey, D., 220–221

Iyengar, S., 87

Jackson, Andrew, 15

Jahoda, M., 47 (box)

Jamieson, K. H., 88

Jancovich, M., 259

Jenkins, H., 241, 246, 247, 251, 252, 254, 256, 258, 281, 291, 305, 316

Jhally, Sut, 104, 105, 190–191, 316

Jibril, Ahmad Musa, 29

Jon & Kate Plus 8 (television series), 163–164

Jones, Alex, 90

Journalists

citizen journalists, 290. *See also* blogs

online analytics and, 279–280 (box). *See also* news media; press

Jowett, Garth, 32

Karpf, D., 290

Katz, Elihu, 49, 138–139, 144, 145, 146, 147, 151–152, 155, 188, 227

Kennedy, John F., 228

Kim, J.-H., 56

Kinder, D. R., 87

Knowledge Workers in the Information Society (McKerche and Mosco), 102

Kosterich, A., 128

Labor

audience, 103–104, 304

free, 295

Labor exploitation, 294–296

Labor-management relations, 101–102

LaMarre, H. L., 47 (box)

Landreville, K. D., 47 (box)

Lasswell, Harold, 147

Last Broadcast, The (Weiler), 305

Lauer, J., 294

Lazarsfeld, Paul F., 38, 48–50

Le Bon, Gustave, 15–16, 31, 32, 37, 38

Leading questions, 79

Lee, K. M., 54

Lee, Thomas, 284 (box)

Lefkowitz, M. M., 52

Leisure time, 17, 102–103, 213, 213 (figure)

Lemish, D., 154

Lennon, John, 240

Lessig, Larry, 283, 285

Lewis, Justin, 83 (box), 190–191

Liberalism, 14–17

Lichty, L. W., 126, 276

Liebert, R. M., 52

Liebes, T., 188

Lifestyle measurements, 123

Liminal events, 227

Limited effects paradigm, 45–50

Linguistics, 175

Lippmann, Walter, 41, 81, 85

Literacy, 10, 13

Literary Digest (magazine), 76–77

Livingstone, Sonia, 219–220, 221, 225 (box), 313, 315, 317

Location

Greco-Roman audiences and, 12

reading and, 13

Locke, John, 14, 65, 74

London Bridge attack, 29

Long tail, 308–309

Longhurst, B., 242

Lord of the Rings, The (film), 313

Lotz, A., 268

Lucas, George, 250, 251, 284 (box), 295 (box)

Lucasfilm, 284 (box)
Lukes, Steven, 21
Lull, James, 138, 153, 214–215, 307

Mackay, H., 220–221
Macready, William, 15
Madison, James, 14n1
Magazines, 186
Mail-administered survey, 78–79
Make Room for TV (Spigel), 211
Management-labor relations, 101–102
Manheim, J. B., 50
Margolis, M., 84–85
Market Opinion Research (MOR), 79
Market research, 80
Market systems, 65. *See also* Institutions
Marketing. *See also* Advertising
    measuring media audiences and, 99
    social media and, 277–278
Marshall, Joshua, 290
Martin, S., 219
Marwick, A. E., 315
Marx, Karl, 169
Marxism, 103, 169–170, 173, 201
Mary Sue stories, 253–254
Maslow, Abraham, 146, 147 (figure), 150, 155
Mass audience, 3, 4–6, 14, 17–18, 27, 120–128
Mass media, 31. *See also* Motion pictures; Television
    production/consumption divide, 102–103
    vulnerability to. *See* media effects
Mass society, 34, 35
Mass suggestibility, 32–34
Massively multiplayer online role-playing games (MMORPGs), 269, 285–286
Mateen, Omar, 29
Mauser, G. A., 84–85
May, M. A., 36
Mayer-Schönberger, V., 274
McCarthy, A., 224
McChesney, Robert, 101
McCombs, M. E., 85
McDonald, S., 309
McFadden Publications, 49
McKerche, Catherine, 102
Meaning, 175, 184, 198, 199
Measurement error, 82
Measurement of audiences, 99, 113–116. *See also* Data; Metrics, audience; Ratings

agency of audiences and, 310
audience engagement, 126–128
automated, server-side audience metrics, 274
consumer-generated data, 274
democratization of audience analytics, 275
fragmentation and, 307–317
media environment and, 118–120
production/consumption divide and, 103
reasons for, 99, 100
web-based audience metrics, 275–276
Measures of engagement, 277–278
Measures of exposure, 277
Media, traditional, 266
Media effects, 30
    audience power and, 157
    characteristics of audience and, 38–40
    compared to uses and gratifications paradigm, 142
    direct effects model, 38–40
    interpersonal relationships in, 49
    limited effects paradigm, 45–50
    long-term, 52–53
    mass persuasion and, 40–45
    mobile media and, 54–56
    motion pictures, 32–34
    Payne Fund Studies, 35–38
    radio, 38–40
    theories of, 30–34
    violence and, 51–56
Media environment. *See also* Information environment; Media landscape, audience measurement and, 118–120
Media Events (Dayan and Katz), 227
Media gap, 5–6
Media landscape
    changes in, 208–209, 266–267, 305
    reception and, 218–221
Media panics, 34
Media rituals, 226–230. *See also* Rituals
Mediated audiences, 12–14
Mediated mode of reception, 198
Meeds, Robert, 137
Meehan, Eileen, 105, 106, 121, 294
Merton, Robert, 48
Message asymmetry, 174–175
Messages
    effects of, 29–57. *See also* media effects
    private consumption of, 65. *See also* mobile media; social media; television

Methodology, 313. *See also* Research
  ethnography, 153, 166, 208, 214, 220–221
  participant observation, 153
  for studying reception, 207–208
Metrics, audience, 274, 279–280 (box). *See also* Data;
    Measurement of audiences; Ratings
Meyrowitz, Joshua, 223, 224
Michelle, Carolyn, 196–199, 201
Mill, John Stuart, 14, 74
Miller, Peter, 106
Minority groups
  advertising and, 123–125
  stereotypical representations of, 190
Minow, Newton, 51
Mobile audience experiences, 305–307
Mobile media, 306–307. *See also* Social media
  activism and, 56
  addiction to, 55
  effects of, 54–56
  sampling and, 78
Mobile privatization, 102, 223
Mollen, A., 314–315
Moore, Ron, 249 (box)
Moores, Shaun, 209, 215, 224
Moral economy, 223
Moral panics, 34
Moral philosophy, 101
Morley, David, 179, 179–182, 191–192, 194, 201,
    208, 214, 216–217, 220, 221, 223, 224, 225
    (box), 307, 312, 313
Mormonism, 157
Morris, J. S., 47 (box)
Morwitz, V. G., 87
Mosco, Vincent, 101, 102, 274
Motion Picture Research Council, 36
Motion pictures, 31
  autobiographical statements and, 140
  beginnings of, 17–18
  fear of crowd and, 31
  ideological domination of society and,
    170–171
  importance of in American life, 31
  mass suggestibility and, 32–34
  media effects and, 32–34
  minority representation in, 190
  online video access and, 305. *See also* mobile media;
    streaming services
  Payne Fund Studies, 35–38

  production of, 101–102
  propaganda and, 44
Motivations, 140. *See also* Active audience; Uses and
    gratifications perspective
  audience decision-making about media and,
    146–149
  categories of, 148, 148 (figure)
  of game players, 286
  for social media use, 149 (box)
Movies. *See* Motion pictures
Movies and Conduct (Blumer), 139–140
Mueller, Robert J. III, 68
Müller, F., 313
Multistage cluster sampling, 109, 110
Multitasking, 56, 219
Münsterberg, Hugo, 32–34, 38
Music-making, 254
My Blood Approves (Hocking), 266–267

Napoli, Philip, 121, 128, 269, 272, 277
Narrowcasting, 123
National Association of Broadcasters, 51
National Institute of Mental Health (NIMH), 52
National Opinion Research Center (NORC), 79–80
Nationwide (news program), 179–182, 181 (figure)
Nationwide Audience, The (Morley), 179–182, 181
    (figure), 191–192, 194, 196, 214, 216, 313
Needs, 144–146. *See also* Uses and gratifications
    perspective
  gratifications and, 150
  motivations and, 146
  shifts in, 152
Needs hierarchy, 146, 147 (figure), 150, 155
Negotiated position, 176, 196
Netflix, 119–120. *See also* Mobile media; Streaming
    services
New Deal, 75
New York Times, The (news outlet), 279 (box), 287
News agenda, 85–87
News environment, 89, 173
News framing, 87
News media
  blogs, 267, 268, 289–290, 293, 303–304
  defining, 173, 177–178 (box)
  fake news, 89–90
  Nationwide, 179–182
  online, two-step flow model and, 50
  online analytics and, 279–280 (box)

Pulse nightclub shooting, 29
Putnam, Robert, 213

Quantification, 74–75, 108. *See also* Surveys
Questions, 79, 82, 83 (box)
Quigley, Bill, 237

Race
  audiences linked to, 14
  decoding and, 189–191
  fans' social position and, 259
  interpretation and, 181, 182
Racial formation, 125
Radicalization, 29
Radio
  effects of, 38–40
  female serial listeners study, 140–143
Radio ratings, 115. *See also* Arbitron; Nielsen Audio
Radway, Janice, 184–186
Rallies, public, 74
Ran, W., 56
Random sampling, 77–78
Rape on campus, news about, 177–178 (box)
Rating, 116, 117 (box)
Ratings, 5, 105, 107. *See also* Nielsen Audio; Nielsen
    Corporation
  assigning market value to mass audiences,
    120–128
  audience created through, 104–106
  C3 ratings, 118–119
  college-aged audiences and, 111 (box), 112 (figure)
  commercial-based, 118
  computation of audience numbers, 117 (box)
  construction of Nielsen sample, 108–113
  definitions and, 113
  measuring audience viewership, 113–116
  methodology of, 106–120
  operationalization of audience concept, 107–108,
    111 (box)
  quantification of audience responses, 108
  television industry and, 116–118
  unit of analysis and, 113
Rayburn, J. D., 151
Reach, 277
Reading
  audience experience and, 13
  de Certeau's conceptualization of, 251–252
  power and, 13

Reading the Romance, 184–186
  as rebellion, 186
Reading the Romance (Radway), 184–186
Readings, contesting, 198
Readings, counterhegemonic, 198
Readings, hegemonic, 198
Readings, oppositional, 176, 196
Read-only (RO) culture, 283
Read-write (RW) culture, 283
Reagan, Ronald, 240
Reality, 222
  expectations of, 41
  fans and, 241
  motion pictures and, 32–34
Receiver, 9. *See also* Audience
  interaction with sender, 3
  separation from sender, 13
Recent Social Trends, 75
Reception, 183, 207–231. *See also* Interpretation
  bedroom culture, 220
  context and, 209–214
  described, 208
  discursive mode of, 198, 199
  in domestic sphere, 214–221
  family and, 214–215
  gender and, 215–216
  Internet/new media and, 220–221
  media and everyday life in domestic context,
    221–226
  media landscape and, 208–209, 218–221
  mobile devices and, 306
  possible contexts, 307
  privatization of media usage and, 220
  radical contextualization of, 223–224
  rituals, 226–230
  social versus individualized television viewing
    behaviors, 219–220
  studying, 207–208
"Rediscovery of 'Ideology,' The" (Hall),
    165–166
Reese, S. D., 174
Referent. *See* Signified/referent
Referential mode of reception, 198, 199
Reliability, 113
Religion, 170
  Durkheim on, 227
  fandom and, 240–241
  intertextuality and, 193

Slash fiction, 254

Smartphones. *See* Mobile media

Smith, Adam, 100

Smythe, Dallas W., 103–104, 105, 294, 316

Snapchat, 271. *See also* Social media

Soap operas, 182–184, 244

Social change, 30, 51. *See also* Industrial Revolution/industrialization

Social contract, 14, 152

Social Contract, The (Rousseau), 74

Social control, 170. *See also* Institutional control

Social critique, political economy and, 101

Social desirability bias, 84

Social dimensions of media use, 144

Social environment. *See also* Context, reception and, 209–211

Social hierarchies, 257–260

Social justice, political economy and, 101

Social learning theory, 52

Social media, 54, 271–272, 272 (figure), 273 (figure). *See also* Facebook; Google; Instagram; Mobile media; Pinterest; Platforms; Snapchat; Twitter; YouTube

  access to user data, 275

  audience marketplace and, 303–304

  audience surveillance and, 293–294

  as daily journal, 289

  election tampering and, 67–68, 90

  gender stereotypes and, 186–187 (box)

  interpretation and, 196

  marketers/advertisers and, 277–278

  motivations for use of, 149 (box)

  as news sources, 88

  one-step flow of communication and, 50

  political changes and, 67–68

  political discourse and, 66

  as public opinion barometers, 88–90

  social TV and, 126

  two-step flow model and, 50

  types of, 273 (figure)

Social media metrics, 277–278

Social networking, 5–6

Social Organization (Cooley), 31

Social research projects, 75

Social TV, 126–128, 127 (figure)

Social uses of media, 151–154, 154 (figure)

Socialization, 147

Sociology, 31–32, 35, 227. *See also* Methodology

Source credibility, 46, 279–280 (box)

Space. *See also* Context

  introduction of television and, 211

  reception and, 209–211, 214–221

  reorganizations of, 224

  time-space distanciation, 222–223

Spectator audience, 12

Speier, H., 69

Spigel, Lynn, 211

Spiral of Silence, 87

Splogs, 293

Star Trek (television series), 240, 241, 245–246, 253–254, 291

Star Wars (film), 240, 249–251, 284–285 (box), 287, 295 (box)

Static-abstraction problem, 152

Status quo

  challenging, 244

  reinforcement of, 170, 171

Stehling, M., 311

Stereotypes, 41, 190

  advertising and, 123–125

  of audiences, 242

  of fans, 241

  gender, 186–187 (box)

Stoddard, George, 36

Stouffer, Sam, 43

Stratified sampling, 109–110

Straw polls, 75, 76–77

Streaming services, 119–120, 305, 308

Streeter, Thomas, 4

Structural Transformation of the Public Sphere, The (Habermas), 71

Structuration theory, 18, 66

Structure, 18–20, 66, 311. *See also* Institutions

Subculture (Hebdige), 244

Subcultures, 235–236, 240, 243–245

Subscription-video-on-demand (SVOD), 119–120. *See also* Mobile media; Streaming services

Suffrage, 14n1, 15

Suggestibility, mass, 32–34

Sun, T., 157

Sunstein, Cass, 89

"Surgeon General's Report," 52

Surveillance, 147, 315. *See also* Data

  advertising and, 309–310

  social media and, 293

Surveillance, lateral, 294

Surveillance capitalism, 310

Surveillance function, 152

Surveillance mechanisms, 100. *See also* Feedback;
    Measurement of audiences; Ratings
Surveillance motivation, 137
Surveys. *See also* Feedback; Public opinion
    criticisms of, 80–85
    cross-sectional, 77
    data gathering for, 78–79
    failures of, 82, 84
    Gallup organization, 77
    methodological challenges, 81–85
    methods, 77–80
    question wording, 83 (box)
    rise of, 75–77
    sampling, random, 77–78
    sampling errors in, 110

Tablets. *See* Mobile media
Talkingpointsmemo.com (TPM), 290
Taste, 256, 258
Taxonomic collective, 106
Telephone interviews, 78
Television. *See also* Ratings
    amount of viewing, 219
    as civil religion, 228–230
    concerns about, 51–53
    digital, 119
    in everyday lives, 225 (box)
    gendered technologies in home and, 217–218
    individualization of viewing, 225 (box)
    introduction of, 211
    long-term effects of, 52–53
    marketing for, 212 (figure)
    media environment, 118–120
    media events, 227–229
    as open text, 192
    program selection, 153
    reality TV, 163–164, 292
    role of, 51
    social TV, 126–128
    social uses of, 153–154, 154 (figure)
    social versus individualized viewing behaviors,
        219–220
    time-shifted viewing, 118–119, 212, 269, 305
Television & New Media (journal), 314
Television Culture (Fiske), 192, 242
Television viewing, defining, 113
Terranova, T., 295
Terrorism, 29–30

Texting, 54, 56. *See also* Mobile media
Texts. *See also* Interpretation
    open, 192, 196
    paratexts, 306
    reinterpretation of, 239. *See also* fan fiction/fanfic
Textual determinism, 171
Textual Poachers (Jenkins), 241, 252
Texture of experience, 2
The Learning Channel (TLC), 163–164
Theater, class and, 15–17
Thomas, C .G, 10
Thombre, A., 189
Thornton, Sarah, 259
Thurstone, L. L., 36–37
Tich, Cecelia, 211
Time. *See also* Context; Leisure time
    Greco-Roman audiences and, 12
    reception and, 211–214
    spent with media, 213 (figure), 213–214
    television and VCR use, 225 (box)
Time for Life (Robinson), 213
Time-shifted viewing, 118–119, 212, 269, 305
Time-space distanciation, 222–223
TNS Media Research, 119
Tocqueville, Alexis de, 74
Toffler, Alvin, 267
Tönnies, Ferdinand, 34–35
Transactional system, 223
Transmedia production, 304, 305–307
Transmedia Television (Evans), 307
Transmission view of communication, 3
Transparent mode of reception, 198, 199
Trimble, Bjo, 245
Trimble, John, 245
Trump, Donald J., 67–68, 89–90
Tufecki, Zeynep, 89
Tulloch, J., 246, 247
Turkle, Sherry, 54
Turner, Victor, 227
Turow, J., 310, 312
2030 agenda, 314–317
Twitter, 271. *See also* Social media
Twitter Analytics, 275, 277, 278, 278 (figure)
Two-step flow model of communication, 50, 50
    (figure), 280 (box)

Underdog effects, 87
United Kingdom, 67

Urbanization, 34–35. *See also* Industrial Revolution/
    industrialization
User data. *See* Data
User-generated content (UGC), 269–272, 291–296.
    See also Producer-audience relationship;
    Producers, audiences as
User-oriented inquiry, 138. *See also* Active audience
Users, audiences as, 9
Uses and dependency approach, 155–157, 156 (figure)
Uses and gratifications perspective, 137–158
    audience power and, 157
    basic assumptions of, 143–144
    criticisms of, 152, 165
    described, 143–149
    early examples of, 138–143
    expectancy-value approaches to, 150–151
    female radio serial listeners, 140–143
    Israeli media, 144–145
    motivation of game players and, 286
    needs and, 145–146
    Payne Fund Studies, 139
    relational uses, 153
    reorientation of, 155
    self-reports, 140
    social media and, 149 (box)
    social uses of media, 151–154
    static-abstraction problem, 152
    structural uses, 153

Validity, 113
Van Gennep, Arnold, 227
VCRs, 212, 217–218. *See also* Time-shifted viewing
Veronica Mars (television series), 246
Victim-blaming, 178 (box)
Video games, 53–54. See also *World of Warcraft*
View, 276
Viewing, operational definition of, 108
Violence, media, 51–56
Viral post, 277
Vlogs, 282
Vulnerability of audiences. *See* Media effects

Walder, L. O., 52
Walmart, 99
War of the Worlds, The (radio broadcast), 39–40
Wasko, Janet, 101
Watching With the Simpsons (Gray), 195 (box)
Wealth of Nations, The (Smith), 100

Web 2.0, 270
Web surfing, 193
Webb, E. K., 10
Webcams, 226
Weblogs, 289–290
Webster, J. G., 7, 8, 126, 276, 309
Weiler, Lance, 305
Welles, Orson, 39
Wells, H. G., 39
Western Canon, The (Bloom), 249
Why We Fight (film), 44
Wikipedia, 288–289
Wikis, 268, 288–289
Will, free, 74
Will of majority, 74
Williams, Mike, 137
Williams, Raymond, 102, 223
Willkie, Wendell, 49
Wilson, Woodrow, 41
Windahl, S., 155, 157
Wired (magazine), 308
Wirthlin Group, 79
Women. *See also* Gender
    fan production by, 253, 254–255
    housewives and mass media, 215–216
    radio listeners, 140–143
    soap operas and, 182–183
World of Warcraft (WoW), 269, 285–286, 295–296
World War I, 41–43
World War II, 43–45, 48, 53
Worthington, Nancy, 177–178 (box)
WoW (*World of Warcraft*), 269, 285–286, 295–296
Wright, Charles, 147

Yankelovich, Skelly, and White, 124
Yee, N., 286
Yoo, C. Y., 306
YouGov, 80
Young People, New Media, 219–220
YouTube, 29–30, 265, 271, 281–286. *See also*
    Social media
Ytre-Arne, Brita, 314–317
Yu, G., 157

Zahn, Timothy, 250
Zaller, J., 81, 82
Zenor, J., 198–199
Zuboff, S., 310

About the Author

John L. Sullivan is a professor of media and communication at Muhlenberg College in Allentown, PA. He earned his BA in German and media studies from Pomona College and his MA and PhD in communication from the Annenberg School for Communication at the University of Pennsylvania. Dr. Sullivan's research explores the links between media industries and systems of social and economic power. More specifically, he focuses on the constructions of audiences within media organizations, the implementation of U.S. media policies, and on the political economy of online cultural production. He has recently begun a long-term study of podcasting production in the United States, focusing on the processes of formalization and monetization of amateur and semiprofessional (or "Pro-Am") labor within this arena. He has published research on a wide variety of other topics, including the U.S. distribution of British science fiction series *Doctor Who*; the development of a social movement around free, open source (F/OSS) software; and issues of artificial scarcity in digital software. Dr. Sullivan teaches a range of undergraduate courses, including Media Industries, Audience Analysis, Free Culture, the Politics of Media Reform, 20th Century Media, Media and Society, and Media, Theory and Methods.